THE
UNBROKEN
MACHINE

CANADA'S
DEMOCRACY
IN ACTION

DALE SMITH

DUNDURN
TORONTO

Cover image: 123RF/mejn
Printer: Webcom

Library and Archives Canada Cataloguing in Publication

Smith, Dale, 1978-, author
    The unbroken machine : Canada's democracy in action / Dale Smith.

Includes bibliographical references and index.
Issued in print and electronic formats.

ISBN 978-1-4597-3825-6 (softcover).--ISBN 978-1-4597-3826-3 (PDF).--ISBN 978-1-4597-3827-0 (EPUB)

1. Political participation--Canada. 2. Democracy--Canada. 3. Civics, Canadian. 4. Canada--Politics and government. I. Title.

JL186.5.S62 2017   323.0971   C2016-907199-5
                                           C2016-907200-2

1 2 3 4 5   21 20 19 18 17

Conseil des Arts du Canada   Canada Council for the Arts   Canadä   ONTARIO ARTS COUNCIL CONSEIL DES ARTS DE L'ONTARIO an Ontario government agency un organisme du gouvernement de l'Ontario

We acknowledge the support of the **Canada Council for the Arts** and the **Ontario Arts Council** for our publishing program. We also acknowledge the financial support of the **Government of Ontario**, through the **Ontario Book Publishing Tax Credit** and the **Ontario Media Development Corporation**, and the **Government of Canada**.

Care has been taken to trace the ownership of copyright material used in this book. The author and the publisher welcome any information enabling them to rectify any references or credits in subsequent editions.
                                                            — *J. Kirk Howard, President*

The publisher is not responsible for websites or their content unless they are owned by the publisher.

Printed and bound in Canada.

VISIT US AT

dundurn.com | @dundurnpress | dundurnpress | dundurnpress

Dundurn
3 Church Street, Suite 500
Toronto, Ontario, Canada
M5E 1M2

For Brian Hodgson, sergeant-at-arms of the Legislative Assembly of Alberta, and to Professor Katherine Binhammer, each of whom helped start me down the path to political journalism

CONTENTS

FOREWORD

The fact that you're reading this means that you have decided to at least try entering the world of electoral reform. The fact that you could read this sentence means your eyes haven't glazed over yet. Good. Keep going. It's worth it.

We are told that there is a terrible problem with our electoral system. It seems to be electing governments that don't represent the will of the voters, or at least don't represent the many views of the voters. A system that crudely crushes political dreams and ensures the hegemony of the established power grid. Apparently, following in the footsteps of Dante on the road to Hell, the only valid sign outside a polling station, should read "Abandon hope all ye who enter here." In short, the way we practice democracy is an absolute mess.

Or so we are told.

Fortunately, there are many solutions, and a virtual army of policy warriors ready to slay the dragon of democratic injustice by dispatching not only the current system, but anyone not adhering to the one true alternative. Just which one that is depends on which army you join, and it's a crowded field.

Here's a simple guide: The smaller parties, like the NDP and the Greens, prefer Proportional Representation, because it's the one system that could give them a secure and influential position in Parliament, despite their limited appeal. The Liberals want ranked ballots, because as a party of the centre, they will likely be the second choice of both those on the right and the left, thus ensuring political dominance for generations. The Conservatives don't want any change, as the current system favours them every decade or so, which is why they are demanding a referendum. Referendums tend to kill change.

Proponents of the various systems will no doubt quibble with some of this. That's fine. In the electoral reform world, simplicity is eschewed and complexity celebrated. Listen to any of the public consultations.

But hang on. Push the pause button.

What if the electoral reformers have got it all wrong? What if this is not a problem of fairness but one of understanding? What if the real issue is a problem of indifference and ignorance, rather than competing systems and outcomes? Is electoral reform then just a solution in search of a problem, while the real issue is the steady erosion of the bonds between citizen and institution? Could be.

Take a look at just two of the seismic political events of the past few years: Brexit and Donald Trump. They have both been seen, and rightly so, as expressions of anger and frustration against the ruling order. In Britain, the fuel for the revolutionary fire was the massive tide of human migration all too near to England's green and pleasant land — the hundreds of thousands people from the war-torn countries of the Middle East and Africa streaming into Europe anyway they could. Their journey headed ever northward, through the Balkans and into the heartland. Tens of thousands tried to get through to England, stopped temporarily in Calais at an encampment known simply as "The jungle." A great many Britons wanted nothing to do with it. While the migrants could travel freely on the continent because of the Schengen Agreement, they didn't have the right to enter the UK, which stayed out of Schengen.

So *what*, you may ask, got enough British voters so worked up that they decided to leave? Fear. Pure and simple. Fear that Europe would grant citizenship to the migrants. If that happened, Britain would be obligated to let them in. All of them, if they wanted to move there. And that didn't include the other tens of millions of Europeans who might fancy a little place near the village common too. Faced with such possibilities, a majority of Britons said enough, we're out.

In the United States it was the middle class, and those who used to be in the middle class, who provided the oxygen for Donald Trump. Yes there were loud overtones of the migrant issue there too, but the larger elephant in the room was the failure of the economy to embrace tens of millions who could no longer afford to even dream about the American dream. Globalization and technology had killed their jobs and their spirits. Elites had all the money and power, they had little of either, and so they used the system to force what they hoped would be a correction.

But in both cases there was something else at play under the surface. That fear evident in England, and that anger felt in the U.S., were magnified by a bigger force. A large number of people in both countries no longer felt any great attachment to their institutions. After all, the institutions had failed to protect them, either from rapid change or from economic hardship. What good is an institution if it can't do something that basic? Besides, for years they had believed that politicians were corrupt, because so many politicians told them so. To be clear, the politicians making that claim were always talking about the other guy in the other party, but few paid much attention to the nuance. Increasingly all anyone knew about the instruments and institutions of government was that they were working against them, the working middle class, the majority of the citizenry.

So with a combination of fear of the future and loathing for those in charge, the people rose up. They didn't care a bit that they were being warned not to do what they were about to do. In fact, they were encouraged. If their vote was going to harm the elites, so much the better. In the case of Britain, a majority didn't much care that it would also hurt them, and in the U.S. the mission was to drain the swamp, regardless of the consequences.

Which, in an odd way, brings us back to electoral reform in Canada. Our middle class is doing better than our American cousins, and our immigration policies aren't creating distress. But that doesn't mean that we love or understand our institutions.

On a recent tour to gauge the mood of the people, a meeting on electoral reform in Yellowknife attracted exactly zero people. Now that doesn't mean people in Yellowknife don't have an opinion or two on the matter, or on all sorts of other things, but engaging with the system may not be the way they want to express it. Ditto for tens of thousands, hundreds of thousands, maybe millions of Canadians in towns and cities across the country.

This disconnect to government could have something to do with the deplorable lack of teaching civics in school. Or it could mean that those in charge are losing the connection to the people.

Either way, it's a red flag that we ignore it at our peril.

Dale Smith has taken on the task of looking at electoral reform through this lens. You may or may not agree with his thesis, but it's an important debate, and his work is an important contribution to it. I commend him for taking this on. The work of a good journalist is to shine light in dark places. He has done just that.

Tom Clark, chief political correspondent, Global News (retired)
Ottawa
December 2016

INTRODUCTION

While books describing the "broken" state of our political system are numerous, and the various proposals for how to fix that state mount, I turn the idea on its head — what if it's not the system that's broken, but rather our understanding of how to use the system?

This book will look at the critical gaps in civic literacy that have become endemic within Canadian political culture, and serve as a kind of layman's guide to the Canadian political system, since it's something we apparently are no longer learning in school. In fact, only one province has a dedicated civics course, and it's one plagued with misinformation and misplaced in the curriculum.

How endemic is the problem? Samara Canada's study has shown that the majority of MPs that we elect don't actually know what their job description entails, which is to hold the government to account by means of controlling the public purse. Meanwhile, Canadian voters have skewed expectations of the electoral system based on false readings of the significance of popular support numbers on the one hand, and on the other, years of people telling them that their votes don't count if they don't vote for the winner.

Furthermore, nobody seems to know what political parties do anymore, and those very same parties have used that gap in knowledge to increase their own power, taking it away from their grassroots membership. And, of course, most Canadians think of our system along American terms because that's what they're exposed to in popular culture and even our own education system. Finally, and perhaps most alarming of all, there is a widespread tendency to treat democracy as a spectator sport where all one has to do is mark a ballot every few years and let everything else take care of itself, when the system is built for constant participation.

Out of these gaps in knowledge have come proposals for reforms that people think will fix the system, and will, in the buzzwords of the modern era, make it "more democratic." What is disconcerting about most of these proposals is not the fact that they won't actually increase the actual democratic value of the system in the pursuit of "fairness," but that most proposals also reduce the systems of accountability that are built into the political setup. For example, one-member-one-vote party leadership contests make leaders less accountable to their membership and allow them to concentrate power without an effective mechanism to be unseated. But if people don't understand how the systems work currently, it's easy to see how they don't see the unintended consequences of their proposals.

As a journalist in the Parliamentary Press Gallery, I have not only observed what happens currently in Parliament first-hand but have also engaged with the public about their participation in the system. I have become increasingly alarmed by their lack of understanding of the system and their reliance on magical thinking and quick-fix proposals that demonstrate a flawed understanding of how a parliamentary democracy operates. *The Unbroken Machine* is an attempt to correct that problem.

THE AGE OF CIVIC ILLITERACY

We will make every vote count.

We are committed to ensuring that 2015 will be the last federal election conducted under the first-past-the-post voting system.

We will convene an all-party Parliamentary committee to review a wide variety of reform, such as ranked ballots, proportional representation, mandatory voting, and online voting.

This committee will deliver its recommendations to Parliament. Within 18 months of forming government, we will introduce legislation to enact electoral reform.

— Liberal Party of Canada

In recent years, Canadian politics has been filled with talk of the need for reform of the system. Political action groups like Fair Vote Canada and RaBIT (the Ranked Ballot Initiative of Toronto) have been advocating for changes to the way votes are cast in this country. A number of political parties have also become involved in attempts to change the political system in Canada. In 2005 the B.C. Liberal Party sponsored a province-wide referendum that asked voters to decide if they wished to replace the existing first-past-the-post system with another system called Single Transferable Vote — an attempt that failed. In the 2015 federal election, Liberal Party leader Justin Trudeau promised that if elected his party would form a committee to consider reforms to the voting process. Since winning the election, they have followed up on that promise and that committee has met to consider proposals for electoral reform.

This movement for political change is fostered by a widespread sense of dissatisfaction with Canadian politics as it exists now and a belief that the perceived problems could be corrected if the system was changed. In short, there is a belief that the machine is broken and that all would be well if somehow it can be fixed.

The machine is not broken. It has a defined purpose and it works — it works well, in fact. At the municipal, provincial, and federal levels, candidate nominations are held. Political parties hold conventions to decide policy and elect leaders. Elections are held in towns and cities across the country to elect councillors and mayors, provinces and territories hold elections for their legislatures, and nationally, federal elections to select MPs, and thereby, a government. Following all of these elections, the various politicians and the government bureaucracies work to keep all of the offices and agencies of state running smoothly.

But many of the people who operate it seem to have forgotten just how it's supposed to work. They keep coming up with ways to "improve" it, to somehow change its outcomes — creating something that will be fantastic and magical, like unicorns. However, when they don't use the machine properly, and when they have unrealistic expectations about what it's supposed to be producing, well, they deem it to be "broken" and in need of an overhaul.

Welcome to the state of Canadian democracy, something that many claim needs reform. While for decades now it has often been said that ours is an age of reform, it would also seem that ours is also an age of civic illiteracy. The demands that we see for electoral reform often spring from unfamiliarity with just how the system operates, and some blatant misrepresentations about the nature of some of our institutions. It doesn't help that we are bombarded by depictions of the American political system in our popular culture, depictions that have created a distorted image of our own system — a fiction that involves elements of the American system mapped over ours in people's minds. Things are made worse by the fact that many Canadians are wrapped up in American political concerns, never mind that they can't actually vote in their elections.

For some Canadians, the level of illiteracy is pretty extreme — you might even say that it is alarming.

"Stephen Harper's the mayor, right?" asked one constituent of a prospective MP who was knocking on doors in a Calgary riding during the 2011 federal election.

Many can't tell you the three levels of government, who the head of state is, and you might be lucky if they know who the prime minister is at any given moment. Others can't distinguish between the public service and the elected officials, between government and Opposition, or between the roles of an MP versus the role of a minister. To them, everything is just "government." Many people don't know about the nomination process that political parties use to select candidates, or the policy conventions that parties hold to draft election platforms, or the roles that parties play within our system, and may instead believe a narrative that fits their world view, which often involves belief that a small cadre of powerful elites pulls the strings and makes our democratic institutions dance to their machinations.

This general confusion about Canada's electoral system and belief that it is "broken" is often encouraged by the very people who do know better. They do this because they have their own ideas about how the system should operate instead, which usually involves changes made for their own partisan advantage. They sow additional confusion into the system and then declare it to be broken because it is in their advantage to do so. Of course, they may not actually have engaged in enough of a consequence-based analysis of just what would happen if they should implement their "reforms," but that doesn't stop them from trying to push their own vision or agenda. "Reform," they feel, will benefit them in the long term.

And more often than not, their visions will go unchallenged by the media or the general public because of a pervasive lack of knowledge of how the systems of our democracy operate, or how they would be affected by changes that may sound novel or interesting.

For many Canadians, this lack of knowledge of our system of government stems from inadequate education in the primary and secondary levels. Most provinces don't require civics education or its equivalent in their social studies curriculums, and when students are offered civics education, they are often taught only a few basic facts without being given an accurate representation of the mechanics of a system. In some cases, such as in Ontario, it was found that the civics course being taught in high schools was imparting wrong information about the roles and responsibilities of the different institutions of government.

Not only are our students being given an inadequate education in civics but they are often being taught by instructors who have a bias against the system as it exists. Studies have shown that teachers with the greatest interest in politics are also those with the greatest belief in the need for reform of the system. This bias among many teachers and political scientists for reform of one form or another, means that students often graduate with a distorted understanding of the system and how it operates currently.

One of the most damaging misunderstandings about how the system operates stems from a pervasive misuse of the term *democracy*, or rather, *democratic*. This leads to the completely false notion that things can be made "more democratic," as though there were a way to assign a point value to the "democraticness" of systems or proposed reforms, and the first one to get to a hundred, wins.

The most popular notions for making things "more democratic" tend to involve adding more votes to the process — votes by the general public, or by members of the House of Commons — or require positions currently held by appointment be made elected ones, or that certain decisions that would ordinarily be under the purview of the Crown be similarly put to a vote. And while votes are a good thing, they need to be held with a specific purpose in mind and within a specific framework — what is this vote going to accomplish and what does the democratic weight behind it mean?

Part of the problem with many of these proposals to hold more votes is that the resulting votes are simply votes held for the sake of holding a vote to put a coat of "more democratic" paint over decisions that are, in fact, foregone conclusions based on how the seats break down in a majority government in the Commons. Others are votes structured in a way to artificially create a "50-percent-plus-one" result, even though that was not the intent of the votes being cast. Still others ignore one of the most fundamentally important mechanisms inherent within the Westminster democratic model: accountability.

As things are currently structured in the Canadian parliamentary system, there is a healthy tension between democracy and accountability. When voters elect MPs, they hold them accountable for their conduct at the next election. When MPs form governments, those governments are held accountable to the Commons by votes of confidence. And when decisions are made by governments, they are made accountable to both the Commons and to the electorate.

But this is where the demand for more votes can turn into a problem. When individual MPs start voting on decisions that the government should make on its own, it dilutes accountability because it means that when things go wrong, those MPs share in the decision. When an appointed position is instead made an elected one, it starts to lose its ability to speak truth to power because it must satisfy the demands of voters rather than holding the government that appointed it to account. The delicate balance between democracy and accountability tilts toward "more democracy," and inevitably what results is less accountability. But unless one understands that the balance exists within the system, then it gets easy to be swept up in the romanticism of "more democracy," and the accumulation of imaginary points toward the supposed perfect one hundred.

Our collective lack of understanding of how the Westminster system — the parliamentary system that Canada inherited from Britain — operates has also allowed for a more presidential political discourse to develop here, and as a result, the role of individual MPs has been reduced in favour of an expansion of the power of party leaders. It's rare to hear anyone discuss the election of local MPs; instead, we focus all of the attention on the leader. Despite the fact that policy is supposed to come from the grassroots membership of a political party, we have become used to the expectation that leadership candidates will develop their own policy platforms during party leadership contests, and so we are now seeing the rise of candidates with no history of political involvement who suddenly decide that they should run for leadership because they have policy ideas they want to present. Never mind that there are already mechanisms in place for parties to decide policy, the fact that the focus has shifted entirely to leadership means that the avenues for ordinary citizens to contribute to the process are being steadily sidelined and starved for oxygen.

This same kind of lack of oxygen for the role of the grassroots also affects MPs. The lack of civic literacy is not only a demonstrated problem for voters but for the MPs they elect as well, and there are studies that show that the vast majority of MPs don't even know their own job descriptions. Canadian politics and elected office has become an exercise in winging it, while all eyes are on the leadership. Backbenchers are increasingly treated as puppets or ciphers for those party leaders. They have become little more than a chorus, background actors who only do as they are told in Parliament. With their reduced status in Ottawa, they are encouraged to take on a vastly inflated role at the constituency level that focuses on "customer service," work that the permanent civil service should be doing, while the work that MPs should be doing — holding the government to account — is left by the wayside.

And a perhaps more damning indictment is that the media itself largely doesn't seem to have a firm enough grasp on civic literacy and the importance to accurately reflect the system. The prorogation crisis of 2008, when Prime Minister Stephen Harper used a procedural tactic to avoid a confidence vote, was a prime example of how the media was largely unable to offer informed commentary on just what prorogation meant. Even fewer offered challenges to the Conservatives who delivered talking points about going over the head of the governor general to take the question of a coalition to the people — in fact, Don Newman seemed to be the only journalist who challenged a minister on that very point. The fact that prorogation became synonymous for an illegitimate attempt at shutting down a legislature from that point on indicates that the media as a whole still hasn't come to terms with a routine operation of Parliament or legitimate power of the Crown.

During elections, media comment immediately moves to a "winner takes all" mode rather than relying on the actual parliamentary process — the election of MPs, the summoning of Parliament, the giving of the incumbent the first opportunity to meet the House of Commons, and the selection of a new first minister only once they inform the governor general or lieutenant governor that they intend to resign in order to let someone else try to form a government that can command the confidence of the chamber.

Media attention is leadership-focused, and as a result, recognition of the importance of individual MPs is reduced. Most MPs gain no attention from the press unless they do or say something outrageous. There is an inherent dichotomy in the competing demands that MPs have a bigger role, while at the same time any glimmer of independent thought or action is immediately accompanied by headlines that the party leader is losing control of the caucus. Policy is written about as being decided by leadership candidates rather than grassroots membership, especially as leadership contests take place. In day-to-day parliamentary coverage, much of the coverage revolves around personalities, in part because of the dramatic narratives that can be drawn from it. Many other aspects are dismissed as "process stories" which, it is assumed, people will not read — despite the fact that the heart of democracy is process and that understanding how that process works and how the issues of the day fit into that process is a critical component of civic literacy and a gateway for citizen engagement. Debate or argument is written off as "squabbling," despite the fact that the Opposition is an inherent and important feature of our system because it is a built-in mechanism for accountability. Entire segments of the parliamentary process are treated with outright derision, in particular the Senate, while there is little awareness of the role of the Crown-in-Parliament.

Add to that the kind of envy that many Canadian political journalists suffer from when it comes to the romance with American politics, and it is perhaps not surprising that undue comparisons are drawn, be it with terminology or job description, or the particular sense of celebrity or personality-led drama that seems inherent in that system.

The media also tends to focus on stories about how to enact political reform of any particular description — to increase decorum in the chamber, to make MPs' jobs somehow more meaningful, to make the electoral system more "reflective," or to reform the Senate — rather than on stories that demonstrate the kind of critical awareness of what those reforms might actually mean. And having journalists who are able to critically challenge the perceptions put forward around reform ideas or characterizations of the system would be of tremendous public benefit if the knowledge were to be found.

Not all of this is the fault of individual journalists or even the media establishment as a whole, either — it is merely a reflection of the broader decline in civic literacy in general society. Most political journalists have the same level of inadequate civics education as the rest of Canadians, and view the parliamentary process through that same lens. They simply don't know enough about how things actually work, and so, as a consequence, they rely on shorthand that elides the actual functions inherent in the Westminster model when they report, or they frame things in American-centric terms. They have expectations of MPs that are bred from the same lack of knowledge that MPs themselves possess, and the distortions that appear in copy are a mere reflection of that. Tightening budgets and the tighter deadlines in the era of the twenty-four-hour news cycle, reporting at the speed of Twitter, only make things worse. The kind of beat system that used to happen in newsrooms in which reporters were able to focus on a specific area and so gain knowledge in that area is by and large a thing of the past. Most reporters are now of necessity generalists. They must develop knowledge of everything rather than cultivate a mastery of specialized areas, and the loss of expertise is the inevitable result.

So where do we go from here? Have the waters been too muddied with misconceptions and wrong-headed notions about how our system works or is meant to accomplish? Is the effect of our collective civic illiteracy so corrosive that there is no hope? Has the discourse around reform become so pervasive that there can be no other ways forward? Have we reached the point where the only thing we can do is burn the system to the ground and start over with some more "modern" and "democratic" way forward, striving for those hundred imaginary points? My answer is no, and will always be no.

I'm not about to suggest that there ever was a "golden age" of Canadian political discourse, or even of civic literacy, because I simply have no metrics by which to compare it. I do believe, however, that in our constant grasping to be more "modern" in our democracy, we have forgotten the reasons why our system evolved the way that it did, and that we should be looking to restore some of the things that we have already abandoned, and turn back to re-engage with those parts of the machine of parliamentary democracy that we have not yet debased. Indeed, many of our attempts at "modernizing" the machinery of governance have wound up being for the worse, whether it's the way in which political party leadership contests are held, the power of party leaders to sign nomination papers, or the way in which prorogation is handled as a matter of course.

None of this is about actual reform — it's about education and understanding of the way our democracy functions. As long as we don't understand how it functions, we can't be expected to actually properly engage with it in a meaningful way. If there is a "democratic deficit" in this country, as has so often been declared, it's because the deficit is in our understanding.

Over the course of this book, I will be looking at the various parts of our democracy, showing the role and proper context of each. I will explain why the various and sundry ideas for "reform" of the system are, in fact, bad ideas, taken in the broader context, and show how the system actually addresses most everyone's concerns provided that they actually engage with it properly. Chapters will look at what responsible government means, how our voting system works, the House of Commons, the Senate, and the Crown in Canada.

The machine works. We need only to relearn how to use it, and understand what its outcomes actually are and what they mean.

2

A REFRESHER ON RESPONSIBLE GOVERNMENT

Before Canadians can relearn how to use their political system, it's necessary to understand how it's structured, what its component parts are, and how they relate to one another. In order to do that, it's necessary to understand the principles that underlie it. In other words, we need to go back to the basics.

As I mentioned before, a fair amount of the political discourse we hear focuses on some pretty American notions, like "checks and balances," rather than on issues such as "accountability" and "maintaining confidence," issues that lie at the heart of the Canadian political system. Of course, it's not hard to understand why — with much of our media dominated by American imports, we Canadians are constantly bombarded by American political discourse and the terminology used in it. The notion that governments need "checks and balances" is one of these imported American terms. I'm not suggesting that there are no checks and balances in Canada's political system; there are, and with the advent of the Charter of Rights and Freedoms, they have multiplied in number and achieved greater prominence in the system. However, they function in a different way in Canada from those in the United States, because our system is constructed differently from the one that operates south of the border.

Canada's political system is based on the one that operates in the United Kingdom, what is known as the Westminster model — Westminster being the London borough where Great Britain's Parliament is located. The British system is made up of the sovereign, the House of Lords, and the House of Commons. There is also a separate and independent judiciary. Over time, the British system evolved, with the general result that the Commons has assumed more and more power at the expense of the sovereign and the Lords. One of the more significant events in this change followed what is known as the Glorious Revolution of 1688, when King James II was overthrown in favour of William of Orange and Mary II. The two were only granted the right to ascend the throne after agreeing to the Bill of Rights, a bill passed by Parliament that ended the absolute power of the monarchy and established a system of constitutional monarchy instead.

This new order of government has been called the "balanced constitution," since the powers of the monarch, the Lords, and the Commons (the monarchy, the aristocracy, and democracy) are held in "balance." Into this mix was added the judiciary, which was gaining ever greater distance from the monarch at the time, although the Lords remained the court of highest appeal. Gradually, the theory of the balanced constitution evolved into one in which the executive, the legislature, and the judiciary acted as checks and balances on one another's powers.

This theory of the balanced constitution is what America based its Constitution on at the time of the American Revolution, and it still dominates the country's political discourse. But Britain and its colonies, including the Canadian ones that joined at the time of Confederation to form Canada, continued along a different path, which culminated in the Reform Act of 1832 that led to the rise of responsible government by 1835.

RESPONSIBLE GOVERNMENT

Responsible government is at the heart of the Westminster parliamentary system. According to its tenets, governments must be responsible to the representatives of the people, which is why Cabinets are drawn from the legislature. Just as important, a government must hold the confidence of the legislature from which it is drawn. In practical terms, the government (the executive) is drawn from and responsible to the legislature (the legislative branch of government). This is entirely different from the American system, with its balanced-constitution-style "separation of powers." In the American system, the executive (the president and Cabinet) are not selected from or responsible to Congress, while in Canada, the executive (the prime minister and Cabinet) are linked to the legislative branch of government because the prime minister and Cabinet are parliamentarians.

But what does this mean?

In the American system, the legislature, executive, and judiciary check one another owing to their overlapping powers and spheres of influence. It is this balancing between the branches that prevents one from becoming too powerful or dominant. Under the system of responsible government, the legislature determines the party affiliation and duration of the governing ministry through the expression or withdrawal of *confidence* (official support). If the government fails to ensure confidence of the legislature, it will fall and a new government will have to be formed, either from the ranks of the Loyal Opposition, or by means of an election.

Unfortunately, we aren't being educated about responsible government, let alone its implications for our political system. As a result, many Canadians don't really understand how our system differs from the American one.

As I mentioned earlier, many provinces are wholly lacking in any kind of decent civics education, and some provinces that do offer it, like Ontario, are, in fact, teaching the wrong thing. Nathan Tidridge explains:

> In the Ontario curriculum, there is no mention of the words Sovereign/monarch/queen, governor general, prime minister, Cabinet or responsible government within the Grade 10 Civics document (the only time government is discussed in high school). The definition — wholly incorrect — of Parliament is given as "An elected assembly responsible for passing legislation and granting the right to levy taxes." In Canada, the federal legislature consists of the Sovereign's representative, the Senate, and the House of Commons."[1]

How can one understand how responsible government operates if we don't even have the basis of knowledge of what the constituent parts of Parliament do, or how they operate and inter-operate? In order to show how these systems operate, we need to step back and break them down a bit more.

CONFIDENCE

The foundation on which the system of responsible government is built is the legislature's support for the government. This means that the government must maintain what is known as the confidence of the legislature. At the federal level in Canada this means that the government must maintain the support of enough MPs in the House of Commons for the political executive — the prime minister and Cabinet — to carry out their policy platform. They carry out their policy platform by spending the money required to do so, but it's the Commons and the MPs that control the public purse. They control the supply of money and decide if the government deserves to spend it to achieve their policy goals. This is the most fundamental check on government that the legislature offers in a system of responsible government. If the Commons doesn't grant supply — the appropriations from the consolidated fund, i.e., money — then the government is deemed to no longer have its confidence, and the government falls.

THE FORMATION OF A GOVERNMENT

Of course, before a government can ask a legislature to approve its spending plans, i.e., its budget, it must first be elected.

How is a government formed?

After a general election, MPs get together and form a government based on who can command the confidence of the chamber (the House of Commons). Or that is what the Constitution states should happen. In reality, over time, we have developed the shorthand of the party that wins the most seats will form the government. The power of the party system, which I'll get to in a moment, is what allows this to happen. The monarch or her representative, the governor general, appoints the leader of the party that can command the confidence of the Commons to become the new prime minister. He or she then selects a Cabinet and forms a government. They usually face their first test of confidence with a Speech from the Throne, whereby they lay out their legislative agenda.

Now, although I stated that the party that wins the most seats in an election forms the government, it should be noted that, in fact, this is not automatic, nor is it automatic that the leader of the party with the most seats becomes prime minister, either — incumbents remain in the position until they either resign because they know they won't be able to command the confidence of the chamber, or they try to find support from outside their party and retain control as long as they can retain confidence. We have simply created the shorthand that the party that wins the most seats forms the government, though we need to remind ourselves that this isn't always the case and that an attempt to find that outside support is neither illegitimate nor undemocratic.

Up until the 1930s it was standard practice that when MPs were named to the Cabinet they had to resign their seats and run in by-elections so as to ask their electors if it was permissible for them to change roles — i.e., to cease being a watchdog of the public purse and instead become someone who would now be dictating its use. It was also a useful test to gauge whether the public approved of the proposed government.[2]

This eventually fell to the wayside, likely out of expediency — it used to be that Parliament sat for only a few months of the year in a prescribed period, and so didn't need to open immediately after an election. However, now, since there is an expectation that the House will sit for the bulk of the year and that it will meet shortly after an election, immediate by-elections for Cabinet posts would be considered by most to be an unacceptable delay, since they would necessitate the opening of a Parliament by several more weeks.

As well, that period of resignations and by-elections had been open to abuse, especially when the dissolution of a government didn't result in an immediate election, but, rather, led to an attempt by the Opposition to form a government. This happened in pre-Confederation times, with an incident known as the "Double Shuffle" in 1858. After losing a vote of confidence and resigning as premier, John A. Macdonald used the period in which prospective ministers were running for by-elections to seize control of the chamber and retake government two days later.[3]

Although there were certainly drawbacks to this practice, the loss of this tradition means that the electorate is no longer reminded of the role of MPs — to hold the government to account.

This has no doubt also contributed to the fact that even most MPs don't know that their principal job is to hold the government to account — even those in the governing party. And so those in the backbenches of the government will try to hold out for a Cabinet post as a reward for good behaviour, rather than doing their jobs as watchdogs of the public purse. If, on the other hand, MPs still needed to fight a by-election in order to claim that reward of a Cabinet post, there would likely be more awareness of the differences in the functions of MPs and ministers on the part of both the electorate and the MPs, and so fewer feelings of entitlement about getting a Cabinet post. However, the costs and delays necessitated by running these by-elections immediately after general elections have resulted in a significant decline in support for them. Perhaps it is not feasible to return to such a system, but it nevertheless should be reinforced that there is a difference between being an MP and being an MP who is also a minister of the Crown.

THE RISE AND ROLE OF PARTIES

Currently, there are 338 seats in the Canadian House of Commons. If all of the MPs were independent, imagine how difficult it would be for an MP to try to gain the confidence of enough of the 337 other MPs long enough to form a government and then trying to maintain their confidence long enough to implement a legislative agenda and pass a budget. It's easy to see how this situation would quickly become unworkable and virtually impossible to maintain. Individual MPs would demand favours in return — patronage, or "pork" for their ridings or for the various special interests they support — and suddenly the budget would become stuffed full of promises for those MPs who pledged support for the government. And if a prime minister wanted to pass bills relating to different areas, well, the negotiation process would come up again for each piece of legislation, since each MP would have his or her own policy concerns, and on and on it would go. The business of governing would grind to a halt pretty quickly.

Of course, that's not the way Parliament functions. Factions have always played a part in government, and the rise of the political party is a by-product of that factionalism and of the needs of those factions to create some way of operating so that they will be able to form a government and win the continued confidence of Parliament. Political parties lie at the very heart of responsible government — they are a means of organizing MPs who share similar beliefs and values in order to form a bloc of votes that will be able to go on to form a government, to maintain the confidence of the chamber, or if their party loses an election, to oppose the government. Parties become necessary to organize support and to seek its continuance in elections.[4]

It is in this way that parties link people to power.[5] While everyone is quick to lament the role that party discipline plays in our system, it also keeps the Commons from turning into 338 independents. Brokerage politics within party ranks keeps the horse-trading that is the lifeblood of politics in check and within reason, and in the Canadian context, acts as an instrument of federalism as parties generally demand support from all areas of the country if they are to have any chance of gaining power.

Parties have had a variety of roles to fill beyond just enabling a government to maintain the confidence of the chamber. Beyond the exercise of disciplining power, they also link people to power, which is the means by which the legislature is the pre-eminent legitimating body in our system.[6] This is why parties exist at a grassroots membership level, and why that grassroots involvement is the bedrock of our democratic system. It is when the parties lose touch with their grassroots base — whether by ignoring them or by not bothering to adequately cultivate them — that the problems of legitimacy start to take hold.

Part of the problem with civic illiteracy in this country is that most Canadians don't understand what a grassroots party organization does, or the role it plays within politics. They don't understand the interplay between their own roles as voters and citizens when it comes to participating in the process. They don't understand that the vehicle for fully participating in democracy is party membership.

"Oh, but …!" they cry. "I don't want to be tied to any one party! They're all corrupt! Nobody represents me!" Most of these sentiments tend to be mere excuses, barriers imposed on themselves to keep from actually getting involved. Such a stance goes hand in hand with the view of democracy as a spectator sport — they think that they can watch the goings-on in Parliament from time to time but that they only have to vote once every four years or so, and then they can wash their hands of it until the next election.

But that's not the way things actually work, and refusing to participate in party politics shows disrespect for the machine that is parliamentary democracy and the way it operates. You see, that machine requires human input and that input comes from political parties and their members.

Do you think that candidates appear on your ballot out of thin air? No — a candidate's name appears on a ballot because the local party members in your riding nominated someone, had a contest, and he or she is the one who was chosen by the membership.

And those very same party members? They contribute to party platforms by suggesting policy ideas, which in turn get voted on at conventions by the party membership, which later become adopted as policy. All of this requires human input.

When there is a decline in input, however, or when those in power alter the normal rules of party operation, problems arise. In the absence of human input, and with the increasingly consolidated power within leaders' offices, those same leaders' offices have been able to take a more active hand in that policy development, vetoing policies the grassroots approved in a convention if the leader feels they don't want to deal with it. For example, despite the fact that the Liberal Party membership voted to make a carbon tax a part of the platform at their April 2009 policy convention, then-leader Michael Ignatieff declared that it wasn't going to happen and left it at that. Never mind that the membership to whom he should theoretically have been accountable made the democratic decision to adopt that policy.

The subversion of party operations by leaders goes beyond just giving an illegitimate veto to policy inputs, however. Party leaders have taken their ability to sign off on nominations — a power that had been granted to them with good intentions — and used it as a means of threatening MPs who step out of line, saying that their nomination papers won't be signed in the next election, or to parachute candidates into ridings without proper nomination races.

Now, as I said, the granting of this power to party leaders was originally done with good intentions; however, lately its use has resulted in a decline of democracy within parties. The change was brought in as part of a whole package of electoral reforms in an age where political parties were not yet legally recognized organizations and they were trying to find a means of controlling who could put a party affiliation on the ballot, but it has lately been perverted in the name of centralizing power.

The worst part is that the grassroots organizations let it happen because they haven't pushed back enough to preserve their vital role within not only the party structure but our very system of parliamentary democracy. Instead of jealously guarding their position of providing that vital input and being the ultimate mechanism of accountability for a sitting MP, seeing as they have the ability to nominate someone other than the incumbent before the next election, they simply let it slide, possibly grumbling a little bit, or maybe quitting in protest, but the result is the same. The party leadership isn't afraid of the membership because they haven't pushed back.

And now the Liberals have proposed getting rid of party memberships altogether in favour of signing up people as "supporters" in order for the leader's office to use their data to target them for fundraising and voting appeals under the guise of canvassing them for opinions and policy ideas. One has to wonder if many of those policy ideas will actually flow upward to the leader's office to translate into policy in the absence of a resolution process that exists now, or if it will be the leader who comes up with policy and uses the data gathered to creatively justify it.

Party membership and its vital role is under additional assault by the urge to "further democratize" the process of things like leadership contests — and here again is where that balance between democracy and accountability becomes an issue. It used to be that the parliamentary caucus decided who would serve as the party leader. MPs would vote to determine who the leader would be, and when that leader wasn't perform-ing the way he or she should be, well, those very same MPs could sack that leader. It made for a very effective system of accountability, and it's one that other Westminster Parliaments still employ — Australia still uses it (that was the mechanism that allowed for the dispute between Kevin Rudd and Julia Gillard; it was also the tool utilized by Malcolm Turnbull to depose Tony Abbott). The U.K. Parliament also employed this system until very recently; however, of late, it has slowly but surely been moving toward the Canadian system.

The Canadian system of membership-driven leadership contests began with the Liberal leadership in 1919 and was later adopted by the Conservatives in 1927. While this has often been hailed as being more "democratic," it allows leaders to escape being accountable to the caucus because they can simply walk into the room and say, "A thousand people elected me into this position — not you, and you can't remove me." It gives them an air of "democratic legitimacy" that resists accountability, and with no removal mechanism in place, they can behave as autocratically as they like.

And that's exactly what's happened. In a confrontation with his caucus, William Lyon Mackenzie King, the first leader chosen by delegated convention, was reported to have reminded his MPs that they had not selected him and so could not remove him, leaving the party without an instrument to constrain the leader.[7] This played out even more spectacularly in the United Kingdom recently. After the "Brexit" vote in 2016, Labour Party leader Jeremy Corbyn refused to step down despite an overwhelming vote of non-confidence by his own caucus.

Restoring the ability for caucus to select and remove a leader can't be a half measure like the one proposed in Aucoin, Jarvis, and Turnbull's *Democratizing the Constitution*, which was echoed by MP Michael Chong's Reform Act 2014. In their proposal, the authors posit that as long as a mechanism is put into place for a party leader to be fired by caucus and an interim leader be appointed until the party can come up with a new leadership process, it is sufficient to ensure accountability.[8] What this half measure fails to address is the democratic legitimacy argument — the fact that even if party constitutions were modified in the manner the authors suggest, a sitting party leader would still wield "moral authority" based on the democratic legitimacy arising from his or her broad-based selection process. This is what Corbyn kept arguing in the United Kingdom. It also played out to a lesser extent in Manitoba in 2015 when then-premier Greg Selinger faced a Cabinet revolt. He ran again in the subsequent leadership vote and won based on grassroots organizing, creating a permanent schism in his New Democratic Party (NDP) caucus, which no doubt contributed to the party's subsequent election loss. In order to overcome this hurdle, which can and will be abused in the court of public opinion, there must be a full measure of reform/restoration — only this will ensure that the MPs of a caucus have their own power restored.

And what about the membership? The power that is accorded to them in this scenario should be transferred to the party president, whose role should be augmented to reflect the difference. This transfer of power would create more tension in party leadership contests. There would be a highly visible struggle between the party president, representing the grassroots membership, and the party leader, representing the caucus.

The membership's loss of power in this instance wouldn't, however, necessarily result in an overall loss of power for them. In fact, this change should restore some of the power traditionally enjoyed by party members. The clear opposition between the party president and the leader could mean that it becomes harder for a leader to dismiss or veto the policy initiatives that the party membership has voted on and adopted, as currently happens now. Another benefit of the change is that it would also force MPs to justify to their own riding associations why they decided to sack a leader, or why they decided to choose a different one in his or her place, and the membership could then use their nomination powers to hold that MP to account for the leadership decision. Again, this ensures a clear line of accountability that the current leadership selection process no longer maintains.

Unfortunately, the pattern has been going in the other direction. For example, the demands to further "democratize" the process of leadership selection has driven the Liberal Party to adopt a system whereby anyone can sign up to become a "supporter" for free and get to vote for the leader. The only proviso is that they have to swear that they're not members of another political party. It's a move intended to populate the party's voter identification database, a move that not only allows for the leadership process to be hijacked but also further insulates the leader chosen by such a process from any accountability, since he or she will enjoy vastly increased "democratic legitimacy." Instead of saying that it was a thousand delegates who chose him or her, the winning candidate will be able to claim tens of thousands of "supporters." And the advocates of such a system want as many supporters as possible to vote, so as to be able to shock and awe critics with the thousands of supporters the leader is able to command. This wild inflation of the numbers permitted to vote in party leadership contests results in leaders almost being able to claim that the Canadian people voted them in. This sea change in party electoral systems is also a crass attempt at aping an American-style presidential primary without the inherent time limit incorporated into that system.

This way madness lies. Not only is there no mechanism in place to ensure the accountability of the leader, no instrument to constrain their powers, no means of removal, but it also further devalues party membership and the role and powers of MPs themselves. When people have to pay their $5 or whatever it is for a party membership, it gives them a reason to care — they have skin in the game. But instant memberships are destructive to the system of accountability, and to the party system itself. Free instant memberships of the type now being proposed are even worse.

In a CBC interview shortly after his retirement, former Senator Lowell Murray looked at the way in which the Progressive Conservative Party in Alberta allowed for instant memberships during its leadership contests, in which one simply had to pay $10 at time of voting in order to cast a ballot. Murray noted of the recent PC leadership in Alberta:

> Between the first and the second ballots, they were out signing up new members to the PC Party. Where's the cohesion in that? Where is the commitment? If the membership of a political party at the constituency level is so fluid and so amorphous, how can that party play its essential role of acting as an interlocutor of the people of that constituency and the caucus and government in Ottawa or Edmonton, or Toronto or wherever? The short answer is that it can't, and then the constituency party is just a sitting duck — it's completely at the mercy of the well-financed and permanent apparatchiks in the nation's or the provincial capital.[9]

Notice how Murray pays particular attention to the role of the party as the "interlocutor" between the constituency and the caucus. This should absolutely be the role of an active and engaged riding association, which will not only provide the policy input to the party itself but will connect the concerns being raised in that community to the relevant MPs in Ottawa, be they ministers or Opposition critics. And while Murray points to the fact that the constituency finds itself at the mercy of the well-financed individuals within the party mechanism, it should also be noted that those without the civic literacy to realize their own roles within this power structure are also targets. If they don't know to push back, they won't.

And this brings us back to the role that parties play within the system. They are the mechanism by which the voters interact with the caucus. The constituency association brings to the attention of the MPs issues facing their community. This is especially true when an MP of their party doesn't represent that constituency. They become the conduit by which the caucus at large is made aware of issues within those ridings.

THE "UTOPIAN" IDEAL

With the rise in negativity toward the role of parties, we're seeing an escalation in a rather "utopian" rhetoric about doing away with them. After all, they're seen as these corrupting influences that keep MPs from voting either with their conscience or according to their voters' wishes, so why not do away with them?

"Wouldn't it be great," some wonder, "if we could just do away with the parties and deal with everything on an issue-by-issue basis?"

Which is about as far as these idealistic plans ever get. Without any real grounding in civic literacy, those who indulge in such fantasies have little awareness of what the actual consequences of such a plan would be. There is no awareness of how a government would be formed in such a party-less system, how confidence would be maintained, and how an MP could gather support for an individual bill without an excessive amount of trading favours — be they political or personal — or outright bribery, let alone what would be necessary in order to achieve enough support for a budget or even a major policy item.

This is part of the problem with popular conceptions of how politics works. Look at the definition of Parliament put forward in the Ontario curriculum: "it's an elected assembly responsible for passing legislation." This entirely confuses the role of an MP with that of an American "lawmaker" when they are nothing of the sort. Passing legislation is only one of the many responsibilities MPs have, and yet it is the responsibility that most people seem to believe to be their most important one. That, as I've said before, is holding the government accountable.

Perhaps what drives the utopian ideal of a party-less legislature is the belief that all policy goals can be achieved rationally; that it's only the party mechanism itself that is the corrupting influence on MPs, who are somehow powerless before their political leadership. There seems to be little conception of the beneficial role that party discipline plays within the broader context of Parliament or its organization, or the fact that it is the party that has the disciplining effect on MPs or their pursuit of power.

If much of politics is about the balance of priorities and finding the right kinds of compromises, then the party is certainly a vehicle by which to do so. Aside from the ability to organize enough members to either form a government and maintain the confidence of the chamber, or to form a loyal Opposition whose role it is to hold the government to account, it uses its collective powers to make those bargains and compromises in a fashion that benefits more than just the narrow interests of individual MPs or their constituencies.

In this way, most parties are federalist entities. They work to ensure that benefits are spread out across the country as widely as possible (provided that it's not a regional party whose concern is less about forming government, which would be virtually impossible, than advocating for a restricted platform), and make the necessary compromises and trade-offs internally to ensure that the limited resources of a government are best distributed. Parties also temper the expectations of MPs hoping to maximize the benefits for their ridings in exchange for support, subordinating personal gain for the greater good of the party as a whole. This enhances Canada's federal structure, if different regions work together to benefit one another within the party.

Party discipline becomes the mechanism by which MPs are held in check so that their own interests don't subordinate those of the larger party and, when their party is in power, the country's. Which isn't to say that sometimes party discipline isn't subverted or abused, such as when ostensible free votes are either officially or unofficially whipped for the purpose of giving the appearance of cohesion when perhaps it doesn't actually exist, or when other MPs bully those who are threatening to go against party policy because they consider it to be unseemly for an MP to oppose the direction set by the leadership.

None of this makes party discipline wholly bad or wrong, either. Its function at its core remains to ensure that a government can continue to maintain the confidence of the chamber, but that doesn't mean MPs must willingly submit to it if it is unjust, or if they feel they must do their duty as backbenchers and hold a government, a prime minister, or a party leader to account for bad decisions. Such actions are integral to the way in which a Westminster system operates, even though the Canadian version thereof seems to have forgotten that. However, we still to this day see backbench revolts within British governing parties when they feel the leadership has gone against its principles — such revolts never go far enough to bring down a government, but they certainly embarrass it and force it to rethink its plans if need be. Such revolts should only be occasional things, though. If a government loses the confidence of the chamber, it will fall. Deciding whether or not that should happen is the fundamental role and responsibility of a backbench MP.

This situation described above can only work in a chamber where the MPs obey party discipline most of the time. One then has to wonder how the "utopian" ideal of a "party-less" Parliament would actually work if that wasn't the case. How would a government be formed? It's hard enough in a minority situation to form coalition governments in some countries — look at Belgium, for example, whose inability to form a government that can command the confidence of its legislature has dragged on for over a year in some cases. Now imagine that with 338 individual MPs. And while this inability to form a government forestalls the actual business of governing, whom is it then turned over to in the interim? Unelected public servants? Such a plan would be even more counter to the supposed democratic ideal of doing away with parties.

How would a government be formed? Would you have each MP trying to gather enough support to form a government? Probably not, but there would be factions that would emerge, be they on regional or ideological grounds. Even without a formal party structure, factionalism is inevitable, and those factions would have to find someone to rally around in order to form that government. (About the only upside here is that said ersatz leader would once again be accountable to the members in his or her de facto caucus, since he or she would need their ongoing support and wouldn't be able to claim the support of party membership or the broader public.) And if the factions happened to fall along regional grounds, then that group's ability to form a government would be further reduced because of the way that support needs to be spread out through the country in order to maintain confidence.

The governor general would always be in a much more active role as a negotiator for the various factions vying to hold power, while the Clerk of the Privy Council would have to act as a caretaker of the permanent civil service that would have to continue to operate in the vacuum of political leadership. There would certainly be less time for the symbolic roles of the governor general, who would need to be ever-present at Rideau Hall for negotiations or in the event that a government lost confidence and a new one had to be formed. Would that inevitability have a detrimental effect on other aspects of national cohesion? Quite possibly.

Should one faction then form a government and assemble a base of support that would be enough to get the nod of appointment from the governor general, then it would immediately have to put that to test with a Speech from the Throne to lay out its policy platform, but that would have to be a pretty thin document because unless the faction could get some kind of blanket approval for the entire platform, it would be negotiating with as many of the 338 MPs as it could for each individual item in that platform. And trying to create a government — meaning executive or Cabinet — that in and of itself would be large enough to maintain a majority in the chamber is simply absurd. Imagine a Cabinet of 169 MPs, each either given a crumb of responsibility or being made "ministers without portfolio" while maintaining Cabinet solidarity. A non-starter to be sure.

Should a Speech from the Throne pass and the government maintain its confidence, a budget would have to be drawn up and passed, which is again a test of confidence. Would every member of the faction supporting the government simply pass the budget unheeded, or would they begin demanding concessions such as public works projects for their ridings in exchange for ongoing support? That's certainly a possibility — after all, there is enough self-interest in wanting to see that they are re-elected, and nothing is a better reminder of an MP's effectiveness and deservingness for re-election as the ability to "bring home the bacon" to his or her riding. Remember that there would no longer be a moderating influence of a party that would try to redistribute that self-interest to the greater good. And who's to say that MPs who pledge support one day wouldn't decide they need a better incentive to maintain support the next? Perhaps an Opposition faction would try to woo votes with promises of even greater largesse should it be allowed to form government instead?

For every aspect of policy outside the budget, there would need to be a renegotiation process to gain support for passage, and that negotiation would likely include a mini-budget in each bill to ensure that the interests of enough MPs were taken care of to ensure their support. This would not only drag out the process but make bills unwieldy, since there would be so many added provisions to ensure passage. And since such bills are considered confidence votes, a government generally can't afford to lose too many — it needs to be allowed to put through a policy agenda. We might even see legislation become all wrapped up into a single omnibus bill to ensure that the whole of the government's agenda can pass with the support it is able to muster.

The lack of a permanent base of support in the chamber, or of a cohesive Opposition, would create an air of instability. The threat of election would be permanent if the MPs in the House could at any moment vote to ensure that they were withdrawing confidence in the government. Then, if a different faction wasn't able to guarantee enough support for its own ability to maintain confidence, well, then an election would have to be called, with the hope that the next group of MPs could put together enough factions to both form a government and maintain confidence. And if not, then perhaps another election would need to be called after that.

The ability for a government to do any kind of long-term planning would be destroyed. It was bad enough in the era of minority governments when all plans would be good for a two-year time span, but in a chamber full of free agents and independents, that would be reduced to planning only far enough for the next vote of confidence. It would likely fall to the Senate to do any kind of substantive policy work within Parliament, given that senators don't need to worry about either bringing home the bacon or ensuring their own re-election. Senators are also much more capable of working as independents, since the Senate isn't a confidence chamber. This inability to bring down a government on a vote blunts the need for party discipline.

And yet this is what the "utopian" ideal would call for. Like most any idea about how to "reform" our system, it is grounded in ignorance of how systems of government operate and in the wishful thinking that everyone can simply get along and work together on an issue-by-issue basis because it's the right thing to do. It makes false assumptions about the roles that parties play currently, and in the absence of those roles, they don't see the anarchy that would result.

If the people calling for this vision of politics had enough of an understanding of civic literacy to see why their vision is so flawed, they could instead turn their energies toward working within the established structures to achieve the ends they're aiming for, rather than creating a wasteland with the best of intentions.

RESPONSIBLE GOVERNMENT IN THE CANADIAN CONTEXT

Responsible government arrived in the Canadian colonies not long after it became the mode of government in Westminster. Where some of the evolution here differs from that experienced in Britain is that in Canada achieving responsible government was more about self-government than it was about parliamentary accountability, and self-government had to do with patronage.

During the 1840s, when debates about self-government were ongoing, the fight for responsible government and the transfer from London to the Canadian colonies of the responsibility over their internal or domestic matters was really a contest between the governor general and Canadian politicians over who should get to dish out patronage.[10] Patronage, after all, was a big part of the lifeblood of politics. It was the means by which support was rewarded, and initially, there was some conception that while the current government might dish out patronage to its heart's content, the government that followed would do just the same for their own supporters, and thus patronage wasn't seen in the same negative light as it is today. Not that I'm suggesting we should return to a system in which patronage continues to be doled out in the same manner, but in order to understand how our system evolved and what the motivating factors are, this is a fact that can't be overlooked.

In the years leading up to the fight for responsible government in the 1840s, including with the rebellions in both Upper and Lower Canada in 1837, political parties emerged on either side of the question of reform and change — Liberals or Reformers favoured it, Conservatives didn't. These parties weren't the same as they are today because they didn't yet have responsible government. As a result, they weren't concerned about ensuring confidence, because as of yet, they couldn't form a government that needed to maintain it.

But in his report, Lord Durham, a British aristocrat sent to try to solve the problems that had given rise to the rebellions in Upper and Lower Canada, recommended, among other things, that the two colonies be merged into one and that they be granted responsible government with a governor as a formal office and that the legislative assembly be given a great deal of power. This recommendation wasn't acted upon, but it did fuel the debate.

It was in the colony of Nova Scotia that responsible government was first achieved, thanks in large part to the efforts of Joseph Howe, a journalist and publisher turned political reformer. Responsible government was declared on January 24, 1848, with a Cabinet selected from members of the Legislative Assembly convened on February 9, 1848. A plaque in Nova Scotia's legislature reads:

> First Responsible Government in the British Empire. The first Executive Council chosen exclusively from the party having a majority in the representative branch of a colonial legislature was formed in Nova Scotia on 2 February 1848. Following a vote of want of confidence in the preceding Council, James Boyle Uniacke, who had moved the resolution, became Attorney General and leader of the Government. Joseph Howe, the long-time campaigner for this "Peaceable Revolution," became Provincial Secretary. Other members of the Council were Hugh Bell, Wm. F. Desbarres, Lawrence O.C. Doyle, Herbert Huntingdon, James McNab, Michael Tobin, and George R. Young.

From that point on, it spread through the other colonies — New Brunswick later in 1848, and in the Province of Canada the following year. Nevertheless, it has been observed that since 1848 Canadian politics has focused more on governing than representation. Control of the legislature required a majority of the constituencies; the vehicle was the national political party and the fuel was patronage.[11]

In the time since, Canada has developed certain practices and conventions of its own form of responsible government that differ from those of other similar Westminster democracies. Many of the differences that can be observed in Canada's form of government have to do with the unique composition of Canada as a federal country with bilingual and cultural considerations that don't factor elsewhere.

One example is Cabinet composition, which dates back to the first federal Cabinets of Sir John A. Macdonald, for which considerations for bilingualism and regional representation were built into the selection process so that Cabinet itself became both a token of and an instrument for federalism. As the country grew, the maintenance of this principle of Cabinet selection led to a move away from Cabinets of a fixed size, of the type that existed early in Canada's history and that still exist in Westminster. The size of Cabinets in the time since has varied greatly from prime minister to prime minister, though the general trend has been one of growth. This growth has led to concerns about Cabinets growing overly large as their size is adjusted to provide gender balance and in order to accommodate as wide a representation as possible of visible, linguistic, religious, regional, and other minorities.

The now common practice of selecting ministers according to region, gender, etc., has led many to be concerned that talented MPs might never make it into Cabinet because they don't happen to fit the right profile for the Cabinet vacancy as it exists.

Canadian Cabinets have used representation from the Senate to round out representation from regions if the Commons caucus is insufficient, and those ministers will typically be held to account during Senate Question Period. Because the Canadian Senate is an appointed body, there is little need to ensure that there is Senate representation in Cabinet beyond the position of Leader of the Government in the Senate, unlike in a country like Australia where elected senators end up filling up to a quarter of Cabinet seats.

Cabinet size versus caucus size is another area where Canada differs from other Westminster systems. Because the Canadian Commons is half the size of that at Westminster, and because its Cabinets tend to be larger, the ratio of backbenchers to Cabinet ministers is much smaller than it would be in the United Kingdom. This has an effect on backbench independence and party discipline, since the rewards for government back-benchers seem closer to attaining than they would be in a Parliament like Westminster. This can create an incentive for backbenchers to toe the line that much more readily, since they feel they are a mere ministerial slip-up away from a Cabinet post. Where there is a larger backbench population, on the other hand, most backbench MPs know they are never going to get into Cabinet. So, assuming they feel their seats are secure enough, they are more likely to step out of line more often and vote their consciences or their constituents' wishes.

These same dynamics play out with committees in Canada's Parliament as well. Our committees are structured differently from those found in other Westminster-style Parliaments. They tend to be less independent because the Prime Minister's Office has been inclined to wield a great deal more author-ity in terms of the selection of chairs (though this is moving toward free votes of prospective chairs), and in some governments, parliamentary secretaries and critics will sit on the committees. (Under the current Trudeau govern-ment, parliamentary secretaries are forbidden from being voting members of committees, but some attend regardless to "provide guidance.")

Another source of difference with Canada's parliamentary committees is the sheer numbers of MPs in play — in some Opposition parties, there wouldn't be enough MPs in the caucus to keep a lead critic off a committee in the way that shadow ministers in the United Kingdom don't sit on select committees. In any case, it should be noted that because Canada doesn't have the same kind of shadow Cabinet system within the Opposition benches as there is in the United Kingdom, where critic portfolios can be somewhat amorphous and not necessarily tied to the positions in Cabinet, there is a far less formal structure to the way Opposition functions are carried out.

Money is the source of another major difference between Canada and other Westminster Parliaments. There is no one single model used for the process by which the Estimates — parliamentary spending — are accounted for. For example, in Australia the Estimates are studied in the Senate alone rather than in both chambers, and in the United Kingdom, there are strict guidelines for when the departmental select committees must report back to the House, and for when the House must respond to those committees. In Canada we have established a rule in the Standing Orders by which the Estimates are deemed to have been adopted by a certain date, whether they have been studied and voted upon or not. While this was no doubt done in order to ensure that Opposition parties couldn't hold the process hostage, it nevertheless reduces the ability of Parliament to hold the government accountable, and the role of scrutinizing of those Estimates has become a largely symbolic one. With the creation of the Parliamentary Budget Office in 2006, there was an attempt to give MPs more assistance with the Estimates process; however, this office has come with its own challenges in terms of powers and resources.

It should be noted here that any weaknesses in the Canadian system of responsible government, the relative lack of independence of backbenchers and committees, or the "deemed to" rule with the Estimates are all the product of Parliament giving up its oversight powers of the government of its own volition and aren't simply the actions of any one particular government.

THE FLAWED PORTABILITY

The outline of responsible government and its constituent parts — confidence and the political party — presented above illustrates just how flawed and inappropriate the attempts to wedge our system of politics into the American model are. The comparisons aren't portable or analogous. Ours is a fundamentally different system, from the linked powers of the executive and the legislature to the differences in the roles of each constituent part.

One can argue all one wants about the merits of one system over the other, whether it's better for a president to not be able to control the legislature the way that a prime minister can by way of party discipline, or whether it's better that a legislature can withdraw confidence from a prime minister rather than have to wait out a four-year time clock for the expiration of a presidential term, or what have you. These are important discussions to have, but when they happen they need to be held in an environment where there is an awareness of context and of how the operation and inter-operation of the whole system works, rather than in a fantasyland where changes are imagined without any real consideration of what the effect the alteration or replacement of one constituent part would have on the functioning of another.

You say you want more "checks and balances" in our system, but how does that impact the established system of accountability as it stands? Does the introduction of new elements help to improve the broader whole, or does it actually interfere with things and make them worse? Think about how the attempts to make politics "more democratic" — as with the opening up of the contests for party leadership — have led to a loss of the accountability of the leadership because the consequences weren't thought through. The imposition of additional "checks and balances" has affected significantly the role of an MP in holding the government to account. In the end, this move to make the system more democratic has reduced the powers of MPs further, and in some ways, it could be argued, reducing them largely into voting machines.

This is why an awareness of civic literacy is important. We can't simply look at pieces in isolation and determine what we think might make them better without seeing how that impacts on the broader whole. Knowing how the machine — the system of parliamentary democracy — works is of vital importance. We can't just mouth the words we hear on American television and expect them to mean the same thing here. We can't expect them to fit into our context nicely — or at all. Our machine works differently from that in the United States, no matter how much we like to think they're similar enough to be interoperable. They're not, and it's our responsibility to treat our own machine with the respect and awareness that it deserves.

3

ELECTIONS AS DEMOCRACY AND ACCOUNTABILITY

A common complaint heard during the 2006–11 minority government years was that the electorate was suffering from "voter fatigue" — that elections had been so frequent (and by frequent people meant every couple of years) that voters were disengaging. As a result, there was a continuing decline in voter participation.

While the notion that it's onerous to have to cast a ballot every couple of years seems fairly absurd, it is by no means an unusual one. Related to this is one of the other significant problems lying at the heart of our crisis of civic literacy: the belief that elections are the be-all and end-all of participation in our system of democracy. Further to that, there is a prevalent attitude that democracy is little more than a spectator sport — elections are seen as championship matches, and once your ballot is cast, you can sit back and wait for everything to sort itself out.

Meanwhile, when elections do roll around, you hear partisans moaning about the quality of their local candidates. There seems very little aware-ness about where those candidates come from — something that's perhaps unsurprising since there is almost no civic education in this country about the nomination process for candidates within parties. This lack of know-ledge is one of the most serious problems with our democracy; the process of selecting candidates is possibly the most fundamental and most import-ant aspect of our system. Despite its importance, it is entirely ignored in what scraps of civics education we do get. The only time that a nomination might make the news is when it's highly contested — and that's usually for a by-election when the leaders' tours aren't eating up the entirety of the news cycle. Even then, since the average voter has little to no understanding about what the process entails, dismissing it as something happening elsewhere and tuning out becomes easy.

It is little wonder that most voters think candidates come out of thin air at best, or at worst, believe them to be on the ballot because they've done enough favours for the party overlords that they were placed there in something akin to a patronage appointment. This perception isn't helped by the increasing tendency of party leaders to make appointments to fill vacant ridings, or to parachute "star candidates" into them, sometimes over the protests of the local membership; nor is it helped when sitting incumbents are given free passes, or "protected nominations," as was the norm in some parties during those minority government years when this practice was championed by party officials who believed it necessary because the party needed to be "election ready." (It also doesn't help when it appears that the party's central office blocks a riding association's attempt to remove a candidate it's not happy with, as happened when there were accusations against Rob Anders in the riding of Calgary West. In the end, though, he lost the nomination in 2015.)

So what, then, is a nomination race?

Ask pretty much any sitting MP and he or she will tell you that the nomination is the most brutal, gut-wrenching part of politics. "Worse than contesting an election itself," MPs will answer almost universally. In a nomination battle, prospective candidates within the party's riding association try to sign up as many members as they can, with the understanding that these members will vote for their candidacy. In the end, the victor of that race — the one who has the most members supporting him or her — gets to have his or her name on the ballot. It seems to be a simple enough process, and in a way it is. But it's crucially important. Everything flows from these contests, but they're almost entirely overlooked. And these battles are so brutal because the candidates are essentially fighting within their own party ranks to win that place on the ballot rather than fighting their political opponents in the other parties. It's hard to draw neat lines in what is de facto internecine warfare, and candidates don't want to play too dirty of a game because they need everyone on their side once the race is over so that they can fight the election.

This, of course, is the broad overview, but generally the major parties all fit within this particular system, with some variation. The NDP has tended to add another level to its own races: to encourage more women and minorities to run for public office, the party's nomination rules state that the riding association needs to find at least one nomination candidate from an "equity-seeking group" — in other words, someone other than a heterosexual white male — in order to better encourage diversity. The NDP's success has been shown in the number of women elected to its caucus (though until the 2011 federal election there was very little uptick in visible minority groups).

In some cases, as with the Liberals, the party leader has at times reserved the right to appoint women candidates in order to boost the number running, but the problem with appointing women or minority community candidates is that this is often done in "no hope" ridings so that the party can claim a certain percentage of candidates that fit the diversity description without making enough effort to have these same candidates in winnable ridings. This applies just as much to the NDP. Despite its rules that nominations can't be held until an "equity-seeking" candidate has been found, the party has at times either appointed names off lists even though the candidates didn't live in the riding (as happened in Quebec during the 2011 election when most of those absent candidates won without running in a nomination contest or without there even being an active riding association). Or it has also engaged in the intellectually dishonest excuse that no equity-seeking candidate could be found in the riding, so a heterosexual white male was "elected" through acclamation — as was the case with Robert Chisholm in 2011, or Joe Cressy in the Trinity-Spadina by-election in 2014.

The various methods used to cheat the innovations supposedly designed to improve representation in the parties' roster of candidates provide a strong argument for holding the nominations races in the "textbook" manner as described above. The traditional method engages the grassroots party membership in the selection of a candidate, in the recruitment of new party members who can then contribute to the ground-up political engagement that our system requires, and it offers an unassailable legitimacy to a candidate that the membership rather than the party leadership has selected. It means that minority candidates who are chosen have earned their places on an equal basis, and so deflects accusations of tokenism that can often accompany appointed candidates. Having said that, there would likely still need to be some kind of encouragement at the riding level to find minority candidates to run for the nomination (a process the Liberals were successful in doing in 2015 with recruiting more women candidates), and to give everybody an equal footing in terms of their democratic legitimacy.

Of course, there are other problems with the nomination process. That is why safeguards are needed. There has always been the risk of a hijacked nomination race, i.e., a race in which an outside candidate with a lot of money signs up a large number of instant members within the requisite period. This led to changes to the Canada Elections Act in 1970 that allowed leaders to sign off on nominations. The change was both an attempt to thwart pro-life groups from hijacking nominations and to keep the chief electoral officer from being dragged into intraparty disputes on who the official candidate could be. This was also the change that put the party name on ballots instead of just the candidates' names, addresses, and occupations, and since political parties weren't legally recognized organizations in the legislation at the time, the power fell to the leader.[1]

Of course, this has led to a situation in which party leaders have increasingly used this ability to wield power over their MPs, something contrary to the principles of the nomination race. I believe a change is needed to prevent this and that it's one of the few reforms to our system that has to happen. Other safeguard mechanisms could also be implemented such as giving the power to a body within the party, for example, a council of riding presidents, who could overturn a controversial nomination. One proposed mechanism, from Conservative MP Michael Chong's Reform Act 2014, was the establishment of a provincial nominations officer elected by the riding presidents to supervise the nomination contests. Vesting the power in such a figure would at least keep the decisions around nominations within the ranks of the party membership and away from the leader, something necessary given the propensity for this power to be abused, or taken away from the grassroots membership. That provision never survived to the final version of the bill that eventually became law; instead, that power is now given to a "designated person" in the party, with no restrictions on how that person is chosen, meaning it can be the leader's chief of staff if the leader so wishes.

One of the other consequences of this ability of a leader to overturn or protect a nomination is that it removes the accountability to the riding members. One of the most fundamental ways ridings can keep their MPs in line is the threat that if the MPs don't do their jobs, or if they ignore the ridings' concerns, or so on, then the riding associations can nominate other candidates in their stead the next time around. And, yes, nomination battles to unseat incumbents are a nasty business, but sometimes they're necessary. They keep both the democratic and accountability mechanisms tied to the grassroots membership. Allowing a leader or party headquarters to either protect an incumbent the membership is dissatisfied with or to parachute in a candidate over the protests of the local membership circumvents those very crucial accountability measures. Even if the parachuting is done with the best of intentions, such as ensuring there are more women on the party's slate or because it's an accomplished individual the party would like elected without going through the usual hassle, it nevertheless is an unacceptable circumvention of the democratic and accountability mechanisms at the very heart of our system. And when the party leadership continually hijacks nomination races, disengagement is fuelled.

One of the other symptoms of voter disengagement from the nomination process is the problem of people now believing they're voting for the prime minister as opposed to their local MPs. This is further promoted by increased media coverage of the leaders' tours and debates, all of which results in a kind of presidentialization of the role of the prime minister in the popular perception. As noted, this focus on the party leaders and the prime minister by the media is itself the product of the kind of envy many Canadian political reporters feel for the American political system and its dramatic presidential races; it contributes to the mimicry they end up engaging in.

By giving the leader more power and prominence, as has increasingly occurred over the years, and allowing party leaders the added broad-based "legitimacy" of being elected by a wider membership (which is about to be exacerbated if the Liberal idea of the "supporter" class takes hold more extensively), the media and party members themselves have elevated the position of party leaders and diminished the status of individual MPs.

As media coverage continues to focus more narrowly on the leaders and as poll questions such as "Who would make the best prime minister?" rather than "Which local candidate would you prefer to represent you as an MP?" become the ones increasingly asked, the distortion is magnified over time. As such, anecdotes about people walking into polling stations to vote for the leader — and only the leader — become not uncommon. And if you look at the 2011 federal election in which a significant percentage of the Quebec electorate "voted for Jack [Layton]," it is clear that a great many of them did so without any knowledge of their local candidates, several of whom had never visited their ridings and some of whom were unilingual anglophones running in francophone ridings. And yet, because media coverage had focused on the leadership, it was acceptable for a significant portion of the electorate to ignore who they were actually casting a ballot for — their local candidates — in favour of an ersatz president.

When you take the lack of awareness of the local nomination race, the lack of active participation of the riding in choosing its local candidate that results from that, and add that to the distortion of the electoral process caused by the focusing of attention on the leadership as opposed to the local candidate, the result is the perfect situation for the promotion of the viewpoint that sees politics as a spectator sport. Because there is no awareness on the part of the average voter of the on-the-ground input necessary for a healthy democracy, be it in buying a membership, helping to select the nominee to become the candidate, or the ongoing policy input process that feeds the party's idea generation, it contributes to the perception that all that's involved in democracy is the act of casting a ballot every few years — if you're not "too busy."

And therein lies one of the biggest dangers stemming from the lack of civic literacy when it comes to the fundamental inputs of the democratic system — if you don't know how to provide input into the system, it fuels disengagement. If you remain unaware of your active responsibilities as citizens to engage with the political process in an ongoing manner, above just the spectator level, then the input that does take place becomes more selective and controlled by those who have agendas of their own — none of which is healthy for our democratic system.

THE VALUE OF "FIRST-PAST-THE-POST"

We are constantly bombarded with the call to reform the electoral system in this country. We are told the system is "antiquated" and is a "relic of the nineteenth century." A great deal of fantasy has been projected onto what an electoral system is "supposed" to look like and how its results are "supposed" to be achieved. But as with so many calls for reform, there seems to be little understanding about how the mechanics would actually work, or the reasons why the system operates the way in which it does.

One of the biggest myths about the single-member plurality or "first-past-the-post" system is that it produces "distortions" and "false majorities." That is, the share of the popular vote isn't reflective of the number of seats that a party wins, that it can get a majority of the seats with some 38 percent of the vote. But there seems little awareness as to what is actually being measured by either count, or of the fact that using the share of the popular vote as a reflection of the number of seats won is in and of itself a distortion.

The biggest common fallacy arising from using the "popular vote" to describe the results from an election is that it treats a general election as a single event when it is, in fact, 338 separate and simultaneous elections. Each riding has its own writ dropped to signal the election — there isn't one signal for the whole affair. This was less of a confusing issue when elections were staggered over several days due to the limitations in transport and communication in the early days of the country. Although such staggered elections made it clear that the election was, in fact, a number of elections, this staggering brought problems with it — occasionally, attempts were made to try to game elections and drop candidates who were assured defeat in eastern ridings that had earlier elections and have them run again in a western riding that wouldn't be voting for several days.

Treating 338 separate elections as a single event with a single popular vote creates national distortions on a major scale. It also misreads what is happening in each of those 338 elections — that a single representative is being chosen in each of those 338 simultaneous elections. By trying to apply the results of each of those contests in the broader context the percentages quickly become meaningless because the context changes once you begin adding up the percentage of the voters' shares and averaging them across the entire country. Suddenly, you're counting two different measures and treating them the same, which they simply aren't.

And then there is the distortion of the overall picture. There is no greater example of how the overall picture can be distorted than the use of Bloc Québécois popular vote figures within the overall national picture — because the Bloc only runs in one province, it is disingenuous to lump that party's results in with every other province in the country. It's the same with the Conservatives, who enjoy overwhelming support in certain parts of the country but limited backing elsewhere. If one assumes that the level of support a party enjoys in one of the areas in which it is popular is the same number as it receives elsewhere, including those areas of the country where it doesn't share the same popularity, perception is distorted, making it appear more popular than it really is in that region.

Of course, statistics are confusing to many people, and most like having a single number they can cite when they talk about election results or polling numbers. This tendency is exacerbated partially by the focus of political coverage. The media concentrates its attention on what are known as the "horse-race" numbers, with its daily polls during writ periods, or weekly polls outside them. But because it's impractical to poll each of the 338 ridings in a statistically significant way and ask the voters which candidate they would vote for outside the writ period — a period when parties other than the incumbent are unlikely to have a nominated candidate in place — the polling questions build a picture of support based on backing for a particular party or leader in the national picture, which isn't the way elections operate. Nevertheless, this number gets compared with the distorted value of the "popular vote," and both of them are treated as significant figures. By perpetuating this fundamental distortion of the system, whereby people believe there is a straight-line comparison between voter share and the number of seats won, it creates false expectations and fuels the disengagement of disappointment.

One of the other problems with the current expectations of the system revolves around the difference between simple majorities and pluralities — the latter involving simply getting more votes than anyone else. When people look at a voter share, they have a notion that 50 percent-plus-one is a sufficient majority for legitimacy and that anything less is, well, "less democratic," and in most of the rhetoric, less legitimate. There seems to be little appreciation for the reality of what a plurality represents, no matter that it's what the system is built on. Instead, there is a rather absurd fixation on the simple majority.

This isn't to suggest there is no place for simple or super-majority decisions within the political system — it's merely to raise the awareness that a plurality decision shouldn't necessarily be seen as illegitimate, nor should it be deemed so by a losing candidate (or his or her supporter) in a fit of sore-loser pique.

Seats are determined by a plurality vote because we have multiple parties running. Such contests can produce minorities or majorities. In those instances in which a majority is produced, the winning party should understand not to "over-read" its own mandate; instead, it should understand that winning a majority of the pluralities isn't the same as winning an outright majority. If as a government it fails to act in a manner that befits that situation, the electorate can punish it for overreaching.

Awareness of the somewhat limited authority that a plurality bestows should inspire a proper degree of modest circumspection in a government, not a fixation on the concept of the simple majority or on ways to create artificial ones. Such a fixation is the product of a "gut feeling" that decisions can't be seen as legitimate unless they are made by majority. As a result, ways are devised to create that majority by artificial means, usually through a mechanism like ranked ballots or run-off elections in which candidates are dropped from the ballot until a binary choice is forced and the simple majority can be achieved — thus, satisfying the "gut feeling."

But that kind of artificiality is also a false reflection of what the true desire of the electorate is. In this way, the current single-member plurality results provide an accurate reflection of the electoral mood of the country — there is no ranking or distortion to produce an artificial majority result designed to placate the fixation on the need for 50-percent-plus-one. Surely, that must count for something.

DEMOCRACY VERSUS ACCOUNTABILITY IN PROPORTIONAL REPRESENTATION

The false understanding of what election results mean, combined with the fixation on fifty-percent-plus-one, has led to a rise in the calls for electoral reform, the most prominent form being those that fall under the category of "proportional representation" — that is, the proportion of seats won are allotted as a reflection of the popular vote. Never mind that the popular vote figure is itself a distortion — in order to satisfy an artificial need, increasingly convoluted systems are dreamed up to provide the artificial sense that the election results are somehow "fairer."

One can argue that there is an inherent illogic in the way we look at proportional representation (PR) schemes. For one, it seeks to apply a result that doesn't reflect the reality of the situation. In the case of a federal election, what is being voted on is who will represent each constituency in the House of Commons. No matter that people might feel they're voting for the party, or the leader, or whatever other consideration they might have in mind, the ballot they are casting is for the representative in that seat in the House of Commons. Saying that seats need to be apportioned otherwise would indicate that the votes being cast were to determine the composition of the House of Commons in an overall cohesive manner rather than to determine its population of individual MPs. There is a massive gap in the underlying logic here that certain PR systems try to bridge with other mechanisms, but it doesn't change the fact that within a Westminster system the individual MPs are the basic representative unit.

It would help at this point if we reminded ourselves of the simple fact of just what an election is about, which is to make a decision. In the case of federal politics, it is a decision about who will fill that particular seat in the House of Commons — nothing more, nothing less. And yet there seems to be a kind of "mandate creep" regarding what the election is supposed to represent. This is not only symptomatic of a failure to understand the simple mechanics of the election and its results, it is the product of the broader move toward giving more weight to the role of the party and the leader in an election result. The logical fallacy produced by tallying vote counts across the country to produce popular support percentages for each party fits entirely within the rubric that holds that elections are held so that parties can be apportioned seats within the Commons rather than so that individual MPs who fall into party affiliations can be elected to fill seats in the House.

The most commonly discussed version of proportional representation bandied about is a kind of "mixed-member proportional" (MMP) system in which voters cast two ballots — one for the candidate of their choice, and the second for the party of their choice. The idea is that the added number of seats designated for party votes will be used to balance out the composition of the Commons to better fit the proportion of the popular vote — no matter that this number is a flawed metric. It is the trade-off to overcome the logic gap of trying to apportion seats to parties based on votes for individual MPs — applying that new metric to artificially legitimize the push toward an arbitrary measure of "fairness." But let's explore the consequences of this proposal.

First and foremost, an MMP system has the immediate effect of increasing the role of the party in the election and diminishing that of an individual MP, because of the two votes cast, one is for the party itself. This immediately creates two classes of MPs — ones who are forced to face nomination races in their constituencies, and those who are appointed from party lists, who will then fill the "proportionate" seats after they are allocated. Each will face different challenges, and each will have a different master.

Constituency MPs will remain accountable to their riding associations, but because the party role will have been increased, they are almost certain to face a more empowered central party leadership, one that has demonstrated few qualms about using whatever weight or power it can bring to bear to get its way with nominations or policies. But list MPs are accountable solely to the party and instead of facing the electorate only need to maintain the favour of the party leadership to whom they owe their positions. This arrangement gives more power to the central party leadership and takes it away from the grassroots membership who would otherwise have the say in who they choose to represent them.

Some proponents of MMP, like former NDP MP Paul Dewar, have suggested that the creation of list MPs would ensure that the value of the Senate (which they would see abolished) wasn't lost, since notable Canadians who wouldn't otherwise run for office could be appointed as senators are currently, and contribute to public life in a similar manner. While it's a nice idea in theory, it falls apart rather quickly once you look a little more closely at it.

One of the biggest differences between an appointed senator and a list MP is that a senator has longevity with which to make considerations — an average of ten to fifteen years, as opposed to a list MP having maybe three to five years. More than that, senators have permanency — they can't be removed if the party loses the next election, and trying to remove them for anything other than criminal convictions is almost impossible. That gives them a level of protection that allows them to act as an effective check on power that doesn't face the consequences of removal when they speak truth to power. Contrast that to list MPs who must continue to curry favour with the party leader who appointed them, lest they face removal from caucus (thus losing their raison d'être for being in the Commons — there is no logic behind an independent list MP). Failure to do that will result in them simply not being reappointed during the next election.

Proponents of the list system tout its ability to appoint more women and visible minorities to the Commons to "fill in the gaps" left by elections, which are still dominated by middle-aged, straight, white men. But this is part of the problem that comes with having a "two-tier" system of MPs and goes to the issue of legitimacy. Politically speaking, using an MMP system to "fill in" the Commons with more women and visible minorities through appointments taints them with the air of tokenism, in contrast to the other MPs who had to fight nomination races and win over the electorate to get elected.

It also sets up a dynamic in which constituency MPs will feel that their votes should count for more than those of list MPs because of the democratic legitimacy attached to them. This establishes difficult party dynamics, and even worse tensions within the Commons, where smaller parties, unable to win constituency seats, might only achieve status by means of list seats, and these based solely on the artificial measure of voter share. These "free" seats would come without having to win a single constituency seat, which is the basis on which our system depends. With the democratic legitimacy of parties who only have list seats in question, the legitimacy of any coalition government (and most governments in an MMP system will be coalitions) will themselves be called into question if any of the partners in that government have only list MPs.

There are also few guarantees concerning the transparency of the process by which these list MPs would be appointed. While proponents of MMP insist that parties can introduce some kind of transparent process by which list MPs are chosen, this again is problematic when an attempt is made to combine that aim with the stated goal of using the power of list appointments to ensure there are more women and visible minorities within the Commons. To achieve such goals, parties must be able to locate potential candidates who aren't currently seeking a seat, individuals who possess enough desirable qualities for the parties to want them in Parliament, and further, the parties must be able to identify appropriate numbers of women and/or visible minorities. It goes without saying that the candidates would all have to be new. If a party were to use its list system to appoint defeated candidates post-election, that would fuel the cynicism of a system whereby a person is defeated and yet still winds up in the Commons regardless of the decision of the voters. And what if a list MP is someone the public is generally dissatisfied with, yet the party seems to like? Once again we find ourselves in a system where the accountability mechanism — in this case the nomination race — has been circumvented, and where list MPs can keep their seats as long as the party continues to appoint them.

Because an MMP system favours smaller parties that generally have difficulty getting seats and rewards them for the artificial metric of voter share, a Commons elected under such a system would almost certainly guarantee perpetual minority governments. Furthermore, because of the rewards offered to smaller parties, such a system would encourage the rise of regional or single-issue parties and would consequently weaken the role of the larger "brokerage" parties, as they are sometimes known. Currently, parties broker within their caucuses to share risk and reward together so that regional tensions are dissipated, and policy is generally decided by the grassroots membership.

In an MMP system, with the rewards of election for regional blocs and single-issue groups being immediately apparent, the ability to moderate the excesses of those demands by disciplining power also weakens, and because they know that at least some of them will be needed by a coalition government, it further empowers them to break apart from the brokerage party. The fact that our current brokerage parties are able to absorb new ideas has led to them being adaptable rather than hidebound to single ideologies, and it can also be argued has kept out hard-right politics from Canada, unlike many countries with MMP systems. One could go as far as to argue that single-issue or regional parties are illegitimate, given that the role of the party within a system of responsible government is to form a government and maintain confidence. There is nothing about regional or single-issue parties that concerns the formation of a government.[2]

While there is nothing inherently wrong with a coalition government, the notion that coalitions must be formed post-election, trading policies and favours for Cabinet posts and assurances of confidence, is again problematic within the context of accountability. Parties are elected based on platforms, but for coalition governments to be formed, whole swaths of policy that a party was elected on must be tossed overboard to satisfy the demands of coalition partners, and those negotiations for the final policy platform of a coalition government happen in backroom deal-making rather than at the ballot box where voters can decide if they want to sign on for that policy platform or not. As well, this kind of backroom negotiation gives rise to a situation in which a radical party with a small percentage of the popular vote can exchange its policy preferences to get a large party into power, in effect, giving that small minority a de facto veto over the majority.

Not only is the development and expression of a political platform a problem in a coalition government, such governments are also difficult to turf from power — they have a tendency to become almost perpetual things. One of the most important ways in which our system is accountable is the ease with which the current system allows the public to "throw the bums out" when it is dissatisfied with them. But what many European Parliaments have demonstrated is that coalition governments have a greater tendency to simply shuffle around coalition partners rather than face outright defeat, keeping them in power for decades in some cases. How this is at all desirable from either a democratic or accountability standpoint is hard to fathom.

WHAT REFORM WE DO NEED

As a complete overhaul of the electoral system is both unfeasible and of dubious value, since it would make the system both less democratic — in fact, it would be less so despite being presented under the guise of being "more fair" — and much less accountable to the electorate, we need to realize that any reforms that do need to be made are minor and rest largely with the electorate itself.

As was mentioned previously, one of the most detrimental changes to our electoral system was made as part of the 1970 revisions to the Canada Elections Act, which gave party leaders the ability to sign off on the nomination forms of prospective candidates. Combing through the debates in *Hansard* and committee transcripts of that era, one scarcely finds mention of this change at all. Nevertheless, it has resulted in some of the biggest unintended consequences that have occurred in our political system — all made in the name of trying to modernize our system of elections.

Bill C-215, as it was then known, was a massive piece of legislation that rewrote the entire electoral framework in the country. This was the bill that lowered the voting age to eighteen from twenty-one, allowed liquor stores and bars to open once the polls closed rather than forcing them to remain shuttered the whole day, and most controversially at the time, removed the candidate's address and occupation from the ballot in favour of the party affiliation instead. There were a number of reasons for doing so. Some candidates had the same last names, others had difficulty putting an occupation down — incumbent MPs, for example (and there was a fair bit of debate as to whether or not it was appropriate to put "politician" or "ex-MP" for incumbents, or if someone could list "football star" rather than "professional athlete" as an occupation).

There was plenty of concern about what having a party affiliation on the ballot would mean, whether it was a "free ride" for parties, how it would play into financing for advertising, and whether it would negatively impact the individualism of candidates on the ballot, since the era of people voting for leaders rather than MPs was already well under way. Concerns were also raised that removing the addresses of candidates from the ballots made it easier for a party to parachute in non-resident candidates whose only legitimacy would be their party affiliation. Others were worried that it would allow for parties to "merchandise" themselves, and have an added effect at the point-of-sale — namely, the ballot box — based solely on brand identity. As it turned out, both concerns weren't entirely unfounded.

The change resulting in party leaders being given sole authority to sign off on candidate nomination papers, however, arose in large part because some mechanism was needed to ensure that prospective candidates couldn't simply declare themselves to be a Liberal or a Progressive Conservative. At the same time, changes were made to guarantee that such individuals didn't invent spoofed parties, such as the "Progressive Conservative Party for Canada" rather than the "Progressive Conservative Party of Canada," in order to try to claim ballots that way. There were also financial concerns coming into play; parties, which were only just gaining legal standing as organizations, needed a method of accountability for tax credits, donations, disclosures, and so on.

At the same time, as well as concerns about people simply declaring themselves to be candidates for this or that party, there were also worries about hijacked nominations, though this has been a problem that was relayed anecdotally rather than in any of the recorded debates. In particular, there was apparently a push by pro-life groups to hijack nominations in the era when Pierre Trudeau was busy decriminalizing homosexuality, birth control, and abortion in certain circumstances, and there would have been a more concerted effort to undermine Liberal votes at the time. Giving the leader the ability to sign off on nominations would be useful for keeping such attempted hijackings from taking place.

Nevertheless, the granting of this one particular power, no matter how well intentioned its institution, has been abused since and has resulted in the removal of the agency of both MPs and the grassroots membership to fulfill their roles. Its usefulness in ensuring that candidates are properly nominated and are legitimate representatives of the party has long since passed, since new legislation has not only formalized the legal standing of political parties but also their financial operations and accountability. New safeguards against hijacking could be implemented within the party mechanism itself, be it the national council or the council of riding presidents, whereby suspect nominations could be declared void and new votes ordered. There is no longer any particular need for party leaders to have this power.

Removing this ability of party leaders would eliminate a cudgel they can wield over the heads of their caucuses. MPs, now understandably concerned about the consequences facing them if they take a stand that goes against the wishes of the leader, would no longer be faced with the threat of not having their nomination papers signed. Not only would that restore some of the power of the MPs — and more can be done on that front — but it would also return power to the riding associations. Grassroots members would no longer have to fret that their choice of a candidate would be overturned by the leadership, while the ability of the leadership to parachute in a candidate of its own choosing would also be diminished.

While on the one hand this change would represent a restoration rather than a reform, it should be noted that in no way am I saying there was a golden age of election laws in this country. The secret ballot wasn't introduced until well after Confederation, and up until that point people had to line up at polls and publicly declare which candidate they supported, and needed the protection of a party gang to ensure they weren't coerced with the threat of violence. Even when ballot boxes were introduced, elections were hardly free from outside interference. Until there were sufficient safeguards in place to protect the privacy of those casting ballots, the era of "rum-bottle" politics ruled. Party organizers were able to see who a voter was voting for and rewarded those who voted for their candidates by handing out either a small bottle of rum to men or a pair of stockings to women as they exited the polling stations.

If there has been some back and forth in the area of protecting the secrecy of the ballot, a great deal of progress has been made since that time ensuring that election financing is as clean as possible. However, this was a problem that was still being addressed even as the 1970 reforms were being debated. At that time donations and expenses were both unlimited and kept secret, and concerns over the influence of corporations were much more tangible, since they could pour massive amounts of money into campaigns without any real transparency. To the greatest possible extent, these kinds of things have changed.

While electoral reform proposals continue to be bandied about, it's important to remember what progress we've already made, and to be mindful that we don't create any additional unintended consequences, as with that apparently harmless suggestion of leaders signing off.

EVERY VOTE DOES COUNT

One of the most dangerous mistruths about our system of elections going around is the claim that we need some kind of proportional representation in order to "make every vote count." What our current system offers is more than just an accurate and undistorted reflection of the mood of the electorate; it provides the ultimate expression of fairness, since it ensures that every ballot counts equally. There is no adjustment to create an artificial simple majority, there are no added mechanisms to create a distorted picture of proportionality based on a logical fallacy, and MPs have equal democratic legitimacy.

The notion that proportional representation would make "every ballot count" is a product of the dangerous belief that the only ballots that count are those that go toward the winning candidate. Not only is it wrong and a threat in and of itself, it also helps to strengthen the wrong view of democracy as a spectator sport — only by aligning yourself with the winning team do you take some small measure of its victory with you. All of this is patently false.

What PR gets away from is the very basic participatory nature of democracy. Democracy is about more than simply casting a ballot every few years; it's about getting involved in the grassroots level of a party, contributing to policy ideas, voting to get a candidate nominated, and then working to ensure that said candidate gets elected. It's about the process more than it is about the outcome.

Nevertheless, the wrong-headed "fairness" arguments and those that would see a vote only counting if it's toward the winning candidate have given rise to the notion that we can implement reforms that would be "quick fixes." These reforms would allow other parties to win power by some other means than the current system of winning enough seats. Much of the discussion of these reforms is couched in the language of "consensus" or "co-operation," without the understanding that it's nearly impossible to create a system in which there is any accountability for decisions made by consensus or co-operation. Not that these considerations are of much importance in the minds of those proposing such reforms usually. Generally, these considerations are partisan in nature and those proposing such reforms either lack understanding of how our system operates and why there need to be mechanisms of accountability, or when they are aware of them, express little interest in maintaining them.

But quick fixes only offer superficial solutions; in fact, often they end up making the situation they're hoping to fix — the "increased democracy" — worse. In the age of "slacktivism" in which all one has to do is join a Facebook group, get a topic to trend on Twitter, or click to sign an online petition, the spectator model reigns supreme. Absent from these discussions is the realization that elections rely on hard work. For politics to be meaningful, it can't rely on the spectator model of simply casting a ballot.

Meaningful participation in our democratic system means volunteering, fundraising, organizing, and building support from the ground up. To get more women or visible minorities in the House of Commons, it's up to the electorate to identify these candidates, encourage them to run, and then organize to build their support. That means paying more than lip service to diversity and overcoming the inherent structural biases and doing the work in finding candidates who can fill the roles — again, the hard work of political organizing instead of quick fixes. That makes the achievement of nomination and election meaningful and legitimate, and it engages the community in a way that an appointment or parachute candidate never can.

But with the awareness that politics is hard work must come another kind of mature realization — that it's not always about winning. As much as the proponents of proportional representation might like to believe it, politics isn't a co-operative board game in which everyone wins. Making decisions — which is what an election is about — means there will always be winners and losers. Does that mean the ballots cast for a losing candidate have been wasted? Of course not. How could they have been when it shows that particular candidate engaged that portion of the electorate?

If candidates don't win, at least they've engaged in the process. Likewise, if the candidate you cast a ballot for didn't win, at least you took part in making that decision. And the more you participate, the greater will be your incentive to get out, organize, fundraise, and participate again to ensure that you engage the community in the hope of bringing them onside. If your riding association is active and involved, then your concerns will still make it to your party's elected representatives in Ottawa, which again showcases the input of the community. It all adds up to active and ongoing participation in the process, which is really what it's all about.

4

THE HOUSE OF COMMONS

Just what is the role of an MP? You would think that would be an easy question, but apparently not. Everybody seems to have a different description — most especially the MPs themselves, who are thrust into their positions with little in the way of orientation and almost no training whatsoever.

In a report by Samara Canada, which conducted exit interviews with sixty-five MPs between the thirty-eighth and thirty-ninth Parliaments, not only did it become clear that MPs don't know what their role is, it also became evident that the Commons is virtually out of control. MPs don't know their own job description, are dissatisfied with the committees they are assigned to, and have very different ideas regarding what their role in the parliamentary system entails.[1] It's indicative of the alarming level of civic illiteracy that we're facing in this country and heralds worse to come if it goes unaddressed. This is particularly true if there are more repeats of the 2011 federal election when a swath of new NDP MPs — MPs who hadn't even campaigned in their own ridings — were elected. If MPs who didn't even campaign for the job can get elected, it paints a grim picture of what we can expect.

So what is the job of an MP? Let's break it down. There are all kinds of theories out there about what it means to be a representative, but none of those theories actually mean anything if one sticks to the strictest definition of an MP's actual job description. You can say that MPs should be representatives of the electorate, representatives of their party. You can say they should represent their constituencies to Ottawa or Ottawa to their constituencies, that they should be role models for their particular communities whether it's geographic, socio-economic, or ethnocultural. You can debate whether it's their job as MPs to vote according to their constituents' wishes, whether they should toe the party line, or whether they should vote their own consciences. All of these are valid points to debate, but none of them addresses the core functions of what that job description actually entails. At its very heart an MP's job is to ensure there is accountability in the system; their job is to hold the government accountable.

MPs ARE NOT PRINCIPALLY LAWMAKERS

MPs are frequently labelled "lawmakers." That is one of the biggest misnomers in Canadian politics. The role of "lawmaker" is a particularly American one. Their congressmen and senators are given that label because they have the ability to put forward legislation and debate it. But in a Westminster-style parliamentary democracy like ours, operating under the rules and conventions of responsible government, laws aren't put forward in the same way. In our system, an MP isn't primarily a lawmaker, despite the fact that the media likes to use this term to describe MPs.

If there is one quote that should be emblazoned upon the walls of all MPs' offices and headlining every single description of an MP in every single school textbook, it is this one by William Ewart Gladstone: "You are not here to govern; rather you are here to hold to account those who do."

This is exactly the rule of thumb that should be adhered to because the first duty of every single MP who isn't a minister is to hold the government to account. Remember that the government is the prime minister and the Cabinet, which means that even backbench MPs of the governing party have an obligation to ensure their own government remains accountable to the chamber. In exercising this power, the MPs continue to hold the balance of power in guaranteeing the government maintains the confidence of the chamber. It's a pretty powerful responsibility, if actually exercised — as it should be.

The way that MPs hold the government to account is by controlling the public purse. If the government wants to spend money to implement its policy platform and to generally run the affairs of the nation, it had better be prepared to answer for its decisions to the House, and MPs had better make it work for every cent it wants to spend and ensure that it remains accountable to the public whose funds it is spending.

Unfortunately, this doesn't seem to be the way things work anymore. A variety of factors, including civic illiteracy, have led to the degradation of the role of MPs. As a result, the first duty of MPs — holding the government to account — seems to be almost entirely absent from the self-reported descriptions of their role in the Samara exit interviews. In the Library of Parliament's "Members of the House of Commons: Their Role" publication, that function is listed far below the discussions on influencing policy and receives a mere mention in the "legislative role" section before a slightly more robust discussion of the "surveillance role" of an MP.[2] What takes precedence is the "representative function" of MPs and their ability to influence policy through debate, committee participation, and private members' legislation. The fact that this function is elevated above the role of an MP in holding the government to account speaks volumes about the way in which MPs and those who study them are enamoured with the "lawmaker" idea. That the role of accountability isn't even mentioned until much further in an official parliamentary document outlining the role of an MP is also indicative of the way in which that most crucial function has been devalued in the face of the "lawmaker" idea.

While there is a time and place for private members' business, and it does have a role to play within the system, it occupies a minor position in the overall function of an MP, and the disproportionate amount of credence given to that role has degraded the accountability function of MPs. It has been argued that private members' business has an increasing role to play with respect to influencing policy decisions — especially after changes to the Standing Orders made more of these bills votable[3] — however, this movement nevertheless continues to take that policy development role away from the grassroots membership. All of this is further complicated by other abuses of private members' business instituted by parties themselves.

If an increase in the amount of private members' business has resulted in an attempt to bolster the status of the average MP, excessive party discipline, unaccountable leadership, and the ability for party leadership to blackmail MPs through the rule of the nomination paper sign-off are all contributing factors to the decline of the role of an MP. Overall, these latter factors have had a much stronger effect on the place of MPs in the system. More than all of the above, however, it is the MPs' own lack of awareness of their own roles that is perhaps at the heart of most of these problems.

Because MPs face the constant challenge of re-election, a tendency has grown for MPs to focus more of their time and attention on constituency work, in which they act as a kind of ombudsman for their constituents when they have dealings with the civil service. While constituency work can be a useful tool for showing constituents that their MPs have their backs when it comes to interacting with the faceless bureaucracy, and while engaging in it can show MPs what the pressing issues are within their ridings for some citizens, problems arise when MPs devote too much time to constituency work, the main one being that it eats away at their time and limits the amount they can spend, and therefore their effectiveness, focusing on their main role as MPs.

As well as there being only so much time, there are only so many resources that an MP has to devote to doing his or her job, and so it becomes a problem when constituency work takes precedence over policy and over-sight. And yet this is exactly what starts happening when some MPs have a constituency staffer devoted full-time to issues such as processing immigration files. This creates an escalating cycle: as MPs and political staffs spend more time and precious resources on playing this ombudsman role and processing paperwork, the expectation that this is part of their job (which it's really not) grows, which feeds the demand, and so MPs begin demanding yet more staff to deal with these kinds of files.

Meanwhile, the amount of staff and resources an MP is able to devote toward the scrutiny of the Estimates or of legislation is further reduced. And because they have very limited budgets, many MPs tend, when hiring staff, to select recent graduates with very little experience because they can be enlisted cheaply, which gives a staffing budget a little more breathing room. This leads to the further degradation of the effectiveness of MPs at their actual job — holding the government to account through their role of scrutiny — because with little time and often only a small number of rather inexperienced staff to help with this kind of work, it becomes impossible to be very effective in that role.

There are further problems that stem from the practice of MPs playing the ombudsman role within their constituencies. A Samara Canada study showed that non-voters have been turned off politics entirely because they had a disappointing interaction with a member of a government establishment over an issue such as accessing daycare spaces, covering tuition costs, or having a speed bump installed in their neighbourhoods, though there seems little awareness that the job of dealing with such matters is not really the concern of elected officials but more the responsibility of the permanent civil service.[4] MPs are encouraged to "reach out" even more to jaded voters with this kind of constituency work, but without any kind of functioning education system for the electorate to realize the difference in levels of government or between elected officials and bureaucrats, it feeds the spiralling disengagement of disappointment.

Despite the fact that playing the ombudsman isn't the proper role of an MP, most still feel the need to "reach out" with pithy political slogans like "working for you." This kind of affirmational marketing repeats to people the message that they are the centre of the universe and that they deserve to be catered to because they are special. That this has become part of the language of political marketing feeds the expectation that an MP's job is to navigate the bureaucracy on behalf of his or her constituents, rather than hold the government to account. This is, of course, not true; nevertheless, the fact that it is held by many to be true has resulted in MPs needing to contort themselves and their roles to suit this ombudsman role. And the more they do so, the further it erodes their ability to do their jobs.

To add to all this, there seems to be a corresponding disconnect within the civil service when it comes to its own role concerning these kinds of files. Anecdotally, in speaking with the staff of an MP, there emerges a common thread of reports that some departments won't even begin to process files until they're forwarded by the MP's office. This should raise some very big flags about the line between politicians and the bureaucracy. If files need to be forwarded by the MP's office before the bureaucracy will act on them, it is a mere half-step away from the kind of corruption we see in other countries. This trend should also raise a flag about the problems that exist within the public service if this issue isn't addressed. And should this trend continue, it will further consume the time and resources of MPs and their staffs, with the result that their most basic function — holding the government to account — will be overwhelmed by the need to simply maintain this burgeoning ombudsman role.

The other danger of having MPs who don't know their roles, and of having young staffers who are cheap to employ, is that the policy expertise moves out of the offices of those MPs and progresses up the ladder into the offices of the party leadership. The MPs haven't spent any time scrutinizing the Estimates, so they don't know what's in them? Have no fear — the leader's office can advise on how to vote on them. The leader's office can supply talking points for Question Period (QP), or prepared speeches for what passes for debate in the chamber, or even lines for media appearances. MPs don't know what's actually contained in the bill they're supposed to be scrutinizing? Don't fear — the leader's office has that covered, too.

It's not hard to see the dangers that immediately creep up. Leaders' offices, already too powerful and without any kind of mechanisms of accountability, thanks to their "democratization," will become ever more powerful as more and more authority continues to be amassed by them, while MPs content themselves with work that isn't actually theirs to perform. They do so, of course, in the hope that engaging in such work will attract voters, who themselves don't know what their MPs' jobs are, and who subsequently expect them to be all things to all people.

If there is one way for us to ensure that our MPs are actually empowered and have meaningful roles, then ensuring that they know what their jobs are is a good start.

LETTING SOMEBODY ELSE DO IT

One of the consequences of MPs not understanding their accountability role, and of spending all their time and resources on constituency matters, is that the actual work of accountability gets passed on to independent officers of Parliament in their stead — people like the auditor general, and the more recent parliamentary budget officer. After all, scrutinizing the Estimates is hard work, and a relatively large proportion of the MPs who are elected these days lack the training and skills with which to read these technical and complex documents, and because their staffs also lack the training — trained and qualified staffs cost money, which MPs generally don't have — well, why not turn these matters over to the experts?

But this is, of course, a rather fraught proposal. For one thing, turning over the scrutiny function of the Commons to independent officers of Parliament weakens accountability because of the nature of those very officers.

Because they exist outside the system of responsible government, there is no accountability for their actions. They are revered because their unelected status affords them a kind of apolitical credibility in an age of cynicism about political parties, and yet their reports nevertheless become political documents used by MPs as tools for scrutinizing the government — a role MPs are supposed to perform. Do these officers of Parliament, existing outside the political system, strengthen or undermine responsible government? Does the auditor general assist the Commons Public Accounts Committee, or does his work supplant it? It can be argued that if taken to the extreme, his independence is at odds with the accountability of the system.[5]

At what point do these independent officers of Parliament usurp the role of MPs rather than strengthen it by assisting them? It's an important question that I don't think enough people have adequately considered — especially MPs. While they may benefit from the assistance provided by those officers in doing the heavy lifting when it comes to the financial scrutiny of government, such assistance conversely diminishes the importance of their role because they have less of an active hand in that exercise in accountability. As David E. Smith wrote in his exploration of the relationship between these independent officers and MPs:

> Each officer becomes tantamount to an external body that relies more on the capacity of public opinion to draw attention and mount pressure on the executive to act, instead of relying on Parliament itself to make an effective and continuous effort to implement the recommendations made in the officers' annual report.[6]

All of this has been further complicated by the creation of the Parliamentary Budget Office as part of the Library of Parliament in 2006, and the appointment of the first parliamentary budget officer (PBO) in 2008. Part of the problem with his office is that it was modelled on the American Congressional Budget Office, which fills a specific role for a very different system from ours. The parliamentary budget officer is not, in fact, an actual independent officer of Parliament, a situation that led to disagreements between Kevin Page, the first PBO, and his putative boss, the parliamentary librarian, over how much independence he actually had. We have also seen that after the appointment of Kevin Page the government disagreed with his projections and calculations and sought to punish him by starving his budget, which hampered his ability to do some of the work he was asked to do simply because he wasn't able to maintain some of the necessary staff.

But while the Conservatives were high-minded in advocating the creation of the PBO as someone who could provide independent analysis of the projections put out by the Department of Finance, which they didn't trust while they were in Opposition, the PBO soon came to be seen as an agent of the Opposition, whose MPs would get the PBO to do their due diligence for them. When the Conservatives were back in Opposition, they immediately began praising the work of the PBO again when criticism was against the Liberal government. The rationale behind all of this isn't hard to understand. After all, reading the Estimates or cost projections is complex, and most MPs don't have the expertise to do it, so since the PBO was independent and operated outside the party system, his analysis was seen as more "credible." Which isn't to say there isn't value in having the PBO as someone who can provide independent analysis of budget projections, for example, or in assisting MPs in navigating the Estimates process, but MPs shouldn't simply stop doing their jobs because the PBO is there.

THE BUSINESS OF SUPPLY

With the auditor general to catch all the misspending on the back end, and the PBO checking cost estimates, MPs now seem to have watchdogs on both sides of the supply cycle. This has led to further abdication of their own duties and responsibilities as stewards of the public purse. Remember that MPs are supposed to be scrutinizing the Estimates process — that means looking over where the government plans to spend money before it actually goes out the door. But the Estimates have become increasingly difficult to read, and MPs have little time for them, spending their resources on constituency work or their own personal policy preoccupations.

All of this would be bad enough, but even when MPs do muster the time and focus to consider the Estimates, rules have been put in place to hinder them in this task. In 1968, when the Liberal government of the day decided it didn't like the fact that MPs were holding up the supply cycle, it put through changes to the Standing Orders so that if the Estimates aren't approved before a certain date, they are automatically deemed to have been adopted.

Think about that for a second — even if nobody bothers to actually scrutinize the Estimates, they're still deemed to have passed because time lapsed on a calendar. That's a pretty glaring lapse in the ensuring of accountability, which the MPs are supposed to be exercising over the government of the day. This practice is about as bad as rubber-stamping the entire main Estimates from start to finish in the space of a couple of hours, as the Commons did in the three-week sitting that followed the 2011 election, and again in the week sitting following the 2015 election. They didn't even pretend to look at them — just rushed through the votes to pass them. In the 2015 post-election vote, MPs missed that the bill didn't contain a crucial schedule, and it was up to the Senate — which spent the week going over those Estimates in detail while the Commons spent mere minutes — to catch the error and send the bill back for correction.

The abuse of the Estimates has become worse in recent years. Governments have begun using different accounting methods for the Estimates and the Public Accounts — the documents published at the end of the fiscal year to show how money was spent — so that MPs aren't able to track the spending. Votes on the Estimates have also been decoupled from the budgetary cycle so that in many years the Estimates have been voted on before the budget has even been tabled, making it impossible to track where money is supposed to be spent.

The Conservative government under Stephen Harper also passed a law hidden in an omnibus bill that took away the power from MPs to approve government borrowing, making it simply a decision of Cabinet. The Liberal senators protested this change but weren't able to thwart it. The current Liberal government has promised to reform the Estimates cycle so that its release will again coincide with the release of the budget. The Liberals have also promised to change the accounting system so that the one used for the Estimates will match that used for the Public Accounts, but that hasn't come to pass yet. Neither have they fully restored the ability of MPs to vote on government borrowing, instead retaining a loophole for Cabinet to approve it on its own during "emergencies" — something that hasn't been defined.

In the bigger picture, this means there is virtually no scrutiny of plans to borrow or spend money. Only after it's been spent, well spent, or misspent, is the auditor general sent in to see if things went okay or not. That seems like a pretty poor way to control the public purse — the fundamental fiduciary responsibility of every single MP in the House of Commons. But if MPs don't know it's their job, and if the public doesn't, either — since they're busy trying to get their MPs to "work for them" — then perhaps it's not all that surprising that MPs aren't doing their jobs, either.

It's also not very remarkable that the notion of supply days has fallen to the wayside in the new political calculus in the Commons. Supply days, or "Opposition days," as they're otherwise known, have a very specific purpose: to give the Opposition an opportunity to demonstrate why supply should be refused.[7] This allows the Opposition to choose the subject of debate on the allotted days, of which it has a certain number in every supply cycle. One of the most important functions of such days is to provide a mechanism for the Opposition to move motions of non-confidence, something extremely important in periods of minority Parliaments when a government could fall on such a motion. But the business of deciding whether or not to vote supply has all but vanished as supply days are currently being exercised.

Supply days have more recently become an exercise for take-note debates. Rather than being used to discuss supply, or why a government should be refused it, supply days are more commonly employed to harangue governments with debate and votes on non-binding motions about any number of subjects, almost none of which have to do with why the government should be denied supply. While it might be laudable to debate what the Opposition feels the government could be spending money on, it nevertheless remains removed from the debate about why supply should be refused.

Even more worrying is the tactic of debating and voting on "mom and apple pie" issues. In such debates, the Opposition hopes to gain some moral clout by getting the government to agree to unanimous motions to address some social problem, which the government is happy to do because it looks as if it's doing something about that problem. When the government doesn't actually follow up that vote with any concrete plan, there is little in the way of harm for it in terms of either public opinion or consequence in the Commons because the votes are on non-binding motions. While there may be a certain symbolism to the use of the moral weight of non-binding motions, the business of supply remains unattended to and the government hasn't had to defend its spending plans before the Commons. In the end, MPs are allowed to remain in the realm of "feel-good" politics rather than focusing on their jobs of scrutiny of the Estimates.

One last note on this point: in recent history there has been some semblance of a resurgence of the awareness of the responsibility of MPs to control the public purse. In the lead-up to the 2011 election, Opposition parties demanded costing figures for the Conservative government's justice agenda, and for its planned purchase of F-35 fighter jets. While committees can compel documents, those documents that the government did turn over didn't contain the full life-cycle costs, which led to the government falling on a loss of confidence brought about by a finding of contempt of Parliament.

But there are two things to note here: number one was that the MPs were more concerned that the figures weren't being turned over to the PBO for review rather than they were with their own ability to review them; and number two, this contest with the government was presented to the public in a manner that made it seem like political gamesmanship and squabbling, and not one of the most fundamental parts of the system of responsible government. This latter indictment is directed both at the governing party and the media, which wasn't making the point about the proper role of the exercise of this responsibility. And thus, the electorate went into the election not thinking about those fundamental responsibilities. Civic illiteracy ruled the day.

PRIVATE MEMBERS' BUSINESS CREEP

As we have established, one of the fundamental misunderstandings about our system of government is that MPs, while legislators in the sense that they are members of the legislative assembly, are not lawmakers. And yet, with the way in which private members' business is being considered these days, it would be hard to think otherwise. The importance placed on this particular role that MPs play has been blown entirely out of proportion, and now it's not uncommon to see MPs devoting an inordinate amount of time to private members' business, introducing bills and motions — especially if they're trying to raise their media profiles.

The creep in importance of this private members' business, and private members' bills (PMBs) in particular, stems in large part from the fact that many people get into politics full of their own ideas about how to change the world, or riding their own personal policy hobby horses. Full of ideas, they want to express them in a meaningful way. For most of them, that meaningful way involves constantly crafting PMBs and introducing them in the House, and getting them onto the Order Paper.

This was made even more problematic in the minority government years between 2006 and 2011 when Opposition parties felt as if they could band together and start passing their own bills contrary to those of the government. Apparently none of them had read the William Gladstone quote about not governing but holding to account those who do. Just because they had more votes didn't make them the government, and yet they believed they could pass these bills with relative impunity. In fact, some Opposition parties went as far as to brand the pithy statement of "We're in proposition, not Opposition." The kind of muscle-flexing challenge contained in this statement makes clear the authors' lack of understanding of their role in Parliament and serves to perpetuate the notion that somehow a "consensus" government is more desirable than the current adversarial system, with its systems of accountability built in. But, of course, there are plenty of restrictions around PMBs, although these did temper the zeal for them a bit. Nevertheless, these restrictions should nevertheless be spelled out a bit more.

Under the current Standing Orders, each MP who isn't a member of the Cabinet or a parliamentary secretary gets one slot for private members' business, whether it's a bill or a motion. That slot is two hours of debate and then a vote whether to adopt the motion or the bill at second reading, at which point it is sent off to committee for another brief amount of scrutiny, usually another couple of hours only.

It's not a lot of time, and only one hour of every day of the House's calendar is devoted to private members' business. The order in which MPs are chosen to present their private members' business is determined by lottery, and they reach the House in lots of thirty.

Even if they do reach the House, such motions are non-binding, and PMBs are strictly limited in that they cannot require the government to spend money. That would need a Royal Recommendation, which the government tends to be pretty reluctant in handing out — as should be the case, considering its job is to govern and not the backbenchers'. As well, it is the role of the Commons to grant supply to the government, not to impose it upon the Crown.

And yet, judging from the number of PMBs and motions on the Order Paper, you would think this was the pressing business of the nation. MPs who want to look as if they're on top of an issue will draft a PMB about it. They'll draft a series of PMBs about their personal policy preoccupations. They'll call press conferences and invite people up to the Hill to talk about how great it would be if this bill got passed. But there's just one little problem — pretty much none of them will ever see the light of day. Since backbench MPs have just one slot in which to put a piece of private members' business through, it is mystifying why certain of them put hundreds of motions on the Order Paper, every new Parliament, followed up by dozens of PMBs, knowing full well they will go nowhere.

"Oh, but it's symbolic," they'll argue. "It shows the government that people care about the issue. And if the government wants to pass a similar bill on its own, I'd be happy to relinquish mine." But if these bills are only intended to be symbolic, then surely the time and effort that goes into drafting them are opportunity costs that could have been better spent doing the actual job of scrutiny. If MPs want debate on a topic, then why not simply debate a motion about it instead of investing all of that added time and energy?

In the end, most of these bills wind up being drafted by clerks in the Library of Parliament (as opposed to legal experts in the Department of Justice), so it's not as if MPs have to spend too much time in the creation process. And it's not as if framing such bills takes away too much time and resources from doing the business of scrutiny because, well, as we've already discussed, MPs aren't exactly doing that.

There is, of course, a real benefit for an MP if one of these bills actually does make it to the chamber. If the bill is passed, suddenly he or she becomes a hero for the cause; if it gets defeated, the government/Opposition/other parliamentarians can be villains.

As is clear, this system is already a badly compromised one. Things were complicated even further during the recent era of minority governments when Opposition parties wanted to put forward their competing governing legislation. Never mind that it wasn't their place to do so (governments propose, the Opposition opposes, as it should be), but this desire by the Opposition parties also meant that their MPs were forced to give up their spots for bills the party wanted passed. Sure, some of them claimed they were happy to do so, but the move by Opposition parties to take over the PMB privileges of their MPs was just one more way in which the independence of MPs was being diminished by overbearing central party leadership. Never mind the blackmail a leader could threaten of not signing nomination papers, there's also the internal party bullying that comes into play in which someone is deemed not to be a "team player" if he or she is unwilling to make even more sacrifices to put on a good show for the public. This latter situation was particularly common with the NDP, which had a small caucus at the time and kept putting forward PMBs "as a party," making a complete mockery of the system.

And then there is the problem of the government actually going ahead and supporting such bills, as has increasingly been the case since the 2006 election. In the minority Parliaments from 2006 to 2011, the Conservative government increasingly employed PMBs to put forward controversial policy it didn't want to treat as government legislation that would then be whipped. This distinction was particularly important when the Conservatives were playing politics around the PMB to dismantle the long-gun registry. The government supported this policy goal, but because it put the matter forward as a PMB, it was able to sow divisions in the Opposition ranks, since most party leaders are reluctant to whip votes on private members' business (though it does happen, either officially or unofficially). What better theatre is there than when you have backbenchers breaking ranks and the media then hovering around to wonder obliquely if the leader is "losing control of the caucus" (even though that iron-fisted control should never be a given in the first place)?

Such government sponsorship of PMBs inevitably leads to conspiracy theory-type thinking. Is every piece of controversial private members' business from a government MP — especially those around issues like abortion — really just a backdoor attempt by the government to put forward the bill? Surely, it must be, some think, if they were really behind the long-gun registry. Even when the answer is an emphatic no, and the prime minister himself says he's voting against the bill, many in the public, and even Opposition MPs, still refuse to change their minds.

I once had an Opposition MP recount to me her belief of what the Conservative government must have been up to — that it had its staff in the Department of Justice comb through the Criminal Code and pull out sections it could tweak to fit its ideology and then draft a PMB it could assign to one of its MPs. I was told this suspicion in full earnestness. The MP believed that must be the way things were happening, since there were so many of these boutique Criminal Code changes on the Order Paper, several of which the government supported.

None of the bills on the Order Paper actually passed. A couple of weeks later I had a conversation with a parliamentary secretary. When the subject of PMBs came up, the answer I got was pretty much the opposite. There was no overarching hand, according to her, although she did admit that wasn't to say certain backbenchers, either lacking in imagination or looking to score points with the leadership, might ask if there was a bill they could champion. The government saw a couple of benefits from this kind of approach: it could appear to be listening to the concerns of its MPs, and in turn, their constituents. This approach also provided a different public face for the issue than just the minister, never mind that it's the minister's job to be that public face. That's why we have a Cabinet, and why we have a system whereby the government proposes and the Opposition opposes. The backbenches aren't part of the government — even if the government media strategy of the day would indicate otherwise.

All of this isn't to say that a government might not see added benefits to shepherding some issues through the House using the PMB route, namely, that a complex issue has to have its debate curtailed to a mere couple of hours, with little committee time for scrutiny, and the government can give the appearance of allowing a free vote on it.

But such a strategy is, of course, double-edged — poorly drafted legislation that isn't properly scrutinized will inevitably face further challenges, whether in the Senate or in the courts. It's also an extremely slow process, unlike government legislation, for which the Government House Leader controls the Order Paper. The House Leader has no control over private members' business, and there is no process by which it can be sped up in the Senate.

As noted, the poor drafting of PMBs is a particular problem because of the relative lack of scrutiny they receive. PMBs are almost invariably drafted by the clerks in the Library of Parliament, since most MPs aren't lawyers and don't know the legal terminology to use to ensure the bill is not only in order but that its wording won't create bigger problems with existing legislation. But the problem is that while these clerks might be lawyers, they often come up with interpretations that differ from those crafted by lawyers in the Department of Justice. This means there are inevitably more problems that need to be addressed with PMBs — or would be if most of the PMBs actually progressed to a meaningful stage of debate — than is the case with government-sponsored bills, a situation that places much greater demands on the resources of the House.

Despite all these issues, there are often proposals to try to increase the amount of private members' business the House is able to clear, and many of these proposals are promoted as things that would help to make MPs' jobs "more meaningful." The problem there, however, is that such proposals remain grounded in the mistaken notion that MPs are lawmakers, which they're not. PMBs have a function to serve in influencing government policy. They can even be seen as legitimate tools for use by MPs in their oversight role, since such bills can be used for correcting gaps in existing legislation, and yes, in giving MPs an outlet for their desire to do something about those hobby horses. But private members' business should only be a small fraction of their actual job.

The job of all MPs remains that of holding the government to account. Trying to elevate the significance of private members' business only serves to confuse the issue and treat our MPs more like American congressmen — a mistaken notion.

THE DECORUM DISTRACTION

Whenever anybody talks about things that need fixing in the House of Commons these days the conversation pretty much begins and ends with a single topic — *decorum*. What the public doesn't seem to realize is that the debate about decorum or the lack thereof in the House is only a distraction from the real problems the Commons faces.

Everybody seems to believe that Question Period (QP) is the real and true expression of how the Commons functions on an ongoing basis, which is simply not true. There seems to be little appreciation that QP is not only political theatre but it's also the occasion to let off some steam in what can otherwise be a crushingly dull day. This is part of the problem — pretty much all of the spark and spontaneity has gone from Canadian politics. If QP wasn't situated in the middle of the day to liven things up a little, we might end up being concerned by the rash of narcolepsy that followed, and shortly after that, by the fact that our MPs are slowly being replaced by mindless robot drones who simply deliver speeches into the record and vote as instructed.

Political theatre is necessary for the proper functioning of democracy. If there was no drama, people would tune out entirely. But it needs to be recognized as such — for as much as Question Period serves as an opportunity in which the Opposition parties and government backbenchers get a daily chance at asking questions of the government in order to hold it to account (and the fact that government backbenchers have turned away from this role and are instead using their allotted questions to either congratulate the government or ask planted questions that will lead to a policy announcement is actually troubling), it also allows MPs to showcase their debating skills. Or it would, if they had any, which is another part of the problem. We can't escape the fact that we do have an adversarial system, and that system exists for a reason. This isn't a campfire where we all get to hold hands and sing songs. It requires a certain amount of cut and thrust if it's to maintain the necessary adversarial functions, and QP is one of the best showcases of that.

"But what about the schoolchildren in the gallery?" is the constant plaintive wail from all the concerned people who seem to think MPs demonstrate worse behaviour than said children. Why not simply tell those same schoolchildren the truth — that this is theatre. It serves a function, and that, really, the rest of the day is dull but rather collegial. It's a bit like gym class for MPs in that way, which may, in fact, be an analogy that might work to explain things better. It's less than an hour out of every day in which they get to have a bit of fun. Should we really be begrudging that when nobody can be bothered to tune into the other seven hours of debate in the chamber in a day?

"But what about the name-calling and the heckling?"

Name-calling is a problem, and one that seems to stem largely from the fact that we don't have the same debating culture in this country that they do in places like the United Kingdom — and that is a problem. But there are easy enough remedies for that. The Speaker can simply not acknowledge those MPs who engage in it until they apologize. Or party whips could discipline unruly MPs if they really wanted to, but there seems little appetite for that, despite the constant protestations that everyone is appalled by the behaviour.

Heckling, however, has its place in the chamber, and in debate — now more than ever, I would argue. It's a necessary antidote to the overwhelming amount of scripted speech that has infected the House.

The parties' desire to script the entire affair has reached the point of absurdity. MPs ask a question that is scripted to focus on issues that the leader's office feels is important (they might be allowed a question of local concern toward the end of QP if they're deemed important enough to merit a turn), and for the most part their delivery is wooden and awkward. They're given a scripted response by a minister or parliamentary secretary, which contains prescribed buzzwords and slogans that have been approved by the Prime Minister's Office. Any variation tends to be the result of the degree to which those speaking — the ministers or parliamentary secretaries — have been able to memorize their talking points. If you're lucky, you might hear one of the few ministers or parliamentary secretaries who actually knows their file and can offer a response that is less obviously scripted — not that it won't have the approved talking points contained therein. (This has improved under the current Trudeau government, but obvious scripting still exists.) There is the added problem of parliamentary secretaries delivering responses on behalf of Cabinet ministers, despite the fact they aren't supposed to be answering questions for Cabinet because they aren't members of Cabinet and can't speak about matters discussed by Cabinet; however, their use as replacement ministers has increased dramatically over the past several Parliaments.

All in all, there has been a massive increase in the degree to which parliamentary debate has been taken over by scripted speech. The value of heckling in knocking ministers off their talking points becomes apparent when it's done properly. Sometimes it involves a clever riposte, but other times it's an actual calling out of false information.

There have been times where the crosstalk was more instructive than the minister's scripted response, such as during the debate over the nuclear isotope shortage in 2009–10 when the minister talked about the use of thallium as an alternative. During her response, one of the Opposition MPs — a medical doctor — shot back that they stopped using thallium for a reason.

None of this got picked up by the microphones or video cameras, but it was still a very instructive and spontaneous exchange that wouldn't have otherwise happened if a complete ban on heckling were in place. Heckling does become a problem if it's boorish, or sexist, or otherwise discriminatory, all of which should be policed by the Speaker and the party whips, but to call all heckling out as a problem is small-minded and diminishes the cut and thrust of QP.

The overall issue of scripted MPs needs to be understood in the larger context because it's one of the factors smothering Parliament as it exists. As bad as the spectacle of scripted questions and responses is during QP, it has become far worse in pretty much all other debate in the Commons itself. Outside of QP, the House is occupied by the bare minimum necessary for quorum, and I use the term *debate* loosely. With precious few exceptions, *debate* has become an exercise of MPs reading prepared speeches into the record, and as soon as they're finished and the next prepared speech begins, they get up and leave. The only person who generally sticks around for the length of the debate is either the minister or the parliamentary secretary, in order to ask questions of the Opposition parties in response to the points raised by them or to respond to their questions, but there is nothing that remotely qualifies as debate in the chamber any longer. There is no actual engagement on the issues, no back and forth, no picking up on points raised before and either disputing them or running with them. Each speech pretty much resets the clock at zero in terms of what is being talked about and is then launched into a vacuum.

As for the other MPs in the chamber who have the misfortune of being assigned to House duty, it's rare to find any of them actually paying attention to the debate. Mostly, they sit doing paperwork at their desks, or worse, they're on their computers, entirely disengaged. I've even witnessed some MPs with headphones on while they use their laptops, completely ignoring the proceedings. And yet the Speaker never said anything about it, and nobody seemed the slightest bit bothered by it, either. This is now how we debate legislation — reading speeches prepared by staffers, with the MP reduced to being a mindless drone whose task it is to deliver it, and to later vote according to the whip's instructions (unless it's a PMB, which is generally a free vote, or unless you're trying to prove your loyalty, in which case you find out which way your leader is voting and cast your vote in the same way).

With this in mind, is it any wonder that decorum slides so badly during QP? When MPs are reduced to this level of mindlessness, it's not astonishing that they're itching for some kind of stimulus by the time 2:00 p.m. (11:00 a.m. on Fridays) rolls around. It's no surprise that the heckling and catcalling is an utter relief, since it offers MPs a welcome opportunity to be the slightest bit spontaneous. And how can you learn how to make witty ripostes when the rest of your time is spent simply reading the script you've been given? It seems like a poor training ground for thinking on your feet or engaging in actual debate.

Of course, none of this has to actually be this way. While there isn't a Standing Order that prohibits an MP from reading a prepared speech, it's a practice that has been frowned upon until recently. In the "Rules of Order and Decorum" section of *House of Commons Procedure and Practice*, Audrey O'Brien and Marc Bosc cite the following 1956 Speaker's ruling:

> A Member addressing the House may refer to notes. The Prime Minister, the cabinet ministers, the Leader of the Opposition, the leaders of other parties or Members speaking on their behalf, may read important policy speeches. New Members may read their [maiden] speeches. The Members speaking in a language other than their mother tongue, the Members speaking in debates involving matters of a technical nature, or in debates on the Address in

Reply to the Speech from the Throne and on the Budget may use full notes or, if they wish, read their speeches.[8]

As the ruling states, this isn't to say you can't have a couple of cue cards or a single sheet on your desk with some bullet points — fair is fair. But getting a small lectern on your desk so that you can recite your speech for any routine debate or even a question in QP is going too far. Holding your prepared speech in front of your face as you read it? That also goes too far. And yet MPs do it, oblivious to how ridiculous they appear.

But as O'Brien and Bosc note in the *House of Commons Procedure and Practice*, subsequent chairs have increasingly made it permissible for these prepared speeches, and we can see what the result has been — debate has died in favour of reading speeches into the void, or the more recent phenomenon of ensuring that a "debate" speech or question in QP is perfectly packaged for news clips or put onto YouTube. The tight scripting and message control imposed to create these media packets has taken the life out of the Commons. If we want MPs to have a more meaningful job, we need to enliven debate in the House, and to do that we need to do away with the scripts and packaging. Yes, it's messier — but that's half the point.

And what of the MPs who will be forced to think on their feet and engage in actual debate? I can only say that if they fear public speaking that much, then it makes their choice of seeking elected office a curious one. If they don't want to actually debate and get involved in the issues under discussion, and if they're content to simply read prepared speeches, then do we need to question why we even elect MPs to do this job? Would it not be easier to hire actors or to build robots? If we want representative democracy to mean something, then treating those who represent us as drones can't be healthy.

WHAT FEW REFORMS WE NEED

If we are to ensure that MPs have jobs that have meaning and that they're doing the jobs they're supposed to be doing, there will need to be a couple of changes — but they're pretty minor, and pretty much all of them involve a restoration of earlier rules that have been altered or that we have let slide in the name of modernity, accommodation, or even "more democracy." There is also one slightly more radical suggestion to be made in the name of improving our democracy, but first the things that we could accomplish immediately if there is the willingness to do so.

The first and most immediate thing we can do is to ban prepared speeches, with the obvious exceptions as listed in the 1956 ruling, such as replies to the Speech from the Throne or the budget. As long as MPs don't bother to actually engage with the subject matter they're debating and instead just read speeches into the void, then we might as well submit the speeches to *Hansard* and save the transcriptionists the trouble. Re-engaging MPs in the debate process by actually forcing them to debate can only be of benefit to the process. It will also make for a more robust discussion of the issues, rather than just writing a speech that lists all of the approved talking points. Yes, there might be some resistance to this change, but public speaking and debate is the name of the game. If you want to be an MP, you'd better be prepared to engage in both.

Removing the list of speakers the House Leaders give to the House Speaker can also be done immediately and to the benefit of the flow of the debate, and to the powers of the Speaker. Prior to 1993, the Speaker chose who got to ask questions during QP and generally tried to come up with a good balance between the parties. In 1993 the five parties in the House decided to come up with a list that would better ensure "fairness" in who got to ask questions. This, of course, just added to the scripted element, and currently some parties are even using this ability so that they can have an anglophone critic ask a question in English, followed by a francophone critic asking the very same question in French. It disrupts the flow of debate and makes for an obviously staged performance that becomes little more than an assemblage of news-ready clips.

Keeping with the list system makes for poor debate in QP as well as in the House. When the prime minister or other Cabinet ministers slip up, the next person to ask a question should be able to leap on it and keep the momentum and the pressure going. But as it stands, with the list and the prepared questions that will reset the discussion to zero, there is almost no ability to maintain the pressure. Any drama that has been created dissipates immediately into another round of canned talking points on both sides, unless there is some kind of miracle and one of the upcoming speakers is deft enough to actually pick up on the points. However, this seems more and more of a rarity lately.

People will argue that parties should be allowed to have QP strategies that they can designate lists for, but that again falls into the realm of spin and prepared media packages, which deprive debate of its meaning. The end of the list might also force government backbenchers to come up with actual questions to ask ministers, rather than giving them the opportunity to have three or four assigned softballs, or as my fellow media colleagues and I refer to them, "designated suck-up questions." If only one government backbencher stands up, with the prepared question du jour, the Speaker should be able to recognize this strategy and be allowed to call on a government backbencher of choice to ask a question of the government, in keeping with his or her own role of holding government to account.

The added benefit of this particular system of restoring control to the Speaker is that he or she can then reward good behaviour and punish bad behaviour by simply not calling on those MPs who continually exhibit bad behaviour. While Speaker Andrew Scheer in 2012 did occasionally skip questions when the party in question was too disruptive "in order to make up the time," it has only been something of a half measure. The party leaders still control who says what and when.

Something else to consider would be the restoration of evening sittings three nights a week, as used to be the case until the early 1990s. While this practice was ended to make Parliament more "family friendly," one of the effects was the detrimental impact on decorum. As it stood, the House would break from 6:00 p.m. until 8:00 p.m. on Tuesday, Wednesday, and Thursday and MPs would travel upstairs to the Parliamentary Restaurant and eat together. This built relationships and collegiality because they had that chance to get to know one another in a more relaxed setting. When that practice ended, so did much of the collegiality. While it does still exist, Parliament is far less collegial a place than it once was.

Of course, evening sittings also allowed for several more hours of debate every week, which simply haven't been replaced elsewhere on the parliamentary calendar. It's also one of the reasons why we shouldn't eliminate standing votes in favour of electronic ones, since this remains one of the few times MPs can see and talk to one another.

To broaden the reform ideas a little further, another practice needs to be restored: a speech from the governor general (or Queen) upon prorogation. This practice, which is still employed in the United Kingdom, existed in Canada up until 1983 when Prime Minister Pierre Elliott Trudeau did away with it. It had already been altered once before, back in 1939, when Prime Minister William Lyon Mackenzie King had the chief justice of the Supreme Court read the prorogation speech instead of the governor general when the PM took advantage of the fact that Lord Tweedsmuir was out of town to prorogue Parliament.[9]

The rationale for restoring this tradition should become apparent in light of the prorogation crisis of 2008 in which Prime Minister Stephen Harper sought prorogation after only three sitting weeks when his government faced a confidence motion it was set to lose. While many political scientists and political partisans have since argued that the rules of the Commons should be changed so that prorogation can only be granted after two-thirds of the House votes to approve it, this heavy-handed approach unnecessarily limits the reserve powers of the Crown and places too much power in the hands of the Opposition parties, especially since it's only necessary to lose a confidence vote by a simple majority to lose confidence and dissolve Parliament entirely.

The purpose of the prorogation speech is to ensure the government lists its accomplishments so that it can start a new session with a blank slate and new priorities as laid out in the Speech from the Throne. With the restoration of the necessity for a prorogation speech, a government would be forced to list its accomplishments before the public to justify ending the session — something any sitting prime minister trying to use prorogation to avoid a confidence vote would be hard-pressed to do. Similarly, forcing the delivery of a prorogation speech draws attention to the event and makes it even harder for a prime minister to treat the power casually, as Stephen Harper did on December 30, 2009, when he requested a prorogation by telephone and was granted it, likely under the political calculation that the pressure his government was under regarding the production of documents would ease off with the holidays and the upcoming Winter Olympics that were being hosted in Vancouver that year.

Such a calculation would have been impossible had he been forced to deliver a prorogation speech. There would have been no eleventh-hour, day before New Year's Eve phone call because it would have meant having to recall both chambers of Parliament to give the speech and lay out all his accomplishments, which could be measured against that session's Speech from the Throne. Any opportunism would be laid bare in that moment. Once again, it's a public accountability mechanism that turning over more power to the Commons does little to achieve, and it respects the Westminster traditions, as they exist.

Perhaps one of the biggest and most important changes that needs to happen would also be one of the most difficult to convince everyone, politicians and the public, of — the restoration of the party caucus's ability to hire and fire party leaders, as discussed earlier. By restoring to MPs the ability to appoint and dismiss their leaders, leaders would again be accountable to their caucuses rather than able to enjoy the lack of any accountability that they now effectively have. Restoration of this power would give backbenchers greater ability to stand up for themselves because the leaders would be far more reluctant to come down on them too hard, lest they start a backbench revolt. Coupled with the loss of a leader's ability to sign a candidate's nomination papers, these two measures would greatly diminish the power wielded by party leaders.

In countries like the United Kingdom until recently, or Australia as it currently stands, the ability for the caucus to fire the leader and appoint a new one has caused leaders to be more deferential and made for stronger backbenchers. They have a bigger stake in the value of leadership, and it adds value to their role within a system of representational democracy. Restoration of this power would actually give back to them a modicum of power and agency, which they have been slowly stripped of. Removal of this power from the leader would cancel a change that didn't really "democratize" the process as much as it created power structures that further alienated those who provide the input into the system.

Another proposal that might be worth considering is to change the physical layout of the House of Commons in a way that better reflects its roots in Westminster. Since the Canadian Commons has reached the physical limits of its capacity, it might be time to take out the desks and shrink the chamber so that it becomes more of a cozy and intimate environment for the MPs. For one thing, the desks have outlived their usefulness in Canada. In the past, MPs did their work at them because they didn't have offices. Even when they did have offices, there was the tradition of banging on one's desk rather than applauding. With the demise of desk-banging (in part because it interfered with the microphones needed for televising debates), and every MP having an accessible office within the parliamentary precinct, the need for the desks has pretty much evaporated. Now they simply give an incentive for MPs to not pay attention to the debates, since they can simply prop up their laptops or tablets upon them and play games or spend QP signing their holiday cards. Removal of the desks would also make it harder for MPs and ministers to have their prepared speeches (which should be largely eliminated, anyway) at hand.

Eliminating the desks and shrinking the chamber would force MPs to sit closer together and make it that much easier for them to look one another in the eye during debates or QP. It becomes harder to engage in cretinous behaviour when you're near one another. Likewise, if the party leaders are in close proximity at the dispatch boxes on the Table, then hurling insults and casual dismissal becomes less of an attractive option and debate can intensify with the nearness. While it's not a panacea by any means, it might nevertheless make the chamber much more suited for debate than its current incarnation has become.

Another U.K. tradition that we might look to adopt (or re-adopt as the case might be) is the practice of Urgent Questions. This practice allows MPs to call ministers to the House to answer questions on an urgent topic — more than just the current "emergency debates" we now have, since those are little more than another excuse for MPs to read speeches into the vacuum. Urgent Questions involves more of a QP-like environment where individual ministers, including the prime minister, can be put on the spot over the urgent question. Again, this further empowers MPs in their oversight role, and if conducted properly (without all the prepared scripts), it could serve as a reminder that the government and Cabinet remain accountable to the Commons and not the other way around.

While we're mentioning reforms, I would like to take a moment to say that any attempt to institute electronic voting within the House should be shot down immediately. It's an MP's job to stand up and be counted for these kinds of measures. It might be a symbolic gesture to have them actually stand up and vote for something, but that symbolism remains important. It doesn't matter that electronic votes would save time or allow

MPs to vote if they're away. Standing votes preserve the importance of the notion that you need to be present in order to be counted.

MPs HAVE MORE AGENCY THAN THEY ADMIT

It should be noted that while most of these changes are not only desirable but necessary, it can't be stated strongly enough that MPs currently have a great deal of power and agency over areas that could be changed — they need only claim it. They have the power to change the rules to re-empower themselves with most of the suggestions I provide above. They could band together to stare down their party leaders if they so chose. They still have far more power than they realize.

But therein lies the rub — they often don't realize they have that much power. Because they don't have a proper grounding in civic literacy, in the requirements of their own jobs, or in the kinds of powers they possess, it becomes easy for them to be dominated by party leadership and then complain about not having any power. If we had MPs who actually understood their roles, who understood the powers at their disposal, and who had a robust understanding of civic literacy in this country, we might see far more empowered MPs and far less central control than we do currently.

5

THE SENATE YOU DON'T KNOW

"Does anyone really know what the Senate does?" a pollster's Twitter account asked me when I commented on the fact that most of the people polled who demand a reformed Senate don't actually know anything about the upper chamber. The simple answer to that question is no. The image most have of the Senate is that which is caricatured in the popular media — the cushy, quasi-retirement home offered to party hacks and bagmen, a "relic of the nineteenth century" that simply offers a costly location for napping. Pushed further, most Canadians will tell you that it's "illegitimate" and "anti-democratic," and that it's in dire need of reform or abolishment. And the Mike Duffy trial didn't do anything to help this reputation, either.

It's a stinging rebuke for an institution that is perhaps the least understood in the panoply of Canadian politics. And while the Senate certainly has its share of problems, particularly with the behaviour of a few bad apples in recent years, it has nevertheless been unfairly cast as the punching bag of the Canadian political system.

Every party wants to blame the Senate for the woes of the system, and each has promised to reform it in some way or another at some point (when they're not threatening to abolish it altogether). Attempts to radically reshape the chamber failed as part of the Meech Lake and Charlottetown Accords, and more recent half-baked attempts at piecemeal reform that attempted to skirt the requirement for a constitutional amendment were shot down by the Supreme Court of Canada in a reference decision in 2014. But, of course, any time a senator defends the status quo, he or she is castigated as trying to maintain the privileges and cushy lifestyle senators supposedly enjoy, which makes any kind of rational debate about the merits of reform versus the status quo difficult to achieve.

But if we are to have any kind of discussion about the Senate as it stands, then we need to at least have a working understanding of the chamber and what it does, starting with a working definition of "sober second thought." While it's a phrase that's used to define the role of the Senate, it's not often that there's a pause to consider what the phrase itself actually means.

The meaning of "second thought" is, of course, rather obvious, given that the Senate acts as a kind of reviewing body for the legislation that passes through the Commons; however, the exact value of the "sobriety" that's tagged onto that other descriptor cuts to the heart of the construction — that it be a check on the "excesses of democracy," or put more plainly, on the populist sentiment that sometimes overrides the kind of judgment necessary within a liberal democracy, especially when it comes to the rights of minorities, whose protection was one of the founding principles of the Senate. In fact, having a Senate that speaks for minorities rather than for provincial interests was one of its federalist principles.[1] And while there is now a greater remedy available for minority rights in the courts since the implementation of the Charter of Rights and Freedoms, that doesn't diminish the role the Senate has to play in terms of the consideration of minorities.

The key component of the sobriety of that second thought, and the check against populist excess, however, lies in the Senate's appointed nature — the very feature that is the source of so much of the criticism levelled against it. The fact that senators don't have to stand for re-election and can't be easily removed by a sitting prime minister gives them a certain freedom of thought and action that MPs simply don't have by virtue of the pressures they face. This ability to speak truth to power couldn't be replicated if the Senate were made an elected body, as many would wish it to be.

But what about legitimacy? Doesn't an unelected body lack the fundamental legitimacy that a legislative body requires? This question implies there is only one form of legitimacy — electoral rather than institutional.

The Senate derives its legitimacy from the Constitution, which spells out the designated role it is to play within the legislative process, a role the founders of this country felt would best serve the needs of Parliament. After all, they had experience with elected Legislative Councils (the upper chambers of the pre-Confederation Legislative Assemblies) and had soured on them as a result. The other source of legitimacy comes from the exercise of responsible government — that a prime minister who makes appointments commands the confidence of the Commons, which gives him or her the authority to make those appointments.

Along the way, various prime ministers have been able to employ their power of appointment to the Senate and put it to good use in the way of representation. While the earliest incarnations of the Senate were concerned with cultural minorities in the country — related to religion, education, and language — this mandate has expanded as the country grew more diverse. More modern incarnations of the Senate have included more women and visible minorities, while still maintaining representation from linguistic minorities, such as francophones from outside Quebec.

The Senate has also given certain public policy experts a means of contributing to the creation of that policy within the country, where they otherwise might never have considered running for office. If the Senate were indeed an elected body, its composition would be much more like that of the Commons — less diverse and made up more of the kinds of career politicians who have the ambition for public office than those who have decided to make their marks elsewhere. The kinds of input that the more diverse appointments make to public policy, both in the review of legislation and with the longer-term studies and reports the Senate produces as the nation's premier "think tank," are invaluable to the parliamentary process.

Those appointments can also be useful when a governing party has weak electoral support in certain regions of the country, such as Liberals in western Canada, or Conservatives in Quebec. Including those senators in caucus or Cabinet can help to give some modicum of redress for the vagaries of the electoral system when necessary.

This is great, but what about all of those party fundraisers, bagmen, and failed candidates who also get appointed as repayment for political favours? Undoubtedly this happens, but we should pause for just a moment before we dismiss those kinds of appointments out of hand. If you think about it for a moment, party fundraisers do perform a valuable role for the democratic process. They are useful as a way of engaging the public to support the parties and visions of the country that they share, and that financial support is no less legitimate than any other kind of support. In many ways, fundraisers are possibly more in touch with the grassroots than many MPs because it is their job to reach out to those members of the public in new ways, lest the party's coffers suffer if they don't. They can often have longer careers of grassroots engagement than many of the MPs, too, which gives them a great deal of experience with the kinds of messages Canadian voters have for their elected officials and the political parties.

Likewise, being a defeated candidate or incumbent MP shouldn't necessarily disqualify that person from serving in the Senate, nor should his or her defeat make the appointment illegitimate. Perhaps such candidates did have something to offer but simply faced formidable opponents just as worthy of election as they might have been, or they faced a superior organizational effort from their opponents. Should this disqualify what they can offer from being considered for the Senate? Not necessarily, and so criticism about these kinds of appointments should be met with a bit more nuance and understanding of the circumstances.

The longevity that senators possess shouldn't be scorned, either. Instead, it should be appreciated for its benefits and how that can be applied to public policy and the review of legislation as it passes through their hands. Because MPs often operate with an eye on the next electoral cycle, be it an average of four years in a majority setting or two in a minority setting, they often possess little long-term perspective when it comes to considering policy goals. The high turnover rate among MPs also means the institutional memory of the Commons is similarly fairly short, which can mean that as a group it simply doesn't think about some of the policy ramifications of what it proposes. On the other hand, since senators can often sit for decades, they are frequently able to come up with reports that are more far-reaching in scope and depth than many of the reports we see from Commons committees, which are often more partisan and more constrained by other pressing business.

On the joint parliamentary committees, the longevity of senators has particular value, most especially with the committee on the scrutiny of regulations. Such work is long, technical, and doubtless very tedious, and having parliamentarians who not only have the institutional memory to take to their roles in this scrutiny but can also provide continuity in a process that sees MPs come and go in a fairly consistent manner, means that better work is the inevitable result, with fewer starts and stops and with seasoned veterans who can bring newcomers up to speed in a way that's difficult in other, more ephemeral committees.

It bears repeating that elections don't confer mystical powers of wisdom upon parliamentarians — though you might hear MPs describe their roles in ways that could lead you to that conclusion. Just because someone has been elected doesn't make his or her perspective any more enlightened; nor does it make that person's decisions any more correct because they have the weight of the electorate behind them. Providing the perspective an appointed body that is able to speak in a "truth-to-power" kind of fashion has its value within a parliamentary system like ours. In the same way that we don't insist that the courts also be elected if they're to have any legitimacy, we need to recognize that the place of the Senate has a similar kind of value. In fact, it's a rather complementary hybrid that is like a halfway point between the Commons and the courts. Given the ways in which the Senate has been able to use its power to improve legislation on a consistent basis, it has doubtlessly reduced the burden on the courts that flawed legislation would have imposed on them. By amending legislation that would have passed otherwise, the Senate serves to streamline the legislative and judicial systems in this country. Everyone who wants to abolish the Senate on the basis of its costs should ask themselves if any of those "savings" will actually happen, given the subsequent increase in cases before the courts that would challenge the flaws in legislation that partisan or populist excess is blind to.

But what about the accountability of the Senate if it's unelected? If there is no way to hold senators to account, is there not greater temptation for them to abuse their position? It's a valid concern, one that people have been particularly prone to question in recent years. There is no easy answer, unfortunately, but something will come to mind if one considers the issue long enough. It's another one of those areas where we must reframe the way in which we define accountability. Just because senators are not themselves held to account by the electoral system doesn't mean that accountability for their appointments doesn't exist. In this case, that measure of accountability rests upon the prime minister who recommended their appointment. If you don't like the quality of senators being appointed, well, there is but one person to answer for that.

Now this isn't to suggest there aren't other internal accountability mechanisms within the Senate itself. After a couple of high-profile, embarrassing incidents of absentee senators, the Senate introduced a number of measures to enforce attendance, such as public attendance records and docked pay for missed days after a certain number of absences. After more recent misspending incidents, tighter financial controls and transparent reporting were instituted. Public pressure does hold the Senate to account to a very great degree. This contrasts with the Commons where MPs don't reveal their self-reported attendance records and there doesn't appear to be any kind of monetary penalty for missed attendance. But again, given the secrecy surrounding the records, we don't really know for sure how these things work out.

THE "THREE KINGDOMS"

The construction of the Senate, though it was a particular sticking point in the creation of the country as a whole, was one of the key compromises that allowed Confederation to happen at all.

Member colonies had concerns about being swamped by the others in a House of Commons that nominally adhered to the principles of representation by population, whether it was Lower Canada (soon to be Quebec) with its linguistic concerns, or Nova Scotia and New Brunswick worried about the comparatively massive populations of both Upper and Lower Canada. At the time New Brunswick and Nova Scotia had populations of less than six hundred thousand combined, compared to Upper and Lower Canada having a million people each. The notion of equality between provinces was distasteful to all parties concerned, and so the concept of regional equality became that balancing factor.

In 1867 three senatorial divisions were created, each with twenty-four seats to provide regional balance and equality. Christopher Dunkin, who was minister of agriculture in 1870 and responsible for the country's first census, described the arrangement as representing "the three kingdoms." Dunkin's comment was an allusion to the United Kingdom, which was composed of England, Scotland, and Ireland, along with the Principality of

Wales. He saw the United Kingdom as the paradigm of a successful nation, in spite of its diversity.[2] Where Dunkin's comparison failed, however, was in the fact that the United Kingdom didn't have a political structure that was required to adjust for expansion. As Canada grew, incorporating other colonies, like Prince Edward Island and British Columbia, and adding to Ontario and Quebec and carving the Prairie Provinces out of Rupert's Land, the enormous tract of land it acquired from the Hudson's Bay Company, the new provinces were solely represented in the House of Commons until a fourth senatorial region was added in 1915, thus extending the allusion to "four kingdoms." When Newfoundland and Labrador joined Confederation, it was granted six Senate seats, and each northern territory was also granted one, but they aren't part of any established division. Nevertheless, the principle of regional equality remains largely intact, overriding the interests of individual provinces.

Despite its superficial patterning on the British House of Lords, the Canadian Senate is a unique upper chamber among all other Western democracies, in large part because its construction reflects a double federalism — both cultural and territorial — unlike any other analogous upper chamber.[3]

Unlike the Lords, the Senate represents a federation and has a fixed upper limit of membership. Whereas the Lords can be "swamped" with the creation of new life peerages in order for a government to pass its legislation, the Senate of Canada has an upper limit, albeit there is the provision for the addition of four or eight additional senators, one or two from each of the four divisions, on the advice of the Queen in extraordinary circumstances (as with the passage of the Goods and Services Tax (GST) under the Brian Mulroney government). Those additional Senate seats aren't filled upon the retirement of those senators, so as to return the chamber to its original composition.

Unlike the Lords, but like most other upper chambers, it is smaller than the lower house. Also unlike the Lords, the Canadian Senate has much more substantial powers at its disposal, being nearly equal to the Commons (with the exception that it isn't a confidence chamber, nor is it able to initiate money bills), whereas since 1911, the Lords has only had a suspensive veto, meaning it can only delay and can't kill legislation it doesn't agree with. As well, the composition of the Lords isn't based on territory or region, whereas that was a foundational principle of the Canadian Senate.[4]

The principle of double federalism also separates the Canadian Senate from its other analogous upper chambers, such as those found in the United States, Australia, and Germany. Those institutions, while federal, don't have the same linguistic or cultural minority concerns that Canada has in its federal construction. Whereas Australia and the United States have upper chambers constructed more along the lines of territorial federalism, Germany's is built along the lines of administrative federalism. And while the Canadian Senate is in theory a legislative body like the American and Australian Senates, it is more in practice a deliberative and investigative body that complements the work of the House of Commons rather than competing with it.[5] This might be one reason why, despite the fact that the Canadian Senate has near-equal powers to the Commons, it hasn't come into major conflict with that chamber, unlike that which occurred during Australia's constitutional crisis, nor does it suffer from the issue (though some would describe it as a feature) of logjam between the two Houses that is indicative of the American system.

It is with these facts in mind that we must then consider the way in which we look at the Canadian Senate. While many would-be reformers believe the chamber is organized along provincial lines, and so many of their reform proposals follow from that mistaken belief, this belief ignores the history and reality of the construction of the Senate and its larger role in the federation. While the model of the "four kingdoms" remains relatively intact, the conception of the Senate as a house of the provinces nevertheless looms large in the imaginations of many.

ABOLITION IS NOT AN ANSWER

Before we discuss the issue of Senate reform, we should get off the table the notion that the Senate can be abolished with any particular ease. Abolition is, of course, one of the cornerstones of NDP policy; however, it should be immediately treated as a non-starter. First and foremost, abolition isn't feasible because it would require a constitutional amendment. Not only is amending the Constitution extremely difficult in the best of cases, according to the various amending formulas, outright abolition of the Senate would require the surmounting of the most difficult hurdle of all: the unanimous consent of the provinces. Such uniform consent is necessary to enact this change because of the fundamental way in which it alters our constitutional framework, as per the Supreme Court's 2014 reference decision. (Most other reform proposals would need to use an amending formula that requires the consent of seven provinces representing at least 50 percent of the population).

Because the smaller Maritime Provinces rely on their Senate representation to counterbalance the situation that exists in the House of Commons, where the use of representation by population allows the more populous provinces to dominate, you can be assured there will be no appetite for the loss of that representation.

You can also be assured that whatever "savings" those in favour of doing away with the Senate claim could be achieved through its abolition, those savings would be counterbalanced by the increase in the costs of the court challenges that would result, given that the legislation that passes the Commons will inevitably have flaws that will no longer be caught by the Senate before being passed into law. Given the number of amendments the Senate makes to legislation on a current basis, it is clear there would be a significant rise in the number of challenges that would make their way to the courts. As well, the kinds of reports the Senate produces on a continual basis are achieved at a fraction of the cost of Royal Commissions or other special reports that governments have commissioned. The fact that there seems to be little awareness that the Senate serves as Parliament's built-in think tank — and the fact that its value as such is dismissed by simple virtue that its member are appointed — is both disappointing and counterproductive.

NDP MPs have also put forward the argument that since the provinces are unicameral, there shouldn't be any need for the federal Parliament to be bicameral. This particular viewpoint ignores the fact that the federal construction of the Senate has a value within the legislative process, when it comes to its deliberative and investigative roles, and entirely ignores the principles of double federalism, which isn't a factor that provincial legislatures have to contend with. While provinces do have their linguistic and cultural minorities, and while some have put into place means to better ensure their representation, such as protected ridings within those regions to better capture the representation of those minorities (though the value of such is currently being disputed in some provinces like Nova Scotia where traditionally Acadian and African-Canadian provincial ridings are no longer electing representatives of those particular communities), the reality is that no province's government has to try to represent anywhere near the range or number of minorities (political, linguistic, ethnic, religious, etc.) as does the federal Parliament.

Trying to accommodate all of those minorities in the House of Commons isn't possible. As mentioned before, trying to do so would mean ignoring the concerns of smaller provinces, which would be dominated by the representation-by-population weight of Ontario and Quebec without any kind of balancing mechanism in place. In fact, the sheer weight of Ontario's population and the fact that Ontario already controls more than a third of the seats in the House of Commons would have a deleterious effect on federalism in the country. For if there were no Senate, as long as the MPs from Ontario and Quebec felt that a bill or spending program was in their interests, the considerations of the other regions of the country needn't matter in the Commons — something that couldn't happen given the regional construction of the Senate.

Senate abolition would also do away with the check on the executive authority held by the prime minister and Cabinet and further allow for the centralization of that power. While many assume that currently the Senate is nothing but a rubber stamp whose loss would mean little, this view ignores the real power the Senate possesses if an occasion arises that demands it be used to stand up to a prime minister. This again goes back to the value of the Senate as an appointed body — its ability to speak truth to power without fear of reprisal derives in part from the fact that its members can't be dismissed at the whim of the prime minister. This is what allows it to serve as a check on that central power. Because of the fact that a prime minister can use party discipline to get a majority caucus in the Commons to vote for legislation that's otherwise flawed or odious, the Commons serves as an inadequate check on that power. The Senate, independent in that it's free of the levers of control that a party leader or prime minister might otherwise employ, has the ability to serve as a check on that power if it so chooses to (though this is something it uses very sparingly, and for good reason). The arguments for abolition don't take this ability into account.

Another consideration that abolitionists fail to contemplate is the role the Senate plays in the current symbolic construction that underlies Parliament and the way in which it conducts its business. When there is a Speech from the Throne or a Royal Assent ceremony, these take place in the Senate chamber because the monarch or her representative — the governor general — doesn't enter the House of Commons, in order to ensure that chamber's independence. This goes back to the days when the king would send for men to arrest members of Parliament when he was displeased with them, and MPs needed that ability to refuse entry to the king or his men.

Most abolitionists no doubt want to abolish the monarchy as well — an even more difficult feat than Senate abolition — but in the absence of that, it seems that some would be content for the time being if the Senate, that symbolic safeguard, were to be removed as a good first step. Perhaps some might want to leave the Senate chamber there for symbolic purpose alone and simply have part-time officers to ensure those elements are maintained in some capacity. Even if that were to happen, there is a great deal of importance placed on symbols, and to simply abandon them in the name of "modernity" and "cost savings" not only strips away hundreds of years of parliamentary history but also strips away the tangible and everyday reminders of why Parliament is the way it is, why we have responsible government, and why the Crown must act on the advice of parliamentarians.

THE PROBLEM WITH "REFORM" PROPOSALS

There is no shortage of Senate "reform" proposals — they have come and gone almost since the advent of Confederation itself. The problem with most of them is that they don't keep the whole of the larger parliamentary perspective in mind, but rather treat the upper chamber in isolation as though it weren't intricately connected with the other two elements of Parliament — the Crown and the Commons. The romance of other systems, be they American, Australian, or German, fails to take into account the double federalism principle that lies at the heart of the Canadian Senate. An awareness of the reasons behind the construction of the Canadian Senate often seems lacking, though one would think it would be germane to any kind of reform discussion.

The other common thread that many of the reform proposals have is that there seems to be a lack of consideration for just what role a reformed Senate is expected to play within the process. Focusing on the perceived ills of the current institution rather than what it accomplishes, they come up with notions that don't take into account the work and perspectives being well served under the current system, notions with little regard as to how that would change under their reform proposals. There is little notice taken of the actual (considerable) power the Senate currently has, such as its near-absolute veto power, and how this power would be affected by the changes they propose. This tendency to ignore the outcomes of reform proposals and to instead focus largely on the inputs (such as the possible election of its members or the regional construction) is a huge blind spot that needs greater consideration.

There have been a great many proposals regarding how to reform the Senate, from the "House of the Federation" proposal in Bill C-60 in 1978 to the Molgat-Cosgrove Report in 1984, the Alberta Select Committee and Macdonald Commission reports in 1985, and the Beaudoin-Dobbie Report and Charlottetown proposal in 1992, to name but a few. None of them has really captured the imagination the way the Triple-E Senate proposal has — elected, equal, and effective — which emerged from Alberta and was championed by the Reform Party. In general, these proposals have had a hard time examining the Senate within the context of Parliament as a whole and haven't really focused on just what kinds of outcomes they were looking for, despite the regional and input rejigging they proposed. The Triple-E proposal was no exception, and it, too, relied on a certain amount of magical thinking.

On its face, Triple-E is an attempt at Americanizing the unique Canadian Senate. In doing so, it ignores the fundamental differences between the two systems and how responsible government diverges from a system with an executive head of state who is elected apart from the legislature. In Canada the government needs to maintain the confidence of the Commons to survive, and that's because the Commons is the confidence chamber. It's the elected House and should have that power.

But how does creating an elected upper chamber of near-equal power not affect that balance of power, especially when you have senators who individually represent a greater number of voters than MPs by virtue of the fact that there are fewer of them? In essence, an Ontario senator could tell any MP that he or she represents the electoral weight of the entire population of Ontario — not the couple of hundred thousand people in a single electoral riding in the Commons. The "democratic legitimacy" of the Triple-E Senate would quickly outweigh that of the Commons and permanently weaken the ability of the Commons to be the confidence chamber.

As well, there is no mechanism to resolve a deadlock between the two chambers. Currently, because senators know they don't have the democratic legitimacy of the electorate, they almost invariably back down when faced with a conflict with the Commons (however, their ability to have an absolute veto over the Commons when necessary remains an important check on the powers of a prime minister with a majority government).

An empowered Triple-E Senate wouldn't have that compunction, and not only would there be continual deadlocks, with no mechanism for resolution, but it would empower a prime minister to look toward pushing the powers of the Crown prerogatives to get around those deadlocks, which would again further weaken the check on the executive.[6]

Along with all of these issues, there would be nothing to suggest that a sitting prime minister couldn't be drawn from the Senate in a Triple-E system, as well as other members of the Cabinet. While there were senators who served as prime ministers in the early 1890s, and while the occasional Cabinet minister has been drawn from the Senate ranks (beyond the nominal Cabinet position of Leader of the Government in the Senate), there would be little reason why, with an elected Senate, this would happen more regularly. If such a situation were to become commonplace, it would present a great many more challenges to the task of holding the government to account, or to holding confidence votes — if the prime minister or key members of the Cabinet weren't even sitting in the confidence chamber, they would be difficult to challenge. Australia did put in place a special rule that the prime minister needs to come from its House of Representatives and not the Senate, though as many as a quarter of that country's Cabinet ministers are drawn from its Senate because that body's elected nature requires the government to draw support from that chamber as well.

The Triple-E proposal, like most other Senate reform proposals, ignores the double federalism principle and looks for representation that strictly focuses on territorial federalism, ignoring the cultural concerns of the present setup.[7] The consideration of the need to ensure representation of linguistic and cultural minorities isn't a factor that was built into plans for the construction of a Triple-E Senate, either; nor was the protection afforded to the smaller provinces under the model of regional representation.

It has been noted that equal representation between states in the American Senate works because under the system of U.S. federalism, states have less constitutional power than do Canadian provinces, and thus they require more representation at the national level. The Triple-E model also ignores the subsequent diminution of powers that the provincial premiers would experience under the enhanced Senate, which would centralize that authority. As well, those same elected senators would claim greater electoral legitimacy. After all, they represent the votes of an entire province, while the premier represents a single provincial riding and the ruling party only a fraction of that province's popular vote. One then has to wonder whether premiers would be willing to let those powers go to a reformed and empowered Senate rather than to continue to wield that influence on the national stage as they do currently.[8]

The other parts of magical thinking that fuel the Triple-E proposal — and most any proposal for an elected Senate for that matter — is the notion that these senators would somehow be divorced from the influence of the national parties of the Commons. The theory, advanced largely after the advent of the National Energy Program under the Liberals in the early 1980s, was that a strong and independent elected Senate could somehow overturn government decisions that negatively affected some provinces. This presupposes not only that such proposals could be defeated in a straight-up regional vote but also that there wouldn't be party pressure on the senators from those provinces, elected or not, to follow the policy platform of the leadership.[9]

Party pressure would, of course, be there, since there would need to be more party money and machinery in play if Senate elections were to go ahead. After all, under most conceived systems, senators would run to represent the entire province, not just an electoral district, and even if there were some form of districting (as Quebec currently employs), the cost of campaigning over such a large geographic area would be many times that of a campaign for a seat in the Commons.

In order to ensure that co-operation for future elections (since the Triple-E proposal doesn't specify non-renewable terms), a much stronger system of party loyalty would be imposed on senators than they currently experience with an appointed model in which they have no actual obligation to the prime minister who appointed them as they don't have to fear removal. Independent Progressive Conservative senator Elaine McCoy has often likened the proposal for an elected Senate to the creation of 105 new backbenchers for the Commons, which would be an apt description of the power relationship that would follow.[10] Likewise, if elected senators are more likely to become ministers of the Crown, they will be just as partisan and deferential to the leader as an MP in the Commons.

HALF MEASURES ARE EVEN WORSE

With full-blown Senate reform proposals currently off the table because of the constitutional difficulty in achieving them, there was an attempt to accomplish part of the hoped-for reforms piecemeal through backdoor mechanisms that the Harper government hoped would be able to skirt the need for a constitutional amendment. These proposals were largely confined to instituting new term limits for senators and allowing for provincial "consultative elections" to form a list from which a prime minister could then draw when it came time to make a new appointment. Despite the fact that the Supreme Court shot these changes down without a constitutional amendment, all were fraught proposals from any particular way that you looked at them.

There seems to be little appreciation for the dangers of what an elected Senate would actually represent to the current state of our parliamentary system. As discussed above, elected senators would feel empowered to stand up to the Commons when it suited their needs, and would use the size of their electoral mandates as particular bullying mechanisms to claim their greater democratic legitimacy. All of this also ignores the fact that in the pre-Confederation colonies, there was already a de facto elected Senate. The

Legislative Councils — the pre-Confederation upper chambers — were mostly elected. However, when the colonies came together at the time of Confederation, it was decided that the new country wouldn't continue with an elected upper chamber.

Australia did choose to go the elected route when it created its own Senate in 1900, fashioning a hybrid Westminster and American model often referred to as a "Washminster model," with a more robust upper chamber whose powers to deny supply led to a constitutional crisis in 1975 and double dissolution in 2016.

The Fathers of Confederation largely saw those elected Legislative Councils of the 1850s as a disaster. While there is still a current zeal for the Triple-E model of a reformed Senate, those who propose this model forget that Canada once had what historian Christopher Moore terms a Triple-R Senate — rich, rural, and reactionary. An elected Senate tends to become less representative of the population than the Commons but has the enhanced mandate to challenge the more representative confidence chamber.[11] One fails to see how any of the current elected Senate proposals would differ from that model, considering the expense and geographic considerations of a Senate election bid.

If senators were chosen in "consultative elections," we would begin to see, as had already begun with the appointment of senators from Alberta, battles within the Senate concerning legitimacy. Those who were "elected" (something that occurred in pretty dubious circumstances, given the way in which Senate "elections" have traditionally been run in the province) would claim greater legitimacy than those senators who were appointed — even though their "election" was, by law, an appointment just as much as any other senator. But the manner in which these provincial selection processes were being handled was building to become a much larger problem, one which only a few of the senators speaking to the Harper government proposals had actually acknowledged.

One of the most immediate problems with the proposal to turn over control of Senate "consultative elections" was that there was no uniformity across the country as to how they should be handled. Rules were to have been drawn up by provincial election agencies. However, that didn't happen, so campaign rules, regulations regarding financing, and even simple decisions about electoral boundaries had no common ground. If there is no level playing field for those "consultative elections," especially around districting, does a senator represent the entire province (as an "elected" senator in Alberta does), or a district (as, traditionally, a senator in Quebec does, based upon pre-Confederation districts designed to protected linguistic and religious minorities in the province, and as had been proposed for New Brunswick during their aborted plans for "consultative elections")? This is an important consideration, given that it speaks to the mandate of that "elected" senator — do they speak for the whole province or just that district?

As well, as currently structured in Alberta, the nominations run along provincial party lines, which don't necessarily correspond to the divisions that exist between the federal parties. Indeed, there is no longer an official federal Progressive Conservative Party, despite the fact that most provinces still run under that banner. In other provinces, like Quebec and British Columbia, the Liberal parties are entirely divorced from the Liberal Party of Canada, but are, rather, internal coalitions of other partisan interests within the province. The fact that the Senate is organized along federal party lines makes the votes being cast more problematic — if the candidate is being endorsed by the provincial party, and yet they declare which federal caucus they intend to sit with, it makes a hash of the party system. As well, the fact that provincial parties are expected to pay for these candidates, and provincial governments for these "consultative elections," when they are for the benefit of the federal Parliament, produces a disconnect. In fact, this disconnect is one of the reasons several provinces that are otherwise in favour of the "consultative election" model haven't gone ahead with such elections. They don't feel they should have to pay for senators bound for Ottawa.

The imposition of term limits could, in fact, constitute a substantial change to the character of the Senate because limits that are too short violate the principles of longevity and institutional memory, as well as the fact that they will allow a prime minister who serves two or three majority mandates to entirely repopulate the Senate with his or her own appointments, which effectively removes the check on said prime minister.

Half measures and piecemeal reform can only make the system worse, especially in the resulting constitutional confusion and battles over legitimacy and mandates. The cry of many politicians and pundits that "surely anything is better than what we have now" fails to look at the actual consequences of their actions and remains blind to the outputs as long as they only concern themselves with inputs seen in a narrow lens.

WHAT REFORMS WE ARE SEEING NOW

Given that most of the proposals for reform neglect the principles of double federalism, regional considerations, or the problems around confidence and deadlock with the Commons, and that abolition is a near impossibility that would create more problems than it would aim to solve, is there anything that can be done about the Senate? While there is a lot of value to the status quo that is underappreciated in the popular conception, there is room for improvement that can be made within the current framework that won't require a constitutional amendment to implement. After all, if reforming the structure will only create more problems — namely, 105 new backbenchers — then why not make some tweaks to its operation?

Some of this kind of internal reform has begun already. A good start involved Liberal leader Justin Trudeau expelling all senators from his caucus in January 2014 under the rubric of building toward a "non-partisan" Senate. While this action did have the immediate effect of making senators more independent — though the Liberal Senate caucus wasn't taking orders from the party leader by that point, anyway — saying that it would build a "non-partisan" chamber wasn't a terribly realistic goal, considering that the Senate, like the Commons, is built along adversarial lines, and most of those senators simply redubbed themselves "Senate Liberals," since they had party affiliations going back decades in many cases, and the fact that the Rules of the Senate dictated that things needed to be organized along caucus lines for the rules to function properly. They did make a few other organizational reforms such as electing their own leadership internally and indicating that all votes going forward would be free ones — the caucus whip was now used solely for the logistical purpose of coordinating things like committee assignments and arranging office and parking spaces.

Some of the problems with this particular move — done with no consultation of the senators themselves — was that it deprived the caucus of having senators from regions that are poorly represented in the Commons in order to get input from them. While there might have been merit in not having senators take national caucus with MPs — creating more distance and independence — the loss of those regional perspectives, as well as institutional memory from the party caucus, could have longer-reaching consequences. The Conservative Senate caucus remains part of that party's national caucus, which is faced with the problem of a lack of regional representation — a particular dilemma since the 2015 election when the party was shut out from all of Atlantic Canada and most of the major urban centres in the country. Senators from those regions are now the Opposition voices for those areas of the nation.

One of the enduring problems with the public's perception of the Senate is the common belief that senators will always act in a partisan manner, beholden to the leader who recommended them. This might often be true for new senators, and the issue is certainly more problematic in periods of high turnover in the chamber, however, within a couple of years most senators tend to realize they actually have much more of a free hand than they initially thought and they begin to test their independence a bit more. Upon appointment there should be the awareness that the party leader can't whip senators. While yes, there is some small measure of party discipline in the Senate, given the organizing principle of responsible government, it is a far less rigorous control than that exerted in the Commons. But just as MPs need to be aware that their job is to scrutinize the Estimates and hold the government to account, senators in a government caucus need to be aware that they aren't actually beholden to the prime minister.

Independence in the Senate does come with time and experience, but often the real accelerating factor behind a growth in independence is a leadership change within the party when the prime minister who recommended the senators is no longer in a position of power. As senators line up behind new leadership candidates they are supporting, their previous allegiances tend to dissolve pretty quickly, and the feeling of being beholden is no longer a factor when making decisions. But as this is a process that takes time, this is one of the dynamics that is harder for outsiders to grasp.

The work that they do also helps to encourage senatorial independence. The long-term projects they work on and the issues they champion also help to accelerate this process, as do those occasions when senators find themselves on the outside of the party leader's current position on an issue. In the end, even those who are generally regarded as poor appointment choices tend to get better with time as they do more meaningful work and find their way past the feelings of being beholden.

The single most important change that can be looked at, however, is that of how to make the appointments process more transparent and accountable. Once again, as part of his move in expelling senators from his caucus, Liberal leader Justin Trudeau announced that should he form a government his intention would be to create an appointments body that would recommend potential senators for appointment based on merit rather than partisan loyalty. When he was elected in 2015, he began this process immediately to start dealing with the backlog of Senate vacancies left by Prime Minister Harper.

It is an idea that has merit, as long as it remains understood that the responsibility — and accountability — for the recommendation rests with the prime minister and not the appointment body, thus respecting the role of responsible government. Otherwise, a prime minister who makes a poor choice would be able to say, "It's not my fault — they picked him or her!" That principle of keeping the accountability in one place is often overlooked in the quest to reduce the powers of appointment. Just as with the impulse to make things "more democratic," we must bear in mind that the need to hold someone to account should also balance out that consideration. There must also be the awareness that just because it's an outside body recommending the appointments, it doesn't mean that the quality of appointments will be any better. After all, most of these appointments to date have been made by a committee internal to the Prime Minister's Office.

The process begun by Trudeau has to date produced independent senators who haven't sworn any particular party allegiance upon appointment, despite invitations from the existing caucuses that they would be welcomed if they wished to join. Around this time a third group of independent senators, many of whom had left their original caucuses within recent months and years, banded together with Independent Progressive Conservative Senator Elaine McCoy to create what they termed the

"Independent Working Group," later renamed the Independent Senators Group, a quasi-caucus that existed to help organize unaffiliated senators with the kinds of logistical challenges that normally party whips would deal with, while at the same time trying to rebalance the power structure within the Senate so that the oligarchy of the Senate party leaders and whips would no longer exclude them from committee assignments or disadvantage them in the rules. At the time of this writing that process is ongoing, particularly when it comes to changing the Rules of the Senate to grant them recognition as a caucus without requiring that they align themselves with an existing federal party.

For future governments that might not wish to continue Trudeau's independent appointment panel, another suggestion would be to make the appointments more transparent through guidelines. Prime ministers could begin their terms by drawing up a list of qualities they would base their Senate appointments on, and when appointments were made, they could be compared to those lists of qualifications. Furthermore, a prime minister could also make clear the reasons why a particular person was chosen to fill a Senate seat rather than someone else. This would not only add transparency but would give the electorate a means by which to hold that government to account — whether or not it kept to its published guidelines.[12]

In David E. Smith's essay "The Improvement of the Senate by Nonconstitutional Means," he adds a few other suggestions. These include more robust internal ethics rules and penalties (a process accelerated during the Mike Duffy trial), more stringent attendance rules (though it should be noted that the Senate already has public attendance records, whereas the House of Commons keeps its self-reported attendance records private), and better public communications so greater rationale is given when the Senate sends a bill back to the Commons with changes, as well as for any suggested changes that happen during pre-study of a bill that's still before the Commons (again, an ongoing process that has been intensified as part of the post-Duffy rehabilitation efforts).

Anecdotally, one of the reasons why the practice of pre-studying bills had greatly diminished was that said bills passed the Senate in little time because they had already largely been dealt with, and the public and media perception was that the upper chamber was merely rubber-stamping the bill, rather than having an awareness that the hard work had already been done and the suggestions incorporated while the bill was still in the Commons. While the Senate has been developing a more active public communications team in recent years, with more staff and resources, this practice could prove to be of enhanced utility when it comes to keeping the public aware of the Senate's activities.

In order to broaden the reforms that are possible, the imposition of term limits is often discussed. This is one place where the Supreme Court decided it wouldn't draw lines around just what limit would be acceptable. Before considering the question of whether or not the limits change the fundamental character of the Senate, however, it is crucial to take into consideration a couple of factors: such terms would need to be non-renewable so that senators would maintain their "sober" and independent principles — not vying for re-appointment; and they would need to be sufficiently long enough in order to maintain the Senate's role with regard to continuity and institutional memory.

As well, in order to keep a single prime minister from turning over the population of the chamber within two or three majority mandates, the length would have to be set between twelve and fifteen years. Thus, the proposals put forward by the Harper government of eight or nine years would fail these tests, since they would fundamentally alter the character of the chamber, and term limits that are too short invite their being made renewable, either by election or appointment. Some of the provincial factums leading up to the Supreme Court reference also pointed out that without the current system of appointment to age seventy-five there is a risk that senators could vie for a post-Senate appointment as the end of their non-renewable terms approached — be it for an ambassadorship or to head an administrative tribunal. This particular argument detracts from "sobriety" and institutional independence, which makes term limits more problematic.

One other suggestion that has been explored to some degree and perhaps could be revisited would be the suggestion to reconsider the regional balance within the chamber's composition — still keeping it based on regional lines, as in the current "four kingdoms" (plus Newfoundland and Labrador and the territories) model that currently exists, but rejigging them somewhat. In 2007 Senators Jack Austin and Lowell Murray proposed the creation of a new senatorial region for British Columbia, with twelve seats, while its previous six seats would be redistributed to the three Prairie Provinces (four to Alberta and one each to Saskatchewan and Manitoba) so that their region still held twenty-four seats. While the suggestion would require a constitutional amendment, it could be a means of redressing some of the perceived regional imbalances within the chamber that exist currently, without diminishing its regional characteristics.

But while there is room for improvements around the edges, the fundamental structure and purpose of the Senate needs to be better understood by the broader public if it is to be rehabilitated in any way. The Senate will still be deserving of the status as the least-understood branch of Parliament and it will continue to suffer from wrong understandings of its role and calls for reform unless there is a better public awareness of just what it is, the role that it plays within the broader parliamentary context, and why "appointed" doesn't mean "undemocratic."

THE MAPLE CROWN

Canada is a constitutional monarchy. Since the country was first settled by the French under François I and the English under Henry VII, there has always been a monarch at the head of our state. As the country's parliamentary traditions evolved into a constitutional monarchy, our country, too, has seen its relationship with the sovereign develop, most significantly with the establishment of the Canadian monarchy in 1931.

Yes, that's right — Canada has a Canadian monarchy, a separate and distinct institution that has existed since the passage of the Statute of Westminster. The passing of that act changed in a fundamental way the country's relationship with the Crown. Since 1931, when the statute came into force, it has been decreed that when acting on behalf of Canada and its Parliament the Crown should act on the advice of Canadian ministers alone, thereby dividing the Crown into Canadian and British entities. This made official the separate Crowns that had been evolving since the nineteenth century, and at this point the British Crown split into six separate Crowns (representing Australia, Canada, Ireland, New Zealand, Newfoundland, and South Africa), after which many more emerged.

In 1937, when George VI ascended to the throne, he was asked during his coronation if he would govern Canada while respecting its laws — the first time that we were singled out as a distinct realm. This evolution of a separate Crown culminated in 1953 with the Royal Styles and Titles Act, whereby Elizabeth II became the first monarch to be distinctively proclaimed as the Canadian monarch by the Canadian government. Thus, when acting as the Queen of Canada, she is styled: "Elizabeth the Second, By the Grace of God, of the United Kingdom, Canada, and Her other Realms and Territories Queen, Head of the Commonwealth, Defender of the Faith."

In other words, we might have the same Queen as the United Kingdom, Australia, New Zealand, and Tuvalu, to name a few of her other realms, but each has a separate Crown.

If you look at an official portrait of the Queen of Canada, you'll notice that it's very different from an official portrait of the Queen of the United Kingdom, for example. The Queen of Canada wears her Canadian insignia as the Sovereign of the Order of Canada and the Order of Military Merit. The Queen of the United Kingdom wears the State Diadem, the blue Garter Riband, and the Royal Family Orders of her grandfather, King George V, and her father, King George VI. So while Elizabeth II might be the same physical Queen between the various realms, the institution of the Crown for each of these realms is different, as demonstrated by the various symbols that each employs, and each of those symbols matters.

And yet, listening to the rhetoric of some, there is the impression that a foreign monarch rules us, or that the "Queen of England" holds sway here. Never mind that there hasn't been a separate English Crown since 1707, people still constantly employ the term. The monarchy is treated as some foreign curiosity in the media and popular discourse, which invariably ends up reinforcing the notion that it's some kind of colonial relic, when it is, in fact, the centrepiece of our entire democracy. During a Royal Tour, people mistakenly roll out Union Jack flags as though a foreign monarch is visiting when, actually, it is the Canadian Royal Family and they should be carrying Canadian flags.

It has only been worse since nationalist sentiment in Quebec has decided to brand the monarchy as a foreign imposition, forgetting, of course, that it is thanks to the Royal Proclamation of 1763 and the Quebec Act of 1774 that the province exists at all and that its people have been allowed to retain their language, religion, and culture.

What makes the current antipathy toward the monarchy in Quebec rather ironic is the fact that the traditional culture that so many strong nationalists in the province claim to want to protect was, in fact, a monarchist society, content to have avoided the horrors of the French Revolution until the Quiet Revolution.

These French-Canadian anti-monarchists aren't alone, of course. They have cousins elsewhere in Canada who, while they might not share all the same views, are also moved by a kind of nationalism to oppose the monarchy. There is a brand of Canadian nationalist that doesn't seem to realize that the Statute of Westminster happened and that Canada now has a separate and distinct monarchy, and such people want a "made-in-Canada" head of state — despite the fact that we've actually already got one.

The Canadian monarchy is unique across other monarchies within the Commonwealth. It's a compound monarchy that represents both the federal and provincial governments, and we have a bilingual monarch who speaks better French than many of her ministers. The role of the governor general and the lieutenant governors are unique among other Commonwealth nations also. We have a heraldic authority that blends our British, French, and First Nations traditions.

The conduct of the Canadian Royal Family is also unique and distinct from the British Royal Family, with the pattern having been set as early as 1878 when John Campbell, Marquess of Lorne, was named governor general, and he and his wife, Princess Louise Caroline Alberta, took up residence in Rideau Hall. They quickly discovered the importance of maintaining an egalitarian, informal society rather than the strict social hierarchy of the British court.[1] These changes to adapt to Canadian society, including visiting the different regions as an expression of our "compound monarchy" and doing away with court etiquette in favour of simple good manners, established the "cultural conditions" that led to a distinct Canadian Crown.[2]

There are no other monarchies that exactly parallel ours — and thus, it is a "made-in-Canada" institution. Now, if Canada should want to change the rules of succession so that after Elizabeth II passes, our monarchy's line might diverge from those of other Commonwealth nations, then certainly we're free to do so (provided we can get the unanimous consent of all of the provinces to change the Constitution). But to consider our central principle of governance to be a "relic" or "foreign" is completely false.

THE CROWN-IN-COUNCIL AND THE CROWN-IN-PARLIAMENT

One of the distinct features of a constitutional monarchy is the relationship between who has power and who exercises it. In our system, it is the monarch who holds power, but it is the political executive that wields it in order to carry out the day-to-day governing of the country. It is through the Crown that our institutions receive their legitimacy, since it is the source of formal authority. The Crown is also the source of justice, and even the fount of honours. It is the central organizing principle by which our entire system of government rests. It is also a means of keeping egos in check, since this relationship reminds the sitting prime minister — the current head of government — that said power is held in trust. Acts are proclaimed in the name of the sovereign and not the head of the government to keep that relationship clear.

The Queen personifies the state — hers is the human face of our system of government and its rules, regulations, and the thousand years of traditions that have evolved into our current system of parliamentary democracy. She is the living embodiment of the state and its citizens. As the head of state, she represents all Canadians in a more immutable way than a flag, political leader, or ideology can. She personalizes those symbols so that no sitting politician can, which again keeps the roles of head of state and head of government separate. The non-partisan civil service exercises its functions in her name because she is removed from the government of the day, and that allows it to retain its independence and permanence when the government of the day changes. With the Queen, as head of state, portrayed on postage stamps, coinage, and in government offices, rather than the head of government, it keeps the state from identifying with the particular government of the day, helps to keep cults of personality from developing, and keeps politicians from seeking adulation.

As the head of state, the Queen is at the centre of governance. The political executive consists of the sovereign or her representatives (the governor general or lieutenant governors), acting on the advice of her ministers, and is known broadly as the Crown-in-Council. In Canada, because those powers are mostly executed by the governor general or lieutenant governors, the exercise of acting on advice is known as the

Governor-in-Council. The Queen's advisers — the Privy Council and its main committee, the Cabinet — are drawn from the legislative branch, primarily from the elected Commons as per responsible government. Occasionally, Cabinet members are drawn from the Senate (and on two occasions in Canada, the prime minister was also — Sir John Abbott in 1891–92, and Sir Mackenzie Bowell in 1894–96), but today, other than the Leader of the Government in the Senate, any senators drawn into Cabinet are usually included only out of consideration for gaps in representation in what has been a de facto federalist institution — that its membership is drawn up from all regions and represents the linguistic duality of the country. Thus, the governing that is done by the Crown on the advice of the Cabinet are termed "Orders-in-Council" — an exercise of the Crown powers on the advice of the Prime Minister-in-Council, or as the spokesperson of the Cabinet.

The relationship of the Crown-in-Council extends beyond just the executive; it relates to all players in the Commons. Former House of Commons Speaker James Jerome asserted the following:

> Parliament has endured because it works, particularly in terms of control. The Queen, who appears to have supreme authority, must act upon the advice of her prime minister. The prime minister, who also appears to have supreme authority, acquires that status only by commanding support of a majority of the members of the House of Commons. Within the House of Commons, responsibility for directing the scrutiny of the actions of the government falls to the leader of the majority opposition party, who fulfils that function as a direct responsibility to the Monarch in the capacity of the Leader of Her Majesty's Loyal Opposition.[3]

In this same way, the Senate acts on the same principles of scrutiny, ensuring the legislation that will be enacted in the sovereign's name will be sound. At the end of the legislative process comes the act of Royal Assent as nominally exercised by the governor general or the lieutenant governors. Royal Assent functions on a number of levels — it grants authority to the new law in the name of the sovereign; the Crown, as guardian of the Constitution, represents the people agreeing to live under the rule of law; and the Queen, as the embodiment of the state and its citizens, emphasizes that we all must live equally under the law. Royal Assent is the legislative power of the Crown-in-Parliament and isn't a prerogative power.

THE RESERVE POWERS

The Queen and her representatives do retain certain powers that are necessary for the proper functioning of our democratic system, but to some degree, they're all exercised on the advice of the prime minister. The powers that the Queen has the most discretion over revolve around the issuing of Letters Patent, and the selection of governors general. While governors general are nominated on the advice of the prime minister, it is implicit in the Constitution that the Queen has to give thought concerning the desirability of her representative, and it is generally believed that she retains a greater say in this particular power.

The issuing of Letters Patent is an important power that rests with the Queen because of her particular responsibilities. While Letters Patent can be changed upon the advice of the government of the day, thus amending the roles and duties of the governor general, it remains a key power that the Queen herself must retain because of her role in safeguarding the Constitution. Allowing a government of the day to change the duties and responsibilities of the governor general could impact on the way in which the roles of the governor general are performed in the capacity of the "safety valve" on said government, making the Queen's role an important one.

The naming of senators and additional senators — necessary in break-ing a deadlock in the Senate — is another of the Queen's personal powers, exercised on the recommendation of the governor general, who acts on the advice of the prime minister. This is one of the duties explicit in the Constitution, and one where she generally accepts the recommendation of the governor general and the prime minister's advice.

The reserve powers of the governor general, as laid out in Letters Patent, in large part revolve around four particular aspects — to summon, prorogue, and dismiss Parliaments, and to name and dismiss prime ministers.

After an election, the incumbent is generally invited to try to form the government to test the confidence of the chamber, and if he or she resigns, then the leader of the party who is best able to command that confidence is invited to form a government. This has generally devolved into a kind of shorthand that says the party that wins the most seats is assumed will be the one that forms the government, though it isn't strictly the case — especially in the event of a minority Parliament. It is the governor general's job to ensure there is a government in place that commands the confidence of the chamber — and likewise with the lieutenant governors in the provinces.

Part of the reserve powers of the Crown involves its ability to dissolve Parliament, again upon the advice of the prime minister. The power to grant prorogation is a reserve power over which there has been some contention in recent history, particularly after the prorogation crisis in 2008 when Prime Minister Stephen Harper went to the governor general to ask for a prorogation rather than face a vote of confidence he was likely to lose.

While there has been a great deal of debate whether or not Her Excellency, the Right Honourable Michaëlle Jean, should have granted Harper the prorogation, the accepted convention is that prorogation shouldn't normally be refused if the prime minister retains confidence, which he still did at that point. But as I argued in a previous chapter, if the traditions of prorogation were restored to their roots, which would require the governor general to make an address to Parliament to list the accomplishments of the session, it would have made it very difficult for Harper to have justified requesting prorogation given that the session was only three weeks old and hadn't passed any legislation.

In exceptional circumstances, the governor general can refuse the advice of a prime minister using the authority of the reserve powers; however, there is some debate as to what the consequences for refusing advice would be. There is a school of thought that believes a prime minister whose advice was refused would have to resign, given that the governor general — and by extension the Queen — no longer has confidence in his or her abilities. While this remains in some dispute, it is an indication of the strength of the reserve powers under our system. To date, every formal refusal of advice has led to prime ministerial resignation — a convention that reminds the governor general that advice should only be refused in the most exceptional of cases.

Given the ambiguity of some of those powers, there have been a number of calls recently, mostly from the academic community, for a "Cabinet Manual" for Canada to enumerate and codify those reserve powers — especially as a check on executive powers, such as with the prorogation crisis in 2008. The argument follows that with Cabinet manuals in place in the United Kingdom and New Zealand, there is no reason why Canada shouldn't have a manual of its own, or at least an updated and transparent version from the one created in 1968 by the Privy Council Office — the *Manual of Official Procedure of the Government of Canada.*

Nevertheless, there are problems with the calls for a manual to solve perceived problems, as well as with the citation of other cases where manuals exist. In the United Kingdom a manual can exist because of the general agreement that the parties involved need to avoid going to the sovereign at all costs (although this has created a host of new problems in the United Kingdom such as those accompanying the adoption of the Fixed-Term Parliaments Act in 2011). This creates the need for guidelines that can act as a normative instrument so that everyone can understand the rules and to try to respect those guidelines. In New Zealand there is less possibility of conflict since the role of the Crown is weaker in its Constitution.

The disadvantages of trying to impose a more codified system such as would accompany a new or enhanced manual in Canada is that we have evolved a system already where the conventions are inherently flexible and can allow for judgment calls to be made on the part of governors general. It becomes inherently difficult to bring logic or a set of rules to bear on what have been judgment calls because they are inherently subjective.

This, of course, is likely the point of those who call for such codification — that it takes away the ability for subjectivity. As with most calls for reforms, there are some potential unforeseen consequences to this particular call.

One of the most important unforeseen consequences is the potential impact this kind of move would have on the practice of responsible government. Under those principles, ministers of the Crown take responsibility for acts of the Crown, and the advice that they give the governor general. Does codification take away the onus from those ministers to provide sound advice, or does it shift the onus onto the governor general now that it is no longer a subjective call? Does the codification take away from the mentality that the reserve powers are generally to be used in exceptional circumstances? Does it create the expectation that the governor general plays a more robust role than he or she generally does by convention? Do those expectations impact on the privacy of advice that governors general give to prime ministers? Remember that an important function of a governor general is to advise and warn the government of the day. By taking away the subjectivity, the quality of that advice might be reduced or entirely diminished, because a prime minister would simply consult the manual rather than the governor general. This is one reason why a Westminster system doesn't always work well with codification.

Another problem with codification is that it creates the expectation that advice becomes justiciable. As with Crown Prerogatives, it is a dangerous game to start subjecting these kinds of powers to the scrutiny of the courts, because of the impact that this has on responsible government. How do we subject governments to legal remedies when Parliament remains the highest court in the land? How does this impact political accountability — that is, how do voters hold governments to account when this becomes the domain of the courts? It also raises the question of how much power we want to give the Supreme Court, considering that it isn't a body that has any accountability. If we ask the Supreme Court's judges to rule on the legality of a greater number of matters previously considered political advice, it will inevitably put them into a political role. This is also an underlying reason for some who advocate making this advice justiciable — so that those who lost at politics can try to re-fight their battle before the courts.

While there is merit to the notion of an updated or enhanced manual, especially when it comes to providing clarity around the formation and operation of minority governments in the future, it is another one of the reforms that must be approached with extreme caution. Simply trying to limit the powers of a sitting prime minister, as many of the motivations for these changes seem to involve, might seem like a good idea at the time, but it can have much more far-reaching consequences, especially when those who propose the reforms don't raise the same questions I've just posed — or answer them. Until those questions are asked, and answered in a way that can ensure the principles of responsible government aren't being impacted, then perhaps we need to take those calls with a few more grains of salt.

LET'S NOT ELECT THE GOVERNOR GENERAL

Among republicans, crypto-republicans, "democrats," and so-called Canadian "nationalists," there has been a call to make the office of the governor general an elected one, either with the aim of taking a first step toward abolishing the monarchy, or at least somehow taking away from the powers of the Queen. However, actually taking the step to abolish the monarchy would require a complete rewrite of the Constitution, given the way in which the Crown serves as the central organizing principle of our system of government. One can't simply invest that same power in the governor general because of the present formulation of the sovereign as a being who embodies the state — that is a fundamental and existential concept that can't simply be transferred to an elected governor general. It changes the entire dynamic of the system, so that sovereignty rests within the people instead.

With that in mind, let's look at just what electing a governor general would actually mean.

Some of the calls for easy so-called reform suggest that the governor general could be elected via a "consultative election," much in the way Alberta has been offering up nominees for Senate appointments to the prime minister. The argument, of course, is that nothing has actually changed, that the prime minister still offers this name to the Queen to be appointed, though it does take away from that reserve power the Queen still retains. This can't be true, however, because an election implies a mandate for which there is democratic legitimacy bestowed, and a governor general can't have a mandate because his or her position is based solely on delegated authority using powers laid out in Letters Patent. The Supreme Court also touched on this contradiction with its Senate reference — that election implies a mandate. Regardless of how a governor general is selected, his or her powers are exercised in the stead of a higher authority — the Queen.

What does a prospective governor general run on as a platform in a "consultative election" if he or she is to remain in a position for which there are no additional duties? How do governors general separate themselves from their competitors? Do they engage in a glorified popularity contest, or do they start to throw around facile initiatives such as "I want to be the education GG!" or "I want to be the health promotion GG!" — despite the fact that again they have no powers with which to be anything other than faces for initiatives. Yes, currently governors general champion some kind of cause, but it's done in a low-key way through self-directed initiatives. With Michaëlle Jean it was youth engagement, and with David Johnston it's families and volunteer work. Translating these kinds of initiatives into a democratic mandate lessens a governor general's ability to be involved in non-partisan initiatives that are used to bring Canadians together. The partisanship inherent in electoral politics would make the unifying aspect that much more difficult to take seriously.

The partisanship of an election would create a very real danger of trans-formational change within the role of the governor general. As it stands, the duties of warning and advising are central to the role of the governor general, and with the lieutenant governors in the provinces. In confidential meetings between prime ministers and governors general, there is an opportunity to engage in a dialogue regarding what each of them hears from Canadians, and as a result such meetings can be more valuable for prime ministers than are their meetings with their Cabinets. In such meetings, a prime minister is more likely to hear from those eager to score political points or tell the PM what they think he or she wants to hear, rather than offer advice from a bit more distance. A certain utility would be lost if the role of the governor general were to become politicized through an election, because said governor general would either be offering partisan advice to what could be his or her party leader, or would be in an oppositional relationship with the prime minister. If the latter were the case, their meeting would be one between two people from differing parties, and there would be increasing pressure on the governor general to act in a partisan manner to thwart the agenda of a prime minister whose agenda is opposed to the party the governor general represents.

And those who believe that electing the governor general could be done outside the party system are sadly deluding themselves. The base logistics of running a national campaign for a single position would require millions of dollars and a massive organization. Only political parties have that fundraising and organizational capacity, and even if there were some kind of restriction on keeping political parties out of that race, their volunteers and political machine would still be employed in an ad hoc capacity.

As well, any suggestion that a governor general "consultative" election could be held simultaneously with a federal election would be absolutely untenable, even if that suggestion were made to cut down on the costs of such an election. Because the role of the governor general is to summon a Parliament and to determine which party can hold the confidence of the chamber, thus inviting a party leader to form a government — assuming that the incumbent is unwilling or unable — it puts too much pressure on a new governor general to do so immediately upon election, with no time to adjust to the role or to learn his or her roles and responsibilities.

It would be all the more untenable for a newly elected governor general who was elected on a partisan banner to immediately render a judgment on a minority Parliament in which his or her party was one of the contenders for holding power. Even if the outgoing governor general were to make this decision, since the recently elected governor general's term might not start for several weeks or months, it would still create a perceptual problem about the legitimacy of a "lame-duck" governor general having to make this kind of a call. In this context, the desirability of an elected governor general becomes all the more suspect.

Which brings us back to the question of why exactly one wants to elect the governor general. What is to be gained from the exercise other than the charade of change, which would only sow more confusion in our political system? Such a construction would only create a host of problems in which none currently exists. The unintended consequences would be enormous, from a governor general demanding a more activist role to go along with a mandate and "democratic legitimacy" to the loss of the warning and advising role.

Even more critically, control over the Canadian Forces would be threatened by a significant change in the role and responsibilities of the governor general. Remember that the governor general is also the commander-in-chief of the Canadian Forces, and therefore has a constitutional concern regarding how the prime minister deploys the troops. This could set up a power struggle in the situation of a politically unpopular war or troop deployment the prime minister's party favours while the governor general's doesn't.

If the goal of electing the governor general is simply to have an election, then one has to wonder about the broader consequences of such a reductionist approach. After all, if one starts to hold elections merely for the sake of holding them, do elections not then begin to become meaningless? If you want to hold an election for a position that has few day-to-day powers, using facile initiatives as the shell of a mandate, the weight and meaning of that vote becomes diluted. It also raises serious questions about the meaning of legitimacy if one simply reduces the legitimacy of an office solely to those who have secured it by means of a vote. What is next on that list? Electing the judiciary, right up to the Supreme Court of Canada? The allure of holding a vote to have a system with the gloss of "modernity" rarely takes these questions into consideration, or the harms that their proposed "reforms" would ultimately cause.

THE CROWN PREROGATIVES

Under the system of responsible government, executive authority resides with the Crown, which is personified by the sovereign and represented in Canada by the governor general, but this is normally exercised on the advice of the prime minister and Cabinet members — the Crown's ministers who, by constitutional convention, are responsible and accountable for the affairs of government.[4] Included in this executive authority are a number of Crown prerogatives that cover appointments, military deployments, and the exercise of foreign affairs, such as the negotiation and ratification of treaties.

While there is a constant litany of complaints by those who feel that the exercise of these powers should be curtailed and devolved to the House of Commons, there remains one very important reason why those powers should rest with the Crown, and that is accountability. Although people might feel that allowing votes in the Commons on the exercise of these powers would be another example of how the system could be made "more democratic," they fail to see that the inverse of this move is to weaken accountability for these decisions. Such a move would, in large part, make ministerial accountability meaningless. There are several concrete examples of why Crown prerogatives are a necessary function of our system of government.

One of the first and foremost is the deployment of the Canadian Forces. With matters of national defence being a Crown prerogative, the country is able to speak with a single voice in international military forums and to take decisive but unpopular action when necessary.[5] It also gives a central point of accountability for these missions — the minister of defence and the prime minister. But if the practice of holding a vote before a combat deployment becomes the norm, as Prime Minister Stephen Harper tried to institute when he first came to power in 2006, the toll on accountability is immediately apparent:

> If the House of Commons decided on military deploy-
> ments, the defence minister and cabinet would no longer
> be wholly responsible for this choice; the responsibility
> for military deployments would be divided between the
> Commons and the governing cabinet. When time came
> to hold the government to account for the missions, it
> would be unclear who is responsible. While the defence
> minister would remain accountable to the House of
> Commons for the conduct of operations, the government
> could claim that it is not fully responsible for the mission
> itself, since the decision was made in conjunction with
> the Commons.[6]

This is precisely the kind of confusion Harper was attempting to sow by holding votes on the extension of the Afghanistan mission, and in particular, by making it a free vote. He was able to divide opinion in the Liberal Party, which not only allowed the deployment to pass in a minority Parliament but made it easy for him to claim the party was divided whenever it expressed criticism of the conduct of the mission, or that it had supported the mission, giving it no room to complain. Likewise, anyone who voted against the deployment could later be castigated for not supporting the troops.

Other examples of the use of votes in the House to avoid accountability have been seen in recent years such as questions surrounding the conduct of Christiane Ouimet, the public sector integrity commissioner from 2007 until 2010. When the matter was brought up in the Commons during Question Period, the government's standard line became "The House voted on her appointment," which was the means of avoiding accountability for the appointment.

The Crown prerogative of appointments is another example of ways in which the power is necessary not only for accountability but for the process to be made in a straightforward manner. Given that high-level civil service positions in Canada are Order-in-Council appointments, devolving that responsibility to the Commons would require an incredible amount of time and resources to ensure the approvals would be made in a timely manner. As it stands, time is precious within the limited number of sitting days in the calendar, and using up time that would otherwise be spent debating legislation or studying the Estimates would be exhausted through approvals.

This would also add in a number of other complicating factors such as to whom these senior bureaucrats become responsible to, and who has the power to remove them. A clear example of this would be the chief of defence staff (CDS). If his or her job comes at the pleasure of the Commons rather than the prime minister, the politicization of military deployments would become egregious and the CDS would be torn in terms of lines of responsibility among the governor general as the commander-in-chief, the minister he or she is obligated to advise, or parliamentarians, who would now hold his or her job as a political tool to be employed at their whim. As well, in a minority Parliament, would Opposition MPs start firing deputy ministers as a means of pressuring the government instead of going after Cabinet ministers? That would seem to be a surefire way of politicizing a civil service that is supposed to remain independent (by swearing allegiance to the Queen rather than the government of the day) and threatening its ability to speak truth to power.

With respect to the exercise of foreign policy, the power of the Crown to sign treaties is an important one that again began to be weakened by the Harper government's practice of submitting treaties for a vote in the Commons prior to ratification by the Cabinet. Once more, this weakens the accountability of a government that enters into a bad deal, but it also has implications for the way in which the country can withdraw from one. If it becomes incumbent upon Parliament to approve treaties before they are ratified, does it not then limit the ability of future governments wanting to withdraw from treaties as well, since it would theoretically require Parliament to vote on doing so? How does this not become a problem when the courts have decided that legislation shouldn't be able to bind future governments?

Shifting the ratification of treaties to Parliament, away from the Crown's prerogative, as they are intended to be, focuses the attention on the treaty itself rather than on its implementation — that remains a responsibility of the government of the day through the exercise of policy and supply. That invites the question of what happens in a situation in which the House signs off on a treaty, but the government doesn't implement it. The government can rightfully say the House voted on the treaty, so it's not really the government's problem that it's not being implemented — there is no follow-through of accountability or responsibility. Parliament already has a requirement to pass enabling legislation for treaties that necessitate changes to Canadian law, meaning it already has a say regarding our most important treaties. That say remains in its proper sphere of authority, and expanding the sphere creates those problems of accountability.

The bizarre situation with the Kyoto Protocol treaty is brought to mind whereby it was ratified, but the minority government of the day didn't abide by its stipulations and ignored it. When the House tried to pass legislation to enforce the treaty, it wasn't able to include any actual enforcement mechanisms beyond public shaming. In one case, a piece of legislation that did pass because of the minority government situation was dragged before the courts, and because the legislation was simply about reporting, there was no real consequences to the government when it pretty much ignored the bill. (This did become an issue around the rule of law, but that's a matter separate from this discussion.) Another attempted reporting bill died in the Senate, in part because it was an illegitimate bill that was trying to determine government policy from the Opposition benches, when it was not their role to do so. Eventually, the government exercised its Crown prerogative to withdraw from the Kyoto Protocol, ending the years of legal and constitutional wrangling — wrangling that will be the inevitable result if the practice of turning over the power of treaties to the Commons continues.

Another Crown prerogative is that of mercy — another example where it becomes inappropriate for the Commons to become involved. While currently the power of mercy and clemency is largely devolved to the Parole Board, which is independent from government because of Crown powers, an attempt to devolve this power to the Commons would again be problematic. Does the democratic House turn over the powers to the Parole Board, making it a technocratic function rather than a democratic one, or does it instead hold votes over who should be pardoned? Would it be like a return to the days when divorces were determined by a private bill in Parliament? And what about unpopular pardons? Would putting those to a vote in the House not spread the blame around rather than focus accountability on the prime minister and Cabinet? Once again, it no longer becomes the government's fault because the House voted on it.

What the exercise of Crown prerogatives ultimately boils down to is a matter of confidence — as long as the prime minister and the government can maintain it within the chamber, then they have the ability to exercise these powers. Otherwise, when these decisions are devolved to the Commons, no matter how much we might wish to "empower" or embolden the duly elected representatives, it muddies the question of who ultimately has responsibility for the exercise of these powers. And while it might be the current fashion in academic and pundit circles to try to remove as many of the Crown prerogatives and reserve powers as possible and turn them over to the House, in part because of the abuse of some of those powers by the Harper government, there seems to be little appreciation for the price in accountability that those changes would mean. The accountability for any of those abuses rests with that prime minister, and it is up to the electorate to decide whether or not to punish or reward the behaviour. In the case of Stephen Harper in 2011, the electorate chose to reward that behaviour. If the accountability and responsibility were spread around the entire House of Commons, it would then become meaningless. That is the danger of reforms made to satisfy knee-jerk reactions rather than those that take the broader system into account.

ON THE OPTICS OF THE MONARCHY

One of the constant complaints about the monarchy is the money spent to support it, and for a class of people who dwell in castles. The twin arguments of it being a waste of taxpayer dollars and why we need to maintain ostentatious displays of wealth and privilege when there is poverty in the country are constant companions of any discussion that surrounds the monarchy, whether it be in Canada or elsewhere. There are a few things that should be said to keep everything in perspective.

First of all is that the monarch and the Royal Family need to be independently wealthy because that ensures their independence. If they relied solely on the handouts of the government for their survival, it would soon become a contest of wills — "do what I say or I'll cut off your funding." Yes, the Royal Family in the United Kingdom receives payments from the government because that's the agreement by which Parliament abides — the government, rather than the monarch, now collects taxes, and in return, the monarch is granted a share in order to perform and fulfill her duties to the public. As it is currently structured, the Crown gets a 15 percent royalty on the Crown Estates in order to pay for the sovereign and the Royal Family's official residences and duties. This payment from the Crown Estates has replaced the Civil List. On top of that, the Queen has property that she owns in her personal capacity — the independent wealth that allows her to do what she wants should there be a government that would try to reduce the amount given through the Crown Estates. And residences like Balmoral Castle, which she owns as a natural person and not the Queen, means that she has a place to go if the government were to lock her out of her official residence at Buckingham Palace. Here, in Canada, we don't pay for the upkeep of the members of the Royal Family — only for their expenses when they tour the country. By sharing our monarch and Royal Family with sixteen other countries, we come in at a costs saving.

In much the same way as the monarch needs wealth, the governor general requires a certain level of payment and pension level in order to ensure he or she, too, doesn't become beholden to the government of the day. One particularly unseemly instance was in 2004 when the House of Commons, under a minority government, voted to reduce the budget of Her Excellency, the Right Honourable Adrienne Clarkson, after it was upset by the price tag of a series of state visits that she had undertaken, no matter that it was at the request of the government and paid for by the Department of Foreign Affairs. That the Commons would behave in a vindictive manner toward a robust governor general in the exercise of her duties is precisely why the office needs to be free from political interference and have its budget protected.

Part of the problem around the populist outrage over the costs of these institutions, be it the monarchy or the governor general, is that the numbers are usually presented in a shock-and-awe manner in the media without the benefit of context or meaningful comparison. One example is the cost of a Royal Tour, which is usually in the low millions of dollars. News pundits wonder whether it's money well spent, or try to create a stir around the price tag without offering the fact that a seven-day Royal Tour still costs less than it did for U.S. President Barack Obama to visit Ottawa for a single afternoon. Another example again hails from Clarkson when the carpet in Rideau Hall needed to be replaced. Once again, there were media stories about how it cost $91,000 to be replaced — never mind that the actual square footage of said carpet was quite impressive and that it needed to be sourced from a Canadian manufacturer. It was simply the big price tag that was the focus of attention — a problem that's endemic in political reporting.

When people complain about the cost of the monarchy or the vice-regal offices, they don't take into account what the additional costs would be to have elected offices for these roles. In fact, a single election for one of these positions would cost more than the salary and operations of that office for a single year of its operation (and as discussed previously, it would make for an untenable situation to elect the governor general at the same time as the Commons). As well, the offices of an elected governor general would demand more funding in order to play the more robust role that would be demanded because of the mandate her or she received, no matter how little direct influence that office might actually hold in the grand scheme of things.

We must also be wary of those who would see that all spending for pomp and ceremony be eliminated in the name of frugality. While no one is looking for the kinds of lavish gold-plated displays of dictators in the Third World, there needs to be an awareness that democracy costs, diplomacy costs, and ceremony plays an important part in our society, with the recognition of excellence through the Canadian Honours system, or the kind of national unity role that's played when the Queen or the governor general makes an official visit domestically or abroad. Simply focusing this kind of attention on the prime minister politicizes these functions, makes them implicitly partisan if not explicitly so, and is inherently polarizing because only one small riding actually elects the prime minister to begin with. And when a prime minister is media-shy and crowd-averse, as with Stephen Harper, that visibility is even further reduced. There is an importance to symbols, and to the kind of engagement the Queen and the governor general has with the general public.

Simply focusing on a price tag without understanding the meaning is to cut off one's nose to spite one's face. Nobody actually wants to live in a drab, colourless society where pomp and ceremony are extinct. Sometimes it's a fact that bears reminding when the discourse becomes so humourless as to try to suggest that we operate the head of state and her representatives in a dollar-store fashion.

It should also be said that if the Canadian monarchy wishes to assert itself as a more independent institution from its U.K. counterpart, more effort needs to be made by the government as well as by other parties in Parliament. While the Conservative government of Stephen Harper put a great deal of effort into restoring the "Royal" moniker of several institutions, including within the Canadian Forces (such as the Royal Canadian Navy and the Royal Canadian Air Force), the fact that changes were done without cross-party consultation and support meant that the restorations were politicized and seen through a lens of glorifying Canada's colonial past. Had there been a greater effort at cross-party support for the restoration or maintenance of monarchical symbols, there wouldn't have been as much damage to the "brand" of the Canadian monarchy along the way.

As well, there needs to be a greater focus on Royal Tours and working visits by members of the Canadian Royal Family to ensure there is a more visible presence in Canada, and that they're viewed less as a foreign imposition. With a younger generation of Royals doing more of the heavy lifting, it would be an ideal opportunity to see an enhanced focus on promoting charitable works in Canada, and duties beyond just those of acting as colonels-in-chief of military regiments across the country. If the desire is that the monarchy doesn't fade away in Canada, then it must be better at asserting itself — something that governments of all stripes must make a greater effort at.

CHANGING THE POISONED CHALICE

As the preceding chapters have illustrated, Canada does have a robust political system that, for the most part, successfully balances the competing needs of democracy and accountability. That being said, more can be done to return the balance closer to its original state. We can restore the machine of Canadian democracy to its true state, undoing some of the changes that have warped it over the years.

But more than anything, changes are needed when it comes to how we view our political culture. The casual dislike of politicians has become so rampant and so part of our political culture, reinforced by the Reform Party years of populist politics, that we have reached a point where even our politicians distance themselves from the term. The warning about this kind of cynicism goes back more than a century and a half. Walter Bagehot wrote in *The English Constitution* in 1867 that, "A nation which does not expect good from a Parliament, cannot check or punish a Parliament." We are very close to being in that kind of situation today.

The Samara Canada studies, culminating in the book *Tragedy in the Commons*, portrays some eighty-six former MPs who all described themselves as "outsiders" to the system, and who spun sob stories about how they were the victims of cruel party manipulations the whole time. While the book does call them out on the kind of self-mythologizing that these kinds of protests are a big part of, what it doesn't do is take the next step and call these same politicians out for not taking any personal responsibility for their predicaments, especially when it came to not knowing their own jobs as MPs.

It is a curious thing that people will run for the job of MP when asked to do so by others but that they won't bother to find out what the job entails, simply trusting others to tell them what they need to know when the time comes. As most of the MPs in the Samara studies discovered, relying on the party to such an extent meant surrendering their power and autonomy — something they could have avoided by educating themselves better about the very role they had agreed to take on. While most of them did it for noble reasons — and let's face it, one doesn't get into Canadian politics to get rich — the fact that there was a sense of willful blindness to their protestations of being so completely unprepared is troubling.

It is much the same with the rank-and-file grassroots membership decline that we have seen in this country. With less than 2 percent of the population actually holding a party membership, we have one of the lowest rates of civic participation in the Western world. It's not a surprise that this is a contributing factor to lower voter turnouts — more people feel disconnected from the process. The fact that they don't know about that process is part of why we need to start educating ourselves and taking that responsibility to engage.

It also becomes incumbent upon us not to get discouraged when we do try to engage and face resistance. This is in part what our civic neglect has sown — powerful central organizations and leaders' offices that have amassed that power because there isn't enough grassroots engagement to push back against it. Small groups have been allowed to amass power because grassroots members and voters have allowed them to, usually through excuses like "not my problem," or "I'm too busy to think about that," never mind that it's their very governance they should be paying more attention to. And nobody who has amassed power wants to give it up easily.

To that end, we often face calls to impose new rules and structures, and all for the wrong reasons. Reform calls, be it for abolishing parties, changing the voting system, or attempts to further "democratize" institutions, aren't actually addressing the problem of engagement with the system but, in fact, put new barriers in place that further alienate citizens from their machinery of governance. If we want people to engage, there needs to be a tangible sense that their engagement matters — that means policy resolutions, nomination races, and a participatory structure in which the ballot box is the culmination and not the be-all and end-all of political life.

But all of this requires us to change our thinking. We have to stop dismissing politics as "boring," because it's really not. Once someone finds an issue they're passionate about, the best way to advance the cause is to promote it within a party structure by means of policy resolutions. More change happens from within the system than merely yelling from the sidelines.

We need to stop thinking of all politicians as corrupt or corruptible, and remember that they're human beings. We most especially need to stop feeding this mythology that they're "different from those other guys," and that they're the non-politicians. It's a sad state of affairs when members of the political class try to distance themselves from one another and from their own work. It's not only false, but it's destructive to the ability to do any work when they're all trying to burnish the image that they're outsiders and that they're all pushing against the machinery. If they were all pushing against it, then we wouldn't be in the situation we're in today where power has centralized to the extent that it has.

More than anything, we all need to stop blaming "politics" or the parties for our problems and to take the responsibility to educate ourselves about our political system — voters and MPs alike. For voters, that means not only using that knowledge to engage but also to hold MPs to account. We need to challenge candidates that they know what they're signing up for, and not simply satisfy ourselves with platitudes like "they want to help," or "they just want to work together," or "I just want to listen to your concerns." Those are all well-meaning sentiments, but they won't actually do anything when it comes to Parliament sitting down to get work done.

None of this change will be easy, because it's not structural — it's cultural. Can it happen? Absolutely. We are constantly being told that the youth of this country are politically engaged, but in "different ways" with NGOs and other organizations. But we need them to get back involved with the parties and with our political structures. Can it happen overnight? Probably not. We'll likely need to go through a few more election cycles, but with dedication and a commitment by voters and candidates to improve themselves, their knowledge, and what they're bringing to the system, that change can and will happen.

Because, after all, it's not the machine that's broken. We just need to remember how to use it.

ACKNOWLEDGEMENTS

This book comes about thanks to a number of people who have helped me on the road to my career as a parliamentary journalist, particularly editors who have worked with me and nurtured me along the way. Many thanks to David Crosson, Brett Taylor, Gareth Kirkby, Marcus McCann, Brent Creelman, Sue Allen, Tom Korski, and Christina Spencer. Thanks to Chris Waddell for his guidance during my master's thesis, and to others whose words of encouragement helped me along the way, especially Rob Russo, Karine Fortin, and Andrew Coyne. A very special thanks to Philippe Lagassé for his invaluable help with the book and in being a sounding board during the writing process. My thanks to the people at Dundurn Press who made this book a reality, in particular Kirk Howard, Carrie Gleason, Kathryn Lane, Dominic Farrell, Jennifer Gallinger, and Kendra Martin. Thanks also to my friends and family for their unwavering support.

NOTES

CHAPTER 2: A REFRESHER ON RESPONSIBLE GOVERNMENT

1. Nathan Tidridge, *Canada's Constitutional Monarchy* (Toronto: Dundurn Press, 2011), 19.
2. David E. Smith, *The People's House of Commons: Theories of Democracy in Contention* (Toronto: University of Toronto Press, 2007), 5.
3. Richard Gwyn, *John A.: The Man Who Made Us* (Toronto: Random House Canada, 2008), 175–77.
4. John Pepall, *Against Reform* (Toronto: University of Toronto Press, 2010), 31.
5. Smith, *The People's House of Commons*, 31.
6. Ibid.
7. Peter Aucoin, Mark D. Jarvis, and Lori Turnbull, *Democratizing the Constitution* (Toronto: Emond Montgomery Publications, 2011), 115.
8. Ibid., 236–37.
9. Lowell Murray, interview by Anna Maria Tremonti, "Retired Senator Lowell Murray," *The Current*, CBC Radio, October 13, 2011.
10. Gwyn, *John A.*, 69.
11. Smith, *The People's House of Commons*, 30.

CHAPTER 3: ELECTIONS AS DEMOCRACY AND ACCOUNTABILITY

1. Aucoin, Jarvis, Turnbull, *Democratizing the Constitution*, 116.
2. Pepall, *Against Reform*, 32.

CHAPTER 4: THE HOUSE OF COMMONS

1. Samara Canada, "Welcome to Parliament: A Job with No Description," 2010, accessed at www.samaracanada.com/docs/default-source/mp-exit-interviews/welcometoparliament_eng25ef579a50cd6a04a19 bff0000c565b1.pdf?sfvrsn=2.

2. Grant Purves and Jack Stilborn, "Members of the House of Commons: Their Role," revised June 1997, Government of Canada Publications, Library of Parliament, accessed at www.lop.parl.gc.ca/content/lop/researchpublications/bp56-e.htm.

3. Kelly Blidook, "Exploring the Role of 'Legislators' in Canada: Do Members of Parliament Influence Policy," *Journal of Legislative Studies* 16, no. 1 (2010): 32–56.

4. Heather Bastedo, Wayne Chu, Jane Hilderman, and André Turcotte, "The Real Outsiders: Politically Disengaged Views on Politics and Democracy" (Toronto: Samara Canada, 2011), 13–15, accessed at www.samaracanada.com/docs/default-document-library/sam_therealoutsiders.pdf.

5. Smith, *The People's House of Commons*, 64.

6. Ibid., 63.

7. Audrey O'Brien and Marc Bosc, eds., "Financial Procedures — The Business of Supply," *House of Commons Procedure and Practice,* 2nd ed., 2009, accessed at http://www.parl.gc.ca/procedure-book-livre/Document.aspx?sbdid=F26EB116-B0B6-490C-B410-33D985B-C9B6B&sbpid=6E039746-E713-40D2-AEB8-46826181F5AB&Language=E&Mode=1.

8. Audrey O'Brien and Marc Bosc, eds., "Rules of Order and Decorum — Manner of Speaking," *House of Commons Procedure and Practice,* 2nd ed., 2009, accessed at www.parl.gc.ca/procedure-book-livre/Document.aspx?sbdid=EA8C92EB-0A42-4C61-A82E-D3ED72C63F0F&sbpid=BFC12DF9-A808-4F9B-9392-7BCC3EC3E6EE&Language=E&Mode=1.

9. Bruce M. Hicks, "The Westminster Approach to Prorogation, Dissolution and Fixed Date Elections," *Canadian Parliamentary Review* 18, no. 5 (Summer 2012): 25, accessed at www.revparl.ca/35/2/35n2_12e_Hicks.pdf.

CHAPTER 5: THE SENATE YOU DON'T KNOW

1. David E. Smith, *Federalism and the Constitution of Canada* (Toronto: University of Toronto Press, 2010), 43.

2. Ibid., 52.

3. Ibid., 77.

4. David E. Smith, *The Canadian Senate in Bicameral Perspective* (Toronto: University of Toronto Press, 2003), 8–10.

5. Smith, *Federalism and the Constitution of Canada*, 81.

6. Lowell Murray, "Which Criticisms Are Founded?" in *Protecting Canadian Democracy: The Senate You Never Knew*, ed. Serge Joyal (Montreal and Kingston: McGill-Queen's University Press, 2003), 140–41.

7. Smith, *Federalism and the Constitution of Canada*, 82.

8. "Which Criticisms Are Founded?" 141.

9. Ibid., 143.

10. Elaine McCoy, "Last Best Hope for Democracy in Canada: An Appointed Senate," *Toronto Star*, February 22, 2010, accessed at www.thestar.com/opinion/article/768518--last-best-hope-for-democracy-in-canada-an-appointed-senate.

11. Christopher Moore, "Wingnuts with Doubts About Senate Reform," accessed at http://christophermoorehistory.blogspot.ca/2011/05/wingnuts-with-doubts-about-senate.html.

12. David E. Smith, "The Improvement of the Senate by Nonconstitutional Means," in *Protecting Canadian Democracy: The Senate You Never Knew*, ed. Serge Joyal (Montreal and Kingston: McGill-Queen's University Press, 2003), 257–61.

CHAPTER 6: THE MAPLE CROWN

1. Carolyn Harris, "Royalty at Rideau Hall: Lord Lorne, Princess Louise, and the Emergence of the Canadian Crown," in *Canada and the Crown: Essays in Constitutional Monarchy*, eds. D. Michael Jackson and Philippe Lagassé (Montreal and Kingston: McGill-Queen's University Press, 2013), 20.

2. Harris, "Royalty at Rideau Hall," 26.

3. Tidridge, *Canada's Constitutional Monarchy*, 63.

4. Philippe Lagassé, "The Crown's Powers of Command-in-Chief: Interpreting Section 15 of Canada's *Constitution Act, 1867*," *Review of Constitutional Studies* 18, no. 2 (2013): 189–220.

5. Philippe Lagassé, "Accountability for National Defence: Ministerial Responsibility, Military Command and Parliamentary Oversight," *IRPP Study* 4 (March 2010): 7.

6. Ibid., 15.

BIBLIOGRAPHY

Aucoin, Peter, Mark D. Jarvis, and Lori Turnbull. *Democratizing the Constitution*. Toronto: Emond Montgomery Publications, 2011.

Bastedo, Heather, Wayne Chu, Jane Hilderman, and André Turcotte. "The Real Outsiders: Politically Disengaged Views on Politics and Democracy." Toronto: Samara Canada, 2011. Accessed at www.samaracanada.com/docs/default-document-library/sam_therealoutsiders.pdf.

Blidook, Kelly. "Exploring the Role of 'Legislators' in Canada: Do Members of Parliament Influence Policy." *Journal of Legislative Studies* 16, no. 1 (2010): 32–56.

Gwyn, Richard. *John A.: The Man Who Made Us*. Toronto: Random House Canada, 2008.

Harris, Carolyn. "Royalty at Rideau Hall: Lord Lorne, Princess Louise, and the Emergence of the Canadian Crown." In *Canada and the Crown: Essays in Constitutional Monarchy*. Eds. D. Michael Jackson and Philippe Lagassé. Montreal and Kingston: McGill-Queen's University Press, 2013.

Hicks, Bruce M. "The Westminster Approach to Prorogation, Dissolution and Fixed Date Elections." *Canadian Parliamentary Review* 18, no. 5 (Summer 2012). Accessed at www.revparl.ca/35/2/35n2_12e_Hicks.pdf.

Joyal, Serge, ed. *Protecting Canadian Democracy: The Senate You Never Knew*. Montreal and Kingston: McGill-Queen's University Press, 2003.

Lagassé, Philippe. "Accountability for National Defence: Ministerial Responsibility, Military Command and Parliamentary Oversight." *IRPP Study* 4 (March 2010).

_____. "The Crown's Powers of Command-in-Chief: Interpreting Section 15 of Canada's *Constitution Act, 1867.*" *Review of Constitutional Studies* 18, no. 2 (2013).

Loat, Allison and Michael MacMillan. *Tragedy in the Commons.* Toronto: Random House Canada, 2014.

McCoy, Elaine. "Last Best Hope for Democracy in Canada: An Appointed Senate." *Toronto Star*, February 22, 2010. Accessed at www.thestar. com/opinion/article/768518--last-best-hope-for-democracy-in-canada-an-appointed-senate.

Moore, Christopher. "Wingnuts with Doubts About Senate Reform." Accessed at http://christophermoorehistory.blogspot.ca/2011/05/wingnuts-with-doubts-about-senate.html.

Murray, Lowell. Interview by Anna Maria Tremonti, "Retired Senator Lowell Murray," *The Current*, CBC Radio, October 13, 2011.

_____. "Which Criticisms Are Founded?" In *Protecting Canadian Democracy: The Senate You Never Knew.* Ed. Serge Joyal. Montreal and Kingston: McGill-Queen's University Press, 2003.

O'Brien, Audrey, and Marc Bosc. "Financial Procedures — The Business of Supply." *House of Commons Procedure and Practice*, 2nd ed., 2009. Accessed at http://www.parl.gc.ca/procedure-book-livre/Document.aspx?sbdid=F26EB116-B0B6-490C-B410-33D985BC9B6B&sbpid=6E039746-E713-40D2-AEB8-46826181F5AB&Language=E& Mode=1.

_____. "Rules of Order and Decorum — Manner of Speaking." *House of Commons Procedure and Practice,* 2nd ed., 2009. Accessed at www.parl.gc.ca/procedure-book-livre/Document.aspx?sbdid=EA8C92EB-0A42-4C61-A82E-D3ED72C63F0F&sbpid=BFC12DF9-A808-4F9B-9392-7BCC3EC3E6EE&Language=E&-Mode=1.

Pepall, John. *Against Reform.* Toronto: University of Toronto Press, 2010.

Purves, Grant, and Jack Stilborn, "Members of the House of Commons: Their Role." Revised June 1997. Government of Canada Publications. Library of Parliament. Accessed at www.lop.parl.gc.ca/content/lop/researchpublications/bp56-e.htm.

Samara Canada. "Welcome to Parliament: A Job with No Description." 2010. Accessed at www.samaracanada.com/docs/default-source/mpexit-interviews/welcometoparliament_eng25ef579a50cd6a04a19bff0000c565b1.pdf?sfvrsn=2.

Smith, David E. *Across the Aisle: Opposition in Canadian Politics.* Toronto: University of Toronto Press, 2013.

____. *The Canadian Senate in Bicameral Perspective.* Toronto: University of Toronto Press, 2003.

____. *Federalism and the Constitution of Canada.* Toronto: University of Toronto Press, 2010.

____. "The Improvement of the Senate by Nonconstitutional Means." In *Protecting Canadian Democracy: The Senate You Never Knew.* Ed. Serge Joyal. Montreal and Kingston: McGill-Queen's University Press, 2003.

____. *The Invisible Crown: The First Principle of Canadian Government.* 2nd ed. Toronto: University of Toronto Press, 2013.

____. *The People's House of Commons: Theories of Democracy in Contention.* Toronto: University of Toronto Press, 2007.

Tidridge, Nathan. *Canada's Constitutional Monarchy.* Toronto: Dundurn Press, 2011.

INDEX

BISMARCK
and His Times

GEORGE O. KENT

Southern Illinois University Press: Carbondale and Edwardsville

Library of Congress Cataloging in Publication Data

Kent, George O. 1919–
  Bismarck and his times.

  Bibliography: p.
  Includes index.
  1. Bismarck, Otto, Fürst von, 1815–1898. 2. Statesmen—Germany—Biography.
3. Germany—Politics and government—19th century. I. Title.
DD218.K36   943.08′092′4 [B]   78-2547
ISBN 0-8093-0858-4
ISBN 0-8093-0859-2 pbk.

88   87   86   85   7   6   5   4

Contents

Preface

This book presents a short account of Otto von Bismarck's life and policies against the background of nineteenth-century Germany and is based on the literature that has appeared since the Second World War. The aim of this study is to acquaint undergraduate and graduate students and the general reader with a summary of that literature.[1]

A generation ago a similar task would have been relatively easy. Then, historians were preoccupied with political history, particularly German nationalism, and with few exceptions, they considered Bismarck one of the greatest statesmen of all time. World War II changed their outlook and their emphasis. Today, though political history still provides the basis and general framework for any Bismarck biography, it is being complemented by economic, social, constitutional, and most recently, psychological history.[2]

As Lincoln and the Civil War dominated United States history in the late nineteenth and early twentieth centuries, Bismarck dominated German political thinking and historical writing from his death in 1898 to the outbreak of the Second World War. As another historian has noted, the changes in the historical interpretations of Bismarck reflect the heights and depths of German historical scholarship in this period.[3] It was only after Germany's defeat in the Second World War that the personality and policies of Bismarck and the events leading toward German unification ceased to be a political issue for German historians. This change in emphasis led to the post–World War II reappraisal and rewriting of modern German history.[4]

The historiographical Notes and Bibliographical Essay in this volume will provide the serious student of history with a guide to the intricacies of historical scholarship pertaining to Bismarck and his

PREFACE

times. For the general reader, the main text presents a picture of the man, the issues, and the age in the light of modern research.

GRATEFUL ACKNOWLEDGMENT IS EXTENDED TO the publishers for permission to quote from the following: Koppel S. Pinson, *Modern Germany: Its History and Civilization* (New York: The Macmillan Company, 1954), Copyright, 1954, by The Macmillan Company; Fritz Stern, *The Failure of Illiberalism: Essays on the Political Culture of Modern Germany* (New York: Alfred A. Knopf, Inc., 1972), Copyright © 1955, 1960, 1967, 1969, 1970, 1971 by Fritz Stern; Fritz Stern, *Gold and Iron: Bismarck, Bleichröder, and the Building of the German Empire* (New York: Alfred A. Knopf, Inc., 1977), Copyright © 1977 by Fritz Stern.

I am grateful to a great number of people who helped me in the preparation of this study, among them some anonymous readers whose comments and criticisms improved earlier drafts and the staff of the McKeldin Library of the University of Maryland, which provided valuable assistance. My greatest indebtedness, however, is to Marthe— *sine ea nihil*.

George O. Kent

Washington, D.C.
June 1977

1

Bismarck's Youth

Otto von Bismarck was born at Schoenhausen in Brandenburg-Prussia on April 1, 1815, during the Hundred Days, and he died at Friedrichsruh near Hamburg, on July 30, 1898, while the European powers were partitioning Africa and extending their dominion over large parts of Asia. His life spanned almost a century, an important period in the development of modern Europe and a crucial one for Germany. To understand the changes which occurred during Bismarck's lifetime, it is necessary to consider the European situation at the time Napoleon was sent to his first exile.

The Congress of Vienna (September 1814–June 1815) settled the political upheavals which followed the revolutionary and Napoleonic wars; in the process, the Congress created a new order in central Europe which survived for almost half a century. This order was based primarily on a new political and territorial arrangement in which the Austrian Empire predominated, and the Kingdom of Prussia (enlarged in the west to form a barrier against France) became the second largest power. Austria, Prussia, thirty-three other principalities, and four free cities formed the German Confederation. Of these thirty-three states, Bavaria, Wuerttemberg, Baden, Hanover, and Saxony were the most important, and these states were usually called the "lesser German states" or the "Third Germany."[1] The confederation was a loose grouping of sovereign states which had its permanent meeting place in the Federal Diet at Frankfurt. The architect and leader of the confederation was the Austrian chancellor, Prince Clemens von Metternich, who lent his name to this system and the period during which it operated.

Napoleon's defeat brought little change in the economic and social conditions in central Europe, though the revolution in France, the French occupation of large parts of Germany,[2] and the wars of liberation had left their marks. What changes occurred were uneven, and they were generally more extensive in the west than in the east. The gradual spread of the industrial and agricultural revolutions was accompanied by an equally gradual abandonment of the vestiges of the feudal system, a decline which benefited the landowners and the bourgeoisie more than the peasants.[3]

The peasants, who were usually unable to support themselves on the land left to them,[4] turned to home industries—primarily weaving and spinning—and when these were taken over by machines in the 1830s and 1840s, these peasants joined the ranks of the discontented landless and urban masses who played such an important role in the initial stages of the mid-century revolutions.

The gains of the bourgeoisie were primarily economic, occasionally social, and rarely political. That the bourgeoisie in central Europe did not gain political power despite their economic achievements (in contrast to the English pattern) led subsequently to the major constitutional and political conflicts in Germany in the second half of the nineteenth century.

The privileges and powers of the nobility remained intact. Land, especially in the east, was still the major source of wealth, and although the influence of the French Revolution had curtailed some noble privileges, the nobility retained its social position. The Stein-Hardenberg reforms of 1807–8 had only been an abortive beginning toward a more equitable social order.[5]

In the *Altmark*, home of the Bismarcks for over five centuries, conditions were no different from those in the north and east of Prussia. At the beginning of the eighteenth century, the Bismarcks acquired Schoenhausen, an estate surrounded by sand and pine forests on the floodplain of the Elbe near Tangermuende and Stendal. It was here that Otto von Bismarck was born. His ancestors came from the nobility and the upper bourgeoisie. On his father's side, the family could be traced back to the thirteenth century, a part of the Brandenburg nobility whose members fought in the Thirty Years War, in French and Swedish armies, all over Europe. They stayed close to the land, served as sheriffs and judges, led frugal and sober lives, and seldom had higher aims. Though loyal to their sovereign, they were an independent lot. Frederick Wilhelm I once noted that the Bismarcks, the Schulenburgs, the Knesebecks, and the Alvenslebens were particularly disobedient toward their sovereign, and advised his successor to keep a sharp eye on them. August Friedrich, Otto's grandfather, was known for his roughness and his drinking capacity, and also for his prowess as a hunter, horseman, and soldier. Otto's father, Ferdinand, of milder disposition, was more interested in improving his estates. When he was thirty-five, he married the seventeen-year-old Wilhelmine Mencken at Potsdam (July 6, 1806).[6]

The Menckens (of whom H. L. Mencken, the American literary critic, was a descendant) came from an Oldenburg merchant family, some of whom became prominent in literary and academic fields during the eighteenth century. The family's most illustrious member, Anastasius Ludwig (born 1752), became a diplomat and secretary of cabinet to Frederick the Great. As a high state official, he proposed some of the administrative changes which provided the basis for the reforms of Baron vom Stein. His daughter Wilhelmine, Otto von Bismarck's mother, shared her father's humane outlook and keen intelligence.[7]

Thus, the nobility, army, and civil service, the classes which dominated Prussia, were prominent among Otto von Bismarck's ancestors; this legacy was to play a considerable role in his own life.[8] His childhood, while not unhappy, held few fond memories for the man. At seven he was sent off to a Berlin boarding school which was considered very progressive. There he stayed until the fall of 1827, when he entered the *Gymnasium* (roughly the equivalent of a preparatory school) and lived in the family's Berlin flat, supervised by a housekeeper and a tutor. In the spring of 1832 he passed his examinations. He was a slightly better than average student and did well in German, Latin, and history; he was average in mathematics, physics, English, and French. He showed no special interests that hinted at his later career, and when his mother suggested that he prepare for the diplomatic service, he did not object. He apparently never considered a military career.[9] In the summer of 1832 he went to the University of Goettingen to study law but left in the fall of the following year. While he does not seem to have accomplished a great deal scholastically, he did apparently have a good time joining the Hanovera fraternity, fighting many duels, and making friends with some foreign students, among them John L. Motley, the American writer and historian.[10]

In October 1834 he registered at the University of Berlin and studied French literature, philosophy, and political science during the fall semester and law during the summer. The following fall he registered for some economic courses but apparently attended only a few lectures. He probably studied with a tutor, for he passed his final examination in Roman and canon law on May 22, 1835. While in Berlin he attended many social functions and was often invited to Court. His mother, an ambitious and strong-minded woman, realized that he lacked the makings of a scholar and wanted him to choose a military career, but Bismarck declined. Though dreaming of the life of a country squire, he entered the Prussian civil service and in June 1835 became a junior official at the Berlin City Court. He was none too happy interviewing witnesses and keeping records and intended to stay only a few years before entering the diplomatic service. A year later, in the summer of 1836, he was assigned to the Aachen district administration. Bismarck himself had chosen Aachen because the district governor, Count Arnim-Boitzenburg, a well-known and highly respected official, was a friend of the family. At Aachen, Bismarck worked in the estate and foresty departments and the military and communal sections. His inquiries about entering the diplomatic service were not well received in Berlin. The Prussian foreign minister, Ancillon, suggested that Bismarck complete his civil service assignments and then enter the foreign ministry laterally, through the German Customs Union section. The implication was unmistakably clear: there was no place in the ministry's European section for a backcountry squire from Pomerania.[11] Though disappointed, Bismarck accepted Ancillon's suggestion, and with the help of Arnim, prepared himself for still another examination.

His social life during this period was noteworthy for two love affairs, both involving English girls, and one of which seriously interfered with his official duties. He took several months' leave without permission from his superiors and followed his ladylove all over Europe, only to lose her, in the end, to an English major. When his request for additional leave (presumably to recover from this affair) was denied, he asked and was given permission to transfer to Potsdam. He arrived there in December 1837.

Bismarck's assignments in Potsdam were no more exciting than those in Aachen, except that he was closer to home and to Berlin. His father urged him to fulfill his military service and though Bismarck dreaded the drill and loss of freedom it entailed, he joined the guard battalion at the end of March 1838. He was becoming increasingly disillusioned with his prospects in the civil service and longed for country life. Thus, when his mother became ill and his father offered to give part of his estate[12] to his two sons, Otto jumped at the chance, obtained leave from the army (September 1838) and resigned from the civil service a year later.

Bismarck's career had so far been a disappointment. Lack of private funds, slow advancement, and most of all, his desire for independence and self-fulfillment had made government service quite unattractive to him. As he wrote to his cousin, "I should like to make music as I want to, or I shall make none at all."[13] He had also incurred many debts, more than he could afford, and another reason to leave the service was to find an independent income to be able to pay his debtors back.[14]

Bismarck's mother died in January 1838, and two years later his father divided the estate between Otto and his brother. Otto now had Kniephof to himself, and he slowly managed to improve the estate's finances.[15] It was during this period that he became known as the "mad Junker." His wild parties, many duels, heavy drinking, and especially his practical jokes provided endless gossip for the Pomeranian squirearchy. This was also his romantic period of "storm and stress." He admired Lord Byron and loved the "revolutionary" music of Beethoven; he developed a deep feeling for Shakespeare's works and was interested in republican ideals and ideas.

At the same time, he was appalled by the mobs at the Hambach Festival (a patriotic meeting on May 27, 1832, which demanded German freedom and unity and advocated revolutionary action if peaceful measures failed) and by the Frankfurt riots.[16] During this time he also had an unhappy affair with Ottilie von Puttkamer (no close relation to Johanna von Puttkamer, Bismarck's future bride), and to get over it, he traveled abroad, visiting England, Scotland, France, and Switzerland from July to October, 1842. He even thought of going to Egypt and India, but this plan was abandoned when his travel companion, Oscar von Arnim, met and decided to marry Bismarck's sister Malvine.[17] Bismarck was restless, bored, and dissatisfied with country life, and possibly as a diversion, he became an official of his district, acting in this capacity as one of the two representatives of the local district chief (*Landrat*).

Bismarck's political views were no different at this time from those of his conservative neighbors. He believed in the moral precepts and Christian ideals of his class and the traditional prerogatives which made him free and independent on his estates and assigned him God-given authority in matters of law, police powers, and economic affairs. He believed that only the nobility had the right and the competence to govern in a German and Christian state, and that these rights had to be defended against outsiders, such as Jews.[18]

In November 1845 Bismarck's father died and Otto moved to Schoenhausen. There he became involved in numerous local matters; as dike reeve (*Deichhauptmann*) on the Elbe, he engaged in an extensive correspondence with local authorities on the proper conditions of the Elbe dikes, suggesting methods to improve them.[19] More significant for his later career, however, was his involvement in a fight for the preservation and reorganization of patrimonial jurisdiction in his district. This and another legal remnant of feudalism, patrimonial police power, were still widely used on the landed estates of Prussia, Silesia, Brandenburg, Saxony, and Pomerania in the first half of the nineteenth century. Police powers were exercised directly by the nobility, while juridical powers were delegated to trained lawyers and jurists who were appointed by, and responsible to, the lord of the manor. The higher state courts supervised the system, which by the late 1830s and early 1840s had generated considerable dissatisfaction all around. Peasants and tenants became increasingly unhappy with the judgments rendered, the nobility was irritated over the time and expense connected with these duties, and the state courts, jealous of their prerogatives, wanted to take over the entire system. Some noblemen, such as the Buelows and the Thaddens, Bismarck's neighbors, defended these rights as part of their manorial duties toward their dependents. Bismarck favored patrimonial jurisdiction in the interest of maintaining manorial privileges and independence and suggested a clear delineation of the powers involved, rather than a doctrinaire defense of the issues. In a circular of January 8, 1847, to the nobility of his home district, Bismarck explained his position in great detail and argued that the loss of manorial jurisdiction would also involve a loss of noble influence and prestige. At the same time he suggested that the nobility should be given an extension of their powers as well as some financial relief. His views became widely known and, when it appeared that manorial police powers might also be abolished, he was asked to lead the opposition in a regional fight against such reforms. Thus Bismarck acquired a reputation as a strong conservative in his district and beyond, and when his name was suggested as the district representative to the United Prussian Diet in 1847, it was not unknown.[20]

During this same period, two incidents occurred that were of considerable importance in Bismarck's life. Through the friendship and influence of Maria von Thadden and Moritz von Blanckenburg, his religious outlook changed, and he became a devout Christian (he had earlier professed atheism, announcing at age sixteen that he had stopped saying his prayers), and through them, too, he met Johanna von Puttkamer, whom he later married (July 28, 1847).

Bismarck's religious conversion and his numerous subsequent expressions of piety are in sharp contrast with his later pronouncements as statesman and politician. This discrepancy might be explained by his often expressed belief that service to king and country was, in the Lutheran tradition, also service to God. Moreover, he believed that the state and the existing order were divinely ordained, and that governments were instituted to defend Christians from non-Christians as well as from evil, a theory that led logically to his conviction that those with responsibility had been charged by God to defend their subjects with the sword against their enemies. He was also aware that there were times when, as a statesman, he had no choice but to sin; he was always confident, however, that whenever he made such a choice—invariably in pursuit of honorable causes—God would forgive him.[21] He often said, and there was no reason to doubt his sincerity, that his only responsibility was to king and God. This was really an ideal solution; it made Bismarck's egoism and quest for power appear to be God's will, and at the same time, spared him pangs of conscience. "I am God's soldier," he wrote to his wife in 1851, "and must go wither He sends me, and I believe that He sends me and shapes my life as He requires."[22]

Bismarck's religious conversion is also of interest in connection with his betrothal. Both occurred at about the same time, in the summer of 1846, and as was the custom, he wrote a formal letter to Heinrich von Puttkamer, Johanna's father, asking permission to marry her. This letter has become famous. Its style and content foreshadow the statesman; its arguments, the diplomat. Bismarck's life and reputation until then had not been such as to inspire confidence even in a sympathetic and unprejudiced person; Johanna's father, a bigoted, narrow-minded conservative, was aghast at the thought of his daughter even considering marriage to this "mad Junker." Bismarck was, of course, aware of old Puttkamer's attitude, and he set out to overcome this formidable obstacle. Using a tactic that he was to employ regularly in the future, he confounded the unsuspecting gentleman with unexpected and complete frankness; rather than asking "for Johanna's hand because he was worthy of God—this would have seemed presumptuous to a Pietist [such as Puttkamer] in someone far more religious"—Bismarck asked for Johanna's hand "because only God could make him worthy." He went on to describe his youthful religious indifference and his recent struggle to find faith in God. What was the father to do? "To reject him would have indicated not lack of faith in the suitor, but an absence of trust in God." In reply, Heinrich von Puttkamer quoted several passages from the Bible which had consoled him in his sorrow and extended Bismarck a lukewarm invitation to visit. When Bismarck arrived at Reinfeld, the Puttkamer estate, he found Johanna's parents ready for further negotiations. In no mood to accommodate them, Bismarck not only embraced Johanna when they met, to the astonishment of all concerned, but later at an informal dinner brazenly announced his intention of marrying her.[23]

Bismarck was, without a doubt, pleased with his conquest and wrote his brother that "speaking frankly [I am] marrying a woman of rare spirit and nobility, charming and easy to live with as I have never known another woman to be. In matters of faith we differ, somewhat more to her sorrow than to mine, though not as much as you may think . . . certain internal and external events have brought about changes in my outlook . . . so that I consider myself now a Christian . . . furthermore, I love Pietism in women."[24] These remarks seem to cast doubt on the sincerity of Bismarck's religious conversion but only if one applies generally accepted standards of ethics. This would be unfair, because Bismarck himself recognized no standards except those that he applied himself; for example, he never accepted the good faith of an opponent, or the validity of any argument not his own. "It was not that Bismarck lied . . . but that he was finely attuned to the subtlest currents of any environment and produced measures precisely adjusted to the need to prevail. The key to Bismarck's success was that he was always sincere."[25]

In May 1847, between his betrothal and marriage, Bismarck was sent as the first alternate delegate to the United Prussian Diet, when v. Brauchitsch, the original delegate, became ill. This was the real beginning of Bismarck's career, and it became obvious that the political arena was his chosen field. He had found himself at last. At the Diet, Bismarck was moderately conservative. He defended the government against the opposition and the nobility against the liberals. His first speech, on May 17, 1847, caused a minor sensation. It was directed against the liberals, whose demand for a constitution was based on the premise that the wars of liberation against Napoleon had been inspired by liberty and patriotism, and that the popular uprising had freed the fatherland from foreign occupation. Bismarck almost contemptuously asserted that one could not demand rewards for having resisted after a prolonged beating. The liberation movement had been a patriotic one, he said, but it had nothing in common with liberty and constitutionalism. During the uproar that followed his speech, he turned his back to the Diet and read a newspaper until the noise subsided. This incident brought him some prominence, and he became a favorite at the royal court and with the ultra-conservatives.

Always defending the government, he soon became an outspoken opponent of Vincke, the liberal leader. Only on the question of emancipation of Jews, an issue which found some favor with the government, did Bismarck disagree with the government's position. He took his stand on medieval Christian principles and against what he called humanitarian and sentimental trash. All European states, he declared, were religious Christian states, and without religious principles they would disintegrate. His views were not based on racial grounds but rather on rural Junker prejudices and on personal experience with

Jewish moneylenders.[26] The Diet recessed on June 26, 1847, and Bismarck, instead of rushing to Reinfeld to see his fiancée, tended to political affairs while visiting friends and colleagues.

In this, Bismarck's initial experience in politics, certain aspects of the attitudes and style that became characteristic of the future chancellor could already be seen: his eagerness to participate in political debates, his love of a good fight, his desire to influence people, his confidence in his own judgment, and his disdain of majority opinions. His political and social views were those of the Prussian conservative nobility of his region, passionately defensive of the status and privileges of the landed aristocracy and the monarchy. At the same time he was keenly aware of the realities of power and was determined to uphold the power of the Prussian state against what he considered to be the narrow interests of political—and especially liberal—parties. The style of his speeches and writings also emerged. It was expressive and to the point, original in concept and economical in language. It was most effective because he unerringly used those arguments which appealed to his listeners without being too obvious. At Court he became the favorite of the royal princes, especially the prince of Prussia, later Wilhelm I, though King Friedrich Wilhelm IV was less impressed with this young and radical deputy. Yet when they met during Bismarck's honeymoon in Venice (the wedding had been on July 28, 1847), the king let Bismarck know that he approved of his activities in the Diet. To the liberals, however, Bismarck was the personification of the conservative, reactionary Junker.

Bismarck
and the
Revolution
of 1848

The central European uprisings of 1848 began when news of the successful revolution in France reached Berlin and Vienna. In contrast to France, the course of the revolution in central Europe was complicated by nationalism, a force which simultaneously threatened to dissolve the Austrian Empire and unify the German states. The revolution's resulting crosscurrents of nationalism, liberalism, and particularism defy simple explanation and obscure a common pattern. The initial successes of the revolutionaries can be attributed to the ineptitude of the local authorities rather than the strength of the revolutionary movement. This was not recognized at the time, and the misjudgment of the relative power of the revolutionaries and their foes contributed to the revolution's ultimate failure.

Liberalism, the most influential creed of the revolutionary and unification movement in the Germanies, was supported by the professional and business classes. Its roots lay in the early phases of the French Revolution of 1789, and its ideals were those of English parliamentarianism. The number and wealth of German businessmen had increased considerably in the decades of the early nineteenth century; conscious of their rising economic strength and importance, they demanded an appropriate share of political representation. They opposed the arbitrary powers and privileges and the corrupt and inefficient methods of aristocratic government; they advocated constitutional, representative, and limited monarchy, abolition of the remnants of the feudal system, equality before the law, extension of the franchise to the propertied classes, and freedom of thought, speech, and association. They did not advocate violence and revolution but aspired to equality with the nobility; like the nobility, they were apprehensive over the growing number of illiterates and workers, who might threaten life and property if not restrained.

The economic demands of the bourgeoisie paralleled their political demands. They advocated abolition of the restrictions and regulations of the mercantilist system (especially those affecting labor and production), freedom of movement for men and goods, repeal of internal road and river tolls (toward which the Prussian Customs Union of 1834 was a promising beginning), uniformity of currency, weights, and measures, and a common law of commerce. These last provisions linked economic reforms to political issues because every businessman realized that national unification would provide a powerful stimulus to business and industrial expansion and lead to abolition of countless local customs and usages left over from the Middle Ages. The liberal merchants and businessmen also demanded noninterference by the government in matters of business and trade, which became known as the laissez faire doctrine.[1] A similar attitude toward government interference was also noticeable in the field of social welfare. The liberals were opposed to any type of welfare legislation, such as child labor laws or the shortening of the working day, and favored instead freedom of contracts and the abolition of usury laws, which set low rates of interest. This attitude of unrestrained individualism, in the face of the increasingly inhuman working conditions in factories and mines, aroused the hostility of the workers against the middle classes and inspired socialist writers to attack liberalism from the very beginning.[2]

The intellectuals, whose freedom of expression had been suppressed after 1812, reemerged after the 1830 revolution in Paris, and at the Hambach Festival in May 1832, they staged the first mass demonstration in the Germanies; they denounced the repressive measures of the Metternich system, such as censorship of press and publication and restriction of the right of association, and demanded a reunited, republican Germany and the liberation of Poland, Hungary, and Italy. The German governments, prodded by Metternich, responded to these demands with more repressive measures which, in turn, popularized the Young German movement. This movement, one of many similar European-wide movements (Young Italy, Young Ireland, and Young Poland) was inspired by French revolutionary ideals and dissatisfaction with the repressive and reactionary measures of the Metternich regime.

A new generation of writers began to use criticism and satire as political weapons and they attacked conditions in Germany in essays, letters, and travel accounts. In doing so they spared neither Goethe, who had died in 1832, nor the romantic movement. They favored the present over the past and had no use for Romanticism's glorification of the Middle Ages, Catholic piety, or the ancient Germanic tribes. Instead they admired Luther, the Reformation and the Enlightenment, Kant, Voltaire, and Schiller and considered liberty the most priceless possession.

Contrary to the movements in Poland, Hungary, Italy, and Ireland, which were primarily nationalistic and directed against foreign occupation, the Young Germans were not, as a whole, in favor of German unification. They were cosmopolitan ("I hate any society which is smaller than the human society," Boerne wrote) but could not agree on what form the ideal state should take. Some preferred a constitutional monarchy, others a republic.

Led by Gutzkow, Buechner, Herwegh, Freiligrath, Boerne, and Heine, the Young Germans laid the foundations of political journalism.[3] But their political influence on events in the Germanies was limited because two of their best known advocates, Heine and Boerne, were exiles in France. Their praise of French culture and criticism of some of the more exaggerated romantic notions of their compatriots were unpopular in this period of rising nationalism. That they and a number of their followers were Jewish did not help the Young German movement.

Another protest movement, smaller in size but more influential, was the group known as the Young Hegelians. Even more radical and critical than Hegel himself, the Young Hegelians considered themselves guardians of rationalism and champions of humanity. They objected to the religious revival, opposed ultramontane Catholicism, the Pietism of the Protestant churches, and the alliance between throne and altar. Initially they considered Prussia the best and most promising state in Germany but were appalled by the Prussian government's handling of the Cologne disturbances in 1837 and by Friedrich Wilhelm IV's concessions to the Catholic church after 1840.[4]

Most intellectuals, like the bourgeoisie, were not true revolutionaries but advocates of peaceful reforms whose native liberal roots
could be found in the writings of Kant and Wilhelm von Humboldt.
Their beliefs were reinforced in the Rhineland and in southern Germany by French ideas, and in northern Germany by English liberalism. Hanover was tied by personal union to the English crown from
1714 to 1837, and the University of Goettingen, in southern Hanover,
became a center of English constitutional studies and a link between
German and English Protestantism. The case of the "Goettingen Sev-
en" became famous throughout Germany: seven professors from the
university were dismissed in 1837 because they refused to take an oath
to the new Hanoverian constitution which omitted the liberal provisions of the old one.

At about the same time, the reading habits of the romantically inclined public turned from the medieval castles of Sir Walter Scott to
the slums of Charles Dickens and Victor Hugo, who glorified the workers and derided the philistine bourgeoisie.[5]

Throughout the late 1830s and early 1840s, many Germans were
aware that the number of poor had increased, that class conflict was
spreading, and that many people sympathized with the ideas of socialism. It was also widely believed that the proletariat, product of
the new industrial age, was incapable of improving its economic and
social position and would, therefore, resort to revolution to overthrow
the existing order.

Economically, the 1840s were particularly bad; poor wheat and rye
crops and a potato blight had disastrous effects throughout western
Europe. Rising food prices, increasing unemployment, and lower
wages combined with widespread business failures to bring about a
severe depression in 1846–47. Popular unrest led to food riots, and
demonstrations and revolts were expected everywhere. Thus, the
specter of socialism became a real one and most governments expected
a revolution to break out at any moment. When the revolution finally
did come to central Europe, the governments bowed before the inevitable.

Following the initial success of the Revolution of 1848 in Austria,
Prussia, and central and southern Germany, an assembly of representatives from all parts of the country was called to Frankfurt on the

Main to prepare for elections to a national parliament, which would, in turn, draft a constitution and organize a government for a united Germany. This preliminary parliament (*Vorparlament*) met in St. Paul's Church on March 31, 1848. Its delegates were asked to choose between a moderate program—a federal union under a liberal monarch with a constitution drafted by a national assembly—and a radical program— a republic, which called for universal manhood suffrage and the abolition of aristocratic privilege. This latter program was decisively defeated. The preliminary parliament recommended, instead, that the delegates to the national parliament be elected by direct, universal suffrage; this provision was largely ignored by the various states, with the result that most delegates were chosen by electors and came from the propertied classes. The great majority of the delegates were political and economic liberals, without any revolutionary fervor, but anxious to achieve national unification. They met on May 18, 1848, under the presidency of Heinrich von Gagern for the opening session of the Frankfurt Assembly.

The Frankfurt Assembly has for a long time (and especially in Germany history textbooks) been derisively labeled the "professors' parliament," mocked for its long, useless speeches, pointless debates, and lack of practical achievement. This characterization, used primarily by conservatives to discredit liberalism and democracy in Germany, has only recently been corrected. It is now fairly well established that there were more lawyers and judges than university professors among the delegates who, on the whole, did not differ in their professional and occupational background from any similar European legislative body of the period. (There were 49 university professors, 40 school principals and teachers, 200 jurists, 35 writers and journalists, 30 merchants and industrialists, 26 clergymen, and 12 physicians.)[6] There were certainly long, learned debates and numerous committee meetings, but the establishment of parliamentary procedures, the drafting of a federal constitution, the discussion of fundamental rights, and the organization of a provisional federal executive had never been discussed in Germany on a national level before, and these were topics and measures that could not be hurried along.

In the end, the Frankfurt Assembly failed not because it discussed useless theoretical concepts, but because the two major powers in

Germany, Austria and Prussia, had recovered their military strength and refused to put their armies under the leadership of Archduke John, the Assembly's elected executive officer (*Reichsverweser*). Without an army, the Frankfurt Assembly lacked the power to enforce its laws and decrees. Parliamentary impotence became especially apparent in the Schleswig-Holstein question.

In the late spring and summer of 1848, German public opinion was aroused over the plight of the German minorities in Schleswig and Holstein and demanded that German troops defend the minorities against an invading Danish army. In accordance with a resolution by the Frankfurt Assembly, Prussia, Hanover, and Brunswick sent troops into the duchies and expelled the Danes. When the defeat of the Danish army seemed imminent, Russia and Britain, alarmed at German expansionist designs, threatened to intervene. Confronted with this threat, Prussia and her allies withdrew and signed an armistice at Malmoe on August 26, 1848. Members of the Frankfurt Assembly and German liberals everywhere considered the armistice a major national defeat and urged the Prussian government to continue the war, but to no avail. The powerlessness of the Frankfurt Assembly became painfully obvious to liberals and conservatives alike, and the Assembly never recovered from the loss of prestige occasioned by the Schleswig-Holstein affair.

There were other issues as well. The question of Austria's exclusion from, or inclusion in, the new Reich—and whether Austria or Prussia should assume the leadership—had agitated German nationalists for a long time. In general, the Protestant population of North Germany was pro-Prussian, while the Catholics south of the Main River were pro-Austrian. At Frankfurt the problem was solved temporarily when the Czech delegates from the Austrian provinces of Bohemia and Moravia refused to join the Assembly, which reduced Austria's delegation to 120, while that of Prussia remained at 198.[7]

The old Grand Duchy of Poznan, divided since 1815 between the Prussian provinces of West Prussia and Posen, which contained about 800,000 Poles, 400,000 Germans and 76,000 (mostly Germanized) Jews, presented another problem. Before the revolution, German liberals strongly supported Polish claims for independence and the Prussian government was ready to grant concessions to the Polish population in the two provinces. When, however, the Poles took control of the local administration in March–April 1848, the German population resisted and, with the help of Prussian military detachments, suppressed the Polish insurrection.

The debates on the Polish question in the Frankfurt Assembly (July 24–27, 1848) centered on the degree of autonomy the Prussian Polish provinces should be granted in the future, and specifically, on whether and how many Germans should come under the jurisdiction of local Polish officials. Only two delegates, Arnold Ruge, a leader of the extreme left, and Janiszewski, the only Polish delegate, pleaded the Polish cause. Wilhelm Jordan, a Berlin Democrat, spoke for the German minority in Posen. His strongly nationalistic speech can be considered "an early example of that fusion of liberal nationalism and Prussian power politics which was completed between 1866 and 1871."[8] An overwhelming majority, 342 to 31, voted to uphold the rights of the German minority, and those areas with a large German population, such as East and West Prussia, the Neisse district, the city of Posen, and the surrounding area to the west of the city, were incorporated into Germany. The area east of Posen, which had an almost exclusively Polish population, was left out of the newly constituted German state though it was still part of Prussia and would be able to adopt whatever degree of autonomy the Prussian government was ready to grant. The predominant attitude in evidence at the Frankfurt Assembly in the Schleswig-Holstein and Polish questions, the ascendancy of nationalism over liberalism, foreshadowed the widespread popular support for Bismarck's foreign policy.

By the end of March 1849, the Frankfurt Assembly had completed its work. It advocated a federal state with a constitutional monarchy, a bicameral parliament (members of the lower house to be elected by universal, direct, and secret ballot; half of those of the upper house to be chosen by the state governments and half by the lower houses of the state legislatures), and a federal supreme court. On March 28, the Assembly offered the crown of the prospective German state to King Friedrich Wilhelm IV of Prussia, who refused it saying that no king by divine right would stoop to the gutter for an imperial crown. In any event, this was an empty gesture because the revolutionaries had been defeated everywhere, and in Bohemia, Hungary, and Austria the old order was once again in command.

For Bismarck the revolutionary events in Prussia were of particular significance. When news of the successful uprising in Berlin reached Schoenhausen on March 19, 1848, Bismarck was incensed. He became even more distressed when he learned that the troops, undefeated and loyal to the king, had been ordered by Friedrich Wilhelm IV to leave the city and retreat to Potsdam, and that the king himself was a prisoner of the revolutionaries in Berlin. Bismarck's deep-seated Prussian royalism was outraged; he felt compelled to do something. After surveying his estates and the neighboring countryside and assuring himself of the loyalty of the peasants, he decided to mobilize the country against the revolutionary towns, march on Berlin, free the king, and crush the revolution. Before carrying out his plans he went to Potsdam, which had not been occupied by the revolutionaries, to learn at firsthand what had actually occurred. There he stayed with his friend Albrecht von Roon, who shared Bismarck's feelings and believed that the revolution could be defeated if only a man could be found to lead the loyal troops. (It never occurred to Roon that Bismarck, then barely thirty-three, could be that man.) Having agreed on a solution, the two friends set out to find Prince Wilhelm, a strong conservative and next in line to the throne, whom they thought would be the man to rescue king and country. But the prince could not be found; there were rumors that he had left the country because of his unpopularity with the people of Berlin.

When Bismarck called on Princess Augusta, Wilhelm's wife, to inquire of the prince's whereabouts and to tell her of their plans, he met with a cold reception. Augusta insisted that her husband was loyal to the king and would not act against the king's orders; she made Bismarck promise that he would use neither her husband's nor her son's name in any disloyal undertaking. It seemed that Augusta had plans of her own. An admirer of Louis Philippe and the July Monarchy in France, she was said to have established contacts with the liberal party in the Prussian National Assembly. Friedrich Wilhelm IV, according to these plans, would abdicate while her husband, Prince Wilhelm, would renounce his rights to the throne, and she herself would be installed as regent for her son. It seems likely that Bismarck learned of Augusta's plans and considered them nothing short of treason, a perversion of the Prussian monarchy, and an opening toward constitutionalism. Bismarck's enmity toward Augusta and her intense dislike of Bismarck took root at this time.[9]

But the king was still a prisoner and the revolutionaries remained in control in Berlin. In the opinion of the army and its officers, the king was not free to act in the best interests of his country, but without royal orders they could not move. Was it possible to save the royal house in spite of itself by acting without, or even against, the king's orders? Could General Yorck's decision at Tauroggen in 1812, when he concluded an agreement with the Russians without the permission of the Prussian government, be repeated? The only man willing to make such a decision was Bismarck. It was inconceivable to Bismarck that a Prussian king would order the army to refrain from firing on a revolutionary mob of his own free will; therefore, the king was being held a prisoner by the mob. Therefore others who could act for the good of Prussia and the royal house must do so for king and country. Bismarck apparently questioned various army commanders in the provinces about their attitude, and though a few seemed ready to go along with his plans, others opposed them. The whole scheme collapsed when Friedrich Wilhelm IV appeared at Potsdam on March 25, 1848, demonstrating that he was not a prisoner, and exhorted his troops once again to abide by his orders and not to fight the revolutionaries in Berlin.

Bismarck returned to Schoenhausen in despair. "The peasants here," he wrote in his diary, "were enraged over the Berliners, but who can support a building whose main support is rotten?"[10] How much the failure of his plan influenced Bismarck's view of subsequent events is difficult to say. In his opinion, the initial success of the revolution was caused by the cowardice of the civil service, the indecision of the crown, and the timidity of the majority of the population which, though loyal, was frightened by barricades and popular assemblies. The roots of revolution, according to Bismarck, were to be found in the new industrial system and the spirit of the times, which was antireligious and questioned authority. It was this spirit that had infected the intellectuals and the bureaucrats. The people, Bismarck believed, were not inclined toward revolution, and the "enemy" was the bourgeoisie. He apparently perceived, early on, the possibilities of an alliance between workers, peasants, and aristocracy against the middle class. For these reasons he believed that the revolutionaries should have been confronted immediately with force of arms and not with negotiations.[11]

For the time being Bismarck was out of favor with his own conservative colleagues, for he was not asked to participate in the organization of the Prussian Conservative party or in founding the conservative newspaper, the *Kreuzzeitung*. His only support came from the prince of Prussia; the king, though recognizing Bismarck's loyalty, considered him too wild and too reactionary and refused to appoint him to a responsible position. There is a trace of ruthlessness in Bismarck's letter to his mother-in-law in November of 1849, in which he dismisses her sympathy for the Hungarian revolutionaries and defends the mass executions of revolutionaries in Austria. She was, he wrote, only following the principles of Rousseau which had guided Louis XVI when, by his reluctance to execute one man, he assumed the guilt for destroying millions.

The years immediately after the revolution were, for Bismarck, contemplative ones. His views and attitudes matured, and he turned from a narrow defense of his own interests, and those of his class, toward a more general conservative outlook, against bourgeois capitalism and intellectual liberalism. His Prussian particularism, however, remained unchanged, and he refused to recognize German nationalism.

In the February 1849 election, Bismarck won a seat in the lower Prussian chamber and on April 3, 1849, when King Friedrich Wilhelm IV refused to accept the imperial crown offered to him by the Frankfurt Assembly, Bismarck defended the king's action. To accept the crown, Bismarck declared, would be to subordinate the monarchy to popular sovereignty and drive Prussia into a war with Austria at a time when the revolution was meeting defeat everywhere in central Europe. Bismarck preferred an independent Prussia to a Germany united under the Frankfurt constitution.

Only a strong and independent Prussia would be able to play her part in Germany and in Europe. This meant a continuous expansion of Prussia's military and economic power north of the Main achieved through military conventions with the lesser states and an extension of the Customs Union. Independence would be achieved with or without Austria.[12] The implications were clear: "with" Austria meant that Prussia would be equal and not subordinate to Austria, and "without" Austria really meant against her. Thus Bismarck's future policies toward Austria, first as Prussian delegate at the Frankfurt Diet and later as Prussian prime minister, began to take shape. For the time being, however, he opposed the king's plan for a German Union, conceived by Radowitz, as much as he had opposed the plan of the Frankfurt Assembly of which the Radowitz plan was but a variant. This plan envisaged a union of north and central German States under Prussian leadership in a wider German federation under Austria. Prussia would have had to submit to a federal executive, and to this Bismarck objected. The Prussian Union project foundered on Austria's objections, for Austria saw in it an attempt to challenge her claim for supremacy in Germany. This situation, combined with the Schleswig-Holstein and the Hessian problems,[13] almost led to a war between Austria and Prussia in the fall of 1850. Only Friedrich Wilhelm IV's submission to combined Russian and Austrian pressure prevented war. With the agreement of Olmuetz, November 29, 1850, Prussia officially abandoned her Union project and recognized the reestablishment of the German Confederation and the Diet at Frankfurt.

Bismarck first attacked the government for giving in to Austria. Following the example of his hero, Frederick the Great, he would rather have gone to war. "In foreign policy," he told his friend Ludwig von Gerlach, "he [Bismarck], like Frederick the Great in 1740, recognized no rights, only conveniences."[14] But Bismarck soon changed his mind. Whether he recognized that Prussia's army was inferior to Austria's or that Friedrich Wilhelm IV was not a Frederick the Great is difficult to determine. In any case, in a speech to the Prussian Parliament he defended the government's policy forcefully on the ground that Prussia could not go to war against two major conservative powers, Austria and Russia, in defense of an unworkable constitution and the principles of the 1848 Revolution.[15] "According to my [Bismarck's] conviction, Prussian honor does not consist in Prussia's playing the Don Quixote all over Germany for the benefit of mortified celebrities from parliament. . . . I look for Prussian honor in Prussia's abstinence before all things from every shameful union with democracy."[16] Bismarck's speech had important consequences.

Unable to agree on a reorganization of the Confederation, the German states decided to return to the prerevolutionary system, and the problem of whom to send as Prussian representative to the Diet at Frankfurt arose. In the aftermath of Olmuetz, this job would have been a thankless task for any man, and many candidates declined. At this point, Ludwig von Gerlach, Bismarck's friend and mentor and the king's chief adjutant, remembered Bismarck's spirited speech in the Assembly and suggested his appointment to the king. Friedrich Wilhelm, mindful of Bismarck's lack of experience in diplomatic matters, was initially reluctant but later agreed, with the proviso that the Prussian minister at St. Petersburg, von Rochow, be transferred temporarily to Frankfurt to familiarize Bismarck with the intricacies of protocol and negotiations with the Austrians. When Bismarck readily agreed to accept the position, the king complimented him on his courage in assuming this difficult assignment. "It is the courage of Your Majesty," Bismarck replied, "to trust me with such a position. I have the courage to obey, if Your Majesty has the courage to give the orders."[17]

Frankfurt
St. Petersburg
Paris
1851–1862

The relationship between Austria and Prussia at the Frankfurt Diet before the 1848 Revolution had been cordial because Prussia had recognized Austria's supremacy without reservation. After the revolution, and especially after Olmuetz, their relationship changed considerably. Vienna expected another Prussian attempt toward German unification and was determined not only to resist but to expand Austrian power and influence throughout the German Confederation. Austrian Prime Minister Schwarzenberg's plan was to unify Germany under Austrian leadership and to create a central European empire—*Mitteleuropa*. Berlin, on the other hand, was equally determined to achieve parity with Austria in the Confederation, and military and economic leadership in north Germany.[1]

In many ways Bismarck's appointment to Frankfurt constituted the fulfillment of his hopes and dreams; at the same time, he continued to long for the peaceful country life. "To be *Landrat* in Schoenhausen is still my ideal," he wrote to his friend Kleist-Retzow at the time. But when, after one year in Frankfurt he had to go to Vienna, he wrote to Johanna, "I long for Frankfurt as if it were Kniephof."[2]

When he came to Frankfurt he was exceedingly suspicious of Austrian aims and intentions. He was convinced that however Prussia might try, she could never appease Austria and that there was simply not enough room in Germany for the two powers to exist side by side. He believed Austria would use any means to subdue Prussia, including allying herself to France, Russia, Prussian liberals, or south German ultramontanes, or involving Germany in a foreign war, if these acts would maintain her supremacy in the Germanies. To forestall these possibilities, Bismarck felt that Prussia had to bring about a solution to the German question whenever the European situation was in her favor. The Prussian government was reluctant to face this issue squarely; while trying to assert itself north of the Main, it was, at the same time, afraid of offending Austria and her many sympathizers throughout the Germanies. Consequently Prussian policy toward Austria vacillated between defiance and compliance. At the Diet, Bismarck's role was a difficult one: preventing Berlin from showing weakness or compliance toward Austria, and simultaneously challenging Austria more forcefully than his instructions permitted. He tried to influence his government to consider the possibility of alliance with Russia and France against Austria, an act which would exert pressure on Austria from outside Germany. By strengthening Prussia's military and economic position through the Customs Union, railroad, postal, and banking agreements, and currency, trade, and military conventions with the lesser states, Bismarck hoped to make Prussia the center of the unity movement in Germany.

On July 15, 1851, Bismarck, who at the time of his appointment had been given the rank of counselor of legation (*geheimer Legationsrat*), became Prussia's minister of the Federal Diet. Von Rochow, who had instructed Bismarck in his new duties, left Frankfurt to return to his post at St. Petersburg, and from August 27 on, Bismarck was on his own. In his first encounter with Count Thun, the Austrian representative, Bismarck made a point of impressing on the count and the representatives of the other German states that, henceforth, Prussia was to be treated as Austria's equal. When Thun appeared in his shirtsleeves for a meeting, Bismarck took off his jacket; and when the Austrian, alone among the assembled diplomats, lit a cigar, Bismarck took one of his own and asked the surprised Thun for matches.[3] These were petty moves, but they stressed a point which was not lost on the representatives of the lesser states.

More serious were the discussions over the Prussian Customs Union and Austria's desire to join it. Because Austria's membership appealed to regional as well as national interests among the lesser states, Prussia could not oppose Austrian membership outright. Instead, the Prussian government decided to procrastinate. This decision was made easier by discussions within Austria. The industrialists demanded protective tariffs for their goods within the Customs Union, while the Austrian government aimed for free trade. Meanwhile, Prussia strengthened her position by concluding trade treaties outside the Customs Union with Hanover, Oldenburg, and Schaumburg-Lippe (September 7, 1851). At a conference in Vienna during January–February 1852, Austria tried unsuccessfully to persuade the lesser German states to support her inclusion in the Union. While these states opposed Prussian political pressure, their economic ties with and through the Customs Union were too strong to be broken.[4] In Frankfurt, Bismarck rejected all Austrian attempts to set up a competing central European Customs Union project and threatened Prussia's withdrawal from the Diet should Austria succeed. He also opposed Austria's intention to enact a stringent federal press law which would have banned all newspapers that advocated socialism, communism, or the overthrow of the monarchy. Bismarck's objections were not based on his belief in freedom of the press but on his opposition to the creation of a strong federal executive which would threaten the interests of Prussia.[5] And though a majority of delegates were in favor of the Austrian proposal, Bismarck was able to defeat it because a unanimous vote was needed to pass it.

At about the same time, Bismarck used the temporary absence of an Austrian representative—Thun was exchanging places with Prokesch, the Austrian minister in Berlin—to press for a revision of voting procedures at the Diet in favor of equality of members, more liberal access to the archives, and a more equitable administrative procedure which, until then, had heavily favored Austria and her allies. Prokesch, the new Austrian representative, a well-known historian and archeologist but a poor diplomat, was not able to stand up to Bismarck's reasonable and well-formulated arguments,[6] especially when they were supported by a majority of the delegates. As a result, a good number of Bismarck's proposals were adopted.[7]

Austria's acquiescent attitude did not signal a change of policy at the Diet so much as recognition of a change in the European diplomatic situation. The approaching Crimean War made it mandatory for Austria to keep the situation in Germany under control and to oppose Russian moves on the lower Danube, which threatened Austria's economic and political interests in this region. Austria was prepared to join Britain and France in their support of Turkey against Russia, and this in turn meant Russian enmity and the possibility of Russian-Prussian collaboration unless Prussia could be persuaded to support and follow Austria's policy.

Bismarck realized the implications of Austria's dilemma and wanted to keep Prussia and all the other German states free of any entanglements in the Balkans. This policy earned him Russia's gratitude, which could later be used against Austria. If, on the other hand, Prussia followed Austria's anti-Russian policy in this crisis, she should demand equality with Austria at the Diet. "No sentimental alliances," he wrote to Gerlach in February 1854, "which, secure in the knowledge of a good deed, find their reward in noble sacrifices." (*Nur keine sentimentalen Buendnisse, bei denen das Bewusstsein der guten Tat den Lohn edler Aufopferung zu bilden hat.*)[8] But Bismarck's advice went unheeded. Instead, partly to accommodate Austria, partly to exercise a restraining influence on her, Prussia concluded an alliance with her on April 20, 1854.[9] But Bismarck was able to thwart Austrian wishes when, in January 1855, she demanded that the German states order a partial mobilization of their troops to back her anti-Russian Crimean policy. Taking account of the lesser states' suspicion and their reluctance to oppose Austria openly and outright, Bismarck persuaded them to declare their armed neutrality against a general threat of war rather than against Russia alone, as Austria had demanded. His original goal had, in this way, been at least partially achieved, and his leadership in this maneuver was recognized in Vienna as well as in St. Petersburg. At the same time, he was aware that the German states had no intention of following Prussia's lead in solving the German question and that Austria was still the major power. These events convinced him that a solution to the German problem would only come about in the context of European political developments.[10]

During the summer of 1855, Bismarck visited Paris and the World's Fair, and to the chagrin of Leopold von Gerlach, made the acquaintance of Napoleon III and other French and English statesmen and politicians. Bismarck tried to calm his friend's fear by assuring him that an eager diplomat could not forever remain politically chaste. He also seems to have considered the possibility of cooperating with France and Russia and to have talked about the inevitability of an Austro-Prussian war. These speculations found no favor with Friedrich Wilhelm IV; he could not see how he, a king by the grace of God, could approach Napoleon III, the son of the revolution, to improve Prussia's position in Germany. But Bismarck refused to recognize this distinction; in a number of letters to Gerlach and Manteuffel, the prime minister, Bismarck tried to explain that eventually all regimes become legitimate and that, indeed, many territorial claims had revolutionary origins.[11]

At Frankfurt, meanwhile, Prokesch had been replaced by Count Rechberg, who would have liked to return to Metternich's policy of cooperation with Prussia; however, Buol, the Austrian prime minister, disagreed. Instead, he insisted that Rechberg, with the cooperation of the lesser states, obtain a majority at the Diet and outvote Prussia on all important issues. For Bismarck this became an intolerable situation. In a long and confidential conversation with Rechberg in June 1857, Bismarck explained that they, the representatives of the two major powers in Germany, should cease to pretend that the interests of Germany were constantly and foremost on their minds and, instead, openly admit and defend the interests of their own countries. He, Bismarck, would prefer an understanding between Prussia and Austria, but should this be impossible, Austria should know that Prussia would not hesitate to go to war against her. Rechberg was much taken aback by this unusual disclosure, but Bismarck's cool behavior toward him after his return from Paris, and his unusual friendliness toward the ministers of France, Russia, and Sardinia (all possible Austrian enemies) seemed to lend credence to his words. Actually, Bismarck was bluffing; the Prussian government was not supporting his tough policy, and an Austrian inquiry in Berlin would have cleared up the matter very quickly. But Bismarck gambled on Austrian reluctance to make such an inquiry and events proved him right.[12] When Austria continued to refuse to recognize Prussia's equality at the Diet, Bismarck started a war of nerves and used even the most insignificant details to assert Prussian rights. This, in turn, led to interminable procedural squabbles, prolonged conferences, and heated discussions. It was, in many ways, a fruitless undertaking which could only emphasize the uselessness of the Assembly and the Confederation. But Bismarck did not care; to him it was a matter of Prussian honor and power, and anything else was of little concern. Still, there was one major achievement to his credit during this period: Denmark's recognition of the Confederation's rights in Holstein and Lauenburg, a partial and temporary solution to the very complicated Schleswig-Holstein question.[13]

In the fall of 1858, Prince Wilhelm became regent of Prussia when his brother, King Friedrich Wilhelm IV, was pronounced insane.[14] Bismarck hoped to find the new ruler more sympathetic to his views, but this was not quite the case. In an earlier memorandum of March 1858, he had explained to Prince Wilhelm that Prussia could only succeed in her German policy if she ceased to court the lesser states, because Austria had more influence with them. Prussia's interests were identical with those of the people of the lesser states but not with those of their governments. Germany, Bismarck warned, was not synonymous with the Federal Diet, which was really an obstacle to Germany's future development.[15] Prussia's independence was being endangered by Austria, and Prussia's future could only be found outside the Confederation. The regent shared these views, but when Bismarck advocated an active and forceful policy of opposition toward Austria and declared that if the need arose, Prussia might even have to go to war against Austria, Wilhelm drew back. He was too much of a traditionalist to entertain such an idea, as his support of Austria during the Crimean War demonstrated. Wilhelm was determined to initiate better relations with Austria. Bismarck was obviously the wrong man for this in Frankfurt. Rumors of his differences with the regent had reached the Diet, where many of his colleagues would have been happy to see him replaced by a more congenial and pliable man, one who would recognize Austria's supremacy and be less of a troublemaker.

In January 1859, the government in Berlin decided on Bismarck's transfer to St. Petersburg. When he learned of it he was less than happy, though the post was considered among the most important in the Prussian diplomatic service. He hated to leave Frankfurt, especially when his policy was about to pay off. With the approach of the Austro-Sardinian War, Prussia's importance to Austria had increased significantly, and it was this moment, in the shifting balance of power, that Bismarck had planned to use to Prussia's advantage. Leaving now meant giving up eight years of hard work and watching his enemies triumph. Powerless, Bismarck was forced to watch Prussia and the Confederation agree to cooperate with Austria during her struggle in

Italy; this meant the end of his plans and his policy. On February 24, 1859, he attended the Diet for the last time, and on March 6 he left Frankfurt for St. Petersburg.[16]

Bismarck's reception in the Russian capital was extremely friendly. His pro-Russian policy during the Crimean War was well remembered, and he quickly established close ties with the czar's mother, Princess Charlotte, sister of the Prussian regent, as well as with the czar and his consort, Maria, a Hessian princess. As a result, the official atmosphere in St. Petersburg turned out to be a great improvement over Frankfurt, and Bismarck had a much easier life at his new post. At the same time, he was aware that his influence in Berlin had diminished considerably and felt that he had been "put on ice on the Neva."[17] But he was not willing to continue to play an inactive part.

Encouraged by the Austro-Sardinian War, Bismarck tried to convince Schleinitz, the new Prussian foreign minister, that the European political situation was uniquely favorable to Prussia. Austria should either agree to a more realistic relationship with Prussia at the Diet, or the Diet and the Confederation would have to be abolished. Prussia should then take over the leadership of a new German Federation, and with it, the leadership of the federal army. The Prussian army should then move into south Germany where there was considerable fear of a French invasion, and when crossing the border, the soldiers should put the frontier posts in their knapsacks and not put them down again until they reached Lake Constance or the southern limits of the Protestant faith.[18] While Schleinitz rejected these extreme views, he was sufficiently impressed by Bismarck's reports and letters to resist Austrian demands and Diet resolutions which would have dragged Prussia into the Austro-Sardinian War. He failed, however, to see the opportunities that the war presented—which Bismarck had pointed out to him—and declined to use Austria's predicament in favor of Prussia. The regent also shared Schleinitz's opinion; having grown up in the peaceful Metternich era, the prince meant to preserve peace. He considered Bismarck's opinions revolutionary and wanted no part of them. That these two men should ever find themselves in as close a relationship as they later did seemed impossible at the time.[19] Prussian public opinion regarding the Austro-Sardinian War was confused and divided. Some saw in Napoleon III's participation a parallel to Napoleon

I's campaign in Italy and wanted to help Austria prevent a repetition of familiar, though half-forgotten, events. Others saw in the defeat of Austria a possibility for Italian unification and a model for German unity. Before the Prussian government could make up its mind which policy to follow, Austria acknowledged her defeat by the combined French and Sardinian forces at Solferino and concluded an armistice at Villafranca on July 11, 1859, by whose terms she lost Lombardy but kept Venetia.

A month earlier Bismarck had contracted an illness which plagued him until the early part of the following year. (It was apparently caused by a neglected shinbone injury which developed into pneumonia, and at one point, brought him close to death.) He had left St. Petersburg for Berlin in July 1859, and although he had tried to return to his post (in October he participated at a meeting of the czar and the regent at Breslau), he was unable to do so because of a recurrent attack. He was forced to spend the winter on the von Below estate in Hohendorf near Elbing. In March 1860, he was finally well enough to go to Berlin, but his return to St. Petersburg was delayed partly because he needed to recuperate and partly because he was being considered as foreign minister to succeed Schleinitz.

Despite strong recommendations from many officials, Wilhelm could not be persuaded to accept Bismarck as foreign minister and asked Schleinitz to serve another term. Bismarck left for St. Petersburg at the end of May. There he won the confidence of Czar Alexander II and Gorchakov, the foreign minister, to such an extent that this relationship, strengthened by the family ties which bound the Romanovs and Hohenzollerns, formed the basis of Prussian-Russian friendship for decades to come. On the political level, this bond was also strengthened by Bismarck's support of the czar's anti-Polish policies during 1861. Bismarck realized, even then, that a liberal attitude toward the Poles by Russia would drive a wedge between Russia and Prussia because of Prussia's Polish minorities. Such an attitude would also strengthen Franco-Russian cooperation because France was a traditional champion of Polish independence. If these developments came to pass, Prussia would be isolated. Russia's anti-Polish policy, on the other hand, would deepen Russo-Prussian cooperation and isolate France. Russo-Prussian cooperation, then, was the key to Bismarck's future policy, best demonstrated by Russo-Prussian cooperation during the Polish revolt of 1863 and Russian neutrality during the Franco-Prussian war. Except for strengthening Russian-Prussian ties, Bismarck had no influence on Prussian policy during this period. He suffered in his honorable exile, as he called it, and chafed at the bit for lack of activity and excitement.[20]

In Berlin, meanwhile, reorganization of the Prussian army became a major issue between the regent and the Parliament. Wilhelm wanted to expand the regular army by reintroducing universal military service, while the deputies of the Prussian Diet favored retaining and strengthening the militia. The power of the crown in relation to that of the Parliament was at stake. Roon, minister of war and an old friend of Bismarck's, wanted to get Bismarck into the cabinet to strengthen the crown's case. He suggested appointing Bismarck, but Wilhelm was too suspicious of the "Pomeranian Junker" to agree. Bismarck and the king talked while Wilhelm was taking the cure in Baden-Baden, and during the conversation it became clear how far apart they were in their political views. Wilhelm was intent on safeguarding the principle of legitimacy everywhere and under all conditions, and had therefore supported Austria in the Crimean and Italian wars and had refused to recognize the illegitimate Kingdom of Italy. Bismarck, for his part, was interested only in what he considered to be the vital interests of Prussia. The end of the Italian mini-states and the overthrow of the Kingdom of Naples were matters of complete indifference to him. On the contrary, he considered the existence of a unified Italian kingdom an important asset for the successful development of Prussian policy. Still, Wilhelm valued Bismarck's judgment enough to ask his opinion about domestic policy, especially in connection with a new plan advocated by Roggenbach, a liberal Baden minister and a confidant of the Prussian crown prince.

Roggenbach's plan envisaged a reform of the German Confederation under the leadership of Prussia without, however, antagonizing Austria. It followed along the lines of the lesser German solution but provided for an alliance with Austria and mutual guarantees of each other's territories. Bismarck ignored the question of how to promote peace between Austria and Prussia and declared that it was rather a question of how to exert German power in Europe. The road to this goal was not by way of the Federal Diet, he said, but through Prussia's Customs Union. By giving the Customs Union members parliamentary representation, Prussia's national aims would be served as well. Not only would there be common trade and traffic legislation, but also a common army supported by Customs Union receipts. Bismarck's plan was carefully attuned to Wilhelm's views. He, too, had advocated a strengthening of the Customs Union, but in Bismarck's plan this was merely a point of departure; the Customs Union Parliament was the core of the matter, since it would assure Prussia's supremacy and Austria's exclusion. When presenting this plan, Bismarck avoided any references to the exercise of power or territorial conquests, but Wilhelm was not impressed and nothing came of it. Still, Bismarck continued to promote this plan while he accompanied the king to the coronation ceremonies at Koenigsberg (Friedrich Wilhelm IV had recently died, and Wilhelm was crowned king of Prussia on January 2, 1861) and back to Berlin.[21]

In the fall of 1861, the Prussian Conservative party published its program, which consisted of a strong endorsement of the principles of legitimacy and an equally strong condemnation of nationalism and popular sovereignty. Bismarck vigorously attacked it and was, in turn, branded as a revolutionary by the conservatives.[22] His old friends, the Gerlachs, Kleist-Retzows, Belows, and Blanckenburgs, were dismayed at his stand, and from then on a deepening rift developed between them.

When Bismarck returned to St. Petersburg toward the end of 1861, his future was not at all clear. There had been rumors of his reassignment to Paris or London, and during the winter when German domestic conditions took a turn for the worse (in connection with federal reforms and a renewal of the Schleswig-Holstein question), there was again talk of his entering the Cabinet. He returned to Berlin on May 10, 1862, but his audience with the king on May 13 brought no decision. Wilhelm still resisted and, possibly under the influence of Queen Augusta, finally decided against Bismarck's appointment. Instead, Bismarck was sent as minister to Paris and advised not to settle down at his new post but to keep himself available.

Paris was not a happy assignment. Bismarck went there alone, without his family and without his favorite mare, and this, combined with the uncertainty about his future, made him edgy and dissatisfied. His reception by Napoleon III was friendly enough, but Bismarck was bored with his duties, and after a few weeks, he went to London to visit the World's Fair. There he met Palmerston, Lord John Russell, and Disraeli; when asked by Disraeli what he planned to do should he become Prussian prime minister, Bismarck apparently replied that he would carry through the pending army reforms, with or without the consent of the Parliament, go to war with Austria, and unify Germany under Prussian leadership.[23] Disraeli was impressed, and years later when these ideas had become realities, he often remembered their conversation.

Upon his return to Paris, Bismarck felt the need to restore his health and asked and was granted leave to go to the south of France in July 1862. In Biarritz he met Nicolai and Kathy Orlow (Nicolai was Russian minister in Brussels), whom he had known in St. Petersburg. Bismarck spent several weeks in their company. He fell in love with Kathy Orlow, who was young, beautiful, and vivacious, played his favorite music, and went on long walks with him. He wrote his wife about the wonderful time he was having, and Johanna, secure in her love and knowledge of her husband, was pleased that he was happy. It was such a fine vacation that he overstayed his leave and did not return to Paris until September 16.

In Berlin, the constitutional conflict between the government and the Parliament had deepened to the point where even the king's conservative ministers advised him to make concessions. But Wilhelm refused; when the ministers would no longer support him, he declared that he would abdicate and called for the crown prince on September 17. On the same day, Roon sent an urgent telegram to Paris, asking Bismarck to come to Berlin, "There is danger in delay. Come at once." When he received the message, Bismarck took the train to Berlin on September 19 and arrived in the capital twenty-four hours later.[24]

Bismarck's Appointment and the Constitutional Conflict in Prussia

Arriving in Berlin on September 20, Bismarck saw Roon, who told him of the king's desire to abdicate. That evening the crown prince asked Bismarck for his views on the political situation. Bismarck evaded the issue, reluctant to discuss matters he thought should properly first be discussed with the king.[1] Roon saw the king the following day after church, and reported his feeling that the rift in the Cabinet could not be healed; appealing to the king's sense of duty, Roon urged him not to abdicate until all possible means of solving the conflict with Parliament had been exhausted. Alluding to Bismarck, Roon reminded the king that there was still one man who had not been called into the Cabinet who was willing to take on the responsibilities of office. Wilhelm hesitated. He still distrusted Bismarck and had mentioned his misgivings to the crown prince who, though he agreed with his father, had been at a loss to suggest an alternative.[2] Roon was insistent, the king evasive. "He [Bismarck] would not want to take over at this stage," he told Roon, "besides, he is not here and one could not discuss this with him." "He is here," Roon replied, "and will gladly follow Your Majesty's call."[3] The king yielded.

Bismarck's audience with the king in the castle and gardens of Babelsberg on September 22, 1862, was as decisive for the future of the two men as it was for the fate of Prussia-Germany. The king explained that he had been unable to find a minister who could resolve the impasse with Parliament, and that he intended to abdicate rather than accede to the delegates' demands. He then asked Bismarck what

CONSTITUTIONAL CONFLICT IN PRUSSIA

conditions he attached to his appointment and when Bismarck replied that he felt like a vassal toward his feudal lord and would support his king unconditionally, Wilhelm was much relieved. The king abandoned all thoughts of abdicating and decided instead to continue the fight against parliamentary opposition. Still, there was the question of how Bismarck intended to resolve the conflict. The king had prepared a lengthy memorandum on domestic and foreign policy, which was intended to hold the new appointee to a definite program. But the future chancellor and prime minister was not to be tied down so easily. He was as unwilling to divulge his plans as he was reluctant to make commitments regarding his future policy. It was, he told the king, a struggle for supremacy between royal government and parliamentary rule, and the parliament could be suppressed by a brief dictatorship, if need be.[4] To dispel any further doubts, Bismarck promised to submit willingly to all royal decisions as long as he was permitted to explain to the king any policies of his which conflicted with the king's commands. If, despite his explanations, the royal decision remained unchanged, Bismarck assured Wilhelm that he "would rather perish together with [him] than abandon [him] . . . in the fight against parliamentary domination."[5] The king was overwhelmed. He appointed Bismarck temporary chairman of the Cabinet, and two weeks later made him prime minister and foreign minister.

Johanna first learned about her husband's appointment through the newspapers. When Bismarck wrote her on September 24, he referred to his appointment, which he had sought and aspired to for over a quarter of a century, as "our misery" and asked her to submit to God's will.[6]

The constitutional conflict in Prussia, the principal reason for Bismarck's appointment, involved military reforms and the budgetary authorizations connected with these reforms. The problem was not whether the reforms were necessary, but how they should be carried out and, more important, whether the Lower House of the Prussian Parliament or the king had the authority to implement these reforms and to appropriate the necessary funds. The parties to this conflict were the king and the conservative delegates on one side and the liberal delegates, who held a majority in the Parliament, on the other. Implicit here was the liberal majority's desire to use the conflict as a test of the budgetary powers of the Lower House. As the struggle dragged on, it became increasingly clear that this was not merely a squabble over constitutional technicalities, but a fight which involved the very spirit and future character of the Prussian state.

General von Roon, minister of war since December 5, 1859, initiated the army reforms. His plan envisaged an increase in the call-up of annual recruits from 40,000 to 63,000 men (with three years of active service) and a corresponding increase of the standing army of 150,000 to 220,000 men. This would give the army an additional 39 infantry and 10 cavalry regiments. There would also be a change in the relationship between regular (line) troops and the militia (*Landwehr*). Under Roon's plan, the future wartime army would be composed entirely of regular troops, while the militia would be confined to garrison and fortress duties and to the supply services. The cost of these reforms was estimated to be about 9.5 million thaler annually.[7]

The value of the militia as a democratic force was a much debated issue. The militia's revolutionary spirit of 1813 had vanished by the 1850s, and its military value had been greatly diminished. The regular army, on the other hand, had become identified with the fatherland in the minds of the prince regent and the officer corps, especially after the shocking experience of the 1848 Revolution. Furthermore, it was believed that three years' service would make the recruits immune to the revolutionary *Zeitgeist* and convinced partisans of the monarchy.[8]

While the need for army reforms was generally recognized, questions over their scope and the authority for their implementation arose almost immediately. Both king and the Lower House of the Prussian Parliament claimed primary jurisdiction; although the king recognized the preeminence of the legislature in budgetary matters, he refused to share his exclusive rights and powers over the army. Wilhelm's position was based on the Prussian constitution of December 1848 and its revisions of January 1850, which left the army under the exclusive jurisdiction of the king. Soldiers swore allegiance to the king, not the constitution, while civil servants were required to uphold the constitution.[9] This was in line with conservative views formulated during the early nineteenth century Prussian reform movement, which advocated strict separation of civilian and military powers. The former could develop along liberal-constitutional lines, while the latter, based on autocratic concepts, belonged exclusively to the crown.[10]

Another point of dispute concerned the character of the future army. The organizational details of a large army based on universal military service could have been worked out between the government and the Lower House had the government been willing to use the army for national defense and to pursue a national German policy. What irked the liberals was the government's well-known intention of using the army to bring about conservative domestic reforms and to guard against future uprisings. The liberals wanted to preserve and expand General Boyen's reforms of 1814–15, which had started with the establishment of a national militia. Boyen's idea had been to replace an army of subjects (*Untertanen*) with an army of citizens—a national people's army.[11] But Wilhelm and his supporters saw in the militia an expression of the liberal national spirit. They wanted a more conservative, royalist army which would be a reliable tool against domestic disturbances. They wished to increase the term of service from two years to three to enhance the prestige of the military, curb civilian influence, and make the army independent of public opinion. Wilhelm and his followers believed that continuation of the shorter term of service would enlarge the status of the militia, further democratize the army, and hamper the government's freedom of decision. Wilhelm believed that the Lower House had the right and the duty to vote on expenditures, but only the king had the power over the army and its organization.[12]

The liberal majority favored army reforms but made them dependent on two conditions: a two-year term of service and the maintenance of the existing ratio between the regular army and the militia. On February 10, 1860, when the government submitted a bill on army reorganization which included an extension of service and a request for 9.5 million thaler, the committee of the Lower House rejected the request. Wilhelm (then prince regent) refused to authorize any of the changes in the bill which the committee had suggested. Instead, the government took the position that it really did not need the Parliament's authorization for a reorganization of the army because the army was under the exclusive jurisdiction of the crown. The government had approached the legislature in a spirit of cooperation, but once rebuffed, the crown invoked its executive powers. At the same time the government reintroduced the request for 9.5 million thaler for the period May 1, 1860 to June 30, 1861, as a provisional measure to increase the battle readiness of the troops. The minister of finance who submitted the request reaffirmed its provisional nature by assuring the delegates that unless funds were renewed, the entire measure could later be rescinded.[13] The delegates, believing they would still have the decisive voice regarding army reorganization and trusting the finance minister's assurances, approved the government's request on May 15, 1860, by a vote of 350 to 2. That same day the government dissolved thirty-six militia regiments; this and subsequent measures made it clear that far from considering these measures provisional, the government regarded them as permanent. During the following legislative session, the government introduced no army reorganization proposal, though the Lower House, by a considerably smaller majority, again approved the "provisional" appropriations. At the same time, it asked the government to submit proposals for army reorganization during the following year.[14]

The conservatives were badly beaten in the elections of 1861. Their number was reduced to 14, while 250 liberals were returned. (These were composed of 91 old liberals [*Altliberale*], 50 of the liberal center [*linkes Zentrum*], and 109 of the radical liberals [*radikale Linke*].)[15] In response to the request of the Lower House, the government submitted a draft for reorganization of the army. It was the same bill that the Lower House had rejected the previous year. Obviously, the government would neither change its policy nor be intimidated by the results of the election. The Lower House, on the other hand, was unwilling to extend the "provisional" army expenditures again, and to forestall any budgetary modifications by the government, a liberal delegate (Hagen) asked that the government submit a detailed budget for the then current fiscal year (1862). This the government was unwilling to do, and Wilhelm dissolved the Parliament on March 11, 1862. Liberal ministers in the government were dismissed and replaced with more conservative ones; the so-called liberal era was at an end.[16]

New elections in May 1862 continued the trend of the previous year and the conservatives were beaten once again. They lost 3 seats, retaining 11, while the liberals gained 35, for a total of 285 or 80 percent of the Lower House. Under these circumstances concessions by the Lower House were unlikely, and several ministers, including Roon, advised the king[17] to compromise with the liberal majority and to consider a two-year term of service for the army. But Wilhelm would not be persuaded. He was ready to govern without a budget, though his ministers advised him, on September 9, 1862, that this was illegal under the constitution. The liberals suggested a compromise: they would agree to create and pay for new regiments of line troops, if the government would agree to a two-year term of service. The king's ministers approved this compromise, but the king insisted on a three-year term. During a crown council on September 17, 1862, Wilhelm reaffirmed his views and expressed his readiness to relinquish the crown if the ministers insisted on a compromise with the Lower House.[18] That day Roon sent his telegram to Paris, asking Bismarck to return to Berlin at once.

It is easy to accuse both parties in this conflict of excessive stubbornness and of concentrating on apparently minor issues while the country was driven into a major constitutional crisis. But the fight over the length of army service was only the tip of the iceberg. Underneath lay the fundamental question of who should exercise power in the state: the Lower House or the crown. The liberals were determined to use the conflict and their control over the budget to attain power in the Parliament; this power could then be used to initiate a national German policy in Prussian foreign affairs. They also intended to achieve parliamentary government and to restrain the powers of the Prussian crown by popular representation. The Prussian liberals tried to achieve, in a legal way, the democratic-constitutional system which had been defeated by the counterrevolution of 1848–49.

It was precisely this effort that Wilhelm opposed with all the means and energy at his command. He was neither ready to permit the erosion of royal privileges nor willing to submit the traditional powers of the monarchy to a popular vote. Should either occur, he wrote to the grand duke of Baden, we would be "slaves of parliament." Wilhelm was convinced that the Prussian crown had been bestowed on the Hohenzollerns by the grace of God and that giving in to the demands (

the Lower House of the Parliament would flout God's will and lead to a bourgeois monarchy. By assuming the final decision over army reorganization and length of service, Wilhelm felt that he was defending the royal prerogative as the indisputable basis of the constitution.[19]

The battle was joined. Bismarck's appointment appeared to contribute nothing to its solution. Most commentators of the time refused to take the appointment seriously and considered Bismarck quite unsuitable to lead the country out of this grave domestic crisis.[20] The liberals considered him an arch-conservative and "his appointment the desperate act of a distraught King."[21] The conservatives believed him too liberal, pragmatic, and unreliable. Bismarck himself was fully aware of the dangers and frustrations of his position. He realized that the queen was antagonistic to him and opposed to his policies and that many at Court and in influential positions were in sympathy with her. He owed his appointment to the king, not to any parliamentary or governmental faction; it was based entirely on Wilhelm's trust and confidence, and only Wilhelm could dismiss him. It had taken Wilhelm a long time to overcome his suspicion of Bismarck, and it had taken a major crisis to force Wilhelm to accept Bismarck's services. Bismarck's apparent submission to the king's views and his posture of a vassal accepting appointment from his feudal lord struck responsive cords and played a decisive part in Wilhelm's decision. And Bismarck was not totally insincere, for he believed deeply in this feudal relationship. His attachment to the king was reinforced by the realization that without the preservation of a strong Prussian monarchy there would be no possibility of solving the major problems which Prussia would have to face in the future. Bismarck was also concerned that Wilhelm's abdication would seriously weaken the royalist cause to which Bismarck was deeply attached. In his view, the majority in the Lower House was not truly representative of the Prussian people, but only of the Prussian bourgeoisie. Prussia was the creation of the Hohenzollern dynasty. It was not a nation, any more than its eastern and western parts could claim national identity. An effective Prussian policy was therefore only possible under strong monarchical leadership, and this required a powerful army under absolute royal control.[22]

Bismarck began his new career by attempting to conciliate the opposition. He offered cabinet posts to the liberal deputies Vincke, Simson, and Sybel, but was unable to grant the two-year army service on which the liberals insisted. Privately, Bismarck promised to persuade the king to adopt the two-year term (which Bismarck preferred because it would result in a greater number of trained reserves), but the prospects for this were remote and the liberals, unwilling to procrastinate on this issue, refused to enter the government.[23] Thus, the new prime minister had to look for new ways to resolve the conflict.

Following royal orders, he withdrew the budget for 1863 which had been submitted to the Lower House with the 1862 budget. By doing this, the government made any attempt by the opposition to eliminate funds for the army reorganization for the current year impossible. At the same time, Bismarck made it clear that if the Lower House refused military funds for 1862, he would govern without a budget. In his speech of September 30, 1862, he defended this policy by reminding the delegates that he had accepted his appointment from the king with the condition that he would, if need be, govern without a budget. The Prussian Parliament, he pointed out, had no exclusive power over appropriations. Instead, it was necessary for the Upper and Lower houses, together with the crown, to come to an agreement. Should one of these three reject a proposed budget, there would be a "tabula rasa"—a clean slate. In this event, which could be considered an emergency, the government had the right to govern without a budget, because the crown retained all those rights not expressly allocated to the Parliament by the constitution. This was Bismarck's famous theory of the "constitutional gap."[24]

Bismarck reminded his listeners that the German people looked to Prussia not for her liberalism but for her power. Several opportunities for Prussia to exert her leadership in Germany had already been missed. Prussia must concentrate her power; her frontiers, as fixed by the Congress of Vienna, were not suitable to healthy development. "Not through speeches and majority decisions will the great questions of the period be decided—those were the mistakes of 1848 and 1849— but through iron and blood."[25] This phrase (soon transposed to "blood and iron") became instantly famous. Its meaning has been debated endlessly. Contrary to many interpretations, the statement simply recognized existing political realities; it said nothing about Bismarck's plans for the unification of Germany. Bismarck realized earlier than most that Austria would not allow Prussia to attain equal status with her in Germany. Therefore, if Prussia wanted to play a leading role in Germany, as the liberals themselves desired, conferences and debates were useless and only force would achieve results.

But the Lower House was not impressed by Bismarck's speech. It accepted the budget for 1862, but deleted all military expenditures. The Upper House, however, accepted the government's budget, including the military items, thus complicating the constitutional conflict still further. As a result, Wilhelm dismissed both houses on October 13, 1862, proclaimed a state of emergency, and announced the government's intention of submitting a bill of indemnity to the Parliament once normal conditions had returned.[26]

The parliamentary session of 1863 was as futile as the previous one, except that Bismarck began a campaign against the liberals in the country at large by restricting the freedom of the press and by admonishing municipal councils not to engage in political (that is, antigovernment) activities. There was considerable popular protest against these measures and the crown prince openly disassociated himself from them.[27] Bismarck ignored the protests. The Parliament was dissolved once more and new elections called for October 28, 1863. An even larger liberal majority was elected. The deadlock continued. The government collected taxes and spent monies without parliamentary authorization; the people did not object.

When Johann Jacoby, a liberal deputy, suggested that the people should refuse to pay taxes, he was arrested for treasonable remarks. Ferdinand Lassalle, a well-known socialist and labor leader, commenting on the situation, compared conditions in England with those in Prussia:

> In England, wrote Lassalle, if the tax collector were to come to demand taxes not voted by parliament he would be thrown out of the house by the citizens. If the citizen were arrested and brought to court, he would be freed by the court and sent home with praise for having resisted illegal force. If the tax collector were to come with troops, the citizen would mobilize his friends and neighbors to oppose force with force. A battle would ensue with possible loss of life. The tax collector would then be haled into court on the charge of murder, and his defense that he acted "on orders" would be rejected by the British court since he had been engaged in "an illegal act." He would

CONSTITUTIONAL CONFLICT IN PRUSSIA

be condemned to death. If the citizen and his friends had killed any soldiers, they would be released because they were resisting illegal force. "And because all the people know this would happen," wrote Lassalle, "everyone would refuse to pay the taxes—even those who are indifferent—in order not to be considered bad citizens. . . ."

In Prussia, Lassalle went on to say, it is different. If the Prussian citizen were to throw out the tax collector who came to collect taxes not approved by the diet he would be haled to court to receive a jail sentence for "resistance to lawful authority." If fighting and killing ensued, the soldiers would be protected from prosecution because they "obeyed orders," while the citizen who attempted to resist by force would be convicted and beheaded. "And because this is so and because from the start all the odds are against those who refuse to pay, the government will feel confident of any action it undertakes and all the officials will be loyal to it!"[28]

A major problem throughout the constitutional conflict was whether the overwhelming liberal majority of the Lower House of the Prussian Parliament accurately reflected the temper of the country at large.[29] Bismarck, who had a better understanding of political realities than most of his contemporaries, doubted that the majority of the Prussian population was as liberal as the delegates in the Lower House. The population, he believed, was for the most part rural and conservative, and the three-class system of voting gave the masses of people no adequate chance to make their voices heard. That was why Bismarck, to the horror of his old conservative friends, favored universal manhood suffrage. He believed, as did Ferdinand Lassalle, that an alliance between the nobility and the workers would defeat the middle class. But this was still in the future. The outcome of the election of 1863 would not have been materially altered by universal suffrage, nor would the deadlock between the government and the opposition have been less severe. Still, the liberals, despite their majority, felt less secure than would appear. They were uncertain of their support in the country and were unable to prevent the government from carrying on its business. Then too, trade and industry were prospering and the economic policies of the government were liberal and progressive.[30]

The Junkers, however, still believed they had inherent rights to leadership. They did not understand that industrial expansion would increase the value of their real estate and the demand for their agrarian products and that these, in turn, would transform the Junkers into upper-class capitalists and add greater political power to their newly acquired wealth.

The liberals seem not to have realized that these developments left them little time to achieve their aims. The liberals' failure to anticipate this shift in political power was due, perhaps, to their unwillingness to pursue radical measures and their lack of political acumen. Bismarck was the first to recognize the weakness of the liberals and the economic possibilities of the Junkers. [31]

By January 1864 both the government and the opposition, recognizing the hopelessness of the situation, looked to foreign affairs as a means of breaking the deadlock. There, in the tangled web of the Schleswig-Holstein question, the possibility of a compromise finally appeared.

Bismarck's
Three Wars

Despite his tough stand and show of confidence, Bismarck was unhappy about the constitutional conflict. He was mindful of public opinion and wanted popular support for government policies, not criticism and opposition. He particularly needed this support in foreign affairs, where, he believed, Prussian aims would have to be realized.

Two developments made his policies more difficult to pursue in 1863, at the height of the constitutional conflict: the Polish revolt against Russia, and Austria's attempt to join the Customs Union. The revolt in Poland in January 1863 provided Bismarck with an opportunity to establish closer ties with Russia, which he had contemplated since his stay as minister in St. Petersburg. When the Russians requested Prussian military assistance along the common border, the Prussian government, following the precedents of 1830–31 and 1848, mobilized half its army and closed its borders to Polish insurgents. General Alvensleben, the king's general adjutant, was sent to St. Petersburg to encourage further cooperation and "to strengthen the tsar's resistance to the pro-Polish party among his advisers."[1] An agreement which became known as the Alvensleben Convention was concluded on February 8, 1863: it stipulated cooperation and mutual assistance by the Russian and Prussian military commanders and permission for each to cross the border in pursuit of Polish revolutionaries. Although meant to be secret, the terms of the agreement became known in the major European capitals and led to a serious diplomatic crisis.[2] Napoleon III was particularly upset because he had pretended that the revolt was an internal Russian affair to avoid jeopardizing his country's friendly relations with Russia. Prussia's intervention made such an interpretation untenable. If a conservative power like Prussia could intervene to suppress the Poles, a liberal power like France should be able to assist them. Unwilling to challenge Russia directly, Napoleon put pressure on Prussia by suggesting that Bismarck's dismissal might ease the tension, and proposing that Britain and Austria present a joint protest in Berlin.

Strong liberal opposition to the Alvensleben Convention in the Prussian Parliament and general dissatisfaction with it throughout Germany were added to the diplomatic uproar.[3] There were rumors in Berlin of a ministerial crisis and Bismarck's resignation.[4] In an attempt to disarm his critics and forestall complications with France and Britian, Bismarck asked Gorchakov, the Russian foreign minister, to release Prussia from her commitments; the latter complied by declaring that the convention had never been in force.[5] Thus, Bismarck's first venture into foreign affairs was not exactly a resounding success (the czar called him a terrible blunderer), though Bismarck and scores of historians after him tried to present it as such.[6] Bismarck had intended to use the convention to earn Russian gratitude, suppress the uprising before the Western powers could intervene, and prevent a Franco-Russian alliance; instead, he was forced to back down in the face of determined domestic and foreign opposition.[7]

The second development in 1863 concerned Austro-Prussian rivalry for supremacy in Germany. The Austrian government realized that Prussia's humiliation at Olmuetz[8] had been only a temporary setback and that Prussia's economic leadership in the Customs Union was of more serious and more lasting consequence. Austria sought to join the Customs Union, hoping to assume leadership of a much larger free trade area in central Europe. This scheme became known as the *Mitteleuropa* plan. A good plan in theory, it foundered on the economic realities of the times. Prussia, whose economy was considerably stronger than Austria's, looked toward western Europe and the free trade opportunities of the Chevalier-Cobden treaty between Britain and France (January 23, 1860), rather than toward the protectionist system of the Austrian Empire. To this end Prussia, supported by the north German states, concluded a trade treaty with France in August 1862.[9] The Austrian government realized that the Franco-Prussian trade treaty strengthened Prussia's economic position in Germany and that Austria's chances for economic leadership in central Europe had been even further limited.

To recapture some of her lost prestige, Austria proposed a reorganization of the German Confederation which, if accepted, would have given her the preponderant influence in that body. It was a two-pronged plan. First, it called for a reorganization of the Diet at Frankfurt, by creating an assembly of delegates chosen by the state diets. Such an assembly would increase the votes of Austria and her allies to the detriment of Prussia. Bismarck countered this move with a proposal for a German parliament elected by universal suffrage. Without taking a stand on the Prussian proposal, the Diet voted on the Austrian plan and defeated it in January 1863. The second Austrian plan involved replacement of the Confederation by an assembly of princes, led by the Austrian emperor. The key to its success, as the Austrians fully realized, was Prussian cooperation. To achieve it, the Austrian emperor, Francis Joseph, personally invited King Wilhelm to an assembly of the German princes at Frankfurt. The king, flattered by the emperor's personal attention, was inclined to accept the invitation, but Bismarck was strongly opposed. In Bismarck's view, the Austrian plan, designed to attract liberal and greater German support, would impede Prussian policy and deny her a significant voice in German affairs. Wilhelm felt he could not refuse the invitation but Bismarck, after long arguments and threats of resignation, finally persuaded the king not to go. Prussia's abstention doomed the Austrian project, but a complete break between the two powers was avoided when Bismarck suggested a joint policy in the Schleswig-Holstein question.

The Danish War   The Schleswig-Holstein question intruded upon the European diplomatic scene again in the spring of 1863, when King Frederick VII of Denmark announced, by royal decree, the incorporation of Schleswig and a new charter for Holstein.[10] This move violated the London Protocol of 1852, which provided for the inseparability of the duchies of Schleswig and Holstein and placed them in personal union with the Danish crown. King Frederick's proclamation was also a breach of the assurances Denmark had given Austria and Prussia in 1852, that the duchies would not be separated from each other or incorporated into Denmark. While the Danes were confident of British and Swedish support, the German Confederation (of which Holstein was a member) was much disturbed, and German public opinion was outraged. Prussia's inglorious campaign and the defeat of the Frankfurt National Assembly on the Danish question in 1848[11] had not been forgotten, and neither the Prussian government nor the people wanted a repetition of those unhappy events. Thus, when the Danish king died on November 15, 1863, German nationalists everywhere championed Duke Frederick of Augustenburg as the legitimate heir of the duchies, and urged their independence from Denmark. According to the London Protocol, however, Prince Christian was to succeed to the Danish crown and to the duchies.

For Bismarck the situation was still more complicated. On the one hand he felt that Prussia, in this instance, could not ignore German national aims if she aspired to leadership in Germany. On the other hand, supporting the duke of Augustenburg would violate the London Protocol and turn Britain, France, and Russia against Prussia. Then too, Bismarck believed that it was hardly in Prussia's interest to go to a great deal of trouble on behalf of German national aims if, in the end, he would be faced with another German state which would cast its vote against Prussia at the Diet. A better policy would be to incorporate the duchies into Prussia, by force if need be. Obviously, Bismarck could not announce these aims. Instead, he cautiously supported German public opinion without, however, endorsing the claims of the duke of Augustenburg. At the same time, he prodded Austria to join Prussia in whatever action might be appropriate against Denmark. (This was meant primarily to impress Britain, France, and Russia, to prevent Prussia's isolation, and to ensure military superiority in case of war.) The Austrians, opposed to warlike policies, would have been content if Denmark returned to the provisions of the London Protocol. King Wilhelm, on the other hand, was full of enthusiasm for the plan to wrest the duchies from Denmark and place them under the duke of Augustenburg.

When the Federal Diet voted in favor of military intervention in Denmark (October 1, 1863) and Hanoverian and Saxon troops invaded Holstein (December 24, 1863), the major powers were forced to reexamine their attitude toward the impending conflict. Britain, whose support of Denmark had been steadfast all along, was embarrassed by the Danish abrogation of the London Protocol and, after prolonged debates, decided that she could not go to war in defense of this Danish breach of an international treaty.[12] Russia, because of Bismarck's recent support during the Polish insurrection, was on Prussia's side, con-

tent to repay Britain and France for their anti-Russian role during the
Polish uprising. Nor did France have any intention of coming to the aid
of the Danes. Indeed, Napoleon III secretly encouraged Bismarck to
annex the duchies, hinting that some territorial compensations along
France's northeastern borders or along the Rhine would be quite welcome in exchange for his neutrality.

On January 16, 1864, Prussia and Austria concluded an alliance and
sent an ultimatum to Denmark. They asked the Danes to revoke the
constitution of November 1863, which had announced the incorporation of Schleswig with Denmark. When Denmark rejected the ultimatum, allied troops marched into Schleswig on February 1, announcing
their intention of preventing the illegal union of Schleswig with the
Danish crown and disclaiming any intent to destroy the Danish kingdom. Under these circumstances, the powers found it impossible to
come to the aid of the Danes and proclaimed their neutrality.

The crisis created a serious dilemma for the Prussian liberals. While
the moderates backed the claims of the duke of Augustenburg and
urged the government to support his cause, the liberals vacillated between supporting outright annexation of the duchies and refusing to
support the government in an aggressive war. It was the old problem
of freedom versus power. The issue became urgent on December 9,
1863, when the government presented a bill to the Lower House asking for 9 million thaler to finance military operations against Denmark.
This was a political maneuver to split the opposition, for the government did not actually need the money. Should the liberal majority in
the Lower House refuse the authorization, public opinion would consider the liberals unpatriotic, and they would be discredited. For the
liberals, the choice was both crucial and painful. Approving the funds
meant acknowledging defeat in the constitutional conflict; rejecting
them meant opposing the German unity movement and losing public
support, which the liberals could ill afford.[13] After long debates the
Lower House rejected the government's request by a vote of 275 to 51
(January 22, 1864). This, the liberals believed, would bring about Bismarck's resignation and resolve the constitutional conflict in their
favor. But they were mistaken. Austro-Prussian military victory
aroused German national enthusiasm, and for the first time Bismarck
enjoyed popular support. An armistice with Denmark was arranged

and the powers met in London on April 25, 1864 to conclude a settlement. When, in the course of the negotiations, Count Bernstorff, the representative of Austria, Prussia, and the lesser German states, declared the London Protocol of 1852 null and void, the powers protested but were unable to agree on a substitute. It was equally impossible to agree upon a solution for Schleswig, so the conference disbanded on June 25 and military operations were resumed the following day. This time the Danes were beaten decisively; at the preliminary peace of Vienna on August 1, they surrendered the duchies of Schleswig, Holstein, and Lauenburg to Austria and Prussia. The final settlement was signed in Vienna on October 30, 1864.

The allies' major problem was how to divide the spoils. At a conference in Schoenbrunn at the end of August, Rechberg, the Austrian foreign minister, suggested a trade-off: Prussia would take over the duchies and, in return, assist Austria in the recovery of Lombardy (lost by the Austrians to the Italians in 1859 at the end of the Austro-Sardinian war). This was an ill-considered suggestion, for it would have meant the dismemberment of recently united Italy and would also have aroused the enmity of a very suspicious Napoleon III, a price Prussia was not willing to pay. Without mentioning these considerations, Wilhelm and Bismarck evaded the Austrian offer and with many expressions of goodwill—and the major problem unresolved—the allies parted.

It had become clear to most observers in the Germanies that Prussia, under Bismarck's skillful leadership, had outmaneuvered Austria in the Schleswig-Holstein question. But what were his plans for the future? Determining Bismarck's policy toward Austria is crucial to an understanding of his long-range aims: it would establish whether or not he planned and wanted war with Austria, and would also reveal his attitude toward German unification. If this initial aim, as some historians believe,[14] was cooperation with Austria in return for Prussian hegemony in North Germany, then unification of all Germany under Prussian leadership was not a serious goal. If, on the other hand, Bismarck favored war with Austria, his avowed policy of Austro-German cooperation was only a pretext, and Prussian leadership in a united Germany was a definite aim.

There was, furthermore, the still unresolved constitutional conflict at home. It limited the government's freedom of action in domestic affairs and lowered Prussia's standing in the eyes of the other German states. If, however, a war with Austria could be used to distract the people's attention from domestic affairs, Bismarck believed that both crises might be solved simultaneously. The liberals' enthusiasm for a national cause would facilitate such a policy, and he hoped that the people in other German states would follow Prussia's lead, or at least be sympathetic to her aims.

After the Danish war, Austria and Prussia outwardly maintained a common front and unity of purpose, while the struggle for economic supremacy continued behind the scenes. Rechberg once again presented Austria's *Mitteleuropa* plan to the members of the German Confederation in the mistaken belief that Prussia had been dependent on Austrian support during the Danish war and needed the support of the lesser German states to get a renewal of the Prussian Customs Union. The Customs Union treaties were due to expire at the end of 1865, but Bismarck had already announced in December 1863 that their renewal was due in 1864, putting the member states under considerable pressure and causing confusion in their ranks. By concluding a trade treaty with Saxony in May 1864, Bismarck further strengthened Prussia's economic position and this, combined with Prussia's manifest leadership in the Danish war, made clear to the lesser states that they could not afford to leave the Customs Union. Politically and culturally most of the states preferred Austria to Prussia; economically, however, their bonds with Prussia were so strong that they simply could not afford a change. Thus it can be said that "the battle for the economic-political domination of Germany was decided when the continuation of the Prussian Customs Union . . . was signed in Berlin on June 28, 1864."[15]

The Austrian War Still, the problem of the division of the spoils of the Danish war remained unresolved. It proved a vexing matter. The joint Austro-Prussian administration of the duchies led to countless irritations and disputes on the local level which could easily become major political disagreements. While this may not have been Bismarck's original intention—especially at the time (October 1864) when Mensdorff replaced Rechberg as Austrian foreign minister—he was conscious of the possibility, and at the beginning of 1865 he informed Austria of Prussia's conditions for the establishment of a Schleswig-Holstein state.[16] For all practical purposes, Prussian demands amounted to complete Prussian domination, especially in communication matters and military affairs (soldiers of Schleswig-Holstein were to swear allegiance to the Prussian king). The question of a future ruler for the duchies was to be left open for the time being. The Austrian government rejected the Prussian note, as Bismarck had expected, basing its case on the incompatibility of the Prussian provisions with the constitution of the German Confederation, particularly the provision that the federation was an assembly of sovereign princes. The Prussian note also constituted a break with the duke of Augustenburg, whom Bismarck suspected of liberal leanings and of being in close touch with his enemies at Court.

A month later the Prussian government transferred its major naval establishment from Danzig to Kiel, a clear indication that it expected to annex the duchies permanently. At a Prussian crown council in May 1865, the king and Moltke (chief of the general staff) expressed themselves in favor of annexation, regardless of the consequences, while the crown prince strongly opposed it. Bismarck appeared undecided. Though he advocated further negotiations toward a peaceful settlement, he did not reject the possibility of war and warned (this was meant for the crown prince) that force could never be ruled out completely. Nor was this idle talk. In preparation for such an eventuality, Bismarck sounded out the French and Italian governments and received reassurances from both. Italy was anxious to get Venetia from Austria, and France, less specific in her territorial expectations, was forever looking for compensation along the Rhine. Napoleon's Mexican adventure was going badly and the possibility of an Austro-Prussian alliance in the center of Europe was not at all to his liking.

It is impossible to point to the exact moment when Bismarck decided to go to war against Austria.[17] As usual, he kept his options open and pursued several policies simultaneously. The European political situation was more favorable to an active Prussian foreign policy than it had been in the past, and Bismarck was aware of this. Using the moment to advantage, he bombarded the government in Vienna with complaints about the administration of the duchies, accusing Austrian officials, among other things, of supporting the revolutionary activities of the duke of Augustenburg, and threatening to take unilateral action unless the Austrians cooperated by removing the duke from the duchies.[18] The Austrians did not know how to deal with these provocations. They had just changed governments (Schmerling-Belcredi, July 1865), were in the midst of a financial and economic crisis, and had troubles with the Hungarians. They suggested direct negotiations; Bismarck agreed, and these led to the Convention of Gastein of August 14, 1865. Under its terms, the joint administration of the duchies was replaced by a "provisional" division: Austria was to administer Holstein, while Prussia assumed responsibility for Schleswig and acquired the rights to Lauenburg from Austria for 2.5 million thalers.

German public opinion was deeply shocked. Not only had the two powers disregarded what were considered the just claims of the duke of Augustenburg, they had violated the ideal for which the Germans believed they had fought the Danes in 1848 and 1864: the unity of the duchies. People in the lesser states were especially disappointed in Austria for having abdicated her leading role in German affairs, and for abandoning her conservative policy. Almost everywhere the Convention of Gastein was considered a victory for Prussia and a defeat for Austria.

Bismarck, however, considered it only a temporary settlement. To prepare for the next phase (and to see Kathy Orlow again), he traveled to Paris and Biarritz. The French had not taken kindly to the Austro-Prussian agreement and, in a circular note of August 29, 1865, had accused the two powers of basing their settlement on power and force.[19] Then too, the French government was suspicious of secret agreements from which it was excluded, and felt sure that Prussia must have given Austria additional compensation to obtain such a favorable settlement.[20] Bismarck went to France to reassure Napoleon III and to ask him for French friendship and understanding. He must have succeeded in his mission. Though he failed to meet Kathy Orlow (she had gone to Torquay and had not notified him of her change of plans) and missed her company, he returned to Berlin in high spirits. "We shall step on Austria's corns," he told Thiele, the undersecretary in the foreign office, "make an alliance with Italy, castrate the Augustenburger, and rape the [German] Confederation."[21]

The situation in the duchies did not improve following the Gastein agreement. The Austrian administration in Holstein was more relaxed than the Prussian in Schleswig, and the different attitudes of the occupying powers to the claims of the duke of Augustenburg contributed to the underlying friction between the powers and between them and the local population. Bismarck was not unhappy about this development. He was determined to keep these and other dissensions alive and, if need be, to exaggerate them. As before, he sent a constant stream of complaints to Vienna, accusing the Austrians of abandoning conservative policies agreed upon at Gastein, and threatening unilateral action in the future.[22] Bismarck's posture of the aggrieved and injured party was meant not only to put the Austrian government in the wrong, but also to stiffen the king's position. His ruse worked, for in the Prussian crown council of February 28, 1866, Wilhelm accused the Austrians of purposely alienating the local population in Schleswig-Holstein from the Prussian government.[23] During discussions of Austro-Prussian relations and the possibility of war, all participants except the crown prince agreed that war was unavoidable, and that it should neither be evaded nor initiated by Prussia. This latter proviso was necessary to make adequate diplomatic preparations and to negotiate with Italy. To this end the king, with Bismarck's prompting, agreed to send a mission to Florence. Moltke was confident of the readiness of the Prussian army, but he considered the diversionary effect of the Italian army essential for a military victory over Austria.

Bismarck's concern about Italian cooperation went back to the Gastein convention; he worried lest the Italians consider Austro-Prussian cooperation permanent and an Italian-Prussian alliance completely futile. This was exactly how the Italian government appraised the situation. Italians were suspicious of Prussian policy and would have preferred to reach a peaceful agreement with Austria on the acquisition of Venetia. But the Austrians, aware of Bismarck's intrigues in Paris and Florence and confident that they could beat the Prussians and Italians, could not make up their minds. Instead of allying themselves with either the Italians or the Prussians, they managed to antagonize both. One reason for their uncompromising attitude was Habsburg pride, which precluded their dealing with the Prussians on an equal basis, or recognizing the Italian government as legitimate.

BISMARCK'S THREE WARS

When the Italians realized late in 1865 that the government in Vienna was not likely to come to an agreement over Venetia, they became more amenable to Prussian approaches. By the end of February 1866 the Italians were ready for a Prussian alliance against Austria and sent General Gavone to Berlin to work out the details.[24] (This made it unnecessary to send a Prussian mission to Florence.) How to reconcile Italian and Prussian aims was a major problem. Italy wanted a short, wartime alliance, expecting an early start of hostilities. Prussia needed more time to prepare and to create a suitable provocation to start a war.

At this point Bismarck seems to have realized that in the eyes of public opinion the question of the duchies would not be sufficient cause for war with Austria; he began to consider, instead, something more in line with common German national aspirations—a reorganization of the German Confederation or a realignment of the Federal Diet. Either would mean a postponement of the war, and this would make the Italians less anxious to enter into an alliance with the Prussians. The key to this alliance, both parties realized, was Napoleon III, and Bismarck took care to keep Benedetti, the French ambassador, fully informed of the progress of the negotiations. Benedetti, in turn, reassured the Italians, stressing especially Bismarck's determination for a war with Austria. The decisive turn came when Napoleon personally advised a special Italian emissary that Italy should sign the alliance with Prussia. The Italians accepted Napoleon's advice and on April 8, 1866, Gavone and Bismarck signed the treaty of alliance in Berlin. It was limited to three months and was in no way binding upon Prussia. If Prussia were to declare war on Austria within that period, Italy was to join, and the two powers agreed not to conclude a separate armistice or peace. In case of victory, Italy was to get Venetia, and Prussia some territory of similar size and population. There can be little doubt that with this treaty Prussia committed a grave breach of law against the provisions of the German Confederation, which forbade any member to ally itself with a foreign power against another member of the federation. Indeed, the king was uncomfortably aware of this breach and kept the treaty a well-guarded secret.

His foreign policy requirements well taken care of, Bismarck still had to find a solution to a very serious problem facing him at home:

how to finance the impending war. For even though taxes were collected without an authorized budget, the Parliament would not approve additional funds, nor would it "allow the government to sell state property without parliamentary approval."[25] In this difficult situation, Bismarck turned to his confidant and private banker, Gerson Bleichroeder.[26] It was Bleichroeder who had originally conceived of the sale of the Cologne-Minden Railroad, which the Parliament had vetoed in January 1866. Now, upon the request of the new minister of finance, August von der Heydt, Bleichroeder and his fellow banker and longtime friend, Hansemann, formed a consortium to buy the government's shares of the Cologne-Minden Railroad and thus provided Bismarck with the necessary funds to prepare for war.[27]

The Austrians, meanwhile, informed of the Italian-Prussian negotiations, hoped that Wilhelm's traditional conservatism would rule out any firm and binding commitments between Italy and Prussia. When this proved futile, the Austrians started negotiations with the French and on June 12, 1866, concluded a secret convention with them. By its terms the Austrians agreed, in return for French neutrality, to cede Venitia to the Italians if the Austrian armies were victorious in Germany. But even if the Austrians were to beat the Italians, Venetia would still be turned over to Italy. As compensation Austria could acquire territory in the Germanies, as long as this did not upset the balance of power in Europe. An oral agreement between Vienna and Paris envisaged territorial gains for Saxony, Wuerttemberg, and Bavaria and—shades of the Rhenish Confederation—the creation of an independent German state west of the Rhine.[28] This would have been a thinly disguised French satellite meant to compensate Napoleon III for his troubles in these negotiations. The Austro-French convention illustrates the shortsightedness of Austrian foreign policy well. Pursuing dynastic policies and cabinet diplomacy, the Austrian statesmen were either unaware of public opinion or of German national aspirations or were undisturbed by them.

Exploiting the German question, Bismarck informed the governments of the lesser states in March 1866[29] of his intention to suggest reforms of the Confederation. At the same time, he asked what their attitude would be in case of a conflict with Austria. Two weeks later he submitted his plan for reform to the Diet.[30] It consisted, essentially, of a national parliament, based on universal suffrage, which was to establish a federal constitution and was much like the plan he had proposed three years earlier.[31]

It had no chance of being accepted, nor had Bismarck intended that it should be. His aim was to gain the support of national liberal forces throughout Germany and to discredit Austrian policy. To the king and the Prussian conservatives it was a revolutionary plan, but to Bismarck the alliance with German nationalism seemed the only way of preserving the powers of the Prussian monarchy in the modern age. Ever since the Revolution of 1848 he had believed that the masses were essentially conservative and that universal suffrage, far from aiding the liberals, would provide a solid basis of support for the existing government in Prussia.

But the support that Bismarck expected from the German people in the spring and summer of 1866 was not forthcoming. Outside Prussia, many people were either indifferent or opposed to Bismarck's aims. Particularism was widespread in the lesser states; though a number of Germans favored Prussian leadership, many were suspicious of her policies, especially in light of the constitutional conflict. The governments also hesitated, but they finally referred Bismarck's proposal for reform to a commission, thus rendering it ineffective for the time being.

Abroad, Bismarck's proposal for a reorganization of the Confederation encountered mixed reactions. The czar opposed it, seeing in it the dread threat of revolution. Napoleon, though flattered that Bismarck should adopt his own methods of universal suffrage, worried lest it lead to a strong and united Germany. In England, public opinion was divided. Some refused to take Bismarck seriously; others considered him a genius.[32] The Austrian government decided in March, despite serious economic difficulties, to strengthen its military forces in Bohemia, the area most exposed to Prussian invasion. It did so for two reasons. First, the army's communication system and its technical services were so poor that mobilization of its forces would require several weeks, much longer than similar Prussian preparations. Then too, Bismarck's bellicose statements had so alarmed the Austrian general staff that it was able to prevail upon the emperor to authorize these measures over the objections of the foreign minister. To Bismarck this was a most welcome development and he used it to convince King Wilhelm of the perfidy of Austrian policy and to induce him to order partial mobilization of the border forces. The immediate threat of war was averted, however, by an Austrian declaration assuring the European powers of her peaceful intentions and by English attempts, through the royal court, to impress upon Wilhelm the inherent dangers of Bismarck's policy. A military confrontation was averted for the time being but could not be avoided for long.

On April 8, Bismarck concluded the alliance with Italy and the Italians, heartened by this alliance, began to prepare for war. When this became known in Vienna on April 21, Austrian troops were mobilized along the southern border. Unlike the earlier military measures in Bohemia, this was a more serious development. The Italians, encouraged by Bismarck, heightened the crisis and, in a wave of patriotic enthusiasm, the Italian parliament voted the necessary war credits and the government informed the European powers that the Italian forces were being mobilized for the defense of their country.[33] While this enabled Bismarck to forego military demobilization in the wake of British mediation attempts, it threatened his carefully laid diplomatic plans. The possibility of an Austrian attack on Italy had not been considered in drafting the Italian-Prussian treaty and the danger of such an attack led to Italian inquiries in Berlin regarding the government's attitude. Bismarck, on the king's orders, had to tell the Italians that the Prussian government would adhere strictly to the treaty's provisions. Rumors of Napoleon's mediation attempts were circulating and Bismarck feared that this, combined with his rejection of the Italians, would lead to their defection from the alliance.

Napoleon's intervention at the beginning of May was indeed a serious threat to Bismarck's plans. The emperor informed the Italian envoy on May 5 that Austria, in exchange for a free hand in Germany, was willing to cede Venetia to France, which would transfer it, unconditionally, to Italy. It was now up to Italy to decide whether there should be peace or war. Clearly, the Italians were on the spot. To them it was primarily a matter of pride. To acquire Venetia without a struggle would not only be degrading, it would also give Napoleon a voice in Italian affairs, and with Italian memories of Plombières and the Austro-Sardinian war[34] still fresh, they rejected such a settlement forthwith. Meanwhile, Bismarck had persuaded the king to order the mobilization of the eastern army corps, thus reassuring the Italians that they could, after all, count on Prussian assistance.[35]

In the midst of full military mobilization by all sides, there now occurred a curious episode that seemed once more to enhance the chances for a peaceful solution: the Gablenz mission. The Gablenz brothers, coming from an old family of imperial knights, seemed especially suited for this mediation attempt. Anton was a former Saxon chamberlain and Prussian deputy; his brother Ludwig was a general in the Austrian army and governor of Holstein. To them, as to many in Germany, the possibility of an Austro-Prussian conflict carried the specter of a fratricidal war and they were determined to prevent it. The authorities in Berlin and Vienna received them and heard their proposals, which entailed, in essence, creation of an independent Schleswig-Holstein state under a Prussian prince, Prussian sovereignty, special rights in the port of Kiel, a 30 million thaler indemnity for Austria, and the division of German military command along the Main between Austria and Prussia. The Austrians accepted the plan in principle, but asked for one concession: a Prussian military commitment against Italy. Bismarck rejected this out of hand. His counterproposal was to give the Prussian king more power as federal commander in chief in Germany. This the Austrians could not accept. They felt they could not, once again, betray what little trust they might have among the lesser states; they also felt they must have some security against Italy. On May 28, 1866, the Austrian government formally rejected the Gablenz plan.[36]

Failure of the Gablenz mission brought about a scramble for the allegiance of the lesser states. Most were pro-Austrian to begin with, and all Bismarck could do was to threaten and cajole them. He did not succeed. On June 1, the Austrians, in defiance of the Convention of Gastein, placed the future fate of the duchies in the hands of the Federal Diet. The die was cast. On the ninth, Prussian troops marched into Holstein, but much to Bismarck's chagrin, they failed to encounter Austrian resistance. Two days later the Austrians asked the Diet to mobilize all federal troops and on the fourteenth, the Diet voted the request by nine to five. On the following day Prussia sent ultimatums, which were rejected, to Saxony, Hanover, and Kassel. That night

Prussian troops started to move and on June 21 they crossed the border into Bohemia.

The military developments were as swift as they were decisive. The Austrians defeated the Italians at Custozza (June 24) and Lissa (July 20). But the Prussians defeated the Hanoverians at Langensalza (June 27–29) and the Austrians at Koeniggraetz/Sadowa (July 3). This was the decisive battle. The victory should be credited to Moltke's superior strategic leadership, utilization of railroads for rapid mobilization and the movement of troops, and to the new breach-loading needle gun, which was faster and more effective than the Austrian muzzleloader.[37]

Prussia's lightning campaign and decisive military victory caught Napoleon completely off guard. He had hoped for a long, drawn-out war and had planned either to intervene or mediate a peace and, at the end, obtain suitable compensations. On July 5 the Austrians had asked for the emperor's mediation and from then on French intervention was a possibility which Bismarck had to consider. He was prepared to counter it in two ways. First, he held out the possibility of territorial compensation on the left bank of the Rhine to the French, and simultaneously threatened to incite a national uprising in Germany against France, if French demands were too high. To counteract the possibility of French military intervention and to defeat Austria more quickly, he was prepared to support a Hungarian and Serbian uprising against the Habsburg monarchy.[38] The victory at Koeniggraetz/Sadowa made it unnecessary to use either plan.

The threat of French intervention, a cholera epidemic in the Prussian army, and the arrival of Austrian reinforcements from Italy persuaded Bismarck to press not only for a quick preliminary peace but also for lenient terms for the Austrians. This was particularly irritating to King Wilhelm who, full of righteous indignation, wanted to punish the Austrians, march into Vienna, and dictate a punitive peace in Schoenbrunn palace. He had the generals on his side and Bismarck, mindful of possible foreign intervention, finally persuaded the king, with the help of the crown prince, to agree to more sensible terms. On July 26, 1866, a preliminary peace was signed at Nikolsburg; the Austrians were required to give Venetia to the Italians and pay an indemnity. Austria's greatest loss was one of prestige: she was forced out of the German Confederation. These terms were confirmed in the final Treaty of Prague on August 23. Prussia's lack of territorial gains from Austria was amply compensated for by generous acquisitions from Austria's allies in north Germany. There, Hanover, electoral Hesse, Nassau, and the city of Frankfurt[39] were incorporated into Prussia, uniting Prussian territory into one contiguous unit for the first time. The deposing of the Hanoverian dynasty, in violation of the monarchical principle, was a severe shock to the czar, who, scandalized by these revolutionary measures and Bismarck's blatant disregard of monarchical solidarity, called for a European congress to discuss these radical changes. But Bismarck angrily rejected such outside interference in German affairs. He threatened to support Polish nationalism against Russia and let it be known in St. Petersburg that "should there be revolution, we would rather make it, than suffer it."[40]

With Austria's elimination from Germany and Prussia's territorial acquisitions, the German Confederation had been destroyed. The states north of the Main now formed the North German Federation under Prussian leadership, while those south of the river were free to form their own union. While bargaining over compensations with France, Bismarck used his talks with Benedetti to impress upon the south German states the continued threat of French aggression and, as a result, concluded secret defense treaties with Baden, Wuerttemberg, and Bavaria which were later incorporated into the peace treaties. The most significant provision in these defense treaties was the king of Prussia's assumption of supreme military command over the forces of the south German states in case of war with France.

The territorial enlargement of Prussia made her the largest and most powerful state in Germany. Her military alliances with the south German states and her economic predominance in the Customs Union made the unification of Germany under Prussian leadership, that is, along lesser German lines, a likely possibility. One major obstacle remained: the settlement of the constitutional conflict. Here, the victory over Austria played a decisive role. Popular enthusiasm knew no bounds; it was accompanied by a massive shift of votes from the liberals to the conservatives. The election of July 3, 1866—the day of the battle of Koeniggraetz/Sadowa—gave the conservatives 136 mandates (up from 35) and the liberals and progressives 148 (from 247). In combination with the old liberals (24 mandates, up from 9), the conservatives now controlled the Lower House of the Prussian Parliament.[41] The election's outcome made it possible for Bismarck to offer the liberals a compromise. He proposed a bill of indemnity which, though acknowledging no wrongdoing by the government, asked the Lower House to approve, retroactively, the government's unauthorized expenditures of past years. After he had won the king's approval—over the strenuous objections of the old conservatives—Bismarck submitted the bill to the Lower House on August 14, 1866. After considerable debate it passed, 230 to 75, on September 3.[42]

The outcome of the war greatly increased Bismarck's power and prestige, but caused considerable upheaval among the major political parties. Both liberals and conservatives split and sought new alignments. The liberals divided into the Progressive and the National Liberal parties; the former contained the core of those Prussian liberals who had opposed Bismarck's domestic policies all along. The latter were mostly those from the newly acquired territories who welcomed and supported Bismarck's economic and national goals.[43] Among conservatives the shock and confusion over Bismarck's policies were, if anything, greater than the frustrations experienced by the liberal camp. Bismarck's advocacy of universal suffrage and a national parliament, his support of Italy, and his dispossession of the legitimate rulers of Hanover, Hesse-Kassel, and Nassau, left the conservatives utterly bewildered. A small group, which grew steadily as time passed, stayed with Bismarck and the government and formed the Free Conservative party. This was composed of civil servants, professional people, industrialists, and big businessmen. Most of the old nobility, the large Prussian landowners, the Lutheran clergy, and some army officers, stayed loyal to the Old Conservative party.

The massive swing to Bismarck was reflected throughout Germany. Prussia's victory of 1866 seemed to convince many of the advantages of the realpolitik of the 1860s over the idealism of the 1840s. People wearied of supporting the unsuccessful policies of Austria and were frustrated by the seemingly unattainable goals of liberalism and constitutionalism. But beyond that, the unification of the country under Prussian leadership now seemed within reach. German nationalism drew its strongest support from the fear of foreign, especially French, aggression. There was a general desire to end German weakness and disunity and to prevent foreign intervention in German affairs such as had occurred in the Danish crisis of 1848 and the Olmuetz confrontation of 1850. The example of the recent unification of Italy also played an important part.[44] To most Germans it became simply a matter of priorities. If the country could be united first, constitutionalism could be achieved later.[45]

Foreign reaction to the formation of the North German Confederation was relatively mild. Bismarck's genius was everywhere admired and recognized; as long as Prussian domination did not extend beyond the Main, the European powers were not especially concerned.

The North German Confederation   Treaties between Prussia and the lesser north German states on August 18, 1866, laid the foundation of the North German Confederation. In these treaties, the governments agreed to elect a parliament by universal suffrage which would draft a federal constitution. The outline for this constitution was based on Bismarck's draft of December 1, 1866—based in turn on the famous Putbus dictations of October 30 and November 19—which, after a number of corrections and additions by various assistants and government agencies, was circulated to the governments of the North German states on December 15.[46] In spite of much adding and redrafting, the North German constitution was very much Bismarck's handiwork. Inasmuch as this constitution became, with minor changes, the constitution of the German Reich in 1871 and lasted in this form until 1918, the significance of Bismarck's work was inestimable.

From the time it was drafted, opinions have varied as to the constitution's intent and meaning: whether it established a German national state or whether it was merely a decoy for an enlarged Prussia, perpetuating Prussian hegemony in Germany. It is impossible to divine Bismarck's true intentions, but it can reasonably be assumed that he wanted to continue his and Prussia's control in any future national government. "The essence of the Bismarckian constitution was its conservation, by the use of revolutionary means, of the Prussian aristocratic-monarchical order in a century of increasingly dynamic economic and social change."[47]

Bismarck's draft and the version that was finally adopted provided for an Upper House, the Federal Council (*Bundesrat*), which was an assembly of representatives from the North German states in which Prussia, because of its size and population, had seventeen out of a total of forty-three votes. Prussia was also given the federal presidency (*Bundespraesidium*), which gave her authority over foreign representation and the conduct of foreign affairs. The Prussian king was made commander in chief of the Confederation's armed forces and executor of federal legislation, and he was given authority to declare war. Thus Prussia's hegemony in the federation was assured.[48] The Lower House (*Reichstag*) was composed of delegates elected for a three year period by universal male and direct suffrage. There was no provision for a supreme court, nor was there a bill of rights.

The most important debates in parliament on the proposed constitution revolved around ministerial responsibility and the Reichstag's budgetary powers. In Bismarck's draft there were no provisions for a federal government or a federal administration. The only parliamentary responsibility within the federation was between the state governments and their local diets and the instructions they issued to their representatives on the Federal Council. The National Liberal majority strongly objected to this "oversight" and asked for a ministry responsible to the Reichstag. Bismarck, who suspected quite rightly that this plan would lead to Reichstag approval of ministerial appointments, declared his firm opposition to such a measure and threatened to dissolve the assembly. Two proposals recommending ministerial responsibility were submitted by Bennigsen on March 26–27, 1867; both were defeated. A compromise establishing *one* responsible minister, without specifying the exact nature of his responsibility, was accepted.[49] The compromise was accepted by the liberals in the hope that they might later attain their goal of full ministerial responsibility.

In Bismarck's original draft, the chairman of the Federal Council was to be a federal chancellor (modeled after the Austrian representative to the Frankfurt Diet). He would be subordinate to the Prussian foreign minister, and would be an undersecretary for German affairs in the Foreign Ministry. He would be chairman at meetings, and would also act as executive secretary to the Federal Council.[50] In the course of the debates it soon became clear that the federal chancellorship would have to be combined with the office of Prussian minister-president and foreign minister; this position was, in effect, created for and around Bismarck. The responsibility of the future chancellor was not spelled out. Whom he would be responsible to and how this responsibility was to be implemented was not stipulated. The chancellor's responsibility was, at best, political or moral, not legal.[51]

By accepting "responsibility," the position of the chancellor had changed considerably from what Bismarck had originally intended it to be. The chancellor now became the chief federal minister. His government could now develop independently of Prussia and establish its own administration. Herein lay the principle that the chancellor was the responsible official for the direction of federal as well as Reich administration. At the same time, the chancellor's office stood between the Federal Council and the Reichstag and thus assumed governmental functions toward the latter as well. This greatly enhanced the position of the chancellor and gave the crown its most powerful weapon: the right to appoint and dismiss the chancellor and with him the leading administrative officials of the Confederation and later of the Reich.

On the question of budgetary powers, the delegates were able to obtain authority over a yearly civilian budget, but control over the military budget eluded them once again. A compromise was found by which the expenditures for the army were fixed by a quota system—1 percent of the population at 225 thaler per soldier—which was to remain unchanged until the end of 1871. (This became known as the "iron budget.") After that, the Reichstag was to have authority over military expenditures as well. (This was not achieved automatically, however, and another parliamentary struggle ensued in 1874 which resulted in a compromise—the *Septennat*, a law which gave the Reichstag the right to vote on the military budget only at intervals of seven years.)

On April 16, 1867, the parliamentary assembly accepted the constitution by a vote of 230 to 53. In opposition were the Progressives, the Poles, the Catholics, and August Bebel, the only socialist. To Bebel the whole Reichstag was "a mere figleaf to cover the nakedness of absolutism."[52] "Unity over freedom and power over law—this was the constellation under which the German Reich was born."[53]

The National Liberals overestimated the effects of their compromise on future constitutional developments, because Bismarck resisted all further attempts toward the creation of a parliamentary government for the rest of his term of office. Thus the dream of German liberals, to create a system modeled after that of Great Britain, was never achieved. Instead, a government of mixed powers was established and fundamental constitutional problems—the budgetary power and ministerial responsibility—were not resolved until half a century later, after a lost war and in the midst of a popular uprising.[54]

The Hohenzollern Candidature to the Spanish Throne and the War with France   After the Austro-Prussian war, the movement toward German unification was in complete disarray. The establishment of the North German Confederation, with the Main River line dividing the north from the south, seemed to make this division permanent and appeared to give Austria, as well as France, more influence in southern Germany than before. At the same time it became clear that both Britain and Russia would probably oppose any military action by the North German Confederation which would force the southern states into a union with the north. An evolutionary development toward unification was unlikely in the predictable future, inasmuch as anti-Prussian and particularist sentiments were widespread in the south. Even in Baden, a traditionally liberal state which favored unification, the pronational, liberal forces were badly divided.[55] Lack of popular support for Prussia was also apparent in the results of the 1868 elections to the Customs Union Parliament, when anti-Prussian forces received overwhelming majorities in Bavaria and Wuerttemberg, and were only narrowly defeated in Baden.

At the beginning of 1870 it seemed that Bismarck's policy toward unification along lesser German lines was not only blocked, but that opposition to his policy was gaining strength. The morale of Bismarck's supporters was correspondingly low, and to raise their morale and, at the same time, to get the national movement going again, the National Liberals suggested that Baden join the North German Confederation.[56] Bismarck, however, refused. This plan would have meant exposing Baden to economic retaliation and placing undue pressure on Bavaria and Wuerttemberg. Baden was the chief exponent of union with the north; if she joined the North German Confederation, the southern unification movement would lose its leader. The French would undoubtedly have been alarmed to see Baden a part of Bismarck's new state. Bismarck also realized that the other southern states would interpret such a move as aggression by the North, thus rendering the anti-French military assistance clauses between the Confederation and the south German states inoperative. This last consideration—that there had to be a clear case of French aggression to put the military alliance between the North and South German states into effect—became Bismarck's foremost concern. This was also essential domestically, to overcome the reluctance of the opposition parties, and equally crucial for foreign policy, to prevent Austria, Britain, or Russia from coming to the aid of France.

Of the three powers, only Austria could really have assisted France. In the aftermath of Koeniggraetz, France and Austria drew closer together, Austria reluctant to accept her exclusion from the Germanies, France concerned about losing her influence in southern Germany. When Napoleon visited the emperor in Salzburg in August 1867 to express his condolences over the death of Maximilian of Mexico, Francis Joseph's brother, the ministers of the two powers began negotiations aimed toward a future alliance. The talks were complicated and drawn out. Napoleon wanted Austrian assistance in maintaining south German independence and some commitments from Vienna in case of war with Prussia. This the Austrians refused. They realized that giving in to French demands would not only alienate Austria's German population, but it would also antagonize the Hungarians, who had recently achieved an equal voice in the affairs of the empire. (The Compromise of 1867.)

A break in the deadlocked Franco-Austrian negotiations occurred when the Italians indicated that they wanted to join a future Austro-French alliance, hoping in this way to gain Tyrol, Rome, and possibly Nice. Taking advantage of the Italian offer, the French circulated a draft treaty in March 1869 which substituted a few clauses stressing security and the peaceful intentions of the participating powers for the anti-Prussian tone of their original draft. The new draft provided for French neutrality in case of a Russo-Prussian war and Austrian neutrality in case of a Franco-Prussian war. Only if Russia or Prussia were to come to each other's aid would France or Austria enter the war. Italy would furnish 200,000 men in either case. But the Austrians were not willing to give up their neutrality under any circumstances and the Italians asked for French evacuation of Rome before they were willing to commit themselves. This Napoleon could not do because of pressure from the French clerics; for these reasons the grand scheme of a triple alliance against Prussia miscarried. France now stood alone.[57]

In the summer of 1866 the Eastern question came alive once more when a revolt in Crete against Turkish rule again brought the plight of Christian minorities to the attention of the powers. Russia, recovered from the Crimean War, hoped to reestablish her prestige among the Balkan peoples. She tried to persuade Britain and France to remind the Turkish government of its responsibilities for reforms promised to its subjects after 1823. But the two western powers were reluctant to get involved in the East at a time when the Luxembourg question focused their attention on the Rhine. Once the Luxembourg crisis was over, Czar Alexander and Gorchakov visited Paris, hoping to gain the diplomatic support that had eluded them earlier. But this visit was a failure; Napoleon III was unwilling to enter into serious commitments and an assassination attempt against the czar spoiled the Russians' stay.[58] French-Russian relations, which had suffered a setback during the Polish insurrection of 1863, reached an even lower ebb. Denied French support at the Straits, Gorchakov saw no reason for backing France on the Rhine. With Britain seemingly disinterested, and Austria openly competitive with Russia in the Balkans, Russia turned to Prussia.[59]

At the beginning of March 1868, Alexander proposed to the North German ambassador that the two countries support each other if one of them were involved in a war. Russia would put 100,000 troops on Austria's eastern frontier to keep her quiet if France attacked Prussia; in return, Alexander expected similar help from Prussia if Russia were involved with Austria in the Balkans. Bismarck welcomed the Russian initiative but was not willing to make any written commitments; instead, he persuaded the Russians to be satisfied with a mutual understanding of common aims and policies. For Bismarck and Prussia, the benefits of such an understanding were substantial and apparent in a little over two years.[60]

Bismarck, and with him German public opinion, was aware that Napoleon's domestic position had been so weakened by the diplomatic

BISMARCK'S THREE WARS

setbacks of the Austro-Prussian war, the Luxembourg question, the military debacle in Mexico, and the political developments in Italy,[61] that he could not possibly survive another diplomatic or military defeat. Following Prussia's victory over Austria, French public opinion began to realize that the country's prestige had suffered considerably. As a result, Napoleon III tried to recapture some of his former glory by looking toward France's northeastern border as a suitable area for expansion. Luxembourg seemed an especially suitable area for compensation. Louis Napoleon hoped to purchase the duchy from the king of the Netherlands and, because it was part of the German Customs Union (and a previous member of the German Confederation), he started negotiations with Bismarck to gain his approval of the scheme. Bismarck indicated that he would acquiesce as long as the arrangements were done quickly and quietly and without involving him in any way. The French, however, mismanaged the affair. News of the impending purchase was made known prematurely, the king of the Netherlands changed his mind when negotiations were almost completed, and Bismarck was asked in the Reichstag about the details involved. The Reichstag inquiry came from Bennigsen, and it is generally assumed that Bennigsen's tone, which was belligerently nationalistic—expressing the utmost determination to stop any and all attempts aimed at ceding ancient German territory from the fatherland—was drafted by Bismarck. Bismarck's reply, however, was cautious and calm, though it was clear that he would not resist popular opinion. The French, needless to say, were outraged and felt betrayed by these goings on.[62] It was equally clear that any move of Bismarck's that challenged, or even appeared to challenge, the position or prestige of France would elicit a violent response from Paris. Given these circumstances, all that was needed to excite French national feelings was a plausible excuse. Bismarck found this in the issue of the Hohenzollern candidature to the Spanish throne.

Contrary to long-cherished opinion, Bismarck was not suddenly inspired in the spring of 1870 to champion Prince Leopold, of the Sigmaringen and Catholic branch of the Hohenzollern family, as the candidate for the Spanish throne.[63] Bismarck apparently considered the situation as early as the fall of 1868, shortly after the Spanish queen's flight. In March 1870, when Salazar, the Spanish envoy, made a formal offer of the crown to Prince Leopold, Leopold accepted subject to the approval of King Wilhelm, head of the Hohenzollern family. Wilhelm was initially reluctant, but finally gave his blessings (June 19, 1870) at Bismarck's urging. Wilhelm was persuaded by the very favorable report of Bucher and Versen, who had been sent to Madrid to report on conditions in Spain. It seems certain now that these "reports" were prepared in Berlin, and probably under Bismarck's supervision.[64] The climate in Spain, contrary to the reports, was most unfavorable for a Hohenzollern prince.

In Spain, Parliament adjourned before it could vote on Prince Leopold's candidature; rumors of the Hohenzollern candidature reached Paris, where French opposition was predictably strong. When asked, Bismarck adopted a most innocent demeanor and insisted that this was entirely a Hohenzollern family affair and that he knew no more than was printed in the newspapers. In the second week of July, Benedetti, the French ambassador, had an audience with King Wilhelm at Ems and expressed his government's grave concern. He asked that the candidacy of Prince Leopold be withdrawn. Wilhelm, entirely unaware of Bismarck's machinations and not in favor of Leopold's candidacy to begin with, told Benedetti that it was up to Leopold, or his father Charles Anthon, to make up their minds in this matter. Privately, Wilhelm wrote to Leopold, advising him to withdraw his name, and on July 12, Charles Anthon did so on behalf of his son.[65]

Bismarck, who had spent several days on his estate at Varzin to demonstrate his lack of involvement in these affairs, was furious at the turn of events. He became still more enraged when he learned that the French government, not satisfied with Leopold's formal renunciation, had requested another interview with King Wilhelm on the following day (July 13). On this occasion Benedetti asked Wilhelm for a written guarantee of Leopold's refusal and a promise not to revive the candidacy in the future. The king refused these requests, politely but firmly, and when Benedetti asked to see him once more, Wilhelm declined to receive him. Wilhelm sent a telegraphic account of this encounter to Bismarck who, upon receiving it, edited it in such a way that it appeared to be a personal affront to Benedetti and a slur on the honor of France.[66] The French, already enraged over the affair, accepted the challenge and, predictably, declared war on Prussia on July 19, 1870.

The course of these events has long been known; what fascinates historians to this day, however, is the extent of Bismarck's involvement and his underlying motives.[67] It now seems fairly certain, on the basis of newly discovered documents and a reinterpretation of old ones, that Bismarck planned a war from the very beginning. In this aim he had much of public opinion and the influential business community solidly behind him.

The center of controversy in the North German Confederation was the constitutional stalemate over the military question. This and the high level of armaments among the major European powers had a deadening effect on business and trade. As the Prussian crown prince noted to Lord Acton, "the persons who had most urged on the war at Berlin, [sic] had been the bankers, who had declared that another six months of armed uncertainty would ruin Germany."[68]

The compromise over the military budget which ended the constitutional conflict in 1866 had led to the adoption of the "iron budget,"[69] which was to be effective until 1871. There are indications that Bismarck, when accepting this compromise, counted on a war with France before 1871 to solve his parliamentary problems as the war with Austria had solved similar problems in 1866. The 1871 session of the North German Parliament would have to deal once again with the explosive issue of the right of Parliament to control military expenditures. For Bismarck the problem could be solved only along the lines of monarchical principles and Prussian militarism, and to this end a victorious war with France was necessary. At the same time, it had to be a war in defense of legitimate German and Prussian interests, so that the secret defense treaties with the South German states would be put into effect, and to achieve the benefit of European and German public opinion.

France's reaction to Prussia's victory in 1866 and her frustration in the Luxembourg crisis made it more than likely that she would react violently to the Spanish crisis. France's susceptibility was common knowledge, and to believe that Bismarck was unable to foresee the consequences, "requires an act of faith."[70] Whether or not Bismarck really aimed at a preventive war with France, particularly after Gramont became foreign minister, has not been established; the answer must await further research and clarification of French foreign policy. But Bismarck's determination to bring about a war "seems to be the predominant trait in his policy toward the Spanish Candidature."[71]

Thus, when France declared war, an irresistible patriotic wave swept Germany, and north and south united to defeat the French aggressor.

Victory by the combined armies of North and South Germany was made possible by the superior military leadership of Helmuth von Moltke, the chief of staff of the Prussian army, and by the organizational talent of Albrecht von Roon, the Prussian war minister. In a rapid campaign reminiscent of the one against Austria, the German armies defeated the French at Woerth and Weissenburg. The decisive victory occurred at Sedan on September 1, 1870. The French army capitulated and Napoleon III was captured. This should have been the end of the war, for Bismarck was ready to enter into peace negotiations with the emperor. But for the French people, and especially the Parisians, the war was not yet over. They proclaimed a republic (September 4), established a government of national defense, and vowed to continue the war until the Germans were defeated and driven out of the country. Their military prowess, however, was not equal to their patriotic fervor. The German armies, sweeping all resistance aside, advanced rapidly and by September 19 had reached the outskirts of Paris. The long siege of the city began.[72]

This unexpected prolongation of the war created serious strains in the Prussian military-political leadership and led to an open break between Bismarck and Moltke. Moltke, with his narrow military outlook, wanted all political and diplomatic negotiations suspended while military operations were in progress, while Bismarck, with a much wider view, was aware of the constant interaction between political and military strategy. Bismarck was willing to explore the possibilities of a Bonapartist regency during the siege of Sedan, while Moltke worried that the negotiations would deprive the army of a well-earned victory. During the siege of Paris a similar dispute regarding the bombardment of the city and negotiations with the provisional French government finally led to a break between the two men, and Moltke denied Bismarck all access to military intelligence and planning. Considering that Bismarck had fought some bitter parliamentary battles not so long ago to preserve the power of the Prussian military establishment, Moltke's opposition to the chancellor seemed especially ironic. It was only through the king's intervention on Bismarck's behalf that unity was restored at the highest level of Prussian leadership. At the heart of the conflict lay the question of timing and methods regarding peace negotiations while military operations were still in progress; though Bismarck eventually gained the upper hand, Moltke's prolonged and stubborn opposition established an important precedent which was to have disastrous results under less able civilian leadership during the First World War.[73]

Diplomatic Negotiations with France for an Armistice and with the South German States for the Establishment of a New Reich   Bismarck's negotiations with Jules Favre, the acting foreign minister, began at Ferrièrs, outside Paris, on September 18. From the very beginning the territorial issue dominated the negotiations. The foremost German war aim was the demand for Alsace-Lorraine. It was met by equally determined French resistance. "Not an inch of our territory or stone of our fortresses,"[74] Favre told Bismarck, and the negotiations were broken off. French defiance was based on its newly organized armies and on an appeal for assistance to the other powers. They were to be disappointed on both counts. The armies were defeated and Thiers's mission to London, Vienna, and St. Petersburg proved futile.[75] Russia's attitude, which was decisive for the French, was influenced by Bismarck's pro-Russian policy in Poland and by the czar's concern over the revolutionary government in Paris. Still, Bismarck wanted to end hostilities before a change in the European diplomatic constellation led to intervention by the powers.

An opportunity to renew the negotiations presented itself at the end of January 1871, when worsening conditions in Paris (there was only enough bread for two more days) led Favre to ask for a meeting with Bismarck on January 23. These negotiations led to an armistice by which the French surrendered the Parisian forts and agreed to pay an indemnity of 200 million francs, but insisted that the Germans not occupy Paris or take Belfort. The armistice was set for 21 days (it was later extended several times) during which elections for a national assembly were to be held to form a new French government.[76]

After the elections, Thiers, who had been elected head of the government, came to Versailles for further negotiations with Bismarck; after long and arduous conferences, a preliminary peace was signed on February 26, 1871. It provided for German annexation of Alsace and part of Lorraine, a French indemnity of 5 billion francs, and German occupation of northern France to ensure payment. Thiers managed to retain Belfort for France but had to allow the Germans to enter Paris. A definite treaty was to be signed later on.[77]

Even while the battles in northern France continued, the problem of the future shape of a united Germany became a major issue. The attitude of the four South German states, Baden, Hesse, Wuerttemburg, and Bavaria, was crucial to this question. The attitude of each toward the new Reich and the conditions under which they were willing to join differed considerably. Baden was willing to recognize the constitution of the North German Confederation and to join unconditionally. Hesse, because of its geographic position, wedged between Baden and the western provinces of Prussia, had little choice but to follow Baden's example. Wuerttemberg, however, fought for special rights and a change in the North German constitution, though she was, in principle, ready to enter the new Reich. Only Bavaria refused outright. Bavaria, along with Saxony, wanted a redrafting of the North German constitution and the founding of a new federation. Their aim was to break Prussian hegemony and create a looser federal organization in which each state retained a wider margin of sovereignty. This Bismarck opposed energetically. He realized that Prussia's dominant position in the new Germany was at stake, and while he was willing to make certain concessions to the sovereign rights and particularist feelings of the southern states, he was not ready to sacrifice substantial power to them. He insisted that the southern states give up their right to an independent foreign policy to the new federal state.

Bismarck's concept of the new Reich was based on the established North German Confederation and union between it and the south German states. The new Reich government would have authority over the army and navy, and its own source of income through tariffs, con-

sumer taxes, and shipping duties. There would be a uniform system of weights and measures, a common currency, and a common law to promote trade and industry. Legislative powers would be exercised through a federal assembly and a parliament (the Reichstag), and the executive powers through the Prussian king, who would also be commander in chief of the army and navy.[78]

Bavaria held the key to the new Reich. If her opposition could be overcome, the other southern states would follow suit. If she stayed out, the Reich would be weakened and susceptible to Austrian and French influence. At the same time Bismarck realized that undue pressure on Bavaria had to be avoided so as not to complicate future developments. After the victory at Sedan, Bavaria reconsidered her position and entered into negotiations with Bismarck. Bavaria demanded the right to send and receive diplomatic representatives, to conclude treaties (so long as they were not contrary to federal interests) and, in time of peace, to maintain her own army, railroad, post and telegraph system, and her own legislative, administrative, and financial powers. The real stumbling block was her refusal to enter the new Reich under the existing North German constitution. The Bavarian negotiators demanded a reorganization of the federal union on a new and less centralized basis which would give Bavaria a special position.

Concurrently, Bismarck held private talks with Bavarian representatives involving the payment of a subsidy to King Ludwig of Bavaria in return for his offering the imperial crown to King Wilhelm.[79] There were, furthermore, negotiations with Baden, Hesse, and Wuerttemberg aimed at isolating Bavaria, and when these were unsuccessful, Bismarck threatened to bypass an assembly of German princes, which was to approve the peace treaty with France and the constitution of the new Reich, and go directly to the people. As he had done so often in the past, he played two tunes simultaneously, the liberal and the conservative. When the latter failed, he turned to German public opinion which, anxious for unification, was kept in a state of excitement by a well-directed press campaign and by the prospect of participating in the final decisions. In the face of these well-orchestrated proceedings, Baden and Hesse signed a treaty with the North German Confederation on November 15, Bavaria joined on November

23, and Wuerttemberg on November 25, 1870. Aside from some minor changes in the North German constitution and certain privileges granted to Bavaria, the new Reich was but an extension of the North German Confederation.[80]

The final ceremony in the great hall of mirrors at Versailles on January 18, 1871, was entirely in character with the course the unification of Germany had taken. Kings and princes of the German states and generals and officers of the victorious armies attended, and, of course, Bismarck. Only the representatives of the German people were missing.[81]

The New Reich

"Now that we have achieved the most cherished dream of our lives, what is there left to live for?" Heinrich von Sybel exclaimed after the unification.[1] Most of his contemporaries, liberals and nationalists alike, expressed similar sentiments. Those who had doubted after the Revolution of 1848 that their country would ever be unified now rejoiced. It had all come true, because of the genius of Bismarck, and praise of his accomplishments echoed across the land. The future looked brilliant, and the first years after unification fulfilled the highest expectations. Then, suddenly, a severe economic and financial crisis led to bitter disillusionment. In the midst of this crisis, Bismarck began his fight with the Catholic church—the *Kulturkampf*—and then, in the late 1870s, his anti-Socialist crusade. These two domestic struggles caused widespread dissatisfaction among Catholics and workers who, through their political parties—the Center party and the Social Democratic party—formed the core of the government's opposition. These dissidents were joined by the French from Alsace-Lorraine, the Guelphs from Hanover, the Danes from Schleswig-Holstein, and the Poles from East and West Prussia. Taken together they made a formidable group whose diversity and size are an index of Bismarck's failure in domestic affairs.

It seems ironic that a man who was able, despite three wars, to convince the European powers of his peaceful intentions was unable to achieve a similar success at home. Bismarck apparently never fully understood the forces that transformed central Europe from an agrarian to an industrial economy and from a rural to an urban society, nor did he appreciate the consequences of these changes for German political life. His aim was to preserve the monarchy and the established social order, based on the nobility, the bureaucracy, and the army. While he was willing to make concessions in economic matters, he refused to do so in political affairs. With foreign wars no longer a necessity after the unification, Bismarck transferred the struggle to the domestic scene; his fight against Catholics and Socialists can be considered a device to divert popular attention from unresolved social and constitutional problems.

Bismarck's personal style of conducting affairs of state brooked no outside interference; he was intolerant of colleagues, and forever suspicious of real or imaginary rivals such as Arnim and Stosch.[2] Nor were his assistants as devoted and loyal as earlier historians have believed. Bismarck was an exacting taskmaster, but he was also a capricious superior. "He disdained stupidity and rebuffed independence. He wanted intelligent servants without private judgment or ambition, well-wrought tools for his master hands."[3] He never quite knew how to deal with party politicians; in Windthorst, for example, Bismarck could only see the defeated Hanoverian minister bent on revenge, never the leader of the Center party.[4] Bismarck was unable to tolerate opposing points of view, however sincere, and always considered opposition to his policies as personal attacks, motivated by selfish or group interests.[5] According to Holstein, one of the chancellor's closest and most faithful subordinates, Bismarck was a cynic in his relationships with his fellowmen, using or dropping people whenever it suited his purpose.[6] Contrary to his methods in foreign affairs, he tended to exaggerate domestic conflicts, declaring open warfare on his opponents instead of working toward peaceful solutions. These attitudes and policies were ill suited to healthy political development, nor were they designed to attract able men to politics.

> The achievements of 1871 had been extraordinary, and an age that glorified heroes rather than analyzed anonymous social and economic forces attributed them to Bismarck's genius. He had forged institutions that would promote Germany's power by providing for common commercial and foreign policies and that would guarantee Germany's survival by a common military establishment under thinly disguised Prussian hegemony. By creating a national parliament, Bismarck had inserted democratic and popular elements into the structure of the Reich without materially weakening the preceding monarchical-conservative order. By making concessions to modernity, the old order prolonged its life. The new Reich facilitated the immense expansion of material power—though the attendant social transformation undermined Bismarck's political structure. Bismarck was slow to appreciate the danger from that quarter. He was more attuned to

foreign dangers. For the great Bismarck was at home abroad, and estranged at home.

He devoted his best efforts to shielding Germany from foreign wars. His greatest accomplishment after 1871 was his assimilation of Germany into the European state system; he persuaded a suspicious Europe that Germany had become a satiated power—and by the time Europe fully believed him, he was dismissed from office, and Germany ceased being satiated.[7]

Thus, his achievements, while remarkable, were mixed and altogether not solid enough to last more than seventy-five years.

The Annexation of Alsace-Lorraine   The final peace treaty with France, signed at Frankfurt on May 10, 1871,[8] contained two provisions which caused major problems in the development of the Reich: the acquisition of Alsace-Lorraine and the French war indemnity of five billion francs. The former became a constant and sometimes major irritant to Franco-German relations and was a contributing factor to the outbreak of World War I, while the latter was one of the more important causes of the economic depression of 1873 which had a major impact on German economic and political affairs.

In retrospect it is easy to see that the annexation of Alsace-Lorraine was a tragic mistake, though it was clear even at the time that France would not suffer the loss of her provinces with equanimity. In view of Bismarck's lenient terms for Austria in 1866 and his avowed desire for peaceful relations with France after the war, his insistence on acquiring this territory (the mineral wealth of which was not known at the time) is difficult to understand. The usual explanation has been that he reluctantly gave in to overwhelming military pressure; the general staff considered the provinces of the utmost importance for the next war against France. But the problem was more complicated than that. In 1870–71, the annexation of Alsace-Lorraine was, for German public opinion, an expression of the popular, national spirit of the unification movement. The acquisition of the French provinces was not the result of old-fashioned power or cabinet diplomacy. This popular aspect was further supported by memories of French invasions of German territory in the revolutionary and Napoleonic wars. Strasbourg, especially, had been a bone of contention between Germany and France for several hundred years, changing rulers whenever the fortunes of war favored one side. Thus, the vast majority of Germans looked upon the acquisition of Alsace-Lorraine as a legitimate and even necessary part of the peace treaty.[9]

There were, however, other considerations, such as the self-determination of the local population, which was overwhelmingly French in the case of Lorraine, and at least partly so in the case of Alsace, and the constitutional problem of the status of the annexed provinces within the Reich. The annexation of Alsace-Lorraine also diminished the chances of a lasting settlement with France within the framework of a new European alignment, and affected Germany's future role among the great powers. Popular demand for annexation appeared shortly after the start of the Franco-Prussian War, first in South Germany and then in the North. These claims appear to have arisen spontaneously: there is no sign of governmental influence on the press. A few liberal papers, such as the *Frankfurter Zeitung*, opposed annexation on the grounds that it would make the war appear to have been aggressive rather than defensive, and to have been directed against the French people rather than Napoleon III and his government, as many Germans believed it to have been. The nationalistic press dismissed these arguments as sentimental drivel. The preference of the local population would soon be changed under German rule, according to these papers, and the principle of self-determination should be secondary to the demands of German nationalism. Or, as a Wuerttemberg liberal expressed it during the first month of the Franco-Prussian War, "the opposition of the population [in Alsace-Lorraine] cannot be taken into account; we are neither sentimental politicians nor doctrinaire fools. Nationalism [that is, pro-Germanism in Alsace-Lorraine] will come to the fore in due time. Until then, the country can be kept in check and governed militarily."[10] At about the same time a majority of Germans became convinced that the French nation, and not Napoleon III, was the real enemy, and that under these circumstances demands for annexation were valid.

Bismarck's own attitude did not follow public opinion. He seems to have decided on annexation at an early stage, though it is impossible to determine exactly when he made up his mind. It is known that during the Revolution of 1848 he asked that Strasbourg be again incorporated into the Reich. He believed that France would hate Germany and seek revenge in any case, and meanwhile Alsace-Lorraine would provide much-needed security for southern Germany. Then too, Bismarck strongly believed in realpolitik,[11] and this called for annexation of territory after a victorious war. (The example of 1866 did not contradict this principle, because Prussia's failure to acquire Austrian territory was compensated for by Prussian annexations in central Germany.) This concept of power politics demanded that France be weakened territorially, militarily, and economically. France, prior to the war, was vastly superior to Germany in military and economic strength and Bismarck, the leader of a relatively minor power, could not have foreseen that Germany would eclipse France in the following decades.

While German public opinion was overwhelmingly in favor of annexation, this was not a decisive factor for Bismarck. He could have led public opinion toward a negotiated peace after Sedan, but he chose instead to emphasize the dangers of foreign intervention and the stubborn resistance of the French. He was neither the exponent nor the opponent of German national opinion. He considered the problem as an aspect of foreign policy, and was not concerned with its future domestic implications—the form of the territory's integration into the new Reich—and, as it turned out, his policy was shortsighted and mistaken on both counts.

Political and Economic Reversals   The five billion franc indemnity that France was forced to pay as part of the peace treaty created an unprecedented economic boom in Germany. Industrial expansion, building construction, and land and stock market speculation reached new heights, and people believed that an age of continuous prosperity had finally arrived.[12] When, in 1873, the bubble burst because of overexpansion, overproduction, and manipulation of the stock market, the consequences were far-reaching.[13] Industrialists and businessmen demanded protective tariffs to strengthen home industries, alleviate unemployment, and avert the threat of socialism. During the War-in-Sight crisis of 1875,[14] they also advocated a strong industrial base to bolster Germany's military strength.[15] Artisans and shopkeepers asked for state protection, curtailment of free trade, and the end of economic individualism. Farmers and peasants united in demanding cheap credit, lower taxes, higher prices for their products, and protection against exploitation by middlemen. And the workers began to organize themselves under the pressure of unemployment and industrial dislocation.[16]

The way out of the economic crisis appeared increasingly to be protective tariffs. At the same time, the need for tax reforms to make the Reich financially independent of the states, the promulgation of a new army budget, and the reorganization of Reich ministries combined to create a deadlock between Bismarck and the liberal majority in the Reichstag. Bismarck's proposal for a fixed and permanent army budget was rejected by the liberals who, for the first time since the unification, opposed the government.[17] Under pressure from public opinion, a compromise was reached and army expenditures were fixed by law for a seven-year period; this law became known as the *Septennat*. Still, the liberals were none too happy. On the question of tax reforms and reorganization of Reich ministries, they wanted ministers of the government to be responsible to the Reichstag, a demand which Bismarck refused.[18]

By 1875–76 Bismarck's domestic policy of moderate liberalism appeared to have failed[19] and his foreign policy of isolating France had proved unsuccessful.[20] A change of allies and policies, both domestic and foreign, seemed clearly in order.[21] At home, Bismarck looked for and found support among leaders of heavy industry and high finance, and by sacrificing Delbrueck, head of the Reich Chancery and the chief proponent of free trade (who resigned April 25, 1876), the chancellor's shift toward protectionism was firmly initiated. In the wake of a severe agricultural depression at the end of 1875, protectionism gained additional support from agrarian interests. As a result of the depression Germany turned from a wheat-exporting to a wheat-importing country, and unrestricted overseas and Russian imports severely endangered German, and especially Prussian, agriculture. Thus agrarian and industrial interests, both traditionally strong supporters of the Church and the monarchy, combined in their demands for protective tariffs.[22] They would also be able to provide solid conservative support for Bismarck, should he ever choose to abandon the liberals.

The economic depression had discredited liberal policies all along the line, and had "laid bare the foundations of *soi-disant* liberalism in the Germano-Prussian state."[23] The 1877 Reichstag election resulted in a conservative majority and a decline in liberal strength. Protectionists, largely with the help of the Center party, also increased their power.[24] This conservative-protectionist alliance in the Reichstag enabled Bismarck to carry through his tax reforms and the reorganization of the Reich administration. These developments meant an increase in the chancellor's authority and a defeat for the liberals; they strengthened the conservative forces and preserved the leading position of the Prussian nobility, the army, the bureaucracy, and the foreign service. This conservative-agrarian-industrial alliance, which became characteristic of the political-economic structure of the Reich, endured long after Bismarck. In domestic affairs, the alliance of conservative interests contributed to Germany's failure to solve her social problems, led to the anti-Socialist struggle, and was also a factor in her pursuit of colonial acquisition and world policy. Thus, 1877–79 can be considered more decisive for the future development of Germany than 1870–71, the years of Germany's unification.[25]

The political-economic reversal from a liberal to a conservative policy and from free trade to protectionism was a major, though not the only, consequential development in Germany in the 1870s. Two significant conflicts—the Prussian government's fight against the Catholic church (the *Kulturkampf*), and the Reich government's campaign against the Socialists—took up most of the two decades of Bismarck's chancellorship.

The Kulturkampf In the new Reichstag which opened in Berlin on March 21, 1871, the fifty-eight delegates of the Center party were second in number only to the National Liberals. The Center party was founded in Prussia in 1870 to represent the interests of the Roman Catholic minority in the Prussian Parliament and, after the unification of Germany, it expanded its organization in the hope of attracting non-Catholics to its ranks. In this it was only partially successful. A few Poles and Guelphs joined the party and supported its opposition to Bismarck, but the overwhelming majority was made up of Catholics from Bavaria, Silesia, the Rhineland, and Westphalia. It was composed of peasants, workers, shopkeepers, and intellectuals. Suspicious of any forces not under his control, and forever looking for conspiracies directed against his person as well as his policies, Bismarck believed that the Center party constituted a major threat to the new Reich. He habitually equated his person with the state, so that an attack on one invariably was seen as an attack on the other. To Bismarck, the Center party was particularly suspicious because of its connection with the papacy, its support of the papal dogma of infallibility,[26] and more recently, its stand in favor of federalism and against the centralizing tendencies within the new Reich.

"Thinking himself far more infallible than the Pope," Lord Russell, the British minister in Berlin, wrote to the Foreign Office, Bismarck could not "tolerate two infallibles in Europe and fancies he can select and appoint the next Pontiff as he could a Prussian general who will carry out his orders to the Catholic clergy in Germany and elsewhere."[27] Bismarck also believed that a Catholic conspiracy, involving Austria, Italy, France, his domestic enemies, and possibly the Empress Augusta, existed.[28]

Politically, the struggle began over two issues: the right of the Catholic church to regulate its own affairs as guaranteed by the Prussian constitution of 1850, and the Center party's support of certain fundamental rights in the Reich constitution. Joining in this struggle for fundamental rights were the Reichstag delegates from Alsace-Lorraine, Schleswig-Holstein, and those of the Polish minorities and other splinter groups, which made the Center party the leader of the opposition.[29] Outside the Reichstag a controversy erupted over the Catholic church's teaching of the dogma of papal infallibility, which the government considered unwarranted interference in its domain. The liberals, who wanted to secularize the schools and rid the Church of its medieval superstitions, vigorously supported the government's stand against the Church. To the liberals, the *Kulturkampf* signified a struggle between modernity and medievalism; the essence of German culture (hence the term *Kulturkampf* or cultural struggle) was at stake. Just as the Holy See defended the powers of the Church against the encroachments of the state and of modern science, the government and the liberals meant to extend the knowledge of science for the improvement of mankind, the recent discoveries of Darwin being a special case in point.

The first incident in the *Kulturkampf* occurred when state-employed Catholic theologians and religious instructors refused to teach

the dogma of papal infallibility. When their superior, Bishop Kre-
mentz, suspended them from all future teaching, the Prussian minister of culture refused to recognize the bishop's decision and, after
extended altercation, terminated all state subsidies to the bishop on
September 25, 1870.[30] The following summer the Catholic section of
the Prussian ministry of culture was dissolved because its officials had
allegedly supported Polish and Catholic, rather than German, interests in Prussia's eastern provinces. This action was followed, in March
1872, by a new school law which substituted state supervision for
ecclesiastical supervision in the schools. That summer the Jesuits were
expelled from Germany (June 1872) and their Society was dissolved. In
May 1873 the Falk Laws, named after Adalbert Falk, the Prussian
minister of education and ecclesiastical affairs, restricted the training
and employment of priests, limited the disciplinary powers of the
Church, made civil marriage obligatory, and made it easier for Prussians to leave the Catholic church.[31]

These measures aroused the unanimous and determined opposition
of Catholic bishops, the lower clergy, and the laity. If the struggle's
aim had been the destruction of the Center party, the results were
disappointing. The party, as well as other Catholic organizations,
emerged stronger and more resolute in its opposition to the government. Taking advantage of the freedom of the press, the Center party
almost doubled its voting strength in the election of 1874 and received
nearly 28 percent of the total popular vote. The effects of the government's measures and the clergy's opposition to them created hardships for Prussia's Catholic population. Young theologians refused
to take the prescribed stated examinations, and the closing of sem-
inaries and the refusal of bishops to fill existing vacancies led to a severe shortage of parish priests and to a crisis in the religious welfare
of many Catholic communities. By 1876 most of Prussia's Catholic
bishops had either been arrested or fled abroad.

The overall effects of the *Kulturkampf* on Prussia and Germany are
difficult to assess. For Bismarck and the liberals it was a struggle for
the supremacy of the state over the Church. In this struggle, the liberals soon found themselves in a very awkward position. While they
were for the separation of church and state and for state education and
opposed to the federalistic and particularistic tendencies of the Center

party, they were forced, in support of the *Kulturkampf*, to agree to a series of coercive measures that were not at all to their liking. The liberals took this stand believing that it would strengthen their powers and those of the Reichstag against the chancellor's semiautocratic policies in other fields. The liberals were not successful in enlarging their powers or that of the Reichstag; they overestimated their powers and political skills compared to those of Bismarck. As the future was to show, Bismarck did not need their support, and by the end of the decade he abandoned them without further ado and switched to the conservatives.

The conservatives, especially the Protestants among them, were also in a dilemma. Many were anti-Catholic; if they did not actively support the *Kulturkampf*, they tacitly approved of it. But while they opposed papal infallibility and were glad to be rid of the Jesuits, they were also opposed to the separation of church and state, the government's educational policies, the provisions for civil marriage, and the limitation of ecclesiastical independence. A relatively small group of Old Conservatives, led by Ludwig von Gerlach, opposed Bismarck outright. They considered his struggle with the Roman Catholic church an attack on Christian religion and Christian principles. In their view, Prussia was a Christian state which had received its original mandate from the Church through the Teutonic Knights; Bismarck's policy was, therefore, against true Prussian interests and tradition.

Caught in the crossfire of conflicting religious emotions and state policies, Emperor Wilhelm probably suffered a great deal. His basic sympathies and loyalties were often—though not always—with the Old Prussian Conservatives, an attitude which was shared by the queen.[32] But the chancellor, by persuasion, tact, persistence, and sheer force of personality, was able to convince the king of the reasonableness and the necessity of the *Kulturkampf*.

Bismarck, like many observers at the time, was unaware that federalist and particularist tendencies, as represented by the Center party and its allies, were still very much in evidence despite unification. Considering that the actual powers of the Reich—as distinct from those of Prussia—were few in number and limited in scope, Bismarck attempted to strengthen the state's position over the Church just at

THE NEW REICH

the time when the Church, through the decisions of the Vatican Council, was trying to redress the imbalance that had existed for centuries in Germany. The fight was not initially directed exclusively against the Catholic church—though it quickly became so because of the Catholic church's strong centralized organization and resistance—but against the Protestant church as well. Thus, Bismarck wanted to abolish the position of *summus episcopus* (ranking bishop; that is, highest church office of the German Protestant territorial princes), to take over the administration of schools, Protestant or Catholic, at least at the secondary level and if possible at the elementary level as well, and to limit the Church to religious instruction. The chancellor also wanted to ensure the state's right to approve all ecclesiastical appointments and to move the administration of religious affairs from the Ministry of Culture to the Ministry of Justice.

Foreign reaction to the *Kulturkampf*, including the pastoral letters of the French bishops in support of German Catholics, and Pius IX's encyclical of November 21, 1873, protesting the *Kulturkampf*, reinforced Bismarck's suspicion that there was an international Catholic conspiracy against Germany; these developments made him more determined than ever to curb the powers of the Church.[33] But the struggle dragged on, the resistance of the Church remained unbroken, and the strength of the Center party even increased. The resistance of the Old Conservatives and of the orthodox wing of the Protestant clergy against the *Kulturkampf* also stiffened, and the government began to lose popular support just at the time when the adverse effects of the economic depression were being felt throughout the country. By the end of the decade, Bismarck had grown tired of the struggle and was ready to seek some form of accommodation. At about the same time, the leadership of the Center party also appeared willing to come to terms with the government. In political outlook, social composition, and geographic distribution, the Center party was particularly well suited to represent the Reich's new economic interests. Since the beginning of the *Kulturkampf* a considerable number of industrialists and landowners who favored higher tariffs and were opposed to liberalism and laissez faire had joined the Center party, and the party was now ready to use its influence for political ends, especially to press for the termination of the *Kulturkampf*.[34] Bismarck's aim had never been the destruction of the Church, nor had he intended to break with the Old Conservatives. The death of Pope Pius IX, in 1878, presented an opportunity to end this futile struggle. Pius's successor, Leo XIII, was more amenable to compromise and negotiations between Prussia and the Holy See started in September 1879.[35] In June of the following year Falk resigned as Prussian minister for education and ecclesiastical affairs, and his resignation made it easier for Bismarck to change his policy toward the Catholic church in Prussia.

Negotiations with the Holy See and a change in Prussian ecclesiastical legislation led to a gradual easing of tension. Eventually, diplomatic relations with the Vatican were restored (1882) and some of the more stringent anti-Catholic laws were repealed (1882–87).[36] The *Kulturkampf* was not a glorious episode in Bismarck's career. He saw it as part of the age-old struggle between church and state, a relationship which had to be redefined periodically. To him it was essentially a political, and not a philosophical, struggle; but in his quest for state supremacy, he was unable to confine it to the political arena. When the *Kulturkampf* spilled over into the religious field, the results were disastrous for the new Reich.[37]

A Change in Political Alignment and the Anti-Socialist Crusade
Bismarck's dislike for and suspicion of parties and organizations with international connections were not limited to the Catholic church. They extended to the Socialist movement as well, particularly since the Socialists had attracted a considerable number of voters and had increased their delegates in the Reichstag from two in 1871 to twelve in 1877. Bismarck's attempts to suppress the Socialists, combined with the economic depression, tended to strengthen rather than weaken the workers' movement. The two existing workers' organizations, Ferdinand Lassalle's General German Workers' Movement (*Allgemeiner Deutscher Arbeiterverein*), founded in Leipzig on May 23, 1863, and August Bebel and Wilhelm Liebknecht's Social Democratic Labor Party, organized in Eisenach on August 7, 1869, were drawn closer together as a result of Bismarck's anti-Socialist policy. From the beginning there had been considerable rivalry and friction between the two parties. Lassalle's faction was more concerned with immediate and practical achievements, while the Bebel-Liebknecht wing was

THE NEW REICH

more ideologically inclined and, at least theoretically, more faithful to the teachings of Marx and Engels. On May 22, 1875, at Gotha, the two parties united to form the Social Democratic Labor Party of Germany (*Sozialdemokratische Deutsche Arbeiter Partei*, SDP).

Bismarck's halfhearted attempts to suppress the Socialist movement in the early 1870s had failed,[38] but when, in 1878, two attempts were made on the emperor's life, Bismarck took advantage of the public outrage and used these incidents to launch an anti-Socialist crusade. The underlying motives for this campaign are difficult to fathom, particularly since the end of the *Kulturkampf* was nowhere in sight and it was not Bismarck's habit to fight two major campaigns simultaneously. He preferred to destroy his enemies one at a time, after having made certain that they were isolated and without friends and allies. In this case he clearly misjudged the situation. He may have believed that with public feeling so strong he would be able to destroy the Social Democratic party in a short time and with little effort. The chancellor considered the party's growth dangerous to the monarchy and to the social and religious makeup of the state; and in foreign affairs, he was concerned that the SDP, like the Catholic Center party, would use its international connections to ally with Germany's enemies. In the aftermath of the economic recession of 1873 and the general antiliberal trend throughout the country, the time seemed propitious for an anti-Socialist campaign. This tendency in Bismarck's thinking was reinforced by his desire to rely on political support from the conservatives rather than the liberals and to abandon the Reich's free trade stance.[39]

With the help of the conservatives, he hoped to get an "exceptional law" (*Ausnahmegesetz*) through the Reichstag which would outlaw the Social Democratic party. The occasion came after the May 11, 1878, attempt to assassinate the emperor. But the bill failed to pass because the conservatives, though eager to fight the Socialists, were afraid of the precedent such a law would create. The following week, however, a second assassination attempt seriously wounded Wilhelm I. Bismarck blamed this act on the Socialists, though their responsibility was never proven, and used the incident as an excuse to dissolve the Reichstag and call for new elections.[40] The chancellor hoped that public outrage would cause the Social Democrats to lose heavily at the polls. His expectations were not fulfilled, for the party only lost three deputies overall; it actually gained strength in Berlin and other major cities. In the same election the liberal parties lost heavily, and in general there was a distinct shift to the right. (The number of National Liberal delegates declined from 127 to 99 and the Progressives lost 9 seats, while the number of Conservatives rose from 40 to 59, the Free Conservatives gained 19 seats, and the Center added 6 deputies to its ranks.)[41]

When the exceptional law came up before the new Reichstag, the Conservatives, Free Conservatives, and National Liberals supported it, while the Progressives and the Center opposed it. (The Center, still suffering under *Kulturkampf* legislation, refused to sanction any repressive bill.) On October 19, however, the Reichstag passed the anti-Socialist bill by a vote of 221 to 149. The measure was not quite as severe as Bismarck had hoped it would be. While it "empowered state and local governments to abolish societies with 'social-democratic, socialistic, or communist' tendencies . . . and to prohibit the publication and distribution of Social Democratic newspapers, periodicals, and books . . . and to impose a Minor State of Siege (*Kleiner Belagerungszustand*) providing the means to expel the most dangerous persons,"[42] it did not prohibit party members from running for elective office. It had simply not occurred to anyone that a party whose publications had been prohibited and whose organization had been shattered could elect anyone to a seat in the Reichstag. Paradoxically, the anti-Socialist law united and strengthened the SDP and ensured its survival.

Bismarck took advantage of the election of 1878 to realign the political balance in the Prussian Parliament and in the Reichstag, and to launch the anti-Socialist crusade. The chancellor had become increasingly unhappy about the influence of the liberals in the Reichstag, and by 1878, the government and the liberals had reached a constitutional impasse.[43] The origins of the crisis can be traced to the elections of 1874, when the National Liberals had gained a key position in the Reichstag which enabled them to choose an opposition policy with the Left, or a policy of cooperation with the Right. They decided to cooperate with the Left and to push for legislation which would lead to constitutional guarantees in financial matters. In particular, the liberals wanted the finance minister to be responsible to the Reichstag.

THE NEW REICH

This development frightened the conservatives, who saw it as a threat to the established order and a move toward liberalization of the government which could lead to parliamentary control. Though the conservatives saw this act as a "red revolt," it was actually no more than a move toward constitutionalism by the liberals, who would have preferred to achieve this goal with the consent of the chancellor rather than in opposition to him. The liberals failed, however, to take Bismarck's attitude into account. They also overlooked the dissension in their own ranks and misjudged the temper of public opinion. (They could not, of course, have foreseen that the assassination attempts on the emperor would spoil whatever chances they may have had.)

Bismarck's tax reform proposals to stabilize Reich finances became the key issue between the liberals and the government. His plan entailed raising the indirect taxes on beer and petroleum, instituting a state monopoly of tobacco and sugar, and placing higher taxes on taverns. These sources would give the Reich an adequate independent income—which it had not had heretofore—and, at the same time, avoid direct taxation. Since the Reichstag had a voice in matters of direct taxation, Bismarck's tax proposals, combined with his moves toward protectionism, were a clear indication of his intention to reduce the political powers of the Reichstag. If his proposals failed, and many signs pointed in that direction, Bismarck appeared to be ready to dispense with the Reichstag and govern without it. The two assassination attempts provided the necessary pretext and the chancellor's first reaction was to dissolve the Reichstag.[44] Remembering the March days of 1848, he was prepared to proclaim a state of emergency and even inquired whether the Berlin garrison was ready to meet an armed rebellion. For a time Bismarck hesitated, unsure whether to submit his tax reform program to the old Reichstag in the hope that the delegates would be sufficiently intimidated to pass it, or to dissolve the Reichstag and call new elections in the expectation that the shock of events would cause the electorate to return a conservative majority. Bismarck decided to dissolve the Reichstag, and the federal states were so informed and asked to give their approval. When some of the southern states expressed reluctance, State Secretary Buelow hinted at the involvement of Socialist agitators and informed the states that a state of emergency might be declared. He also pointed out the dangers of opposing Prussian policy. The threat was unmistakable. The states could choose either to comply voluntarily or do so under the threat of Prussian military force.[45] Not since 1866 had there been such a confrontation between North and South. In a special directive to Baden, Buelow added that if Prussia's proposals failed to receive a majority in the Federal Council, it would be an indication of the inadequacy of the Reich constitution and a revision of the constitution would have to be considered. This was the first time that a legal dissolution of the Reich and its reorganization under Prussian control was seriously contemplated.

Bismarck apparently considered the threat to Prussia's dominant position in the Reich great enough to warrant the most radical solution. "If I don't make a coup d'état," he told the Wuerttemberg envoy, "I won't get anything done."[46] In the end, Bismarck did not have to carry out his threat. The Federal Council voted unanimously in favor of the Prussian proposal. The rattling of Prussian sabers had been effective and had shown the South Germans just how much influence they had on Reich policy. The dissolution of the Reichstag in 1878 marked the end of the liberal era.

The dissolution of the Reichstag was followed by the government's successful anti-Socialist and antiliberal campaign, and resulted in an election victory for the conservatives. Bismarck had broken the domination of the liberals in the Prussian Parliament and in the Reichstag. The constitutional crisis was at an end. But this was only a temporary solution which failed to solve the underlying constitutional problems. In a rapidly growing urban and industrial society, Bismarck tried to preserve the ancient privileges of the ruling classes without making any concessions to the new forces. A coalition based on the interests of heavy industry and large landowners now formed the parliamentary base for the chancellor's antiliberal policy; this coalition favored the economic interests of these two classes to the disadvantage of the liberals. The landowners and industrialists, in turn, were satisfied with the existing system and grateful to have a strong government representing their interests and supporting law and order.

The new Reichstag was more conservative and less likely to challenge Bismarck's policies than the old one had been. His tariff and tax reform proposals had, however, not been acted on, and until they

THE NEW REICH

were, his policy against the Socialists—and this meant against liberalism, free trade, and parliamentarianism as well—was bound to fail. In an effort to achieve a solid majority for his program, Bismarck tried various coalitions of parties, as well as foreign diversions.[47] None of these arrangements worked for very long, and the threat of a revolution from above remained. There was no solution to the contradictions of the German constitutional system. Just as the outcome of the Prussian constitutional conflict had failed to resolve the inherent contradiction between the Prussian monarchy and constitutional government, so, too, Bismarck's Reich failed to reconcile royal power and parliamentary responsibility. The only means of maintaining the existing order against the new and rising forces of the Left was the threat of a coup d'état from above.[48]

For Bismarck, the Socialist movement was not only a grave peril to the newly created state—its international aspects made its members *ipso facto Reichsfeinde* [enemies of the Reich]—but socialism was also an ungodly philosophy and an immoral movement which sought to change the God-given order of society. In his eyes this was rebellion, and rebellion had to be crushed.[49] Bismarck's attitude toward socialism and the labor movement had probably undergone little change since the March days of 1848 when, outraged at the successful uprisings in Berlin, he wanted to crush them singlehandedly. If anything, his convictions had deepened. He was, like most Germans, confirmed in his conservative beliefs by the republican developments in France and especially by the uprising of the Paris Commune in 1870–71. The very one-sided press reports of these events, which exaggerated the "red peril" but were silent about the excesses perpetrated by the French troops, frightened the public and made the labor movement appear a deadly threat to the state and to society. The declaration of the German workers' movement, expressing solidarity with the Commune, greatly enhanced these fears.[50]

It is curious that Bismarck, like Napoleon III, recognized and used the emerging industrial masses for political purposes and that both men also feared them. Like Napoleon, he believed he could control them by introducing universal suffrage and giving them a voice in the Reichstag. Convinced of the righteousness of his cause and the reasonableness of his policy, Bismarck attempted to deal with the workers in two ways: repressive measures to destroy the workers' organizations and turn them away from the antireligious, materialistic teachings of Marx and Engels, and governmental social measures which would, at the same time, bind them to the state. "He wanted to satisfy their physical needs so as to dull their spirit and break their will."[51] Bismarck's sincerity toward social measures is open to question, inasmuch as his legislative proposals were somewhat lopsided. He approached the problem from the employer's point of view, and never believed that the social question could or would be solved by protective legislation. Though his sickness, accident, and old-age insurance laws failed to protect children and women workers and did not shorten the work day or seven-day week, they were a progressive and pioneering series of measures and became the model for similar laws in many other countries.[52]

The social laws presented the Social Democratic Party with a very serious dilemma. These laws, combined with certain proposals for nationalization and monopolization of certain industries, were the clearest examples of state socialism in Germany. State socialism forced the party to decide whether democratic-political principles or socialistic-economic ideas should prevail in its program. If democratic-political principles were to dominate, Bismarck's policies would have to be opposed, but if socialistic-economic ideas were paramount, accommodation with the government was possible. Thus, when the accident, sickness, and invalid insurance laws were presented to the Reichstag in November 1881, and the proposals for a state tobacco monopoly the following year, the party was faced with a serious crisis. Accepting the insurance program meant giving up opposition to the government in the Reichstag; at the same time, however, the party could not completely reject the government's program on political grounds, having demanded similar improvements for the workers for so long. The course the Social Democratic party finally adopted was to approve the program in principle but to declare that it did not go far enough and to demand many more benefits for the workers.[53] "Since their [the Party's] amendments were never incorporated into the final bills, they could always vote against the welfare legislation on the ground that it was wholly inadequate and therefore fraudulent."[54]

After 1882, increasing urbanization and steady improvement in economic conditions led to a strengthening of the party and the trade union movement. The success of the SDP in the election of 1884 clearly demonstrated the failure of Bismarck's anti-Socialist policies: the party gained 13 delegates and over 100,000 votes.[55] The government parties failed to achieve an absolute majority, which further enhanced the importance of the SDP's Reichstag position. But Bismarck was not ready to give up the fight. The strengthening of the labor movement in Germany and throughout Europe led to an increase of trade union activity, and an increasing number of demonstrations and strikes. By 1886, when the anti-Socialist legislation came up for renewal, the chancellor could argue that labor's revolutionary activities had to be curbed and that there were signs that anarchists had penetrated the Socialist movement. His arguments, coupled with disunity within the opposition parties—the Center and the SDP—enabled the government to achieve its aim; the anti-Socialist laws were passed for another two-year term by a 173 to 146 margin.[56] The government used this victory in a further attempt to destroy the labor movement and cripple the party. By forbidding strikes, closing meetings, and expelling and arresting party officials, it almost succeeded in its aims. But the leadership of the party continued its fight for social and political reforms in the Reichstag, and by using all legal and some illegal means, the party succeeded in keeping its organizational structure intact. During the November 1886 parliamentary session it opposed Bismarck's seven-year army bill, the *Septennat*, and helped to bring about its defeat (January 14, 1887). As a result, Bismarck dissolved the Reichstag and called for new elections. The outcome was a slight increase of the SDP's share of the popular vote (from 9.7 percent in 1884 to 10.1 percent in 1887), but a decline in its parliamentary strength, from 24 to 11 deputies, caused primarily by the government's failure to reapportion the growing urban districts. During this period the party overcame most of its internal differences. August Bebel assumed the party leadership, which diminished the strength of the moderate wing; Marxism, as interpreted by Karl Kautsky, became the official party creed. Kautsky and his followers stressed the economic and revolutionary aspects of Marxism and downgraded political action, except when it affected economic developments. This suited the party's parliamentary faction, which drew increasingly closer to the liberal parties in its actions and outlook.

The beginning of 1890 saw the final defeat of Bismarck's anti-Socialist crusade. The Reichstag's refusal to renew the anti-Socialist laws (January 25), and the party's victory at the polls (to 35 seats from 11), played an important part in the crisis of Bismarck's dismissal. A coal miners' strike in the Ruhr in May 1889 had brought young Kaiser Wilhelm II (who succeeded to the throne at the time of his father's death in 1888) face to face with the plight of the German workers and had impressed upon him the need for more extensive labor legislation. This attitude deepened the emperor's conflict with the chancellor and contributed materially to the latter's dismissal. At the same time Wilhelm's openly expressed concern for the workers lent respectability to the party. The party's impressive electoral victory, confined largely to the North German, Protestant areas, can be explained to some extent by the growing alienation of the workers from German bourgeois society, with its emphasis on education and property (*Besitz und Bildung*).[57]

German Society and Culture   The impact of the bitter and prolonged struggles against the Catholics and Socialists on German society was deep and long lasting. The immediate effect on German political life was to create a large though unorganized mass of disaffected citizens, composed of minorities—Poles, Danes, French, and Guelphs—and Catholics and workers. The fact that this opposition was disorganized made it easier for the nobility, the army, and the bureaucracy to maintain their hold on the government and the country, and made governmental or constitutional reforms seem superfluous. This situation was reinforced by the middle class's exaggerated emphasis on culture and learning and its disdainful attitude toward politics. This belief was expressed in the slogan, "the Buerger is meant to work, not rule, and a statesman's primary task is to rule,"[58] an attitude which led to the so-called apolitical German. In fact, the apolitical German bourgeois was afraid of the masses, suspicious of democratic government, and consistent in its support of conservative policies.[59] The bourgeois ideal was the scholar, immersed in learning and completely disinterested in daily affairs or practical knowledge. Unlike his English or French counterpart, the German university professor had no connection with the business community or the cosmopolitan world of the aristocracy. Separated from contact with the petite bourgeoisie and the artisans, the German academic remained isolated and developed an exaggerated faith in education and equally strong dislike of practical affairs. Education had traditionally been the only way for members of the German middle class to improve their position, and since the eighteenth century many had chosen this route to enter the civil service and the universities.

The prestige of a German university degree before 1890 surpassed that attached to any similar degree anywhere else. Economically and socially, German university professors ranked with the highest state and church officials and were considered the intellectual leaders of the nation. Practical politics were considered beneath their dignity and, "in this sense . . . the German intellectual was and considered himself apolitical: he had an aversion for the practical aspect of the political process."[60] This attitude was further reinforced after 1870 when the political parties openly competed for the vote of the masses. Many feared that under democracy the victorious mobs would sweep away "the aristocracy of birth, the aristocracy of money, and finally the aristocracy of education," as they had allegedly done in France.[61]

Thus, a majority of German professors, themselves conservatives, approved the antiliberal and anti-Socialist measures of successive governments and opposed any trend toward political or social reform. By the late 1880s they were concerned about the general decline of German culture and learning, and blamed the developments on industrialization and rising materialism. They felt powerless and confused, though their social prestige continued to remain high well into the twentieth century.

To the bourgeoisie's general and widespread disinterest and disdainful attitude toward practical politics was added the belief that the threat to liberty was greater and more serious from below than from above. These beliefs, combined with Bismarck's inability to attract new talent into government service, stifled a healthy and meaningful political life.

As one perceptive observer noted,

It is a common enough error among newcomers and superficial observers in Berlin to take for real the parliamentary system as it exists
here; with more experience and reflection, one quickly recognizes that
Germany is endowed with a fine and beautiful facade, remarkably
embellished on the surface, faithfully representing a picture of a parliamentary and constitutional system; the rules are correctly applied,
the customs observed, the external prerogatives respected; the play
of parties, turmoil in the corridors, lively debate, stormy sessions,
defeats inflicted on the government and even on the powerful Chancellor (only in matters of course that he considers of secondary importance), in short everything is done that can give the illusion and
make one believe in the gravity of the debates or the importance of
the votes; but behind this scenery, at the back of the stage, interven-
ing always at the decisive hour and having their way, appear Emperor and Chancellor, supported by the vital forces of the nation—the
army dedicated to the point of fanaticism, the bureaucracy disciplined
by the master's hand, the bench [*magistrature*] no less obedient, and
the population, sceptical occasionally of their judgments, quick to crit-
icize, quicker still to bow to the supreme will.[62]

After the depression of 1873–79 the bureaucracy, under Bismarck's
leadership, heeded the call for increased state intervention in economic
and social matters and effectively bypassed the Reichstag and the
political parties by issuing administrative rules and regulations. Thus
the political system began to resemble Bonapartism, with its monarchical trappings, bureaucratic tradition, constitutional compromises, universal manhood suffrage, and pseudo-parliamentarianism.
It was able to deal effectively with trade and economic problems, taxes
and the codification of laws, and was supported by large segments of
the middle class and the aristocracy because it prevented the take-
over of the state by the Socialists.[63]

The conservative coalition of the nobility and the upper and middle
bourgeoisie, "knitted together by common fears and common interests
. . . and the institutions they dominated, formed an almost irresistible
barrier to substantial social and political reform."[64]

In the social and cultural spheres, the consequences of the anti-Catholic and anti-Socialist struggles are difficult to assess. In combination
with the disillusionment which followed the *Gruenderzeit* (the period
of excessive building and speculation after the Franco-Prussian War)
and the subsequent economic slump, these internecine struggles contributed to the general mood of frustration and dissatisfaction. The

new Reich, despite its military trappings and efficient organization, failed to create its own ideology. Attempts to define and expand on the "ideas of 1871" proved an abysmal failure.[65] The hope that military victory in war would result in a triumph for German culture abroad was not borne out, though popular writers and patriotic historians continued to equate power with culture. There were, of course, exceptions. Nietzsche expressed the fear as early as 1873 that German culture (*Geist*) was being sacrificed to unification. Others noted that the new and widespread fashion of imitating army slang and behavior did little for the improvement of German culture and society. Love for imitations and fakes characterized the period—cardboard for wood, glass for onyx, gypsum for marble. Useless copper kettles, pewter jugs, and medieval swords graced fake beams, and imitation oak furniture was the fashion of the day. The paintings of Hans Makart and the operas of Richard Wagner were representative of German civilization in the latter part of the nineteenth century; the contrast between this period and the neoclassical age of German culture of the eighteenth and early nineteenth centuries was startling.

There was, on the other hand, a decided advance in the historical sciences. Schliemann's excavations of Troy and Mycenae, Ranke's *World History*, Mommsen's *History of Roman Law*, and Treitschke's *German History* were the foremost examples. But the greatest advances were in the natural and technical sciences. There Bunsen, Helmholtz, Virchow, Koch, Siemens, Daimler, Benz, Bayer, and Hertz combined to give Germany a preponderant lead.

Thus two divergent moods dominated popular consciousness. On the one hand, technological and scientific achievements and confidence in the political and economic potential of the newly established empire created considerable pride and optimism. No task seemed too difficult, no goal too distant. A mixture of romantic idealism, belief in Germany's world mission, and an increasingly aggressive nationalism, "rejecting the pacifistic tendencies of the western world," led to imperialism and world policy.[66] On the other hand, the gross materialism of the period underscored the widening gap between material achievement and moral and artistic development, producing a pessimistic world outlook (*Kulturpessimismus*).[67] This widespread pessimism, based on unfulfilled hopes and the realization of the discrepancies between idealism and reality, led to a rejection of many aspects of modern life. The squalor of urban living, the unemployed masses, poor living conditions, and false values, industrialization and its ravages, the decay of small towns and the decline of peasant holdings, all symptoms of a changing society (which were present then, as they are present now), led many to look into the past and to long for a better and simpler life. These people found what they were looking for in an idealization of the agrarian, feudal society of the Middle Ages, when there were few large towns and everyone knew his place in society.

From this longing the Volkish movement emerged, a mixture of conservatism and nationalism. It rejected modernism, liberalism, and western democracy. As in neoromanticism, the Volkish movement stressed feelings and emotions over reason and intellect, sought simple solutions, and longed for the simple life. The peasant, rooted in the soil, became the Volkish ideal; both rural and primitive society were glorified. Its emphasis on the simple virtues contrasted favorably with the complexity and rootlessness of contemporary society, whose uprooted workers and "alien" Jews became the favorite targets of Volkish propaganda. Volkish ideology, disseminated in the writings of Paul de Lagarde and Julius Langbehn, was elaborated into a Germanic faith.[68]

The Volkish movement attracted an increasingly large following in Germany in the last decades of the nineteenth and the early years of the twentieth centuries and appealed to two totally different groups. On the one hand it attracted those who opposed science and modernism and dreamed of the Middle Ages and the glories of the Germanic tribes. On the other hand, a considerable segment of the Volkish movement followed Ernst Haeckel, the foremost popularizer of Social Darwinism in Germany and a recognized and reputable zoologist and biologist.

"The form which Social Darwinism took in Germany was a pseudo-scientific religion of nature worship and nature mysticism combined with notions of racism. It was based on both the social Darwinian ideas of Haeckel and the ideology of Volkism which was related to and largely inspired by his writings."[69] Haeckel made Volkish ideas respectable, and through him large segments of the academic community, including university students and primary and secondary school teachers, were attracted to the movement.

Haeckel's study of evolution and the works of Darwin led him to see man as an integral part of nature and of his environment, and he developed this view of man and society into a new philosophy, Monism. His stress on the animal origin and nature of man opposed the traditional views of western civilization, which looked upon man as an individual, separate from and above his animal ancestors. Stressing the Darwinian concepts of the "struggle for existence" and the "survival of the fittest," the Monists blamed the false humanitarianism and misleading individualism of western society for the general decline and degeneration of the major European states. Rather than believing in the equality of mankind, the Monists emphasized racial differences, which included differences in color and intelligence. Among the various races, they believed that only the Germanic race had any value.

The racial nationalism of the Monists set the racial and Volkish community and the state above the individual citizen. Instead of individual and natural rights, they stressed community and the mutual obligations of the individual to society. They opposed civil rights, constitutionalism, and the supremacy of the individual, and believed that Monism would free Germany from the shackles of western civilization and might lead to a regeneration of her social and political life. At home the Monists advocated abolition of political parties and the establishment of a corporative state. Abroad they supported German colonial expansion and the construction of a powerful navy. They were especially active in the Pan German League and the various colonial and naval organizations.

The impact of Haeckel's interpretation of Social Darwinism and of his monistic philosophy in Germany was considerable. He had popularized his views in his best-selling work *Die Weltraethsel* (published in London in 1900 as *The Riddle of the Universe at the Close of the Nineteenth Century*), which, because of its readable style and the scientific reputation of its author, was read avidly by the literate and semiliterate masses. Thus, while others—such as H. S. Chamberlain and Ludwig Scheman, the founder of the Gobineau Society—also contributed and spread racial nationalism throughout Germany, Haeckel added scientific authority and academic respectability to this move-ment.[70]

Anti-Semitism had roots other than Haeckel's Social Darwinist and racial theories, however. The anti-Semitic movement had received its greatest impetus during the *Gruenderzeit* and the subsequent eco-nomic crash. Its leaders, Konstantin Frantz, Rudolf Meyer, and Paul de Lagarde, were conservative intellectuals, opposed to liberalism and concerned with the Jewish question mainly from an economic and reli-gious aspect. By the middle 1870s, the *Kruezzeitung* and other conser-vative publications blamed the Jews not only for the depression but also for the *Kulturkampf*. In January 1878, Adolf Stoecker, the Berlin Court preacher, founded the Christian Social Workers' Party and started anti-Semitism as a mass movement. His greatest success was not among the workers (he dropped "Worker" from his party's name in 1881) but among small shopkeepers, artisans, businessmen, and officials. Still, Stoecker's anti-Semitism was based on religious grounds while others, such as Bernhard Foerster, Max Liebermann von Son-nenberg, and Ernst Henrici, began to propagate racism and the elimi-nation of Jews.[71]

Bismarck's attitude toward Jews had undergone a change since his Landtag speech in 1847.[72] When he said in 1871 that he favored "the joining of a gentile stallion with a Jewish mare [because] the money had to get into circulation once more and the resulting race would not be so bad either," he probably meant it.[73] His banker, Bleichroeder, his physician, Cohen, and his lawyer, Philip, were all Jews, and his good relationship with all of them was well known, much to the an-noyance of his conservative friends.

While Stoecker's anti-Semitic agitation continued, however,

> the government's refusal to take an unequivocal stand . . . lent further respectability to the agitation and foreshadowed later prevarication and concealed discrimination on the part of the government. In the 1880s the Bismarck regime began a policy of covert discrimination against Jews . . . and Bismarck's own role in setting this policy was far more decisive than has previously been noted.
>
> Bismarck's moral insouciance hid a more complicated opportunism. Anti-Semitism was no part of his creed; he had come to discover the usefulness of Jews to the state and to himself. There was, moreover,

a presumption against extreme demagoguery, partly because of concern over foreign reaction. On the other hand, Bismarck lacked the principles that would automatically shield him from the temptation of political anti-Semitism. He had no basic commitment to what we call civil rights; he had no attachment to any kind of equality; the very idea affronted him. At best he had come to accept the civic equality of Jews.[74]

At the same time that anti-Semitism was increasing, German society took on an exaggeratedly militaristic aspect. The Prussian officers' corps had always been a narrow, self-sufficient organization composed almost entirely of East Elbian Junkers. The expansion of the army after 1871 did not change this pattern appreciably. Admittance of commoners was discouraged and training at the War Academy and service schools was restricted to specialized military subjects; general knowledge, especially politics and economics, was discouraged. In this way the officers' corps was immunized against the evils of the times, but it was also incapable even of understanding the political realities of the period. Thus, the nonpolitical soldier, who believed that war was exclusively a matter for the military and that politics had to be set aside during wartime, came into being. This attitude became apparent before and during the First World War and continued in the *Reichswehr* during the interwar years. The narrow base of the officers' corps and its antidemocratic and reactionary outlook contributed to the widening gap between the army and society, and especially between soldiers and workers.[75] The prestige of the military was enhanced by the father figure of Emperor Wilhelm I and even by Bismarck who, though no militarist, wore the uniform at all official functions.

The adoption by civilians of military slang and barracks behavior became characteristic of German society in the last quarter of the nineteenth century. The highest ambition of the petite bourgeoisie was to attain the rank of lieutenant in the reserve. Contrary to developments in western Europe, universal military service in Germany did not lead to a "civilizing" of the military establishment, but rather to a militarization of civilian life. The widespread view that in Germany the human being started with the officer became more than just a *bon mot*.[76]

Bismarck's Foreign Policy

Bismarck's fame has always rested on his achievements in diplomacy. His handling of the Schleswig-Holstein question, his struggle for supremacy in Germany, and the treatment of the Hohenzollern candidature were great successes in foreign policy, achieved against considerable odds. And though each of these crucial events in German history caused war, they were limited wars which led, in the end, to the unification of Germany. As a unified major power in the center of the continent, Germany changed the balance of power in Europe. Bismarck had fought three victorious wars in a very short time and the question was whether he would continue a belligerent, expansionist policy or would follow a more peaceful course. Bismarck decided for peace, not only for Germany, but for Europe. He recognized Germany's limitations and realized that localized wars were no longer possible in Europe, since all the major powers would be drawn into any larger war, no matter where it started. As far as Bismarck was concerned, Germany was satiated; what had been accomplished could not be risked for the sake of any conquest, no matter how tempting. His successors, less restrained toward war and convinced that Germany's power was overwhelming, willingly risked her position and reputation; in so doing they brought about her eventual defeat and ruin.[1]

The attitude of the powers toward Germany in the aftermath of the Franco-Prussian War was restrained and suspicious. France, thinking of revenge, looked to Russia and Austria as possible allies in case of future war with Germany. Austria, still smarting from her defeat at Koeniggraetz, was jealous of Germany's newly acquired big power status and kept her reserve toward Germany. Russia, though worried about the revolutionary developments in France, was disturbed by Prussia's vastly increased power and by the emergence of a unified Germany. Britain alone seemed unconcerned.

BISMARCK'S FOREIGN POLICY

In this situation, preserving Germany's newly won position of pre-eminence was difficult. Ideally Bismarck thought Germany should seek no further territorial conquests; instead, all the powers except France should vie with each other in an attempt to gain Germany's friendship. At the same time, the tension among the powers would be great enough so that they would not combine against the Reich.[2] Bismarck's system was an extremely complicated one, requiring a continuous assessment of the relationship among all the possible combinations of powers to see that the ideal balance was maintained. Bismarck's policies after the Congress of Berlin toward Austria, Russia, Britain, France, and Italy were attempts to achieve this ideal condition.

After 1871, Bismarck consistently supported a republican regime in France, for he believed that no monarchical government in Europe would enter into an alliance with a republic out of fear of revolutionary intrigues.[3] He concentrated his initial efforts at alliance on Austria and Russia. An alliance with Russia and Austria accomplished both of Bismarck's goals: it isolated France, and at the same time gave him a majority of three among the five great powers of Europe. Bismarck also used alliances to restrain his alliance partners—he compared alliances to a rider and a horse—and he endeavored at all times to be the rider. This tactic was particularly successful in his alliance with Austria.

Bismarck's success in foreign policy was based on three factors. He had a realistic appreciation of the international scene and the interests and relationships of the powers involved. He kept his ultimate aims in mind and always considered several methods of achieving them. Most importantly, his close relationship with Wilhelm I enabled him to carry out his policies. In addition, a combination of circumstances enabled Bismarck to unfold his diplomatic talents to their fullest extent. The age of the masses and the impact of public opinion on foreign affairs had barely emerged in the latter part of the nineteenth century in Europe; while public opinion was a factor that could not be ignored, it was a relatively minor irritant and could be manipulated, as Bismarck had shown prior to the Danish and French wars. Foreign policy could still be conducted on the cabinet level. Diplomacy had accepted rules, a restricted area (Europe), a fixed number of players (the five great powers), and more or less limited aims. Under these conditions Bismarck performed brilliantly. He was the last of the great diplomats, in the tradition of Richelieu, Kaunitz, and Metternich. At the same time, Bismarck's understanding and manipulation of public opinion in the conduct of foreign affairs rivaled that of Napoleon III, whom Bismarck surpassed in methods as well as achievements.[4]

Following the 1871 peace treaty with France, Bismarck set out to repair relations with Austria. The Austrians, prodded by their Hungarian partners, were willing to come to terms with their powerful neighbor.[5] The Austrian and German emperors and their foreign ministers met at Ischl and Salzburg during August and September 1871 to clear up past misunderstandings and lay the foundation for a future alliance. A year later the two emperors and Alexander II of Russia met in Berlin and in a series of informal conversations agreed to maintain the status quo in Europe. Formal negotiations which resulted in military agreements were concluded between Germany and Russia on the occasion of Wilhelm and Bismarck's visit to St. Petersburg in May 1873; similar negotiations between Austria and Russia took place at Schoenbrunn, outside Vienna, in June of the same year. The outcome of these negotiations was the Three Emperors' League, whose purpose was to demonstrate monarchical solidarity and preserve the status quo. For Bismarck, the League meant support against France and was a means of preventing a possible Austro-Russian conflict over the Balkans.[6]

A crisis in German-French relations, initiated by the fall of Thiers, was soon to test the strength of this newly formed Emperors' League.[7] French economic recovery had been faster and more thorough than had been expected and the French government was able to pay off the five billion franc war indemnity ahead of schedule, which resulted in the complete evacuation of French territory by German troops in September 1873. This, combined with the reorganization and strengthening of the French army, caused the German general staff considerable anxiety. After the defeat of 1870, the French army had reorganized its training and organizational structure, adding a fourth battalion to each regiment early in 1875. At the same time, rumors of extensive French purchases of horses and fodder alarmed the German military command and led Moltke, chief of the general staff, to advocate a preventive war against France.[8]

BISMARCK'S FOREIGN POLICY

Bismarck's concern over these developments in France was heightened by his fear of a Catholic conspiracy, involving France, the papacy, and Belgium. He believed that such a conspiracy might actively support German Catholics in their struggle against him and the *Kulturkampf*. The French, on the other hand, were alarmed by Radowitz's mission to St. Petersburg in February 1875; they believed that Radowitz, then German minister in Athens, had been sent by Bismarck to secure Russian support for a preventive war against France. It seems highly unlikely, however, that Bismarck actually contemplated war. Whatever his motives, whether to frighten the French or to mollify the German general staff, a front-page article under the banner headline, "Is War In Sight?" appeared on April 8 in the Berlin *Post*. It had been written on Bismarck's instructions and was followed by a similar piece in the *Norddeutsche Allgemeine Zeitung*.[9] The two articles created a sensation and a war scare throughout Europe. French apprehensions were increased when, at a dinner on April 21, Radowitz told the French ambassador that it was logical for the Germans to consider a preventive war in such circumstances. At this point Decazes, the French foreign minister, appealed to Britain and Russia for support; at the same time, he placed an anonymous article in the London *Times*,[10] accusing Germany of planning an invasion of France. For once Bismarck was on the defensive. The British and Russian governments asked Bismarck to refrain from warlike measures, the former by a letter from Queen Victoria, the latter through Gorchakov, the foreign minister who was then in Berlin with the czar. Bismarck was intensely annoyed, and protested that it had all been a misunderstanding and a false alarm. The crisis blew over. Its significance, not lost on Bismarck, was that for the first time Britain and Russia were willing to come to the aid of France. It did not mean that the two powers intended to restore France to her pre-1870 status, but neither were they willing to tolerate further German aggression. They were satisfied with the status quo and, for that matter, so was Bismarck.

The weakness of the Three Emperors' League in this crisis forced Bismarck to reexamine Germany's relationship to her two partners. This became even more urgent when, in July 1875, an insurrection against Turkish rule broke out in the Balkans. Any trouble in the Balkans, where Austrian and Russian interests clashed, was potentially threatening to Germany and the peace of Europe. Reconciling Austro-Russian differences became Bismarck's most pressing task, second only to the French problem. Recognizing the potential explosiveness of the situation, Bismarck realized—as some of his successors did not—that Germany's attitude toward the two eastern powers was of crucial importance. Only an evenhanded and disinterested Balkan policy had any chance of success. As far as he was concerned, active German participation in Balkan affairs "was not worth the healthy bones of a single Pomeranian grenadier."[11]

Except for the years of struggle leading to unification, Prussia, and after 1871, Germany, had maintained close and friendly relations with Austria as well as with Russia. Germany had a common bond of language and culture with Austria, and although the struggle for supremacy had left some unhappy memories, the feelings of kinship and understanding between Germany and Austria outweighed any lingering resentments. Germany's relationship with Russia was somewhat more complicated. There were close dynastic ties between the Hohenzollerns and the Romanovs—Nicholas I had married a sister of Wilhelm I—in addition to memories of the united struggle against Napoleon I and their common policy toward Poland. The dynastic influence was apparent at the end of the Franco-Prussian War, when the Russians agreed that Germany should take Alsace-Lorraine. According to Bismarck, this was the result not of official Russian policy, but of the personal policy of Alexander II.[12]

The impressions Bismarck had gathered during his ambassadorship in St. Petersburg in 1859–62 played an important part in his Russian diplomacy. He had noted the decline of pro-German sentiments and the rise of prorevolutionary and prowestern sympathies among the ruling classes, and had seen the beginning of the Pan-Slav movement.[13] Prior to the Russo-Turkish war of 1877, Bismarck encouraged Russia to pursue her own policy, regardless of the approval or disapproval of the other European powers, because in such circumstances the Russians would be more grateful for German assistance, however limited. Bismarck's Russian policy proceeded along two tracks. On the one hand he had the emperor write personal letters to the czar, expressing his and Prussia's eternal gratitude for Russia's benevolent neutrality in

1866 and 1870–71 and indicating his government's readiness to support Russia unconditionally. The emperor, Bismarck, and most Russian diplomats realized that these letters were only expressions of good will to influence and reassure the czar, not firm policy commitments. On the other hand, Bismarck's official policy was designed to keep Russia friendly to Germany and out of the French orbit; Germany needed both Russia and Austria, and could therefore not afford to become involved in the Near East or the Balkans.[14]

Austro-Russian relations, strained since the Crimean War (1854–56), threatened to deteriorate further as Austrian interests in the Balkans increased. Austria's defeat at Koeniggraetz, her losses in Italy, and her subsequent exclusion from Germany made her turn East in an attempt to regain her lost prestige and territories. For the Austrians, this was neither a new role nor an unknown region. The Habsburg Empire had expanded toward the southeast ever since the defeat of the Turks at the gates of Vienna in 1683. There, along the Danube, the Austrian drive toward the Black Sea clashed with Russia's centuries-old push south toward Constantinople and the Straits. The economic-strategic competition between the two powers was further complicated by the religious and nationalistic struggle of the Balkan peoples. The majority of them were southern Slavs under Turkish sovereignty who belonged to the Eastern Orthodox Church. They looked to Russia for national as well as religious protection. Since the end of the Napoleonic wars, nationalistic revolts had loosened the ties between the sultan and some of his non-Turkish subjects and the independence movements during the last quarter of the nineteenth century threatened the very existence of the Ottoman Empire. Due to the rise of Pan-Slavism, the Russian government frequently supported these movements, thereby coming into open conflict with Turkey. The Austrians, though not averse to partitioning the Turkish Empire in Europe, opposed Russian support of nationalistic and revolutionary movements in the Balkans, fearful that these movements, once set in motion, would disrupt the Habsburg Empire. "Once the Balkan Slavs were astir, the Russian government dared not let them fail; Austria-Hungary dared not let them succeed."[15]

Thus, the Austro-Russian struggle for the domination of the Balkans became one of the major problems of European diplomacy. That Bismarck was able to contain it even temporarily was one of his great achievements. It was not an easy task. For the longest time he maintained a policy of strict neutrality but when, in October 1876, the Russians wanted to know what Germany's position would be if the difficulties in the Balkans led to a Russo-Austrian war, Bismarck had to take sides. He expressed the hope that peace would be preserved, but let it be known that if war did occur, Germany would not allow Austria's position to be weakened nor the balance of power to be upset.[16]

The insurrection, which had started in Bosnia and Herzegovina in July 1875, spread to Bulgaria in May of the following year, where it was bloodily suppressed by the Turks. When Serbia, later joined by Montenegro, declared war on Turkey on June 30, 1876, she was decisively defeated by the Turkish army at Alexinatz on September 1, 1876. Now it was Russia's turn. She wanted to aid her Serbian "brothers" and occupy Constantinople and the Straits, but not if this meant fighting the European powers. To avoid this and before going to war with Turkey, Russia had to prevent the resurrection of the Crimean coalition of Britain, France, and Austria. In a loosely worded agreement concluded at Reichstadt on July 8, 1876, and confirmed at Budapest on January 15, 1877, Andrassy and Gorchakov, the foreign ministers of Austria and Russia, agreed on Austrian neutrality in case of a Russo-Turkish war, on Austria's claim to the occupation of Bosnia and Herzegovina, and on Russia's right to regain Bessarabia. Assured of Austria's benevolent neutrality, Russia joined France and Britain at a conference at Constantinople in December 1876 for a settlement of the Balkan problem. It was agreed, with Turkey assenting, that Bulgaria would be divided into an eastern and western part, that Bosnia and Herzegovina would be united into one province, that there would be reforms in the Turkish Empire, and that the powers would supervise these reforms and, if necessary, enforce them. These terms were confirmed when Ignatiev, then Russian ambassador in Constantinople, toured the major European capitals during February and March 1877 and a protocol (with slightly less favorable terms for Russia) was signed in London on March 31, 1877.[17]

Thus, the Russians believed that they had obtained a free hand from the powers to carry out their mandate should the Turkish government fail to live up to its commitments. If Russia could do so quickly and decisively, she had a good chance to impose her will upon Turkey without outside interference. Her opportunity came when the sultan rejected the London Protocol on April 9. On April 24, Russia declared war on Turkey. Despite Russia's military superiority and her initial successes, the Turks were able to halt the Russian advance at Plevna. When the fortress finally fell on December 10, the Russian troops were too exhausted to capture Constantinople and an armistice was arranged on January 31, 1878, with the Russian army camped just outside the city limits. A treaty between the two belligerents was signed at San Stefano on March 3. The provisions of the treaty were quite severe for Turkey. Serbia, Montenegro, and Rumania would become independent, Bulgaria would be autonomous, considerably enlarged by the inclusion of Macedonia and an outlet to the Aegean Sea, and occupied by Russian troops for two years. Russia was to receive Kars, Batum, and Bessarabia, in addition to a large indemnity.[18]

The powers, especially Britain, were alarmed at these sweeping Russian terms. A European congress was called to redress the balance of power in the Balkans and to settle existing differences. Britain, anxious to keep the Russians out of Constantinople and to bolster Turkey, demanded that the size of Bulgaria be reduced. Britain wanted Bulgaria to be divided into a northern part, Bulgaria proper, and a southern part, Eastern Rumelia, with Macedonia excluded from the new Bulgarian state. The Russians, in no condition to resist, signed a secret agreement with Britain along these lines on May 30, 1878. Turkey, after obtaining British guarantees, signed an agreement on June 4, handing Cyprus to Britain in appreciation for her services. An Austro-British agreement on June 6—in which Britain supported Austria's claims to Bosnia and Herzegovina, and Austria supported Britain's settlement of the Bulgarian frontiers—completed the arrangements. The stage was set for the Congress of Berlin.

That the Congress met at Berlin (June 13, 1878) was an indication of Germany's preponderance in Europe and of Bismarck's eminence among her statesmen.[19] The chancellor had been reluctant to assume the presidency of the Congress, which met in a time of domestic crisis (the two assassination attempts on the emperor of May 11 and June 2, and the dissolution of the Reichstag on June 11). Bismarck's role at the Congress was not so much that of "honest broker" as it has been traditionally described and as he himself characterized it (in a speech to the Reichstag of February 19, 1878),[20] but rather that of umpire. His major interests were to safeguard the peace, to support Britain and her agreements with Austria and Russia, and to make the settlement palatable to the Russians. For the Balkan people he showed no concern whatever.[21] The settlement agreed upon at the Congress was based on the military balance of power—Russia's inability to take Constantinople—and on the agreements concluded by Britain, Austria, and Russia. It meant, essentially, a lesser Bulgaria (divided into two parts and without an outlet to the Aegean Sea) and a considerable loss of prestige for Russia. Though they lost no territory, the Russians were furious and blamed Bismarck for their diplomatic "defeat."

The Three Emperors' League was, for all practical purposes, dead. It was not a great loss. Its effectiveness had been marginal at best, and the Russo-Turkish war had exposed the underlying rivalry between the Habsburg and the Romanov empires. Bismarck took this rivalry seriously and considered it a potential threat to the European balance of power. With the Russians sulking, Bismarck turned to Austria.

The alliance with Austria, the Dual Alliance of October 1879, marks a change in Bismarck's foreign policy from a policy of a free hand to one of firm and definite commitments. It was the beginning of a complicated system of alliances by which Bismarck maintained Germany's predominant position and peace in Europe. The reasons for this drastic change are complex and not altogether clear.[22] Initially Bismarck seems to have favored the renewal of the Three Emperors' League, but Russian dissatisfaction with the outcome of the Congress of Berlin, for which Bismarck was blamed, made it unlikely that Gorchakov or the czar would agree to such a step. After the Congress there were numerous incidents which contributed to further Russo-German estrangement. German representatives at the various commissions set up by the Congress generally voted with Austria and often against Russian interests. The Austro-German agreement on the abrogation of Article 5 of the Treaty of Prague (August 1866), requiring a plebiscite in North Schleswig (made public February 4, 1879, signed on February 13, 1878, but postdated to October 11, 1878) was considered by the Russians as Austria's payment to Germany for services rendered at the Congress. Finally, an outbreak of the plague on the lower Volga at the end of 1878 produced swift German and Austrian countermea-sures and inspired articles in the press, which the Russians resented. This, combined with higher German tariffs on Russian grain which greatly reduced Russian exports, severely limited her earnings of foreign exchange, and slowed down her economic expansion, resulted in bitter and widespread anti-German feeling within the Russian gov-ernment.[23] On the German side, the expansion of the Russian rail net-work on Germany's eastern border and an increase of Russian troops in the same area caused considerable anxiety in Berlin.[24]

At the same time, Bismarck had to deal with the Rumanian ques-tion. This involved the recognition of Rumanian independence by the powers as soon as Rumania emancipated her Jewish citizens, as stipu-lated by the Congress of Berlin; a settlement of German claims in con-nection with the construction of Rumanian railroads was also in-volved.[25] Thus, while Bismarck might have preferred to maintain his independent position in foreign affairs, the Russian and Rumanian problems were too complicated to continue a policy of the free hand. To cope with the Russian difficulties, he began to rely increasingly on Austria and to look to the British and French for assistance with Rumanian problems. In this way his foreign policy, which had earlier concentrated on the isolation of France, became more and more com-plex.[26]

At times the threat (whether it was real or imagined does not really matter) of an unfriendly coalition—Austro-Russian, French-Russian, or even Austro-French-Russian, the old Kaunitz alliance—seems to have overwhelmed him and spurred him on to more frenzied activities. This may have been the case just prior to the conclusion of the alliance with Austria. The announcement of Andrassy's impending resignation as Austria's foreign minister caused Bismarck to press for the conclu-sion of an alliance.[27] Andrassy and Bismarck drafted the terms in Vienna on September 24, and signed the alliance on October 7, 1879.[28]

From a domestic point of view, an alliance with Austria would be popular with large segments of the German population, especially among liberals and Catholics; East Elbian agricultural interests, which favored protective tariffs, would be glad to see the elimination of duty-free imports of Russian grain. Only Emperor Wilhelm strongly opposed his chancellor's proposals. For Wilhelm, brought up in the old

Hohenzollern tradition of friendship with Russia, a break in this age-old pattern was utterly inconceivable. Bismarck had to use his most persuasive arguments, fabricate some unlikely threats and, finally, submit his and the Prussian cabinet's resignation, before Wilhelm relented.[29]

The Dual Alliance which formed the cornerstone of Bismarck's alliance system lasted until November 1918. As long as he was in power, his restraining influence—and prevailing international conditions—kept the peace, and the Austrian alliance was a major factor in this achievement. Bismarck did not intend the Dual Alliance to be anti-Russian. On the contrary, he expected that Russia would come around and, possibly to frighten her into making up her mind, he approached Britain, inquiring about her attitude in case of a Russo-German war.[30] The British reply was noncommittal, promising only that Britain would keep France quiet.

In January 1880 Saburov, now Russian ambassador in Berlin, suggested reviving the Three Emperors' League; Bismarck showed considerable interest, but the Austrians refused. They would have preferred an alliance with Britain, with Austria dominating the Balkans, Britain Asia Minor, Germany supporting both, and Russia left out altogether. But Gladstone's victory in the general election of April 1880 changed British foreign policy and put an end to Austria's plans for an alliance. By September the Austrians were ready to join the League, and after extensive negotiations the Three Emperors' Alliance, as it became known, was signed on June 18, 1881. "The basis of agreement was the Austrian belief that Germany would automatically support her and the Russian belief that she would not."[31]

The alliance had little in common with its predecessor, the Three Emperors' League of 1873. Instead of vague generalities regarding conservative principles of solidarity, it contained specific clauses, the most important of which stipulated neutrality of the partners should one of them go to war with a fourth power. This meant Russian neutrality in case of a Franco-German war, and German neutrality in case of a Russo-British war. As to the Balkans, the Russians recognized Austria's right to annex Bosnia and Herzegovina, while Austria and Germany agreed not to object to the union of Bulgaria with Eastern Rumelia. The main beneficiary of the Alliance was Russia, which achieved a certain security against British encroachment toward the Straits; it also brought Russia out of the isolation she had suffered since the Congress of Berlin. For Bismarck, the Alliance meant that he did not have to choose between his two incompatible allies.[32]

But Bismarck's pleasure with the Russians was short lived. The rise of Pan-Slavism, together with attempts in St. Petersburg to revive interest in a Franco-Russian alliance, culminated in the Skobelev affair, which alarmed Bismarck and led him to seek additional safeguards against Russia and France.[33] By including Italy in the Austro-German alliance, Bismarck believed that he had found his safeguard. Emerging empty-handed from the Congress of Berlin, Italy felt isolated and deceived. Having lost Tunis to France (the Treaty of Bardo of May 12, 1881, established a French protectorate over this territory), and faced with a renewed conflict with the papacy, Italy was looking for security and assistance. Thus, despite Austrian reluctance—mainly because of Italian irredentist activities in South Tyrol and Istria—Bismarck was able to conclude the negotiations which led to the Triple Alliance, signed on May 20, 1882. Germany and Austria promised the Italians their assistance in case of war with France, and Italy was to reciprocate in case of a Franco-German war. Italy was to be neutral in an Austro-Russian war, but would come to the aid of her allies if they had to fight a Russo-French combination. For the rest, the partners assured each other of the maintenance of the status quo in their respective countries. This clause was designed to reassure Italy that no power would interfere in her internal affairs as France had done. The alliance looked good on paper, but its actual worth was debatable. Italy probably gained the most, having obtained assistance against France and great power status through her association with Germany and Austria.

Two more alliances were concluded in this period to round out the Bismarckian system, the Austrian alliance with Serbia of June 28, 1881, which consolidated Austria's hold of the region and made Serbia a satellite of the Habsburg monarchy, and the Rumanian alliance of October 30, 1883, with Austria. The Rumanian alliance resulted from Austrian and Rumanian concern over alleged Russian designs on Rumania and was meant to be a pact of mutual assistance against Russia. Germany later joined the Austro-Rumanian alliance.[34]

The Three Emperors' Alliance was renewed in 1884, but before another year had passed, trouble in the Balkans tested it once again. Austria and Russia had been peacefully extending their economic interests in the Balkans by building railroads.[35] The Austrians were pushing a line through Serbia and Montenegro which would connect Vienna with Salonika. The Russians, going through Rumania and Bulgaria, hoped to build a line to Constantinople. But Russia's economic situation was such that she could not compete with the other powers even in Bulgaria where she enjoyed a predominant position. To overcome this disadvantage, Russia invested in large railroad concessions which were guaranteed by the Bulgarian government. This enabled her to put pressure on Bulgarian officials to obtain preferential treatment.[36] At the same time, it contributed to Russian unpopularity, and when a revolt broke out in Eastern Rumelia against Turkish rule in September 1885, Alexander of Battenberg (who had been installed by the Russians as prince of Bulgaria following the Congress of Berlin) followed a Bulgarian national policy and was openly anti-Russian. The revolutionaries demanded the union of Eastern Rumelia and Bulgaria, the greater Bulgaria which Russia had demanded in the Treaty of San Stefano and which the powers had opposed at the Congress of Berlin. In a complete reversal of roles, Russia, angry at Alexander for pursuing an anti-Russian policy, refused to support the union, while the British favored it.

Inevitably, Germany and Austria were drawn into this conflict, the more so since Serbia, unwilling to see Bulgarian power increased, declared war on Bulgaria on November 13, 1885. The Serbs were decisively defeated by the Bulgarians, and only Austrian intervention saved them from complete annihilation. A compromise among the powers was finally worked out and Alexander of Battenberg was made governor of Eastern Rumelia, which established, in effect, a greater Bulgaria. The Russians rejected this settlement and Alexander, after being kidnapped and held for a week by Russian officers, resigned on September 7. The struggle over a successor led to increased Austro-Russian tension because neither country was prepared to accept the other's candidate for the Bulgarian throne. Bismarck tried in vain to persuade the two powers to divide the Balkans into two spheres of influence, Russia taking the eastern half with Bulgaria, and Austria the western half with Serbia. When the Austrians asked for German assistance, Bismarck reminded them of the defensive nature of the Dual Alliance and of Germany's disinterested policy in the Balkans. Instead, he suggested that Austria approach Great Britain. The British wanted to keep the Russians away from Constantinople and the Straits, but they were afraid to escalate their already serious conflict with Russia any further.[37] When the Austrians suggested cooperation, Great Britain refused. A solution to the dilemma was found by shifting the focus from the Balkans to the Mediterranean and by including Italy in the arrangements. (The inclusion of Italy bolstered Britain's position against France in Egypt, while Italy gained support in her tariff war with France and her territorial aspirations in North Africa.) In an exchange of notes—to bypass Parliament—Britain and Italy agreed on February 12, 1887, to maintain the status quo in the Mediterranean, the Adriatic, the Aegean, and the Black Sea. Austria joined the agreement on March 24, and Spain on May 4. This First Mediterranean Agreement, as it became known, was strongly supported by Bismarck, particularly because it strengthened Austria against Russia without directly involving Germany.

Bismarck's concern over Russia continued, not only because of Austro-Russian tension in the Balkans but also because of renewed nationalistic agitation in France. There, Paul Deroulède and his League of Patriots preached revenge against Germany and alliance with Russia. General Boulanger, minister of war (and the prototype of the "man on horseback"), became the symbol and the rallying point of this movement. The pro-Russian and anti-German agitation in France was paralleled in Russia by Katkov's Pan-Slav activities and by increasing demands for an alliance with France.

Giers, Gorchakov's successor in the Russian foreign ministry, wanted to renew the Three Emperors' Alliance but the czar, many of his advisors, and public opinion were anti-Austrian and strongly opposed to such a course.[38] At the same time Bismarck pressured the Russian government to conclude a separate German-Russian agreement, and the Russians finally agreed. This secret treaty (known as the Reinsurance Treaty), in which the two powers agreed to stay neutral should one go to war with a third power, was signed on June 18, 1887. The agreement was not to apply in case of aggressive war by

Germany against France or by Russia against Austria. A special clause recognized Russia's preponderent influence in Bulgaria and Germany's moral and diplomatic support of Russia in her quest for an outlet to the high seas through the Straits.

Bismarck's motive in supporting this rather risky undertaking was his desire to keep Russia away from France and to tie her to Germany as closely as possible. When the terms of the Reinsurance Treaty became known after Bismarck's dismissal, it was called "a protective immunization for the Czar against a French infection," "political bigamy," "the finest example of diplomatic duplicity," and much more.[39] These epithets usually referred to the treaty's apparent incompatibility with Germany's alliance with Austria. Actually, the Reinsurance Treaty conflicted more with the Second Mediterranean Agreement (December 1887) than with the Dual Alliance. The agreement, also known as the Near Eastern Entente, between Britain, Austria, and Italy, reaffirmed the status quo in the Near East and the independence of Turkey. Bismarck, who had been instrumental in its formation, refused to join it, preferring to let Britain and Austria emerge as the defenders of Turkish independence. Thus, while he pledged his support for Russia's drive toward the Straits in the Reinsurance Treaty, he knew that Britain, Austria, and Italy were bound by the Second Mediterranean Agreement to halt such a drive.[40]

The benefits as well as the effects of the Reinsurance Treaty have been exaggerated. The relationship between Russia and Germany actually deteriorated during this period, mainly because of Bismarck's directive of November 10, 1887, which forbade the placing of Russian loans and the acceptance of Russian securities (*Lombardverbot*) in Germany.[41] The effects of this move were immediate and far-reaching. Having been denied access to the German capital market, the Russians turned to France, whose bankers and politicians were only too happy to accommodate them. A year later, in November 1888, France granted Russia a 500 million franc loan and agreed to supply the Russian army with 500,000 rifles.[42] Other economic and financial agreements followed, and in August 1891 France and Russia concluded a political agreement, followed by a draft for a military convention in 1892. There were, of course, other reasons for the conclusion of the Franco-Russian alliance[43] but whether it would have come so soon and developed so rapidly without Bismarck's interference seems highly unlikely. Thus, the question of Bismarck's motivation and his awareness of the consequences of his actions is of considerable importance.

There were several reasons for Bismarck's action. By the fall of 1887 many army leaders, Moltke and Waldersee among them, were convinced that a conflict with Russia was inevitable; they urged preventive war.[44] They were especially disturbed by the extensive Russian construction on Germany's eastern border and charged that German loans to Russia had financed these undertakings. Some German industrialists supported the military leaders by pointing out that these funds could be better invested at home, where they would lower the interest rates and help German industry to overcome the Russian tariff barrier. Because of high Russian tariffs against German industrial goods, German exports to Russia had declined while Russian imports to Germany had increased; so had British imports to Russia, while Russian industrial production had expanded to satisfy the greater demands of her home markets.[45] In Germany, large landowners and wealthy agrarians also complained about the scarcity of capital and the exorbitant interest rates. They objected to sending money to Russia to build railroads which facilitated Russian grain exports.

Though strongly opposed to preventive war himself, Bismarck's denial of funds to Russia appeased those who advocated it, and this move also strengthened the agrarian and industrial interests whose political support he needed. At the same time, there was a general feeling that Russia was about to disintegrate and that in such a case, or in case of war, German loans would be lost. Government officials were dissatisfied with German policy and believed that Russia had for too long accepted German economic and political favors without giving much in return. If her loans were stopped, Russia would realize that she was dependent on Germany and, according to Herbert Bismarck, the chancellor's son, would see that without German help she could do very little in the field of European power politics.[46]

So much for Bismarck's motives; but what about his ability to foresee the consequences of his action? In general he was quite capable of evaluating economic factors correctly, though he apparently believed that politics and economics could be neatly separated. In Germany's relationships with Austria and Russia he always stressed political considerations, monarchical solidarity, and common interests to the exclusion of economic factors. In the case of denying loans to Russia he may have underestimated the economic consequences, misjudged the readiness of French financial institutions to accept Russian securities, and overlooked the political consequences of Franco-Russian financial cooperation. Nor was this a momentary misconception. Bismarck continued to refuse the acceptance of Russian loans and securities in Germany and would not allow German banks to subscribe to the Russian loan of 1888.[47]

For Russia the cutting off of German funds in addition to the curtailment of Russian grain imports (German agrarian tariffs reached their highest point in 1887) created severe economic hardship. German investment capital and the earnings from the sale of grain were the major sources for Russian industrial expansion, which was at a crucial stage at the end of the 1880s. To maintain the pace of its industrialization Russia had to look for an alternate source of capital; this could only come from France. Ironically, shifting to France strengthened Russian finances and thus, Bismarck's ill-conceived move hastened, rather than retarded, the possibility of a future Russo-German conflict and with it the specter of a two-front war.[48]

Bismarck's colonial policy, initiated in the 1880s, was as complicated as his Russian policy. Why Bismarck decided to acquire colonies, and whether he was an imperialist or not, is an interesting question. Bismarck's foreign policy had been peaceful from 1870 on; he had carefully avoided unnecessary friction and potential conflicts. He told the explorer Eugen Wolff, "Your map of Africa is very pretty; but mine is here in Europe. Here is Russia, and here is France, and we are in the middle; that is my map of Africa."[49] He also maintained that, "so long as I am Chancellor, we shan't pursue a colonial policy."[50] He considered colonies a temporary European folly and wanted no part of them. He admired Britain's informal mid-Victorian empire and was horrified by the prospects of installing an extensive administration, bureaucracy, and military garrison overseas.[51] To Bismarck, colonial possessions were "a source of weakness rather than strength," as he wrote to Wilhelm I in 1873.[52] If business and other interests were clamoring for overseas possessions, let them go ahead on their own and administer and exploit them through private syndicates and chartered companies. Government support would have involved the Reichstag, because "colonial administration would be an extension of Parliament's parade ground," and giving the Reichstag more power was the last thing Bismarck wanted.[53] At the same time, he believed that there was not enough popular support for an active colonial policy. He seems to have been right about this, for the majority of the Reichstag refused to extend government guarantees to an old established German trading company in Samoa that had run into financial difficulties in 1880.[54]

But public opinion was slowly changing, and in December 1882 Prince Hohenlohe-Langenburg and Johannes Miquel founded the German Colonial Society in Frankfurt. German economic and financial interests, like those of other countries, began to look toward overseas trade and investments as a new and possibly profitable activity. This colonial interest coincided with a period of economic fluctuation when, after a short recovery from the great depression of 1873–79, another recession in 1882 rekindled earlier fears and brought renewed demands for economic and political changes. There was widespread fear of social unrest and talk of a "red peril"; though this may have been exaggerated, it was not completely unfounded.

After the 1873–79 depression, Bismarck had abandoned free trade and had adopted a moderate protective tariff policy in 1879. But the changes in economic policy that higher tariffs entailed neither satisfied the business community nor alleviated the consequences of the recession of the early 1880s. At the same time, as the pressure for colonies increased, Bismarck responded to it.[55] He did so for several reasons. He hoped that by winning foreign markets, economic prosperity and stability would be achieved at home and social tradition would remain undisturbed.

The acquisition of foreign markets, however, required a national commitment, because individual German traders could no longer compete with nationally subsidized British and French colonial enterprises. There were ample German precedents for state-subsidized undertakings, such as steamship lines, railroad companies, and financial institutions. As Bismarck told the French ambassador in the fall of 1884, "The aim of German policy was the expansion of unrestricted trade and not the territorial expansion of German colonial possessions."[56] There were also other considerations. Colonial acquisitions could be used to divert public opinion from the divisive domestic struggle against the Catholics and Socialists. From 1884 on, Bismarck used the colonial issue to stir up national sentiment; the press attacks against Britain in connection with the establishment of a German settlement in Angra Pequena in Southwest Africa are an example of this tactic. Colonies also provided a much-needed rallying point—an ideological substitute as it were—on which the dissident elements at home could agree. Bismarck also used the colonial issue for electoral and parliamentary maneuvers, and to enhance his own position and prestige. This was successful in the election of 1884, when the conservatives won a decisive victory and the progressives were badly beaten.[57] But Bismarck never used colonial policy as a basis for Germany's claim to status as a world power, nor did he believe in the superiority of the German race or in her "mission" in the world. And though others, extreme nationalists and Pan-Germans, did later believe in a German "mission," Bismarck's aims were far more restricted. He wanted to alleviate economic hardships and preserve the social and political status quo. By 1889 he was "sick and tired of colonies," but by then it was too late to change course.[58]

Germany's major colonial activity was concentrated within a short two-year period from 1883 to 1885 and was led by merchants and explorers. In 1883 the Bremen merchant Adolf Luederitz acquired Angra Pequena, which later became German Southwest Africa. The explorer Gustav Nachtigal became German *Reichskommissar* for Cameroon and Togo, on the west coast of Africa, in July 1884, after several Hamburg merchants had established trading posts on the Gulf of Guinea in 1882. The explorer Carl Peters (who had founded the Society for German Colonization in 1884) concluded several treaties with native chiefs on the east coast of Africa in 1884 and obtained an imperial charter in February 1885 for the territory which became German East Africa in the following year. This led to friction with neighboring British colonial interests, which was settled by the Anglo-German colonial agreement of July 1, 1890. Under the terms of this treaty, Germany obtained Helgoland from Britain in exchange for territory in East Africa. In the Pacific, the New Guinea Company, under the leadership of the Berlin banker Adolf von Hansemann, obtained a protectorate over territories on the north coast of New Guinea and adjacent islands which became, in 1885, the colony of Emperor Wilhelm Land and the Bismarck Archipelago.

The German colonial empire came into being during a period of intense imperial rivalries among the European powers, such as the Anglo-Russian competition in Asia and the Anglo-French struggle in Egypt and the Sudan. Bismarck used these rivalries in a way that avoided major confrontations and shifted his support first to one, then to another power, always keeping in mind that colonial issues were second to Germany's prime interests, which were in Europe.[59]

Bismarck's Dismissal

The colonial enthusiasm of the early 1880s gave way to disillusionment at the end of the decade. The exaggerated hopes and promises had not been fulfilled; disappointment in colonial affairs was thus added to the discontent caused by the *Kulturkampf* and the anti-Socialist campaign. On March 9, 1888, Emperor Wilhelm I died and his son, Friedrich III, who succeeded him, died three months later (June 15) of cancer of the throat. Wilhelm II became emperor at age twenty-nine; he was unlike his father or grandfather in behavior or outlook. Wilhelm II was of medium height, fair complexion, and restless temperament. He was sensitive all his life about his withered left arm, which had been crippled at birth. His main interest was the army, but instead of concentrating on military affairs, he occupied himself with the trappings and trivia of military life and wore a uniform at all times. (He is said to have appeared in the full dress uniform of an admiral at a performance of *The Flying Dutchman*.) He admired and tried to emulate his grandfather, Wilhelm I, but he was closer to his granduncle, Friedrich Wilhelm IV, in his indecision, bombastic and deceptive oratory, and narrow view of royal prerogatives.[1]

Apart from these characteristics, the difference in age between the new emperor and the chancellor, now seventy-three, would have made it difficult even under the most favorable conditions to continue the close cooperation that had existed between Bismarck and Wilhelm I. For Bismarck such cooperation was crucial because his office and power were based exclusively on the confidence of the emperor. Inasmuch as the Reichstag in Germany (and the Parliament in Prussia) lacked the power to choose a government, the Reich chancellor and Prussian prime minister were appointed by the German emperor and king of Prussia (combined in the person of Wilhelm II) and served at his pleasure. It is well to remember that it was Bismarck himself who, during his entire term in office, vigorously opposed all attempts to strengthen parliamentary powers and to bring about a constitutional monarchy in Germany. And though public opinion and the Reichstag delegates played an increasingly important role in governmental affairs, the right of appointing and dismissing ministers was still exclusively the crown's.

Wilhelm II had already indicated, at an early date, his intention either to curtail the chancellor's duties or to dismiss him altogether. He had told Adolf von Scholz, the finance minister, in December 1887 that "Prince Bismarck was, of course, very much needed for a few more years, but then his functions would be distributed and some of them taken over by the Emperor." And according to Court Chaplain Stoecker, the emperor had said, "we'll give the old man a six months' breather, then I shall govern myself."[2]

But there were other, more substantive issues that precipitated a major crisis between the two men. An increasingly difficult domestic situation seemed to indicate the failure of Bismarck's mixed system of government by the end of the 1880s. The combined pressure of liberals and Socialists for political recognition and for a more responsible parliamentary government could no longer be resisted; the manipulation of parliamentary majorities, threats of foreign wars, and colonial adventures were no longer producing the desired results. Two issues needed almost immediate attention: the extension of the anti-Socialist laws and the adoption of a new army budget. It was generally assumed that neither one would get Reichstag approval.[3]

Aware of the emperor's desire to dismiss him and determined to stay in office, Bismarck decided that he could survive only in a political situation so utterly chaotic that he would be asked to remain as his country's savior. Since no such situation was likely to occur in time to save him, he set about creating one. To begin with, he worked behind the scenes against the government's coalition parties. The *Kartell*, as the coalition was called, was composed of the National Liberals, Free Conservatives, and the moderate, or national, wing of the Conservative party. Through Bismarck's secret machinations, these parties suffered heavy losses in the election of February 1890, while the opposition parties, the Social Democrats and the Center, and the ultra Conservatives made considerable gains. (Heretofore Bismarck's dismissal has been linked to the outcome of this election, with the implication that the political parties, and with them the Reichstag, had played an important role in this crisis. It was not known that Bismarck was actually behind these activities, nor that the Reichstag or the parties had nothing to do with these developments.)[4] The outcome of the election was a great disappointment to the emperor, who had supported the *Kartell*, and especially to the National Liberals, whom Bismarck had disagreed with as early as 1889. The program of the National Liberals called for colonial expansion, an anti-Russian stance, more social welfare legislation, and tax reforms, all measures which Bismarck opposed. Had Bismarck supported the *Kartell* parties, he would have been following the emperor's lead, thereby surrendering his unique position as political leader of the Reich. Backing the Center and the extreme Conservatives meant defeat of the government's coalition, which would deprive Wilhelm II of much of his political support.

The liberal and moderate conservative elements saw the Center party's victory as a major threat to the established order, and feared that, as a result, Catholic Bavaria would henceforth replace Protestant Prussia as the leading power in Germany. At the same time they expected a disruption of the Triple Alliance, because a German government based on the Center party would lend its support to the establishment of temporal powers of the pope and thus alienate Italy. (The same threat and fear of a Catholic conspiracy at home and abroad that Bismarck himself had so successfully propagated during the *Kulturkampf* was now used by the emperor's supporters against him.) The gains of the Social Democrats, on the other hand, meant to the conservatives that the revolution was just around the corner. In this very confusing situation it was reasonable for Bismarck to assume that his position would be strengthened and that no thought would be given to his dismissal; for who else in Germany would be able to master these chaotic political conditions and still preserve the established order?

But apparently Bismarck's plans went still further. He appears to have considered the possibility of serious and continuing trouble inside Germany and to have prepared for it in two ways: constitutionally and militarily. The chancellor explained at a ministerial council on March 2, 1890, that the federation on which the Reich was based had been formed by an agreement between the federal princes and not by the individual states, and therefore it would be possible for the princes to withdraw from this agreement and get rid of the Reichstag if elections continued to turn out badly for the government.[5] The military aspects were dealt with in a directive drafted on March 12, 1890, by General Verdy, the minister of war. It pertained to supervision of the activities of the Social Democratic party and was submitted to Bismarck for his approval. The directive advised the commanders of the major military districts to watch the Social Democratic clubs in their areas and to be ready to proclaim a state of emergency or war as soon as necessary. In such an event, the constitution and civil rights were to be suspended, ringleaders arrested, newspapers suppressed, and war tribunals established. Preparations for such an emergency were to be made covertly, and included gathering sufficient troops to crush a revolt at its very beginning and providing prison facilities to detain suspects.[6] The most efficient use of firearms during such an emergency was also considered. Bismarck approved these measures and it can be inferred that he and the minister of war looked upon these precautions as rational responses to an immediate threat to the safety of the country.

There can be little doubt that Bismarck would have implemented these plans had circumstances warranted. It can also be assumed that he was willing and able to manipulate events to suit his policies. Thus Bismarck's readiness to stage a coup d'état to secure his position and prolong his tenure should be recognized as a major factor in the dismissal crisis.[7]

These maneuvers make it clear that party politics were much more involved in the crisis than has hitherto been assumed. Bismarck's dismissal should not be seen as a popular vote of no confidence, nor as indication of the Reichstag's power, but rather as a matter of power politics. The *Kartell*, an alliance of eastern landowners and western industrialists, felt threatened by what it perceived as erratic domestic and misguided foreign policies; by exerting sufficient pressure and supporting the young emperor, the *Kartell* was able to oust the chancellor.

There was, in addition, the personal conflict between Wilhelm II and Bismarck. Wilhelm wished to be his own master and a popular monarch. He wanted to appear progressive and, having successfully intervened in a miner's strike in 1889, he intended to introduce comprehensive labor legislation to forestall social upheavals. To this Bismarck was strongly opposed. He was still fighting the Social Democrats, and rather than settle the conflict, he intended to intensify it. By March 1890, with the election results indicating a clear victory for the chancellor and an equally clear defeat for the emperor, an open break was only a matter of time. On March 15, Wilhelm had Bismarck dragged out of bed at nine o'clock in the morning, accused him of negotiating behind his back with Windthorst, the Center party's leader, and ordered him to repeal the Prussian Cabinet order of September 8, 1852. This order, which Bismarck had recently called to the attention of his ministerial colleagues because of their intrigues against him, required that the Prussian prime minister be informed before cabinet ministers made important presentations to the king. Bismarck defended himself against these trumped-up charges, as well as against accusations of having withheld reports on changes in Russian policy,[8] but to no avail—Wilhelm wanted his resignation. Bismarck was trapped. His letter of resignation of March 18, 1890, a memorable document which blames the crisis and his retirement squarely on the emperor, was accepted on March 20. Wilhelm suppressed its publication and instead published his own reply, which indicated that the chancellor had insisted on retiring because of ill health, much against the emperor's wishes.[9]

Bismarck's dismissal marked the end of an era. There was, however, no immediate popular reaction, and public opinion seemed indifferent. The bureaucracy was content to be rid of an autocratic chief and the army remained loyal to the emperor. At seventy-five, after twenty-eight years of faithful service, Bismarck was effectively isolated. His dismissal, like his appointment, was brought about by the personal wish of the monarch; perhaps here more than anywhere else, the tragedy and failure of Bismarck's accomplishments can be seen. Despite his considerable political and diplomatic skill, he had no base of support in the country or among the people. At a time when popular support for domestic and foreign policy was becoming increasingly important, as he himself recognized, Bismarck deliberately shunned becoming involved in party politics. He considered himself throughout his term of office a loyal subject of his master and a faithful servant to his king. This feeling is reflected in the epitaph which he chose to have inscribed on his tombstone: "A faithful German servant of Emperor Wilhelm I."

Bismarck took his retirement with bad grace. He considered his health good enough to carry on for some time, and he expected to be recalled at any moment. He began to loathe the emperor and freely predicted disastrous consequences for his policies. In support of his own views, Bismarck wrote and inspired articles in the *Hamburger Nachrichten* and, with the help of Lothar Bucher, prepared his memoirs. Originally planned for six volumes, only two appeared after Bismarck's death. A third, dealing with his dismissal, was released after the fall of the monarchy in 1919.[10]

Soon after Bismarck's dismissal popular opinion rallied around the former chancellor and a constant stream of visitors came to see him at Varzin and Friedrichsruh. Delegations of students, fraternities, and corporations bestowed honorary memberships, politicians sought advice, and journalists and historians asked for interviews. For a while Bismarck tried to exploit these occasions to express his opposition to the emperor, and in one famous speech at Jena he recalled Goethe's *Goetz von Berlichingen*.[11] All of these gestures did not succeed. The emperor was anxious for a reconciliation, and when Bismarck became ill in January 1894, Wilhelm took the occasion to send him a bottle of wine with his adjutant. A return visit by Bismarck to the emperor in Berlin publicly reconciled the two. On November 27, 1894, Bismarck's wife died, and from then on Bismarck's health, none too good for most of his life, declined steadily; on July 30, 1898, he died.

Bismarck
Reassessed

The nineteenth century was for Germany more than for any other country a period of change. At its beginning—at the Congress of Vienna—a German state did not even exist; instead, there was a conglomeration of medium and small states, monarchies, dukedoms, ecclesiastical states, and free cities, most of them impoverished and rural, with few large towns, connected by a few major rivers and some ill-kept roads. By the end of the century, on the eve of the First World War, Germany was the foremost industrial country on the continent, unified, strong, largely urban, bursting at its seams with energy and expanding its trade and commerce to the four corners of the globe.

These social, economic, and political changes, from a rural to an urban society, from an agricultural to an industrial economy, and from particularism to unification in a period of less than fifty years may explain the problems as well as the challenges which Bismarck faced during his term of office. Combining in his ancestry the two dominant strands of German society—the bureaucratic bourgeoisie and the military nobility—Bismarck's fighting nature and strong will led him to the premiership of Prussia in a time of grave constitutional crisis. By sheer force of personality, cold calculation, and favorable circumstances, he was able to unify Germany under Prussian leadership with considerable popular support. Propelled from the provincial German to the cosmopolitan European stage, and performing simultaneously on both, Bismarck managed for two decades to guide his country through increasingly difficult situations.

At home, he maintained the power of the old order—monarchy, aristocracy, army—in the face of major economic and social changes. His two major struggles against the Catholic church and the Social Democratic party ended in failure and left the country deeply divided. In foreign affairs he preserved Germany's preeminent position and the peace of Europe until his dismissal. To do so he created a system so complicated and contradictory that it began to disintegrate even before he left office. His less able successors, unwilling to follow his tortuous path and dealing with vastly different circumstances, were unable to reconcile the opposing factions within Germany or to agree on a sensible policy abroad.

Bismarck, like most men, had some noticeable blind spots. His creative imagination and energy and his rare political insight were marred by an apparent inability to assess correctly such powerful contemporary trends as socialism and industrialization. He believed throughout his career that he could control and direct these forces and maintain the established order with only minor changes. On a more personal level (and affecting domestic policy more than foreign affairs), his willingness to use moral and immoral means, truth or falsehood, and his intense suspicion and lack of respect for people made it difficult for him to attract and work with bright and independent men.

The great hopes of 1870–71, that the Reich would become a stable and integrated modern state, were not fulfilled. Bismarck failed to adjust to the new and changing order and was unwilling (or perhaps unable) to provide even for an orderly and lasting succession.

How different is the picture of Bismark that emerges from the recent reappraisals and reexaminations? His stature, still impressively large, is marred by serious flaws and shortcomings. His work can no longer be looked upon as the perfect creation it once was believed to be. Instead, it should be regarded as one man's attempt to solve the monumental problem of creating a German state in the latter part of the nineteenth century, an attempt which, in the end, was conceived too narrowly and maintained too rigidly for too long. He was also responsible for setting Germany on her future course, though his successors had ample time to change or modify that course and chose not to do so. That the state Bismarck created lasted less than a century is ample testimony to its basic flaws.

Notes

*Bibliographical
Essay*

Index

Notes

PREFACE

1. The best comprehensive survey of historians' views on Bismarck from the 1920s to the 1950s is by Otto Pflanze, *Bismarck and the Development of Germany*, vol. 1, *The Period of Unification, 1815–1871* (Princeton, 1963), pp. 3–8. I have indicated some of the more significant changes of the recent historical literature in notes.
2. To those familiar with American history and the writings of Charles A. Beard, it will seem strange that economic, social, and constitutional aspects in German historical writings were neglected for so long. A survey of the most popular pre-1940 books on Bismarck and the German unification will show, however, that the overwhelming majority dealt with political history to the neglect of all other.
3. M. Stuermer, ed., *Bismarck und die Preussisch-Deutsche Politik, 1871–1890*, (Munich, 1970), p. 25.
4. For a review of new writings on recent German history see Geoffrey Barraclough, "Mandarins and Nazis: Part I," *The New York Review of Books*, Oct. 19, 1972, pp. 37–43; "The Liberals and German History: Part II," ibid., Nov. 2, 1972, pp. 32–38; "A New View of German History: Part III," ibid., Nov. 16, 1972, pp. 25–31.

1. BISMARCK'S YOUTH

1. E. R. Huber, *Deutsche Verfassungsgeschichte seit 1789* (Stuttgart, 1957), 1:583–84.
2. There was, strictly speaking, no "Germany" before 1871, and the correct reference should either be "in the Germanies" or "in central Europe." Both are awkward and I have used "Germany" whenever it seems more convenient.
3. W. L. Langer, *Political and Social Upheaval, 1832–1852* (New York, 1969), pp. 12–14.
4. "In return for abolition of feudal dues the peasants paid with one-third to one-half of their land, while in the enclosure of the common lands they received only 14 percent, mostly wasteland. Large numbers of small holdings were completely liquidated and absorbed in the larger estates." (Langer, *Political and Social Upheaval, 1832–1852*, p. 12.) See also the excellent article by Jerome Blum, "The Conditions of the European Peasantry on the Eve of Emancipation," *Journal of Modern History* 46, no. 3 (Sept. 1974):395–424, especially 418–20.
5. "In the provinces East of the Elbe, agrarian reforms worked almost invariably to the advantage of the large landowners. The peasantry as a whole was weak-

ened." (H. J. Puhle, *Agrarische Interessenpolitik und Preussischer Konservatis-mus* [Hannover 1966], p. 18.)

6. Erich Marcks, *Bismarcks Jugend, 1815–1848* (Stuttgart, 1915), pp. 12–18.
7. Ibid., pp. 22–23.
8. Some recent Bismarck studies using a psychoanalytic approach have tried to trace the parental influence on Bismarck's later development and to explain his intense drive for power by pointing to his failure to integrate the two different traditions which his parents represented. Otto Pflanze, "Toward a Psychoanalytic Interpreta-tion of Bismarck," *American Historical Review* 77, no. 2 (Apr. 1972):419–44, and Charlotte Sempell, *Otto von Bismarck* (New York, 1972).
9. Marcks, *Bismarcks Jugend*, pp. 54–64.
10. For a fictionalized description of Bismarck's life in Goettingen see Motley's *Mor-ton's Hope* (New York, 1839), where Otto von Rabenmark is unmistakably Bis-marck. Marcks, *Bismarcks Jugend*, pp. 94–95.
11. Marcks, *Bismarcks Jugend*, pp. 131–33.
12. Bismarck's parents had left Schoenhausen a year after Otto was born and moved to their recently acquired estate, Kniephof, near Naugard in Pomerania. Marcks, *Bismarcks Jugend*, p. 41.
13. "Ich will aber Musik machen, wie ich sie fuer gut erkenne, oder gar keine." Marcks, *Bismarcks Jugend*, p. 167.
14. C. Sempell, "Unbekannte Briefstellen Bismarcks," *Historische Zeitschrift* 207, no. 3 (Dec. 1968):610–11.
15. At the beginning of 1847, Kniephof was still indebted by 45,000 thaler and Schoenhausen by 60,000. Sempell, "Unbekannte Briefstellen Bismarcks," p. 613.
16. A plot of April 3, 1833, to seize Frankfurt, dissolve the Diet and unify Germany along liberal lines. G. A. Rein, *Die Revolution in der Politik Bismarcks* (Goet-tingen, 1957), p. 53.
17. Marcks, *Bismarcks Jugend*, p. 198.
18. Ibid., pp. 237–38.
19. Ibid., pp. 293–305.
20. Ibid., pp. 306–94.
21. H. Kober, *Studien zur Rechtsanschauung Bismarcks* (Tuebingen, 1961), pp. 21–32.
22. Pflanze, "Toward a Psychoanalytic Interpretation of Bismarck," p. 424. Older and more traditional studies and biographies, e.g., E. Marcks, *Der Aufstieg des Reiches: Deutsche Geschichte von 1807–1871/78*, 2 vols. (Stuttgart, 1936), E. Bran-denburg, *Reichsgruendung*, 2 vols. (Leipzig, 1916), A. O. Meyer, *Bismarck: Der Mensch und der Staatsmann* (Stuttgart, 1949), take the chancellor's religious pro-nouncements at face value, if they deal with them at all.
23. H. A. Kissinger, "The White Revolutionary: Reflections on Bismarck," *Daedalus* (Summer 1968), p. 897.
24. Ibid., p. 898.
25. Ibid.
26. See F. Stern, *Gold and Iron: Bismarck, Bleichröder, and the Building of the Ger-man Empire* (New York, 1977), p. 12.

2. BISMARCK AND THE REVOLUTION OF 1848

1. The equivalent American slogans were "that government is best that governs least," and "the government of business is no business of government." "The coin-

age of the attractive and celebrated phrase laissez-faire is generally attributed to J. C. M. Vincent de Gournay, an eighteenth century French businessman and economic administrator. It was in an impatient outburst against the clutter of regulations and internal barriers to trade that Gournay is said to have said 'Laissez-faire, morbleu, laissez-passer! le monde va de lui-meme! ('Leave things alone, for heaven's sake, let things move! things will take care of themselves!). The heart of laissez-faire as a precept, as the tag for a whole doctrine and as a trend in policy and practice that promised to dominate the western world in the nineteenth century, was the proposition that any interference by the state must inevitably yield less than the optimum allocation of resources, which would result from the decision of competing individuals guided by a rational calculation of their interests. Exceptions had to be made to preserve internal order and national security, but it was hoped that the progressively unimpeded extension of division of labor and the flow of international trade would eventually produce a world at peace." (E. O. Golob in *Handbook of World History*, ed. J. Dunner [New York, 1967], p. 496.)

2. Langer, *Political and Social Upheaval, 1832–52*, pp. 54–56.
3. Jost Hermand, ed., *Das Junge Deutschland: Text und Dokumente* (Stuttgart, 1966), pp. 370 ff.
4. O. J. Hammen, *The Red '48ers: Karl Marx and Friedrich Engels* (New York, 1969), pp. 20 ff. The Cologne disturbances started in November 1837 when Archbishop Clemens August von Droste-Vischering, following papal guidance, declined to carry out the government's policy regarding mixed marriages. When the archbishop also refused to resign, "the Prussian government had him arrested and incarcerated in the fortress of Minden. . . . This arbitrary action, which lacked any legal justification, caused enormous sensation." The Rhinelanders, who already chafed under the government's anti-Catholic attitude, now took to the streets. The conflict was not settled until Friedrich Wilhelm IV ascended the throne in 1840, when most of the anti-Catholic measures were abandoned. (H. Holborn, *A History of Modern Germany, 1684–1840*, [New York 1964], pp. 505, 508.)
5. Hammen, *The Red '48ers*, pp. 68–69.
6. T. S. Hamerow, *Restoration, Revolution, Reaction* (Princeton, N.J., 1958), p. 124. German historians of the interwar period looked upon the delegates to the Frankfurt Parliament either as impractical idealists (E. Marcks, *Bismarck und die deutsche Revolution, 1848–1851*, published posthumously [Stuttgart, 1939]), or humanitarian liberals (V. Valentine, *Geschichte der deutschen Revolution*, 2 vols. [Berlin, 1939]). During the Nazi period the Frankfurt Assembly was scorned and its failure and lack of real power were emphasized (R. Suchenwirth, *Deutsche Geschichte* [Leipzig, 1937]). Historians in the Federal Republic, after the Second World War, held differing views on the Frankfurt Assembly. F. Meinecke believed that the threat of the mob and its communistic slogans played a major role in the deliberations of the representatives in the Paulskirche by frightening them into compromises with the established authorities. ("The Year of 1848 in German History. Reflections on a Centenary," *Review of Politics* 10 [1948], pp. 475–92.) H. Rothfels maintains that the delegates' efforts and devotion to liberal ideals should be commemorated. ("1848—One Hundred Years After," *Journal of Modern History* 2, no. 4, Dec. 1948.) Historians of the German Democratic Republic, on the other hand, point out that the petit bourgeois democrats at Frankfurt were strong on speeches and declarations, but weak in their determination for revolutionary action. They were divided among themselves and incapable of revolutionary leadership. (H. J. Bartmuss et al., *Deutsche Geschichte*, 3 vols. [Berlin, 1967–68].) Of non-German historians, A. J. P. Taylor in his *Course of German History* (New York, 1946),

believes that the Frankfurt Assembly "suffered from too much experience rather than too little: too much calculation, too much foresight, too many elaborate combinations, too much statesmanship" and that "the essence of Frankfurt was the idea of unity by persuasion." To L. B. Namier, "the aim of the Frankfurt Parliament was a real Pan Germany, not a Greater Prussia or Great Austria" (L. B. Namier *Vanished Supremacies* [London, 1958], p. 28; see also L. B. Namier, *1848: The Revolution of the Intellectuals* [London, 1946], an expanded version of his Raleigh Lecture of 1944). The most detailed and balanced account is provided by F. Eyck, *The Frankfurt Parliament, 1848–1849* (New York, 1968). According to him, the moderate liberals and the radicals considered "unification and constitutional progress . . . aspects of the same problem." The Frankfurt Assembly failed to unify Germany because of insufficient public support and lack of interest by either Prussia or Austria. Friedrich Wilhelm IV's rejection of the crown was not so much a failure by the Frankfurt delegates to write a proper constitution, but rather his realization "that his acceptance would involve Germany and possibly Europe in a war."

7. Langer, *Political and Social Upheaval, 1832–1852*, p. 412. The Czechs of Bohemia and Moravia, led by Frantisek Palacky, refused to attend the Assembly. "The rulers of our people," he wrote to the Assembly on April 11, 1848, "have for centuries participated in the Federation of German Princes but the *people* [emphasis added] never looked upon itself as part of the German nation." (Quoted by Namier, *1848: The Revolution of the Intellectuals*, p. 91.)

8. R. Pascal, "The Frankfurt Parliament, 1848, and the Drang nach Osten" *Journal of Modern History* 18 (1946), p. 115; see also Namier, *1848: The Revolution of the Intellectuals*, passim.

9. G. A. Rein, "Bismarcks gegenrevolutionaere Aktion in den Maerztagen 1848," *Die Welt als Geschichte* 18 (1953), pp. 246–62; see also E. Eyck, *Bismarck: Leben und Werk*, 3 vols. (Zuerich, 1941–44), 1: 85–90.

10. Rein, "Bismarcks gegenrevolutionaere Aktion," p. 261.

11. Rein, *Die Revolution in der Politik Bismarcks*, pp. 71–75. As Fritz Stern has pointed out, no one has assessed the impact of the 1848 Revolution on Bismarck. "The Revolution gave Bismarck (like Marx) a new élan and a new direction. The death of a woman he loved brought a new religious commitment to his life: the near death of his monarchy left him with a new political resolve. The first had taught him the powerlessness of all men; the second, the frailty of most men. Both together gave him a stronger sense of his own duty and destiny." (Stern, *Gold and Iron*, p. 13.)

12. O. Becker, *Bismarcks Ringen um Deutschlands Gestaltung* (Heidelberg, 1958), pp. 59–69.

13. For details see Meyer, *Bismarck*, pp. 66 ff.

14. Ibid., p. 67.

15. Bismarck, *Die Gesammelten Werke*, 19 vols. (Friedrichsruh, 1924–32), 10: 101 ff.; henceforth cited *GW*.

16. Quoted by Stern, *Gold and Iron*, p. 14.

17. Quoted by Meyer, *Bismarck*, p. 74.

3. FRANKFURT, ST. PETERSBURG, PARIS, 1851–1862

1. O. Becker, *Bismarcks Ringen um Deutschlands Gestaltung*, pp. 68–69.

2. Quoted by Meyer, *Bismarck*, pp. 76–77.

3. Ibid., p. 89.

4. H. Boehme, *Deutschlands Weg zur Grossmacht* (Cologne, 1966), pp. 23–41.
5. Meyer, *Bismarck*, pp. 98–100.
6. Bismarck's memorandum of April 6, 1853, *GW*, 1:323, n. 1.
7. A. O. Meyer, *Bismarcks Kampf mit Oesterreich am Bundestag zu Frankfurt, 1851 bis 1859* (Berlin, 1927), pp. 189–206.
8. Quoted by Meyer, *Bismarck*, p. 105.
9. In concluding the alliance Austria meant to secure her flank in case of complications with Russia. Prussia, largely pro-Russian in her sympathies, was bent on neutrality and by concluding the alliance hoped to influence Austrian policy toward this goal.
10. Meyer, *Bismarck*, pp. 106–7.
11. Ibid., pp. 108–10.
12. Ibid., pp. 107–11.
13. For details see Meyer, *Bismarcks Kampf*, pp. 324–66.
14. The king's insanity disabled him in October 1857, and Prince Wilhelm had been acting regent since that time.
15. *GW*, 3:302–23.
16. Meyer, *Bismarck*, pp. 119–24.
17. Ibid., p. 126.
18. O. Becker, *Bismarcks Ringen um Deutschlands Gestaltung*, p. 74; *GW*, 14, pt. 1, p. 517; 3:37, 38.
19. Meyer, *Bismarck*, pp. 127–30.
20. Ibid., pp. 145–47.
21. H. Oncken, "Die Baden-Badener Denkschrift Bismarcks," *Historische Zeitschrift* 145 (1932), pp. 124 ff.
22. He criticized the negative and defensive aspects of the conservative program and ridiculed the idea of a solidarity of conservative interest throughout Europe. He characterized the existing constitution of the Confederation as a hothouse for dangerous revolutionary and particularist ideas and expressed surprise that people should be so sensitive to the idea of popular representation in the Confederate Diet or in the Customs Union Parliament. (Bismarck to Alexander Below-Hohendorf, Sept. 18, 1861 [*GW*, 14, pt. 1, p. 578].)
23. Meyer, *Bismarck*, p. 161 and reference.
24. Ibid., pp. 162–68.

4. BISMARCK'S APPOINTMENT AND THE CONSTITUTIONAL CONFLICT IN PRUSSIA

1. Meyer, *Bismarck*, p. 172.
2. Ibid., p. 171.
3. Ibid., p. 172.
4. *GW*, 15:179.
5. Ibid.
6. *Fuerst Bismarcks Briefe an seine Braut und Gattin*, ed. H. Bismarck (Stuttgart, 1900), pp. 513–14.
7. Huber, *Deutsche Verfassungsgeschichte seit 1789*, 3:280.
8. M. Messerschmidt, "Die Armee in Staat und Gesellschaft—Die Bismarckzeit," in M. Stuermer, *Das kaiserliche Deutschland: Politik und Gesellschaft, 1870–1918* (Duesseldorf, 1970), pp. 90–94.
9. O. Becker, *Bismarcks Ringen um Deutschlands Gestaltung*, p. 94.
10. Huber, *Deutsche Verfassungsgeschichte seit 1789*, 3:278. See also W. Sauer, "Das

Problem des deutschen Nationalstaates," in H. U. Wehler, ed., *Moderne deutsche Sozialgeschichte* (Cologne, 1968), p. 427.

11. O. Becker, *Bismarcks Ringen um Deutschlands Gestaltung*, p. 96.
12. Ibid., p. 97. Transcending the military and financial question was a fundamental split between the outlooks of the bourgeoisie and the nobility: "as the political representatives of an economically emancipated middle class, the Prussian liberals had little understanding of the remnants of the old regime, of its political and financial privileges, of the burden of unproductive military expenditures on the economy and of its often patronizing attitude toward the bureaucracy. To get rid of these chains they [the liberals] needed, according to their views, not only economic but political power. These were the issues of the 1860's." (H. A. Winkler, *Preussischer Liberalismus und Deutscher Nationalstaat: Studien zur Geschichte der Deutschen Fortschrittspartei 1861–1866*, [Tuebingen, 1964], p. 20.)
13. Huber, *Deutsche Verfassungsgeschichte seit 1789*, 3:280–87.
14. O. Becker, *Bismarcks Ringen um Deutschlands Gestaltung*, p. 98.
15. Huber, *Deutsche Verfassungsgeschichte seit 1789*, 3:291–93.
16. Winkler, *Preussischer Liberalismus*, pp. 14–15.
17. Wilhelm was crowned king of Prussia at Koenigsberg on January 2, 1861.
18. Huber, *Deutsche Verfassungsgeschichte seit 1789*, 3:294–97.
19. Ibid., pp. 298–99.
20. L. Reiners, *Bismarcks Aufstieg, 1815–1864* (Munich, 1965), pp. 354–56.
21. T. S. Hamerow, *The Social Foundations of German Unification, 1858–1871: Struggles and Accomplishments*, 2 vols. (Princeton, N.J., 1972), 2:158.
22. O. Becker, *Bismarcks Ringen um Deutschlands Gestaltung*, p. 103.
23. Huber, *Deutsche Verfassungsgeschichte seit 1789*, 3:305.
24. Ibid., pp. 306–7; O. Pflanze, "Juridical and Political Responsibility in 19th Century Germany," In L. Krieger and F. Stern, eds., *The Responsibility of Power* (Garden City, N.Y., 1967), p. 179.
25. *GW*, 10:140.
26. Huber, *Deutsche Verfassungsgeschichte seit 1789*, 3:308–9.
27. Ibid., p. 318–19.
28. Quoted by K. S. Pinson, *Modern Germany* (New York, 1954), pp. 130–31.
29. The constitutional conflict in Prussia is probably the best and clearest issue with which to demonstrate the disparate views of historians over the last half century. Erich Marcks, Bismarck's defender and one of the foremost German nationalist historians of the older generation, believed that the chancellor's theory of the constitutional gap could not be considered legally wrong, though the government was in effect exercising dictatorial powers. According to Marcks, the liberals and the moderates, supported by public opinion, were aiming for west European parliamentarism. Bismarck, unable to achieve a compromise, threw himself into the fight with great enthusiasm and carried the king with him. The opposition, in turn, was ready to deny its support even in case of war. The liberals were convinced that without the people's support, Prussia would be defeated in such a war. This stand was necessary to get rid of Bismarck and the hated government. The liberals' fight against their own state was a heavy and tragic responsibility, according to Marcks, but in the end, they vastly overestimated their strength because the Prussian people, basically patriotic, did not follow them. (E. Marcks, *Der Aufstieg des Reiches*.)

    Presenting the traditional, liberal point of view, Eugene N. Anderson, an American historian who has written extensively on modern European and Germany history, closely analyzes the parties and issues involved in his *Social and Political Conflict in Prussia, 1858–1864* (Lincoln, Nebr., 1954). He believes "that the Prussian people overwhelmingly opposed the preservation of the vestiges of the Old Regime and desired reform." They understood the issues involved but because of their inexperience in self-government and their fear of using force, they failed in their aims. The liberals did not surrender, however, until the Austro-Prussian War provided the basis for one of their major objectives, German unity. Bismarck, according to Anderson, was not only adept at using power, he was also lucky in benefiting from an upswing of the economy.

Focusing on the Progressive party, Heinrich August Winkler, in his *Preussischer Liberalismus und Deutscher Nationalstaat: Studien zur Geschichte der Deutschen Fortschrittspartei, 1861–1866* (Tuebingen, 1964), believes that the issues involved were more complicated than either Marcks or Anderson will admit. He disputes the latter's judgment on the election of July 1866 (Winkler, *Preussischer Liberalismus*, p. 92, n. 4) and asserts that the Liberal's views on foreign policy in the 1860s were "considerably more aggressive and militant than those of Bismarck" (p. 112, fn. 59). Winkler also maintains that the so-called capitulation of German liberals in 1866 has been misinterpreted by the older historians, E. Marcks (*Der Aufstieg des Reiches*) and E. Brandenburg (*Die Reichsgruendung*), and by the more recent ones, F. C. Sell (*Die Tragoedie des deutschen Liberalismus* [Stuttgart, 1953]) and H. Kohn (*The Mind of Germany* [New York, 1960]). According to Winkler, the resistance to the rise of liberalism was much stronger in Germany than in western Europe because of the greater power and firmer foundation of the various local dynasties; the Reformation and the strong particularistic feeling throughout Germany had also established close ties between the people and their princes, closer ties than those between other people in western Europe and their local nobility. For these reasons, the Prussian liberals were justified, according to Winkler, in trusting the nobility which, under Stein and Hardenberg, had effected a revolution from above (pp. 115–16).

Breaking new ground by getting away from the usual preoccupation with diplomatic and political affairs, Theodore S. Hamerow focuses on the social and economic aspects of nineteenth-century history in his two-volume study *The Social Foundations of German Unification, 1858–1871*. From a vast array of hitherto neglected sources and statistical data, he concludes that the majority of people were indifferent to the constitutional conflict. "The struggle between Crown and Parliament did not arise out of a deliberate confrontation. It was rather the inadvertent result of political strategems whose effect had not been foreseen." Bismarck, according to Hamerow, "rejected the possibility of an overt coup d'état. He felt that under the political conditions of modern society, parliamentary institutions were essential for monarchical rule. Prussia's experience with constitutionalism convinced him of the compatibility of a representative assembly with royal authority." For the latest study see M. Gugel, *Industrieller Aufstieg und buergerliche Herrschaft: Sozio-oekonomische Interessen und politische Ziele des liberalen Buergertums in Preussen zur Zeit des Verfassungskonflikts, 1857–1867* (Cologne, 1975).

30. Winkler, *Preussischer Liberalismus*, pp. 24–27.
31. Shlomo Na'aman, *Lassalle* (Hannover, 1970), p. 431.

5. BISMARCK'S THREE WARS

1. Quoted by R. H. Lord, "Bismarck and Russia in 1863," *American Historical Review* 29 (October 1923), p. 26.
2. Gorchakov mentioned the Convention to the French ambassador, while Bismarck

bragged to Behrend, vice-president of the Prussian Diet, about Prussian incursions into Poland as far as Warsaw; in addition, German newspapers had printed several stories about Russia's inability to cope with the revolt. (E. Eyck, *Bismarck*, 1:469.)

3. Ibid., p. 472. On the attitude of the liberals to the Polish question, see Winkler, *Preussischer Liberalismus*, pp. 34–41.

4. Lord, "Bismarck and Russia in 1863," p. 32.

5. W. E. Mosse, *The European Powers and the German Question, 1848–1871* (Cambridge, 1958), pp. 115–16.

6. Lord, "Bismarck and Russia in 1863," p. 24; see also A. Hillgruber, *Bismarcks Aussenpolitik* (Freiburg, 1972), pp. 49 ff., and W. Bussmann, *Das Zeitalter Bismarcks* (Frankfurt, 1968), pp. 71 ff.

7. It has been suggested that Bismarck might have wanted to use the crisis and an ensuing war to alleviate and perhaps solve the constitutional crisis at home. (Lord, "Bismarck and Russia in 1863," pp. 47–48.)

8. See chap. 2.

9. Boehme, *Deutschlands Weg zur Grossmacht*, pp. 100–117.

10. The standard work is still L. D. Steefel, *The Schleswig-Holstein Question* (Cambridge, Mass., 1932).

11. See chap. 2.

12. K. A. P. Sandiford, *Great Britain and the Schleswig-Holstein Question, 1848–1864* (Toronto, 1975), pp. 67 ff.

13. For a detailed account of the Prussian liberals' concern regarding the Schleswig-Holstein question, see Winkler, *Preussischer Liberalismus*, pp. 41 ff.

14. F. Thimme, editor of Bismarck's political writings (*GW*, vols. 4–6b), believed that Bismarck's foreign policy toward Austria was strongly influenced by domestic conservative considerations (the desire to repress liberal opposition and reestablish and increase royal power) and that his cooperation with Austria in the Schleswig-Holstein question was not designed to achieve greater power for Prussia. Bismarck's real aim, according to Thimme, was an alliance with Austria to gain Austria's trust and favor, and in this way achieve Prussian predominance in North Germany. With Prussia's vital interests secured, and a trusting and long-lasting cooperation between the two German powers established, they could both fight against the common enemy: constitutionalism and revolution. It was only after the Gastein Convention that Bismarck considered all possibilities for cooperation with Austria lost. Austria's secret agreement with France was a much stronger indication of her pro-war policy than Bismarck's earlier agreement with Italy was in the case of Prussia. (Introduction to *GW*, 5:x–xii).

15. Boehme, *Deutschlands Weg zur Grossmacht*, p. 165.

16. *GW*, 5:96–103.

17. In an interesting and penetrating study on the possibility of war in the summer of 1865 ("Kriegsgefahr und Gasteiner Konvention: Bismarck, Eulenburg und die Vertagung des preussisch-oesterreichischen Krieges im Sommer 1865," in I. Geiss and B. J. Wendt, eds., *Deutschland in der Weltpolitik des 19. und 20. Jahrhunderts* [Duesseldorf, 1973], pp. 89–103), J. C. G. Roehl agrees with R. Stadelmann, who believes that the European political situation in the summer of 1865 was an ideal moment for Bismarck to declare war on Austria. Britain was preoccupied with the American Civil War, France with her Mexican adventure, and Russia with internal affairs in the aftermath of the Crimean War. None of these powers could have come to Austria's assistance and, in addition, Austria had constitutional and financial troubles of her own. Since this situation could not be expected to last, time was against Bismarck; why he failed to take advantage of this favorable moment is an

intriguing question. Either he genuinely wanted to avoid war and come to terms with Austria, or he had already decided on war but had not completed all his preparations. Stadelmann tends toward the latter explanation, though he also considers the influence of public opinion and the possibility that Bismarck may have pursued both courses simultaneously. (Stadelmann shows that Wilhelm I and his advisors favored a much stronger anti-Austrian policy than German historians of the older school have heretofore assumed. R. Stadelmann, *Das Jahr 1865 und das Problem von Bismarcks deutscher Politik, Historische Zeitschrift* supplement no. 29 [Munich, 1933], quoted by Roehl, "Kriegsgefahr," pp. 90–91.)

Roehl concludes, on the basis of newly discovered letters from Bismarck to the Prussian minister of the interior, Eulenburg, that Bismarck's reasons for postponing war in July 1865 were predominantly financial. The failure of some important financial transactions, for which he blamed the Prussian finance minister Bodelschwingh and the Prussian minister for trade Itzenpiltz, left the government short of funds for the war effort. "During the year 1865, Bismarck did not honestly work for an understanding with Austria. The Convention of Gastein cannot be judged as proof of a desire to achieve a peaceful dualism; it was nothing but an attempt to gain time." (Roehl, "Kriegsgefahr," p. 103.)

18. E. Eyck, *Bismarck*, 2:68–69.
19. Ibid., p. 86.
20. *GW*, 5:307–11.
21. Quoted by E. Eyck, *Bismarck*, 2:101.
22. *GW*, 5:365–68.
23. E. Eyck, *Bismarck*, 2:112.
24. Ibid., p. 124.
25. Stern, *Gold and Iron*, p. 69. The property involved was the Cologne-Minden Railroad.
26. Although Bleichroeder's relationship to Bismarck had been known for a long time, the details of their relationship and the importance of Bleichroeder's role has only been dealt with recently by Fritz Stern in his penetrating and well-written study, *Gold and Iron*.
27. Ibid., chaps. 3 and 4.
28. A. J. P. Taylor, *The Struggle for Mastery in Europe, 1848–1918* (Oxford, 1954), pp. 163–65.
29. *GW*, 5:416–19.
30. Ibid., pp. 432–34, 447–49.
31. See chap. 3.
32. E. Eyck, *Bismarck*, 2:162.
33. Ibid., p. 169.
34. On July 20, 1858, Napoleon III and Cavour met at Plombières and agreed to join forces in a war against Austria. For details see Taylor, *The Struggle for Mastery in Europe*, pp. 103–4.
35. E. Eyck, *Bismarck*, 2:170–72.
36. The motives which caused Bismarck to consider the plan at all are not entirely clear. They were probably part of his two-track effort to gain Prussian supremacy in Germany. One track followed a warlike policy, the other a peaceful one. The Gablenz plan was part of the second track and also served to strengthen the king's resolve, should the peaceful policy fail. (E. Eyck, *Bismarck*, 2:174–81.) For a presentation of various views by historians on the Gablenz mission and Bismarck's attitude toward it, see O. Becker, *Bismarcks Ringen um Deutschlands Gestaltung*, chap. 4, n. 4, pp. 843–44.

37. Reorganization of the Prussian army in connection with the constitutional conflict played no part in the army's effectiveness, for victory could also have been achieved by employment of the militia and other Boyen reforms. O. Becker, *Bismarcks Ringen um Deutschlands Gestaltung*, p. 98.

38. Pflanze, *Bismarck and the Development of Germany*, vol. 1, pp. 301–3. "Bleich-roeder . . . transmitted 400,000 thaler to the Hungarian revolutionaries" (F. Stern, *The Failure of Illiberalism* [New York, 1972], p. 62). See also Stern, *Gold and Iron*, pp. 89–90.

39. On Bismarck's treatment of Frankfurt, see Stern, *Gold and Iron*, pp. 90–91.

40. *GW*, 6:120. Pflanze, *Bismarck and the Development of Germany*, vol. 1, pp. 306–10.

41. Winkler, *Preussischer Liberalismus*, pp. 91–92.

42. Huber, *Deutsche Verfassungsgeschichte seit 1789*, 3:353, 358.

43. On the split of the liberals, see Winkler, *Preussischer Liberalismus*, pp. 93 ff.

44. G. A. Kertesz, "Reflections on a Centenary," *Historical Studies of Australia and New Zealand* 12 (Oct. 1966), pp. 333–42.

45. K. G. Faber, "Realpolitik als Ideologie," *Historische Zeitschrift* 203 (Aug. 1966), pp. 1–45. Winkler believes it would be wrong to accuse the liberals of having opted for power and against freedom in 1866. From their point of view it was quite reasonable to hope that Prussia's strongly authoritarian position would be diluted by the unification of Germany. (Winkler, *Preussischer Liberalismus*, p. 122). See also G. R. Mork, "Bismarck and the 'Capitulation' of German Liberalism," *Journal of Modern History* 43, no. 1 (March 1971): 59–75.

46. Bismarck spent the latter part of October and early November at Putbus on the Baltic Sea, recuperating from an illness. Bussman, *Das Zeitalter Bismarcks*, p. 96.

47. Pflanze, *Bismarck and the Development of Germany*, vol. 1, p. 338.

48. H. Hefter, *Die deutsche Selbstverwaltung im 19. Jahrhundert*, 2d ed. (Stuttgart, 1969), believes that Prussian hegemony in the North German Confederation and later in the Reich preserved Prussian particularism. By the same token, the particularism of the lesser German states was preserved, and the door was left open for the South German states to enter the Confederation later on (p. 468).

49. The text of this clause provided that "the regulations and decrees of the Federal President are issued in the name of the Confederation and require for their validity the counter signature of the Federal Chancellor who accepts with it the responsibility." Article 172/2 as quoted by R. Morsey, *Die oberste Reichsverwaltung unter Bismarck, 1867–1890* (Muenster, 1957), p. 19. See also E. Hahn, "Ministerial Responsibility and Impeachment in Prussia 1848–63," *Central European History* 10, no. 1 (Mar. 1977): 3–27.

50. Morsey, *Die oberste Reichsverwaltung*, pp. 20–21.

51. During Bismarck's term of office he was responsible neither to the Reichstag nor to the Federal Council, only to the king. His dismissal in 1890 was not for any loss of confidence by any legislative bodies, but only because the king had lost confidence in his minister. Morsey, *Die oberste Reichsverwaltung*, pp. 21–23; Pflanze, "Juridical and Political Responsibility," p. 173, n. 17. For Bismarck's views on ministerial responsibility, see Hahn, "Ministerial Responsibility," pp. 24–25.

52. Quoted by G. P. Gooch, *Studies in Modern History* (New York, 1968), p. 227.

53. Pflanze, *Bismarck and the Development of Germany*, vol. 1, p. 361.

54. Morsey, *Die oberste Reichsverwaltung*, pp. 24, 25.

55. J. Becker, "Zum Problem der Bismarckschen Politik in der Spanischen Thronfrage 1870," *Historische Zeitschrift* 212, no. 3 (June 1971): 529–607.

56. E. Eyck, *Bismarck*, 2:424.

57. Taylor, *The Struggle for Mastery in Europe*, p. 185.

58. Alexander had come to Paris in June 1867 to visit the exhibition and to meet his mistress, Princess Catherine Dolgoruky. W. E. Mosse, *The European Powers and the German Question, 1848–1871*, p. 270, n. 3.
59. There were firm indications of a French-Austrian understanding at the time (November 1867–January 1869) and rumors of an Austro-Prussian rapprochement. The latter was strongly denied by Bismarck. W. E. Mosse, *The European Powers*, pp. 279–83.
60. Ibid., pp. 284–90.
61. Following the defeat of the republican forces under Garibaldi, French forces occupied Rome in 1849 to ensure the future safety of the pope and of the Church. By 1864 Napoleon III changed his policy, to the dismay of many Catholics in France and, in an attempt to curry favor with the Italians, he signed the September Convention with the Italian government. By its terms, the Italians promised not to attack papal territory and, in return, the French government agreed to withdraw its troops within two years, which it did in December 1866. By October of the following year, French troops returned after an insurrection in Rome had failed and volunteers under Garibaldi had defeated the papal forces. The combined French and papal forces defeated the volunteers in the battle of Mentana, November 3, 1867, and Garibaldi was captured. The Italians were deeply resentful and though Napoleon tried to come to terms with them, French public opinion, spurred by the Church, precluded any concessions. Thus, the Roman question remained a major point of dispute and crippled Franco-Italian relations until the fall of the Second Empire.
62. E. Eyck, *Bismarck*, 2: 342–46, 348–51, 355–58.
63. The Spanish throne had become vacant after Queen Isabella fled to France, September 29, 1868, following the defeat of the royal forces. In May 1869, the Spanish Parliament voted for a constitutional monarchy and looked for a suitable candidate for the Spanish throne among the royal houses of Europe.

    The material on the Hohenzollern candidature is voluminous; the original German documents, with minor exceptions, were kept secret until the Second World War when Allied troops captured them as part of the German Foreign Ministry archives. The documents on the Hohenzollern candidature plus some documents from the Hohenzollern-Sigmaringen archives were compiled and edited by Georges Bonnin in *Bismarck and the Hohenzollern Candidature for the Spanish Throne: The Documents in the German Diplomatic Archives* (London, 1957). Bonnin's introduction is a fascinating account of how German Foreign Office officials suppressed the key documents. The publication of Bonnin's volume was welcomed by most historians as an important contribution and clarification of a major problem in modern European history. Only Gerhard Ritter, the doyen of German national historians, was unimpressed. In his introduction to J. Dittrich's book (see below) he asserted that most of the material that Bonnin had discovered had been known to German historians since 1913. (One can only wonder why German historians did nothing with the material in that interval.) He deplored the fact that the documents had been translated into English and regretted that they were published by a foreigner.

    Historical opinion on Bismarck's role in this crisis can be roughly divided into three views: historians who believed that Bismarck used the Hohenzollern candidature from the very beginning to go to war with France, those who considered Bismarck completely blameless in the affair, and those who believed that while he did not cause or even want the war, he took advantage of the situation and confronted France with a choice of war or diplomatic defeat.

    To the first group belong the French historians who published prior to World War

I. E. Ollivier, *L'Empire Liberal*, 16 vols. (Paris 1895–1912); H. Welschinger, *La Guerre de 1870: Causes et Responsibilités*, 2 vols., (Paris, 1875); A. Sorel, *Histoire Diplomatique de la Guerre Franco-Allemande* (Paris, 1875); P. de la Gorce, *Histoire du Second Empire*, 7 vols. (Paris, 1896–1903). German historians whose studies came out after World War II also shared this view. E. Eyck, *Bismarck*, believed Bismarck set a trap for Napoleon III from which there was no escape but war (2:487). H. U. Wehler, *Bismarck und der Imperialismus* (Cologne, 1969), sees in Bismarck's policy a "revolution from above" with aspects of Bonapartism designed to preserve the existing order through foreign diversions and limited concessions at home (p. 456). J. Becker, "Zum Problem der Bismarckschen Politik in der Spanischen Thronfrage 1870," in *Historische Zeitschrift* 212, no. 3 (June 1971): 529–607, the most recent and most comprehensive account, concludes that Bismarck was determined that his policy should lead to war with France from the very beginning (pp. 604–5).

The second group, which considers Bismarck blameless, is composed of historians, mostly Germans, who wrote before or after World War I, but there are some who, even after 1945 and the considerable amount of new evidence, still consider Bismarck innocent of an aggressive policy toward France. H. v. Sybel, the official historian of German unification, asserted in his *Die Begruendung des deutschen Reiches durch Wilhelm I*, 7 vols. (Munich, 1913), that Bismarck had nothing to do with the Hohenzollern candidature. Hans Delbrueck, in "Das Geheimnis der Napoleonischen Politik im Jahre 1870," in his *Erinnerungen, Aufsaetze und Reden* (Berlin, 1902) and H. Oncken, in *Das deutsche Reich und die Vorgeschichte des Weltkrieges* (Leipzig, 1933), believed that Bismarck's policy was primarily defensive and a reaction to Napoleon's attempt to encircle Prussia by his alliances with Austria and Italy. This is also E. Brandenburg's opinion in *Die Reichsgruendung*. L. Reiners, *Bismarck gruendet das Reich, 1864–1871* (Munich, 1957), asserts that although Bismarck favored Leopold's candidacy, he had no intention of letting it lead to war, nor did he want to set a trap for Napoleon III (p. 381). A. J. P. Taylor, *Bismarck: The Man and the Statesman* (London, 1955), considers the question of Bismarck's involvement "the most difficult to answer" and concludes that "there is not a scrap of evidence that he worked deliberately for a war with France, still less that he timed it precisely for the summer of 1870 . . . the Hohenzollern Candidature, far from being designed to provoke a war with France which would complete the unification with Germany, was intended rather to make German unification possible without war. . . . He [Bismarck] had neither planned the war nor foreseen it. But he claimed it as his own once it became inevitable. He wished to present himself as the creator of Germany, not as a man who had been mastered by events" (pp. 115, 116, 118, 121).

The third and largest group consists of those historians who occupy a position between the two extremes; they are Germans, Americans, and Englishmen, most of whom have reevaluated old evidence or have used new documents appearing since the end of World War II.

H. Geuss, in *Bismarck und Napoleon III* (Cologne, 1959), believes that Bismarck estimated that a Hohenzollern in Spain would tie up 40,000–80,000 French soldiers; that is, one-eighth to one-quarter of the French wartime army. The diversion of such a large part of his army would persuade Napoleon to abandon the French war faction in the government and turn toward a liberal course in domestic policies. This, in turn, would have allowed Bismarck to pursue a peaceful policy of German unification. "The Hohenzollern Candidature was thus primarily a lever for Bismarck to move the uncertain French domestic situation . . . toward German unification and peace as he had intended all along" (p. 266). The plan misfired because one of its key factors—total secrecy—was not maintained. B. Schot, "Die Entstehung des deutsch-franzoesischen Krieges und die Gruendung des deutschen Reiches," in H. Boehme, ed., *Probleme der Reichsgruendungszeit, 1848–1879* (Cologne, 1968), pp. 269–95, maintains that Bismarck did not plan a war from the beginning, but at the same time, he did nothing to calm the excitement aroused by the premature news of the candidature; on the contrary, he cleverly utilized the situation created by the exaggerated French demands. And he confronted the French government with the alternatives of war to save French national prestige or diplomatic defeat. It was imperative for German and European public opinion that France take the initiative and appear as the disturber of the peace. Bismarck had achieved his aim, but in a different way than he had originally imagined (p. 291). J. Dittrich, *Bismarck, Frankreich und die spanische Thronkandidature der Hohenzollern: Die "Kriegschuldfrage" von 1870* (Munich, 1962), concludes that Bismarck engineered (*gemacht*) the candidature and that he used it to bring about a decision (p. 2), but does not believe that Bismarck wanted war (p. 289). L. D. Steefel, *Bismarck, the Hohenzollern Candidacy and the Origins of the Franco-German War of 1870* (Cambridge, Mass., 1962), states that "the Franco-German War of 1870 was not the product of reasoned long-term policy" (p. 221). He stresses repeatedly that France declared war and that war was not inevitable until then. "Bismarck did not create the Hohenzollern Candidacy as a countermine to explode the projected triple alliance, but the fear of such an alliance was a major factor, perhaps the major factor, in his decision to urge the Spanish offer" (p. 239). "[The candidacy] provided Bismarck with the means to create a European crisis. What form it would take could not be predicted with certainty" (p. 244). Pflanze, *Bismarck and the Development of Germany*, vol. 1, considers that "the Hohenzollern candidature was an offensive, not a defensive act. . . . Bismarck's goal was . . . a crisis with France. He deliberately set sail on a collision course with the intent of provoking either war or a French internal collapse" (pp. 448, 449). W. N. Medlicott, *Bismarck and Modern Germany* (London, 1965), believes that "Bismarck undoubtedly instigated the candidature, and he undoubtedly welcomed the outbreak of war which resulted from it" (p. 81). The Franco-Prussian War was certainly not an unprovoked attack on Prussia's part: "but who can deny that Bismarck's conduct since 1866 had provoked the provocation?" (p. 84). A. Mitchell, *Bismarck and the French Nation, 1848–1890,* (New York, 1971), calls attention to Bismarck's concern with French domestic policies, especially the outcome of the national election for the legislature in May 1869, which returned a liberal majority. Contrary to some opinion which feared that the election results heralded a return to domestic unrest and foreign adventures, Bismarck believed it "strengthened Napoleon's throne." Mitchell believes that this was unsettling to Bismarck, because he "would no longer be able to count on a maladroit French initiative to provide a convenient diplomatic complication to be exploited" (p. 51). In his foreword to G. Bonnin, ed., *Bismarck and the Hohenzollern Candidature for the Spanish Throne. The Documents in the German Diplomatic Archives* (London, 1957), G. P. Gooch writes that "Bismarck welcomed the prospect of a conflict with France in which military victory seemed reasonably certain and which he believed would remove the last obstacle to the voluntary incorporation of the south German states in a federal empire with the King of Prussia at its head. Of his desire for war there is of course not a trace in his letters and dispatches" (pp. 10–11).

64. J. Becker, "Zum Problem der Bismarckschen Politik in der Spanischen Thronfrage 1870," pp. 569–70.

148

65. D. W. Houston, "Emile Ollivier and the Hohenzollern Candidature," *French Historical Studies* 4 (Fall 1965), pp. 125–49.
66. W. L. Langer, "Bismarck as a Dramatist," in A. O. Sarkissian, ed., *Studies in Diplomatic History and Historiography in Honor of G. P. Gooch* (New York, 1962), pp. 199–216. The original of this famous dispatch, with Bismarck's corrections, is missing, if it ever existed. J. Becker, "Zum Problem der Bismarckschen Politik in der Spanischen Thronfrage 1870," p. 531.
67. A correct appraisal would shed important light on Bismarck's personality and methods, and would also clarify his policy toward German unification and explain subsequent German-French relations prior to World War I. For the following, I have relied heavily on J. Becker, "Zum Problem der Bismarckschen Politik in der Spanischen Thronfrage 1870."
68. Quoted by J. Becker, "Zum Problem der Bismarckschen Politik in der Spanischen Thronfrage 1870," p. 597.
69. The "iron budget" of 1867, "provided for an army equivalent to 1 per cent. of the population, supported by an automatic annual grant of the 225 thaler per man. Originally scheduled to expire in December 1871, this law was extended for an additional three years." G. Craig, *The Politics of the Prussian Army, 1640–1945* (Oxford, 1955), p. 220.
70. Pflanze, *Bismarck and the Development of Germany*, vol. 1, p. 449.
71. J. Becker, "Zum Problem der Bismarckschen Politik in der Spanischen Thronfrage 1870," p. 605. Mitchell, *Bismarck and the French Nation*, pp. 51–52.
72. The best account of the war is M. Howard, *The Franco-Prussian War* (New York, 1961).
73. E. Kolb, "Kriegsfuehrung und Politik 1870/71," in T. Schieder and E. Deuerlein, eds., *Reichsgruendung 1870/71* (Stuttgart, 1970), pp. 95–118.
74. Quoted by Taylor, *The Struggle for Mastery in Europe*, p. 212.
75. Ibid., pp. 212–14.
76. R. I. Giesberg, *The Treaty of Frankfort* (Philadelphia, 1966), pp. 87–98.
77. Ibid., pp. 107–26.
78. The unified German state, Bismarck's greatest achievement, did not survive the Second World War. The methods Bismarck used to unify Germany were admired and praised during his lifetime, but were increasingly questioned as the Reich failed to meet a series of external and domestic crises and was finally crushed.

    Before and during the First World War, historians stressed the patriotic and national aspects of the unification movement and praised Bismarck and Wilhelm I, thus indirectly criticizing Wilhelm II. Some writers during the Weimar Republic, which followed World War I, attempted to discover whether faults in the founding of the Reich could explain its recent defeat, while others extolled Bismarck's glorious achievements, which they compared favorably to the petty and harmful policies of the politicians of the Republic.

    In the Third Reich Nazi historians compared Bismarck's establishment of a lesser German Reich unfavorably to Hitler's Greater Germany; some saw in Bismarck's creation the forerunner to Hitler's Reich. After the collapse in 1945, German historians have tried to reassess the unification of 1871.

    The following is but a sample of some historians' views. H. v. Treitschke in his *Historische und Politische Aufsaetze*, 3 vols. (Leipzig, 1911–15), written in 1886, credited the Prussian monarchy with the creation of the Reich; accomplished by military might, it had the power of a *fait accompli* and the irresistible force of awakened national feeling behind it (2:551). But the masses played no part in the unification movement, "it was not even desirable that they should do so," according to Treitschke, "because such a movement on German soil usually produced a lot of noise and anarchy" (3:544). Nor did the Customs Union parliament play a constructive role in the larger movement. Particularism and the hatred of Prussia among the South German states made German unity appear unattainable for a long time. At this point, "a kind providence sent us the war with France. And indeed, only such a tremendous event, only such an act of violence, so brutal and impudent that it would arouse even the most indolent conscience, was able to lead the South back into the greater fatherland" (3:548).

E. Brandenburg, in *Die Reichsgruendung*, believed that while leading statesmen and generals played an important role in the unification and military and diplomatic events may have been decisive, the national feeling and the cooperation of the German people should not be underestimated; the existence of a strong national movement was the indispensable basis for the achievements of the statesmen. Everyone who had carried a gun during the struggles from 1813 to 1870, or had fought for national ideals by making speeches and writing pamphlets, had participated in the founding of the new Germany. The decisive deeds, however, came from the men around King Wilhelm, and the biggest among them was Bismarck (2:413, 417–18).

J. Ziekursch, in the *Politische Geschichte des neuen deutschen Kaiserreiches*, 3 vols. (Frankfurt, 1925–30), asserted that Bismarck's work was accomplished against the wishes of a majority of the German people. It was done in the interests and with the help of the Hohenzollern dynasty, the Prussian nobility, the officer corps, and high civil servants. This created tensions at home and pressures from abroad. In spite of these difficulties Bismarck led Germany to glory and power, but when he was forced to resign, nobody was able to continue his work or take his place (1:328–29).

Writing only a few years later, E. Marcks, a nationalist and an ardent admirer of Bismarck, completed the first part of his Bismarck biography and his life's work with *Der Aufstieg des Reiches: Deutsche Geschichte von 1807–1871/78*, 2 vols. (Stuttgart, 1936). He believed that Germany's unification was Bismarck's own work; and while others, such as the king, Moltke, Roon, the army, public opinion, and the German people were involved, it was Bismarck who unified the country (1:xii–xiii; 2:514–15).

H. v. Srbik, the Austrian historian and foremost proponent of the all-German historical view (*gesamtdeutsche Geschichtsauffassung*), asserted in his *Deutsche Einheit: Idee und Wirklichkeit von Villafranca bis Koeniggraetz*, 4 vols. (Munich, 1940–42), that it was on the battlefield of Sadowa/Koeniggraetz in 1866 rather than in the palace of Versailles in 1871 that the German empire was founded (4:464). And Srbik regretted Bismarck's failure to establish a Greater German Reich.

Writing during World War II, W. Mommsen, in "Bismarcks kleindeutscher Staat und das grossdeutsche Reich" originally printed in the *Historische Zeitschrift* (vol. 167, pp. 66–82), now reprinted in H. Boehme, ed., *Probleme der Reichsgruendungszeit, 1848–1879* (Cologne, 1968), pp. 355–68, saw Bismarck's Germany as a direct antecedent to Hitler's Greater Germany, not a detour. And he believed that the particular form which German unification took was the only possible solution at the time (p. 356).

L. v. Muralt, in *Bismarcks Verantwortlichkeit* (Goettingen, 1955), sees the problem in a similar light. "Bismarck created the German Reich in the only way possible at that time, i.e., under the leadership of Prussia's power" (p. 33).

Golo Mann, on the other hand, in his *Deutsche Geschichte des 19. und 20. Jahrhunderts* (Frankfurt, 1958), believes that German unification was accomplished by the states, that is by Prussia, the big state, forcing the lesser states to follow its lead. Prussia's coercion was hidden by the fact that large segments of the population wanted and worked for unity though the people themselves did not achieve it. Once unity was accomplished, only a minority was satisfied with the results (p. 378). In the end it was not even a real national state, inasmuch as large parts of the nation remained outside forever (p. 386).

H. Bartel, an east German historian, in "Zur Stellung der Reichsgruendung von 1871 und zum Charakter des preussisch-deutschen Reiches," in H. Bartel and E. Engelberg, eds., *Die grosspreussische militaeristische Reichsgruendung 1871*, 2 vols. (Berlin, 1971), pp. 1–20, sees the founding of the Reich primarily as the result of successful capitalism. Quoting Engels, he asserts that trade and industry had developed in Germany to such a high level and German trade relations were so extensive that particularism at home and lack of protection abroad could no longer be tolerated. The path toward unification proceeded along bourgeois, counter-revolutionary lines and ended without a complete victory for the people. The old monarchy was transformed into a bourgeois-imperialist monarchy with the privileges of the nobility intact, to the great disadvantage of the workers. Thus, class differences were reinforced and the divergence between the character of the state and the developing needs of the nation was further accentuated which led, among other things, to an aggressive foreign policy (2:4–6).

Among non-German historians, G. Barraclough in his *Origins of Modern Germany* (New York, 1946), states "that the new Reich of 1871—whatever the theory—was in practice a Prussian Reich, shaped to accord with Prussian interests, constructed in conformity with Prussian tradition, ruled by the dynasty of the Hohenzollern, and dominated by the Prussian Junker class" (pp. 442–23).

A. J. P. Taylor, in *The Course of German History* (New York, 1946), asserts that "the Bismarck Reich was a dictatorship imposed on the conflicting forces, not an agreement between them. The parties did not compromise; they were manipulated by Bismarck—pushed down when they threatened to become strong, helped up when they appeared weak. Bismarck stood at the center of a multiple seesaw tilting it now this way, now that in order to keep his artificial creation in some sort of equilibrium; but the inevitable result was to give Germany ever more violent and uncontrollable oscillations" (pp. 115–16).

In *The Catholics and German Unity, 1866–1871* (Minneapolis, 1954), G. G. Windell writes that "the particularists had lost, but only by the slimmest of margins. The nationalists had won but only with the aid of some who were in their hearts chagrined at what they had done . . . throughout the country many individuals of both faiths had come to regard the war, and the future of Germany, as another stage in the centuries-old struggle between Wittenberg and Rome" (pp. 273–74).

T. S. Hamerow in *The Social Foundations of German Unification, 1858–1871* believes that, "even in the hour of its greatest triumph the policy of centralization was received by most Germans with indifference and suspicion. National unification was the achievement of a determined, influential, prosperous, intelligent, and indefatigable minority. . . . Bismarck had succeeded in adapting the structure of the state to the needs of an economy which was increasingly industrialized. He had negotiated an unwritten compromise between aristocracy and bourgeoisie through which the interests of the old order would be safe within the framework of the new. Authoritarian rule was disguised by a facade of parliamentary control, while material progress was assured by the achievement of economic integration. Military and political success enabled Germany to satisfy the demands of industrial capitalism without altering her traditional class system" (pp. 425–26).

79. Pflanze, *Bismarck and the Development of Germany*, vol. 1, p. 491. On attempts by

some representatives of the lesser states to weaken the predominance of Prussia in the new Reich and strengthen the federal aspects of the new constitution, see R. Dietrich, "Das Reich, Preussen und die Einzelstaaten bis zur Entlassung Bismarcks," in D. Kurze, ed., *Aus Theorie und Praxis der Geschichtswissenschaft: Festschrift fuer Hans Herzfeld*, (Berlin, 1972), pp. 236–56. For details on the negotiations with Bavaria and especially Bleichroeder's role, see Stern, *Gold and Iron*, pp. 133–34.

80. Pflanze, *Bismarck and the Development of Germany*, vol. 1, pp. 480–90.
81. K. Bosl, "Die Verhandlungen ueber den Eintritt der Sueddeutschen Staaten in den Norddeutschen Bund und die Entstehung der Reichsverfassung," in Schieder and Deuerlein, eds., *Reichsgruendung 1870/71*, pp. 148–63.

6. THE NEW REICH

1. W. Heyderhoff and P. Wentzke, eds., *Deutscher Liberalismus im Zeitalter Bismarcks* (Bonn, 1925), 1:494.
2. G. O. Kent, *Arnim and Bismarck* (Oxford, 1968); F. B. M. Hollyday, *Bismarck's Rival: A Political Biography of General and Admiral Albrecht von Stosch* (Durham, N.C., 1960).
3. Stern, *The Failure of Illiberalism*, pp. 50–51.
4. L. Gall, ed., *Das Bismarck-Problem in der Geschichtsschreibung nach 1945* (Cologne, 1971), p. 106.
5. Ibid., p. 134.
6. Ibid., p. 338.
7. Stern, *The Failure of Illiberalism*, pp. 47–48.
8. For text see J. Lepsius, A. Mendelssohn Bartholdy, F. Thimme, eds., *Die Grosse Politik der Europaeischen Kabinette, 1871–1914*, 40 vols., (Berlin, 1922–27), vol. 1, no. 17, pp. 38–43, henceforth cited *GP*.
9. The annexation of Alsace-Lorraine after the war of 1870–71 became one of the major problems in German-French relations, and contributed to the outbreak of the First World War. The question of responsibility for the annexation has long interested historians and has understandably focused on Bismarck. Lately the controversy over Bismarck's role has been revived and a series of articles in the *Historische Zeitschrift* and elsewhere has produced some interesting opinions.

    The latest account, by H. U. Wehler, "Das 'Reichsland' Elsass-Lothringen von 1870 bis 1918," in H. U. Wehler, ed., *Krisenherde des Kaiserreichs, 1871–1918* (Goettingen, 1970), with an exhaustive bibliography tucked away in footnotes, shows that far from resisting the annexation of Alsace (which no serious historian ever proposed), Bismarck favored it. The question of how much and how openly he favored it has aroused a certain amount of controversy. W. Lipgens, in two articles in the *Historische Zeitschrift* ("Bismarck, die oeffentliche Meinung und die Annexion von 1870," *HZ* 199 (1964): 31–112, and "Bismarck und die Frage der Annexion von 1870," *HZ* 206 (1968): 486–617, believes that Bismarck stimulated popular demand for annexation through a well-coordinated press campaign in July–August 1870. Arguing against this are L. Gall, "Zur Frage der Annexion von Elsass-Lothringen 1870," *HZ* 206 (1968): 265–326, and E. Kolb, "Bismarck und das Aufkommen der Annexionsforderungen 1870," *HZ* 209 (1969): 318–56. The latter, also supported by J. Becker, "Baden, Bismarck und die Annexion von Elsass und Lothringen," in *Zeitschrift fuer die Geschichte des Oberrheins* 115 (1967): 167–204, shows convincingly that rather than encouraging annexation demands, Bismarck had no influence on public opinion, at least until the middle of August 1870. On the contrary, the recovery of Alsace was demanded unanimously by all sections of German public opinion from the end of July, and with increasing frequency as German military successes mounted (E. Kolb, *Bismarck und das Aufkommen*, p. 353).

While Wehler does not touch upon these finer points, he mentions that German public opinion was strongly reinforced by the views of prominent professors and publicists such as Sybel, Treitschke, Mommsen, Maurenbrecher, and Lenz, who warned the people not to repeat the mistakes of 1815. Wehler also believes that Bismarck kept these annexation demands alive and manipulated them for political purposes. The army demanded annexation for military and strategic reasons, though the extensive economic and industrial benefits of the Longwy-Brie iron ore deposits were not known at the time. (See, however, G. W. F. Hallgarten, *Imperialismus vor 1914*, 2d ed., 2 vols. [Munich, 1963], 1:157–58; H. Boehme, *Deutschlands Weg zur Grossmacht* [Cologne, 1966], pp. 301–2; and R. Hartshorne, "The Franco-German Boundary of 1871," *World Politics* 2 [1949–50], pp. 209–50.) From the military point of view Alsace-Lorraine and the fortresses of Belfort, Metz, and Strasbourg were the keys to the defense of northeastern France, which the German high command wanted to use as a jumping off point in the next war. The two provinces and the fortresses also provided a much needed defense for southwestern Germany, especially Baden and the Palatinate.

That Bismarck always believed in strong safeguards against French revenge is also stated by G. Ritter, *The Sword and the Scepter*, 4 vols. (Coral Gables, Fla., 1969–73). "Bismarck himself . . . helped fan the flames of nationalist passions," though he himself was never swayed by it, "and proclaimed from the outset as one of the war aims . . . the slogan that Alsace-Lorraine must become German." According to Ritter, Bismarck's primary aim was a durable peace, and the annexation of the provinces was "not to vindicate old property rights . . . but to protect [Germany] . . . against the next attack" (1:226, 254, 258).

R. I. Giesberg in *The Treaty of Frankfort* (Philadelphia, 1966) also believes that military strategic considerations were uppermost in Bismarck's mind, that he was not swayed by national sentiments and had no intention of resisting popular demands (pp. 24–25).

The only Germans who were not persuaded by military arguments were Marx and Engels. The latter wrote that only "the asses of the official Prussian press" would believe that France could be held back by Germany's annexation of Alsace-Lorraine (quoted by Wehler, "Das 'Reichsland' Elsass-Lothringen," p. 22); while Marx believed that rather than guarantee the peace, as some German generals and publicists maintained, the annexation of Alsace-Lorraine would lead either to total German dependency on Russia or to a "racial war against the allied Roman and Slav races." (Karl Marx, *Der Buergerkrieg in Frankreich* [Berlin, 1949], p. 36.)

Seventeen years later, in 1887, Bismarck himself admitted that there was a possibility that Germany might have to fight both France and Russia in the not too distant future (*GW*, 7:378).

Wehler believes that annexations were inevitable, considering the overwhelming military victory and the nationalistic sentiments of German public opinion. This thought was also expressed by Wilhelm I. "I did not ask for Alsace-Lorraine at the beginning of the last war," he said to his reading companion, "but, at the same time, I would not have dared to let it go if I wanted to keep my army and my people." (Quoted by Wehler, "Das 'Reichsland' Elsass-Lothringen," p. 330, n. 16.)

See also D. P. Silverman, *Reluctant Union: Alsace-Lorraine and Imperial Germany, 1871–1918* (University Park, Pa., 1972), pp. 29–30 and n. 37.

10. L. Gall, "Das Problem Elsass-Lothringen," in Schieder and Deuerlein, eds., *Reichsgruendung 1870/71*, pp. 366–85; the quotation is on p. 375, n. 26.
11. On Bismarck's realpolitik, see the essays under this title by O. Pflanze, in *The Review of Politics* 20 (Oct. 1958), pp. 492–514; and H. Holborn, in *The Journal of the History of Ideas* 21 (Jan., Mar. 1960), pp. 84–98.
12. On the rapid development of industrialization, see K. E. Born, "Structural Changes in German Social and Economic Development at the End of the 19th Century," in J. J. Sheehan, ed., *Imperial Germany* (New York, 1976), pp. 17–18.
13. For a very detailed account, see Wehler, *Bismarck und der Imperialismus*, pp. 53–84; also Stern, *Gold and Iron*, pp. 182–83.
14. See chap. 7.
15. Boehme, *Deutschlands Weg zur Grossmacht*, pp. 354–59.
16. H. Rosenberg, "The Political and Social Consequences of the Great Depression of 1873–96 in Central Europe," *The Economic History Review* 13 (1943), pp. 58–73. Rosenberg expanded this topic in his *Grosse Depression und Bismarckzeit: Wirtschaftsablauf, Gesellschaft und Politik in Mitteleuropa* (Berlin, 1967). In this study Rosenberg links Bismarck's cautious foreign policy and his aggressive domestic policy to the consequences of the depression of 1873–79, which coincided with Kondratiev's "long wave" of 1873–96. For a different view, see A. Gerschenkron, "The Great Depression in Germany," in his *Continuity in History and Other Essays* (Cambridge, Mass., 1968), pp. 405–8.
17. Up to that time, 1874, the army budget was governed by the so-called iron budget of 1867. Craig, *The Politics of the Prussian Army*, pp. 219 ff.
18. D. S. White, *The Splintered Party: National Liberalism in Hessen and the Reich, 1867–1918* (Cambridge, Mass., 1976), pp. 55 ff.
19. A good example is the attempt to reform the Prussian district administration (*Kreisordnung*). After 1866 there was general agreement that reform and a certain measure of decentralization were necessary, and Bismarck supported this trend. The measure failed in 1869 because of conservative opposition in the upper house; in 1872, when it came up again, Bismarck had lost his interest and insisted that reforms of the upper house—where there was considerable opposition to his policies—take precedent. In this instance he was outmaneuvered by Count Eulenburg, the Prussian minister of the interior, and the new *Kreisordnung* became law on December 13, 1872. Contrary to general expectations, it did not liberalize or decentralize the established power structure in the country districts as the municipal order (*Staedteordnung*) had done in the cities. (Hefter, *Die Deutsche Selbstverwaltung in 19. Jahrhundert*, pp. 489–555.)
20. See chap. 7.
21. Boehme, *Deutschlands Weg zur Grossmacht*, pp. 380–86.
22. The development from free trade to protectionism was, of course, much more complicated than described in this short survey. For details see, *inter alia*, H. Boehme, "Big-Business Pressure Groups and Bismarck's Turn to Protectionism 1873–79," *Historical Journal* 2 (1967); I. Lambi, *Free Trade and Protection in Germany, 1868–1879*, (Wiesbaden, 1963), and Born, "Structural Changes in German Social and Economic Development at the End of the 19th Century."
23. Knut Borchardt, "The Industrial Revolution in Germany, 1700–1914," in C. M. Cipolla, ed., *The Fontana Economic History of Europe*, (London, 1971–), 4, pt. 1, p. 155.
24. Aside from economic interests, Center party officials believed that by favoring protectionism they might force Bismarck to terminate the *Kulturkampf*.
25. Boehme, *Deutschlands Weg zur Grossmacht*, pp. 419, 566–67. The single most deci-

sive shift in recent German historiography is the change of emphasis from 1871, the founding of the empire, to 1879, the turn toward protectionism. This new attitude de-emphasizes the political and organizational aspects connected with 1870–71 and stresses the economic, social, and domestic changes that took place after 1875 as a result of the depression of 1873. The foremost proponent of this new view is H. Boehme, who sees Bismarck's shift in the years 1875–81 from laissez-faire to protectionism and from cooperation with the liberals to alliance with the conservatives as more significant in the development of Prussia-Germany than the unification and founding of the Reich at Versailles in 1871. "The reconciliation with the Center and, most of all, the change-over by the large landowners to protectionism constituted [important] points on the road to the reorganization of the Prussian-German state by Bismarck; a reorganization which was equivalent to a new founding of the Reich." (Boehme, *Deutschlands Weg zur Grossmacht*, p. 419.)

26. Promulgated at the Vatican Council on July 18, 1870, it asserted that the pope, when speaking *ex cathedra*, was infallible in matters of faith and morals.

27. Quoted by Stern, *The Failure of Illiberalism*, p. 53.

28. On Augusta's pro-Catholic sympathies, see, *GW*, 15:336 and M. Busch, *Bismarck, Some Secret Pages of His History*, 3 vols. (London, 1893), 2:416. Interpretations of the *Kulturkampf* and Bismarck's motives for embarking on this fateful struggle have been influenced by religious and ideological considerations, and no balanced, definitive study has appeared so far.

One of the earliest works by a Catholic historian, J. B. Kissling, *Geschichte des Kulturkampfes im Deutschen Reiche*, 3 vols. (Freiburg, 1911–16), is sharply antiliberal. In Kissling's opinion, Bismarck's alliance with the liberals after 1871 led to concessions in religious and educational matters and sacrificed conservative Christian principles in the process. The chancellor's support of the liberal government in Bavaria was another reason for the struggle (1:365, 390). But there was no overall definite plan; it started very gradually. Neither the Polish question nor the Center party had any real influence on Bismarck's policies, contrary to what he may have said later on (3:357, 360). Originally, Bismarck had no intentions of fighting the Center; instead, he wanted to reconcile the Center and the National Liberals, and maintain friendly relations with the pope. But when the National Liberals introduced the question of German intervention in behalf of the pope's temporal powers, Bismarck had to take sides. He still hoped, however, to get the Center's support, and asked Antonelli, the papal secretary of state, to direct the Center along those lines. When Antonelli refused, Bismarck labeled the pope a *Reichsfeind* (enemy of the state) and applied this by extension to the Center party (3:361–63).

Following World War I and the publication of 40 volumes of pre-1914 German Foreign Office documents, German historical writing concentrated on foreign policy. In this vein, A. Wahl, *Vom Bismarck der siebziger Jahre* (Tuebingen, 1920) and *Deutsche Geschichte, 1871–1914*, 4 vols. (Stuttgart, 1926–36), believed that Bismarck started the *Kulturkampf* primarily to isolate France and to tie Russia and Italy (which had their own troubles with the Church) closer to Germany. No domestic political considerations played a role in this decision.

Paul Sattler, "Bismarcks Entschluss zum Kulturkampf," in F. Hartung and W. Hoppe, eds., *Forschungen zur Brandenburgischen und Preussischen Geschichte*, vol. 52 (Berlin, 1940), writing during the Nazi period, saw the *Kulturkampf* as a struggle against the forces of internationalism (represented by the Center and the Social Democratic parties) in which Bismarck was unsuccessful; only Hitler had been able to overcome these enemies of the state. The immediate causes of the

Kulturkampf were the first Vatican Council and its consequences, the Roman question and the loss of the pope's temporal power, and the appearance of a political party organized along confessional lines (pp. 66–67).

Writing during the same period but taking a less extreme position, E. Schmidt, *Bismarcks Kampf mit dem politischen Katholizismus* (Hamburg, 1942), believed that political Catholicism tried to put its own imprint on the newly established Reich and, when this failed, joined the opposition against Bismarck. Thus, Bismarck was forced into the *Kulturkampf* to defend his life's work (p. 6).

A more balanced view is presented by H. Bornkamm, *Die Staatsidee im Kulturkampf* (Munich, 1950), who maintains that domestic as well as foreign considerations influenced Bismarck. Domestically, Bismarck was threatened by the Center's use of parliamentary tactics to further its program. For the safety of the new Reich, this party had to be destroyed, and this was Bismarck's only aim in the struggle. His motives were not based on any theory of state, nor on ideological grounds, but rested entirely on political considerations. "He fought for no ideas, nor in the name of a Protestant, Hegelian, National Liberal, or critical philosophy in which modern science was pitted against medieval dogma. His only principle was to achieve a clear-cut division between the religious and political sphere, which he saw dangerously mixed-up by the very existence and policy of the Center Party . . . [to him], the *Kulturkampf* was a preventive war on the domestic scene" (pp. 65–66).

F. Nova, "The Motivation in Bismarck's Kulturkampf," *Dusquesne Review* 10 (Spring 1965), sees the essence of the *Kulturkampf* in the collision between the pope's desire to reaffirm his preeminent position after his loss of temporal power in 1870, and "the similar dynamic demands and aspirations of modern civilization, nationalism, statism, liberalism, materialism and secularism, manifested most clearly in the newly established German Empire" (p. 43).

J. Becker, on the other hand, sees Bismarck's *Kulturkampf* primarily as a political device. The chancellor used it to unite the diverse liberal parties for his own purpose, while at the same time corrupting their ideals and diverting them from their constitutional goals. (J. Becker, *Liberaler Staat und Kirche in der Aera der Reichsgruendung und Kulturkampf* [Mainz 1973], pp. 375–76.)

29. Bornkamm, *Die Staatsidee im Kulturkampf*, p. 9.
30. Bussmann, *Das Zeitalter Bismarcks*, p. 158.
31. Ibid., pp. 166–67.
32. A. Constable, *Vorgeschichte des Kulturkampfes* (Berlin, 1956), passim.
33. Kent, *Arnim and Bismarck*, pp. 124, 127.
34. Bussmann, *Das Zeitalter Bismarcks*, p. 216.
35. Ibid., p. 215. Talks between the Prussian government and the papal nuncio started in July 1878.
36. Bornkamm, *Die Staatsidee im Kulturkampf*, pp. 65–71.
37. Ibid.
38. Bismarck had accused leaders of the SDP of high treason for opposing the annexation of Alsace-Lorraine and expressing sympathy with the Paris Commune.
39. V. Lidtke, *The Outlawed Party: Social Democracy in Germany, 1878–90* (Princeton, 1966), pp. 70 ff.
40. "Fear of the revolution, fear of losing economic status, fear of the future—these were the basic underlying presumptions of the election in the summer of 1878." (M. Stuermer, *Regierung und Reichstag im Bismarckstaat, 1871–1880* [Duesseldorf, 1974], p. 231.)
41. Lidtke, *The Outlawed Party*, p. 74.

42. Ibid., p. 78.
43. The following is based on M. Stuermer, "Staatsstreichgedanken im Bismarckreich," *Historische Zeitschrift* 209 (Dec. 1969), pp. 566–615, esp. 582 ff.
44. Ibid., p. 593, n. 66.
45. Ibid., p. 599, n. 77.
46. Ibid., p. 601.
47. This was primarily in the colonial sphere; see H. P. v. Strandmann, "Domestic Origins of Germany's Colonial Expansion under Bismarck," *Past and Present* 42 (Feb. 1969); and H. U. Wehler, "Bismarck's Imperialism, 1862–90," *Past and Present* 48 (Aug. 1970).
48. According to Steuermer, *Regierung und Reichstag im Bismarckstaat*, p. 291, the essence of the German constitutional problem during the empire revolved around the unresolved conflict between parliamentarianism and Caesarism. Bismarck used some aspects of the latter to undermine parliamentary representation, while at the same time appealing for popular plebiscites and threatening a coup d'état.
49. O. Vossler, "Bismarcks Ethos," *Historische Zeitschrift* 171 (Mar. 1951), p. 290.
50. H. J. Steinberg, "Socialismus,. Internationalismus und Reichsgruendung," in Schieder and Deuerlein, eds., *Reichsgruendung 1870/71*, pp. 319–44.
51. Quoted by H. U. Wehler, *Das Deutsche Kaiserreich, 1871–1918* (Goettingen, 1973), p. 136.
52. E. Eyck, *Bismarck*, 3: 368–75.
53. Lidtke, *The Outlawed Party*, p. 159.
54. Ibid., p. 160.
55. Ibid., pp. 74, 185.
56. Ibid., pp. 241–44.
57. Ibid., pp. 256–301.
58. Quoted by Stern, *The Failure of Illiberalism*, p. 13.
59. Ibid., p. 15.
60. F. K. Ringer, *The Decline of the German Mandarins: The German Academic Community, 1890–1933* (Cambridge, Mass., 1969), p. 121.
61. Ibid., p. 128.
62. Quoted by Stern, *Gold and Iron*, pp. 205–6.
63. Stuermer, *Regierung und Reichstag im Bismarckstaat*, pp. 296–308. For an interesting and stimulating article on the idea that Napoleon III and Guizot were models for Bismarck, see A. Mitchell, "Bonapartism as a Model for Bismarckian Politics" and subsequent comments by O. Pflanze, C. Fohlen, and M. Stuermer, in *Journal of Modern History* 49, no. 2 (June 1977): 181–209.
64. J. J. Sheehan, "Conflict and Cohesion among German Elites in the 19th Century," in Sheehan, ed., *Imperial Germany*, pp. 62–92; the quotation is on pp. 82–83.
65. Bussman, "Europa und das Bismarckreich," in Gall, ed., *Das Bismarck-Problem*, pp. 325–27.
66. F. Fischer, *Der Krieg der Illusionen* (Duesseldorf, 1969), p. 64.
67. E. Deuerlein, "Die Konfrontation von Nationalstaat und national bestimmter Kultur," in Schieder and Deuerlein, eds., *Reichsgruendung 1870/71*, pp. 226–58.
68. G. L. Mosse, *The Crisis of German Ideology* (New York, 1964); F. Stern, *The Politics of Cultural Despair* (Berkeley, Calif., 1961), passim.
69. D. Gasman, *The Scientific Origins of National Socialism* (New York, 1971), p. xxiii. See also H. G. Zmarzlik, "Social Darwinism in Germany, Seen as an Historical Problem" in H. Holborn, ed., *Republic to Reich* (New York, 1973), pp. 435.
70. Gasman, *The Scientific Origins of National Socialism*, passim.

71. P. Pulzer, *The Rise of Political Anti-Semitism in Germany and Austria* (New York, 1964), pp. 76–96.
72. See chap. 1.
73. M. Busch, *Tagebuchblaetter*, 3 vols. (Leipzig, 1902), 2:33.
74. Stern, *Gold and Iron*, p. 528. See also W. T. Angress, "Prussia's Army and the Jewish Reserve Officer Controversy before World War I," in Sheehan, ed., *Imperial Germany*, pp. 97–100.
75. Messerschmidt, "Die Armee in Staat und Gesellschaft—Die Bismarckzeit," pp. 102–7.
76. K. H. Hoefele, *Geist und Gesellschaft der Bismarckzeit, 1870–1890* (Goettingen, 1967), pp. 22 ff.

7. BISMARCK'S FOREIGN POLICY

1. F. Fischer, *Der Krieg der Illusionen*, chaps. 4–6 passim.
2. *GP* vol. 2, no. 294. This is known as the Kissingen Memorandum.
3. Mitchell, *Bismarck and the French Nation*, p. 74.
4. The appraisal of Bismarck's foreign policy, similar to that of his policy at home, has undergone considerable change since the publication of the *Grosse Politik* in the 1920s. W. L. Langer, in his *European Alliances and Alignments* (New York, 1931) believed that "no other statesman of his standing had ever before shown the same great moderation and sound political sense of the possible and the desirable" (pp. 503–4). Twenty-five years later, and after another world war, opinions were not quite as favorable. A. J. P. Taylor considers the chancellor's " 'system' . . . something of a conjuring trick, a piece of conscious virtuosity. Once started on the path of alliances, Bismarck treated them as the solution for every problem." (*The Struggle for Mastery in Europe*, p. 278.) And W. N. Medlicott in *Bismarck, Gladstone and the Concert of Europe* (London, 1956), writes that "if Bismarck wanted peace, it was on his own terms; his philosophy of international life remained fundamentally combative and pessimistic, and he could discover no reliable basis for national survival other than the accumulation and manoeuvering of superior force. . . . Bismarck was singularly unconvincing as the great architect of peace: foreign states were mainly conscious of the aggressive potentialities of his diplomacy. . . . A considerable problem that faces the student of his later diplomacy is, indeed, to decide how far he was alarmed by nightmares of his own creation" (pp. 11, 12).

Beyond political and diplomatic considerations, there were attempts, especially after 1945, to look at Bismarck's foreign policy from wider perspectives. The dogma of the primacy of foreign policy expressed by Ranke in the first half of the nineteenth century and upheld by German historians well into the second half of the twentieth century, was challenged for the first time by E. Kehr in his *Schlachtflottenbau und Parteipolitik, 1894–1901* (Berlin, 1930). His innovative method of examining domestic problems and policies and their influence on foreign policy was not well received at the time, and his lead was not followed until after World War II. Since then such West German historians as Rosenberg, Boehme, and Wehler have linked economic and social conditions with foreign policy, while in East Germany, Jerusalimski, Wolters, Kumpf-Korfes, and Engelberg followed the tradition of Marxist historiography which has traditionally considered economic and social conditions as the basis of foreign policy. (H. Wolters, "Neue Aspekte in der Buergerlichen Historiographie der BRD zur Bismarckschen Aussenpolitik 1871 bis

1890," *Jahrbuch fuer Geschichte* 10 [1974], pp. 507–39, and G. G. Iggers, *New Directions in European Historiography* [Middletown, Conn., 1975], pp. 96–98.)

5. After Austria's defeat at Koeniggraetz in 1866, a new constitutional system was established and under the terms of the Compromise of 1867 Hungary was given a large measure of autonomy within the empire. Its official title from then until 1918 was the Austro-Hungarian Monarchy. Throughout this study the more convenient term, "Austria," will be used to describe the empire and its government.

6. A. J. P. Taylor, *Bismarck*, p. 143.

7. Kent, *Arnim and Bismarck*, pp. 117 ff.

8. Craig, *The Politics of the Prussian Army*, p. 275, n. 2.

9. E. Eyck, *Bismarck*, 3:160–61: For a recent treatment of the crisis, see Hillgruber, *Deutsche Grossmacht-und Weltpolitik* (Duesseldorf, 1977), pp. 35–52.

10. For Henri de Blowitz's role in this affair, see H. S. de Blowitz, *My Memoirs* (London, 1903), pp. 106 ff., and F. Giles, *A Prince of Journalists: The Life and Times of Henri Stefan Opper de Blowitz* (London, 1962), pp. 80 ff.

11. *GW*, 11:476.

12. N. Rich and M. H. Fisher, eds., *The Holstein Papers*, 4 vols. (London, 1955–63), 1:124.

13. "Pan Slavism was a poorly coordinated movement among the Slavic-speaking peoples of Europe (Great Russians, Byelorussians, Ukrainians, Lusatians, Poles, Czechs, Slovaks, Serbs, Croats, Slovenes, Macedonians, and Bulgarians), chiefly during the 19th century, in which they affirmed their cultural unity and sometimes expressed the desire for political union. Pan-Slavism was not Russian in origin. Nevertheless, it was widely regarded and feared in western Europe, usually without justification, as Russian instigated and directed, as a device to strengthen Russia's hand in international affairs and facilitate its expansion on the Continent." (J. Dunner, ed., *Handbook of World History* (New York, 1967), pp. 680–81.)

14. R. Wittram, "Bismarcks Russlandpolitik nach der Reichsgruendung," *Historische Zeitschrift* 186 (Dec. 1958), pp. 261–84.

15. Taylor, *The Struggle for Mastery in Europe*, p. 229.

16. The Russian inquiry of October 1, 1876, was a result of Wilhelm's letter to the czar, in which the German emperor expressed his appreciation for Russia's policy toward Prussia from 1864 to 1870–71. This attitude, Wilhelm wrote, "will determine my policy toward Russia whatever may come." (Quoted by Bussman, *Das Zeitalter Bismarcks*, p. 133; see also Wittram, "Bismarcks Russlandpolitik," pp. 269–70.)

17. M. S. Anderson, *The Eastern Question, 1774–1923* (New York, 1966), p. 193.

18. See W. N. Medlicott, *The Congress of Berlin and After* (London, 1938), pp. 10–13.

19. Ibid., chaps. 2 and 3. Why Berlin was chosen and who suggested this site are not quite clear. It seems that Andrassy proposed Vienna at the end of January 1878 and, when Russia objected, suggested Brussels or Baden-Baden. According to another version it was Bismarck who suggested Vienna, and Andrassy, Berlin; Gorchakov, too, apparently suggested Berlin. The choice of Berlin was, without a doubt, a concession to Russia to induce her to participate in the Congress, and Gorchakov appreciated this gesture. (A. Novotny, *Quellen und Studien zur Geschichte des Berliner Kongresses 1878* [Graz, 1957], 1:51–52.)

20. E. Eyck, *Bismarck*, 3:253; see, however, Medlicott, *The Congress of Berlin and After*, p. 22, "Bismarck played an essentially negative part during this crisis in Russia's fortunes, and if Russia had no right to claim his support, she also had no reason to be grateful for his friendship."

21. E. Eyck, *Bismarck*, 3:267. Bismarck's support for Britain was in recognition of the close cooperation between Andrassy and Disraeli and the existing agreements be-

tween Russia and Austria. His aim was to avoid a general war but to keep the Balkan question open so that Germany, by holding back, would profit from it. (Hillgruber, *Bismarcks Aussenpolitik*, p. 152.)

22. Various explanations for the Dual Alliance with Austria have been offered by historianŝ. The old school, as represented by Erich Brandenburg, saw it as a simple and straightforward foreign policy matter: Bismarck concluded the alliance as a defensive measure against a threatening Russian attack, though he did not intend to make Russia a permanent enemy. (*Von Bismarck zum Weltkrieg*, 2d ed. [Berlin, 1924], p. 11.) A similar point is made by W. Windelband, *Bismarck und die europaeischen Grossmaechte, 1879–1885* (Essen, 1942) who, on the basis of much new and hitherto unpublished material, concluded that Bismarck was forced to look to Austria because of the greatly increased size of the Russian army and the possibility that Russia might join an anti-German coalition (p. 54).

A. J. P. Taylor cites more complicated causes in his masterful and provocative study on nineteenth-century European diplomacy. Bismarck, according to Taylor, would have preferred to recreate the Holy Alliance, but Austrian suspicion of Russia prevented it; he was more afraid of Austria's restlessness than Russia's aggression and one way to control Austria was to conclude an alliance with her. It "was a sop to the liberals whom he was deserting in home affairs. Though he did not give them 'greater Germany,' he gave them a union of the two German powers, based on national sentiment." (*The Struggle for Mastery in Europe*, p. 259.) Walter Bussman, in *Das Zeitalter Bismarcks*, believes the alliance embodies the concept of *Mitteleuropa*. The possible threat of an Austro-French-Russian alliance, the old Kaunitz coalition of the Seven Years' War, compelled Bismarck to form the Dual Alliance (pp. 140–41). In A. Hillgruber's opinion, Bismarck concluded the alliance at the very moment when Russia was approaching Germany to reestablish friendly relations, and the purpose of the alliance with Austria was to hasten the formalization of the good relationship with Russia (*Bismarcks Aussenpolitik*, p. 156). The most recent and detailed treatment of the Dual Alliance is presented by B. Waller, *Bismarck at the Crossroads* (London, 1974). Waller believes that a personal feud between Bismarck and Gorchakov, combined with the Rumanian question, made a German alliance with Austria desirable (chaps. 4, 7–9).

23. Waller, *Bismarck at the Crossroads*, pp. 102–5.

24. Ibid., pp. 135–44.

25. Stern, *Gold and Iron*, pp. 351 ff.

26. For example, at the Congress of Berlin, Bismarck encouraged French ambitions in Tunisia, which would simultaneously embroil her with Italy, distract her from Alsace-Lorraine, and preoccupy her in case of Russo-German difficulties in Europe. Another example was Bismarck's backing of Britain in Egypt, designed to involve Britain with France and, at the same time, make Britain dependent on Bismarck's good will and assistance. Both cases illustrate Bismarck's thinking as outlined in the Kissingen Memorandum.

27. An ill-tempered letter by Alexander to Wilhelm of August 15, 1879, complaining about the deterioration of Russo-German relations and foreseeing disastrous consequences, did not change Bismarck's decision, but was used by him to persuade the emperor that an alliance with Austria was necessary. Bismarck also used the announcement of Andrassy's pending resignation to convince Wilhelm that under Andrassy's successor Austria might change her policy and turn toward Russia. (Waller, *Bismarck at the Crossroads*, pp. 183 ff.; Hillgruber, *Bismarcks Aussenpolitik*, pp. 155 ff.; Bussmann, *Das Zeitalter Bismarcks*, pp. 139 ff.)

28. It was a defensive treaty directed against Russia, providing for the partners to

come to each other's aid if one or the other were attacked by Russia. It contained no similar provision for an attack by France. In that or any other instance, the party not directly involved would remain neutral.

29. Taylor, *The Struggle for Mastery in Europe*, p. 261. For Bismarck's struggle with the emperor, see Waller, *Bismarck at the Crossroads*, p. 192 and n. 40.

30. *GP*, vol. 4, pp. 7 ff.

31. Taylor, *The Struggle for Mastery in Europe*, pp. 267–69.

32. Ibid., pp. 270–71.

33. General Skobelev, a hero of the Russo-Turkish war and a Pan-Slavist, went on a mission to Paris in January 1882 and made several belligerent speeches which were well received by French nationalists but had no visible effects on either French or Russian policies. (Taylor, *The Struggle for Mastery in Europe*, pp. 272–76.)

34. Hillgruber, *Bismarcks Aussenpolitik*, p. 161.

35. See, in this connection, Hallgarten, *Imperialismus vor 1914*, 1:227 ff.

36. Medlicott, *Bismarck, Gladstone and the Concert of Europe*, pp. 335–36.

37. There was an Anglo-Russian crisis over Afghanistan from March 1885 to June 1886.

38. For the views of the pro-German and pro-French factions within the Russian government and at the Russian court, see S. Kumpf-Korfes, *Bismarcks "Draht nach Russland"* (Berlin, 1968), pp. 77 ff.

39. Gall, ed., *Das Bismarck-Problem*, p. 40; the first two quotations are in Wittram, "Bismarcks Russlandpolitik," pp. 261–84. For a defense of the Reinsurance Treaty, see H. Krausnick, "Rueckversicherungsvertrag und Optionsproblem 1887–90," in M. Goehring and A. Scharff, eds., *Geschichtliche Kraefte und Entscheidungen: Festschrift fuer Otto Becker* (Wiesbaden, 1954), pp. 210–32.

40. It has been suggested that Bismarck, not Giers, inserted the Straits clause, and there are some indications that Bismarck favored Russian aspirations toward the Straits. The possibility that Bismarck wanted Russia to embroil herself in a drive toward Constantinople is expressed in a letter of May 3, 1888, to Prince Reuss, German ambassador in Vienna, and in another one of May 9, 1888, to the crown prince. In the former, Bismarck expressed the belief that Germany could hasten Russia's disintegration by encouraging her to get involved in the "oriental [that is, Balkan] dead end street." To the latter he wrote that the secret treaty (the Reinsurance Treaty) guaranteed that Russia would in the future be trapped in the cul-de-sac of Constantinople, as she would already have been but for German restraint of Austria. (Wittram, "Bismarcks Russlandpolitik," p. 278, n. 1.)

41. For the following, I rely on H. U. Wehler, "Bismarcks spaete Russlandpolitik 1879–90," in Wehler, ed., *Krisenherde des Kaiserreichs, 1871–1918*, pp. 163–80, based on an exhaustive and exhausting source collection, and on Kumpf-Korfes, *Bismarcks "Draht nach Russland."*

42. Kumpf-Korfes, *Bismarcks "Draht nach Russland,"* p. 162.

43. W. L. Langer, *The Diplomacy of Imperialism*, 2d ed. (New York, 1951), chap. 1 passim.

44. Craig, *The Politics of the Prussian Army*, p. 268.

45. Kumpf-Korfes, *Bismarcks "Draht nach Russland,"* pp. 115 ff.

46. Wehler, *Krisenherde des Kaiserreichs, 1871–1918*, p. 176.

47. Ibid., p. 178. See also Stern, *Gold and Iron*, pp. 440–50.

48. Wehler, *Krisenherde des Kaiserreichs, 1871–1918*, pp. 179–80, esp. n. 44. I do not believe, as Wehler does, that Bismarck's action set Germany on her fatal course. Bismarck may indeed have pointed German policy in this direction, but his successors chose to reinforce, rather than reverse, this trend.

49. Quoted by G. W. F. Hallgarten, "War Bismarck ein Imperialist?" *Geschichte in Wissenschaft und Unterricht* (May 1971), p. 262.
50. Rich and Fisher, eds., *The Holstein Papers*, 2:138.
51. Strandmann, "Domestic Origins of Germany's Colonial Expansion under Bismarck," p. 149, n. 36; *GW*, 13:383.
52. Wehler, "Bismarck's Imperialism, 1862–90," p. 129, n. 17.
53. Ibid., p. 129, n. 18. The argument whether Bismarck was or was not an imperialist has aroused much interest among historians. (For one of the more recent exchanges, see the Hallgarten-Wehler articles listed in the Bibliographical Essay.) In A. J. P. Taylor's view, Bismarck used the colonial issue in 1884 for his own ends. "If it is absurd to suppose that Bismarck allowed a few colonial enthusiasts to divert and injure his foreign policy, it is even more absurd to believe that Bismarck, who refused to condone German ambitions in Europe, himself succumbed to ambitions overseas." (*The Struggle for Mastery in Europe*, pp. 293–94.) According to K. Buettner, *Die Anfaenge der deutschen Kolonialpolitik in Ostafrika* (Berlin, 1959), however, Bismarck's initial opposition to and later enthusiasm for colonies was entirely in the spirit of the period. His opposition in 1868 was in line with the prevailing mood of laissez faire and his later conversion to colonies followed the changing trends of business and commercial interests. Bismarck had no blueprint for acquiring colonies, and until the 1880s the German flag followed German trade. The attitude toward colonies was but an expression of domestic political struggles and, as a practical politician, Bismarck changed his views around 1885 (pp. 23–25).

G. W. F. Hallgarten in *Imperialismus vor 1914* believes that it was von Kusserow, an official in the German Foreign Office, who established the major lines of German colonial policy and persuaded a reluctant Bismarck to follow them (1:206–22). H. U. Wehler, in "Bismarck's Imperialism 1862–90," in Wehler, ed., *Krisenherde des Kaiserreichs, 1871–1918*, pp. 113–34, considers Bismarck's imperialism the result of an insolvable tension at home. According to Wehler, there was no break in Bismarck's views in 1884–86; he still believed that an informal empire was preferable to state-directed colonial administration. Bismarck was a pragmatic imperialist, not motivated by prestige, a German mission, or world power. He believed that colonies would assure safe and secure economic growth and preserve the existing social hierarchy and political structure. To alleviate the effects of the economic crisis in the fall of 1882, the government had little choice but to accelerate overseas expansion, which it did by providing subsidies for exports and steamship lines, and by promoting new trade agreements. The end of free trade policies by other nations and increased commercial competition made direct state intervention inevitable. There was also a feeling in German government circles and among the business community that the international race for colonies was just about over, and if Germany did not act quickly, she would be too late. To Bismarck, colonies were a means to assist German export trade and thus the German economy. He also used colonial policies for election purposes, to cover up serious social and political tensions, to strengthen his Bonapartist-dictatorial power position, and to enhance the dwindling popularity and prestige of the government. See also P. M. Kennedy, "German Colonal Expansion," *Past and Present* 54 (Feb. 1972), pp. 134–41, and K. J. Bade, *Friedrich Fabri und der Imperialismus in der Bismarckzeit: Revolution-Depression-Expansion* (Zuerich, 1975), passim.
54. P. M. Kennedy, *The Samoan Tangle: A Study in Anglo-German-American Relations, 1878–1900* (New York, 1973), passim.
55. For an interesting study of the development of business and industrial organizations

in Germany, and their relationship to the government and their attitude toward colonies, see W. Fischer, *Wirtschaft und Gesellschaft im Zeitalter der Industrialisierung* (Goettingen, 1972), especially p. 211.

56. Wehler, "Bismarck's Imperialism, 1862–90," p. 129, n. 18.
57. Hallgarten, "War Bismarck ein Imperialist?" p. 261.
58. Strandmann, "Domestic Origins of Germany's Colonial Expansion under Bismarck," p. 158, n. 74.
59. Bussmann, *Das Zeitalter Bismarcks*, pp. 148–51.

8. BISMARCK'S DISMISSAL

1. M. Balfour, *The Kaiser and His Times* (New York, 1972), pp. 139–40; Craig, *The Politics of the Prussian Army*, p. 239.
2. Quoted by Bussman, *Das Zeitalter Bismarcks*, p. 236.
3. The following is based on J. C. G. Roehl, "The Disintegration of the Kartell and the Politics of Bismarck's Fall from Power 1887–89," *Historical Journal* 9 (1966), pp. 60–89; and by the same author, "Staatsstreichplan oder Staatsstreichbereitschaft? Bismarcks Politik in der Entlassungskrise," *Historische Zeitschrift* 203 (Dec. 1966), pp. 610–24.
4. One of the earliest books on the dismissal crisis, P. Liman, *Fuerst Bismarck und seine Entlassung* (Berlin, 1904), gives a most adulatory account of the chancellor and his policies and blames Bismarck's dismissal on the difference in age and temperament between the emperor and the chancellor. The book is based primarily on Bismarck's memoirs and is only mildly critical of Wilhelm II. Liman blames the crisis on bureaucratic and court intrigues.

   G. Freiherr von Eppstein, *Fuerst Bismarcks Entlassung* (Berlin, 1920), using the private posthumous papers of the former minister of state and state secretary of the interior, Boetticher, and the former chief of the Reich Chancellery, Rottenburg, believes that the clash between youth impatiently forging ahead and cautious old age accounts for Bismarck's removal, but he discounts intrigue as a factor. Boetticher, one of Bismarck's closest collaborators during the chancellor's last ten years in office, was suspected and accused by Bismarck of having intrigued against him. Boetticher denied these accusations in his papers and, in turn, accused Herbert Bismarck, the chancellor's oldest son, of having created bad blood between the emperor, the chancellor, and himself.

   The first comprehensive account of the dismissal crisis is by W. Schuessler, *Bismarcks Sturz* (Berlin, 1922). It presents the chancellor's fall partly in terms of a morality play: "Who can doubt that our calamities started at that time? . . . [It was] a tragedy because the hero—guilty or innocent—was the victim of his fate which was partly created by himself, partly by the Gods . . . but all this, the many misunderstandings, the loneliness of the genius, the passing of an age, and the struggle for power, cannot absolve Wilhelm II who was found guilty before history: the day of judgment was November 9, 1918" (pp. vii–viii).

   Schuessler's account, written in a time of humiliation and distress, was also meant to remind his countrymen of their great past. In this context he saw the conflict between the emperor and the chancellor essentially as a struggle for power (p. 185).

   Wilhelm Mommsen, *Bismarcks Sturz und die Parteien* (Berlin, 1924), looks at the problem from the point of view of the political parties. Had the parties supported Bismarck, Wilhelm II would not have dared to let him go. None of the chancellor's opponents, according to Mommsen, would have been able to justify his dismissal and in the end his fall was due to the combined pressure of various personal interests and demands (pp. 7–9). The petty and self-serving policies of party hacks and politicians, some of whom (like Miquel) saw the dangers ahead but were afraid to mention them and followed the rest, reassured the emperor of his rightness in this matter and thus made future criticism of his policies extremely difficult. The politicians' lack of responsibility and courage made them at least partially responsible for Germany's future fate (pp. 155–59).

Egmont Zechlin, *Staatsstreichplaene Bismarcks und Wilhelm II, 1890–1894* (Stuttgart, 1929) concentrates on Bismarck's plan for a coup d'etat as outlined in the state council's meeting of March 2, 1890. According to the protocol of this meeting, Bismarck intended to have the German princes and representatives of the Free Cities who had signed the federal treaty establishing the Reich revoke the treaty and establish a new constitution for the Reich if the parliamentary elections continued to turn out badly for the government. The chancellor also intended to neutralize the Reichstag by refusing to nominate federal members (*Bundesratsmitglieder*) to attend its sessions (p. 47). Zechlin considers Bismarck's fall the result of the conflict between chancellor and Reichstag, a conflict which Bismarck saw as inevitable. Bismarck hoped to eliminate the Reichstag, or at least the Social Democrats, in this conflict. The emperor, however, decided finally to postpone or avoid such a conflict with the Reichstag.

5. Roehl, "Staatsstreichplaene," p. 610, n. 1.
6. For the text of this directive, see Roehl, "Staasstreichplaene," pp. 623–24.
7. Bismarck's willingness to use the threat of coup d'état throughout his term of office is persuasively presented by Stuermer, "Staatsstreichgedanken im Bismarckreich," pp. 566–615.
8. Bussmann, *Das Zeitalter Bismarcks*, p. 244.
9. Balfour, *The Kaiser and His Times*, p. 132.
10. A critical, up-to-date edition of the *Reflections and Reminiscences* can be found in the *Gesammelten Werke*, vol. 15.
11. *Goetz von Berlichingen*, one of Goethe's earliest and best known dramas, deals with Goetz, the freedom-loving, independent knight during the Peasant Wars who, though disrespectful of laws and lesser men, remained loyal to the emperor.

Bibliographical Essay

This essay deals primarily with books and articles published after 1945; those in English appear first, followed by those in German.

The literature on Bismarck and the unification of Germany is continuously expanding and there seems to be no end in sight. On Bismarck alone, a listing published several years ago mentioned over six thousand items (Karl E. Born, *Bismarck Bibliographie* [Cologne, 1966]).

In English the foremost biography is O. Pflanze, *Bismarck and the Development of Germany* (Princeton, 1963–), but only the first volume covering the period 1815–71 has been published to date. Shorter biographies include: A. J. P. Taylor, *Bismarck: The Man and the Statesman* (New York, 1955), a provocative and stimulating study; W. N. Medlicott, *Bismarck and Modern Germany* (Mystic, Conn., 1965), a concise, well-informed account; E. Eyck, *Bismarck and the German Empire* (London, 1950), a condensed translation of his three-volume work (see below); W. M. Simon, *Germany in the Age of Bismarck* (New York, 1968), an introductory essay with a documentary section; and C. Sempell, *Otto von Bismarck* (New York, 1972), which concentrates on the chancellor's personality.

The economic, intellectual, and social aspects of the period prior to unification are covered by the excellent volumes of T. S. Hamerow: *Restoration, Revolution, Reaction: Economics and Politics in Germany, 1815–1871* (Princeton, 1958); *The Social Foundations of German Unification, 1858–1871*, vol. 1, *Ideas and Institutions* (Princeton, 1969), vol. 2, *Struggles and Accomplishments* (Princeton, 1972).

On the Customs Union, A. Price, *The Evolution of the Zollverein* (Ann Arbor, 1949) deals with ideas and institutions between 1815 and 1833 and supplements W. O. Henderson, *The Zollverein* (Chicago, 1939). I. N. Lambi, *Free Trade and Protection in Germany, 1868–1879* (Wiesbaden, 1963), is a reexamination of Bismarck's tariff policy and its consequences, and H. Rosenberg, "Political and Social Consequences of the Great Depression of 1873–96 in Central Europe," *Economic History Review* 12 (1943), is an excellent survey of a hitherto much neglected subject. Frank B. Tipton, "The National Consensus

BIBLIOGRAPHICAL ESSAY

in German Economic History," *Central European History* 7 (Sept. 1974), pp. 195–224, points out the lack of agreement on industrial and economic development in nineteenth-century Germany. This is further developed in his study *Regional Variations in the Economic Development of Germany During the Nineteenth Century* (Middletown, Conn., 1976). Three review articles are of more than passing interest: Klaus Epstein, "The Socio-Economic History of the Second German Empire," *Review of Politics* 29 (1967), deals with E. Kehr's *Der Primat der Innenpolitik* (Berlin, 1965) and H. Boehme's *Deutschlands Weg zur Grossmacht* (Cologne, 1966); O. Pflanze, "Another Crisis among German Historians? Helmut Boehme's *Deutschlands Weg zur Grossmacht*: A Review Article," *Journal of Modern History* 40 (1968); and J. F. Harris, "Social-Economic Analysis and the Bismarckzeit," *Maryland Historian* 2 (Fall 1971), which reviews Boehme, H. Rosenberg's *Grosse Depression und Bismarckzeit* (Berlin, 1967), and T. S. Hamerow's *The Social Foundations of German Unification*, vol. 1.

There is no recent, comprehensive study of Bismarck's foreign policy in English. Special studies are: W. E. Mosse, *The European Powers and the German Question, 1848–1871* (Cambridge, 1958); Richard Millman, *British Foreign Policy and the Coming of the Franco-Prussian War* (Oxford, 1965); R. I. Giesberg, *The Treaty of Frankfort: A Study in Diplomatic History, September 1870–September 1873* (Philadelphia, 1966); G. O. Kent, *Arnim and Bismarck* (Oxford, 1968); A. Mitchell, *Bismarck and the French Nation, 1348–1890* (New York, 1971); W. N. Medlicott, *The Congress of Berlin and After* (London, 1938), and *Bismarck, Gladstone, and the Concert of Europe* (London, 1956); B. Waller, *Bismarck at the Crossroads: The Reorientation of German Foreign Policy after the Congress of Berlin, 1878–1880* (London, 1974); E. A. Pottinger, *Napoleon III and the German Crisis, 1865–1866* (Cambridge, Mass., 1966); G. Bonnin, ed., *Bismarck and the Hohenzollern Candidature for the Spanish Throne: The Documents in the German Diplomatic Archives* (London, 1957); L. D. Steefel, *Bismarck, the Hohenzollern Candidacy and the Origins of the Franco-German War of 1870* (Cambridge, Mass., 1962); and his *The Schleswig-Holstein Question* (Cambridge, Mass., 1932), and K. A. P. Sandiford, *Great Britain and the Schleswig-Holstein Question, 1848–1864* (Toronto, 1975); L. Cecil, *The German Diplomatic Service, 1871–1914* (Princeton, 1976).

There are some articles on Bismarck's foreign policy that should be mentioned. W. L. Langer, "Bismarck as a Dramatist," in A. O. Sarkissian, ed., *Studies in Diplomatic History and Historiography in Honour of G. P. Gooch* (New York, 1962), is a gem on Bismarck and the Ems dispatch. O. Pflanze, "Bismarck's Realpolitik," *The Review of Politics* 20 (1958), and H. Holborn, "Bismarck's Realpolitik," *Journal of the History of Ideas* 21 (1960), are the best treatments of a difficult subject. R. H. Lord, "Bismarck and Russia in 1863," *American Historical Review* 29 (Oct. 1923), evaluates the Alvensleben

BIBLIOGRAPHICAL ESSAY

Convention on the basis of Russian documents. G. A. Kertesz, "Reflections on a Centenary: The Austro-Prussian War of 1866," *Historical Studies of Australia and New Zealand* (1966), is well written and includes some interesting material. S. W. Halperin, "The Origins of the Franco-Prussian War Revisited: Bismarck and the Hohenzollern Candidature for the Spanish Throne," *Journal of Modern History* 45 (1973), is a critical review of E. Kolb, *Der Kriegsausbruch 1870* (see below). On Bismarck's colonial policies, H. P. v. Strandmann, "Domestic Origins of Germany's Colonial Expansion under Bismarck," *Past and Present* 42 (1969), and H. U. Wehler, "Bismarck's Imperialism 1862–90," *Past and Present* 48 (1970), are the most recent contributions. A good collection of essays appears in P. Gifford and W. R. Louis, eds., *Britain and Germany in Africa* (New Haven, 1967). Also of considerable interest are P. M. Kennedy, "German Colonial Expansion," *Past and Present* 54 (1972), and by the same author, *The Samoan Tangle: A Study in Anglo-German-American Relations, 1878–1900* (New York, 1973). H. D. Andrews, "Bismarck's Foreign Policy and German Historiography 1919–1945," *Journal of Modern History* 37 (1965), is a useful survey. G. Ritter, *The Sword and the Scepter: The Problem of Militarism in Germany*, 4 vols. (Coral Gables, Fla., 1969–73) covers the Bismarckian period in the first volume in a traditional and conservative nationalistic manner.

There are a great number of studies on Bismarck's domestic policies; some of the more noteworthy are the following: F. Stern, *Gold and Iron: Bismarck, Bleichröder, and the Building of the German Empire* (New York, 1977); F. Stern, "Money, Morals, and the Pillars of Bismarck's Society," *Central European History* 3 (1970); H. Boehme, "Big-Business Pressure Groups and Bismarck's Turn to Protectionism 1873–79," *Historical Journal* 2 (1967); A. Dorpalen, "The German Historians and Bismarck," *Review of Politics* 11 (1953); H. A. Kissinger, "The White Revolutionary: Reflections on Bismarck," *Daedalus* (Summer 1968); V. L. Lidtke, "German Social Democracy and German State Socialism 1876–84," *International Review of Social History* 9 (1964). On anti-Semitism, P. Pulzer, *The Rise of Political Anti-Semitism in Germany and Austria* (New York, 1964), is the best study. There are a number of interesting essays on Jewish life in Germany during the nineteenth century in the recent volumes of the Leo Baeck Institute; one of the more noteworthy is M. A. Mayer, "The Great Debate on Anti-Semitism: Jewish Reaction to New Hostility in Germany, 1879–81," *Leo Baeck Institute Yearbook* 9 (1966). G. R. Mork, "Bismarck and the 'Capitulation' of German Liberalism," *Journal of Modern History* 43 (1971); J. L. Snell and H. A. Schmitt, *The Democratic Movement in Germany, 1789–1914* (Chapel Hill, N.C., 1976); O. Pflanze, "Juridical and Political Responsibility in 19th Century Germany," in L. Krieger and F. Stern, eds., *The Responsibility of Power* (Garden City, N.Y., 1967); O. Pflanze, "Bismarck and German Nationalism," *American Historical Review* 60 (1955); H. Pross, "Reflections on German

BIBLIOGRAPHICAL ESSAY

Nationalism, 1866–1966," *Orbis* (Winter 1967); S. A. Stehlin, "Bismarck and the New Province of Hanover," *Canadian Journal of History* 4 (1969); A. Vagts, "Bismarck's Fortune," *Central European History* 1 (1968); F. Nova, "The Motivations in Bismarck's *Kulturkampf*," *Dusquesne Review* 1 (1965); F. B. M. Hollyday, *Bismarck's Rival: A Political Biography of General and Admiral Albrecht von Stosch* (Durham, N.C., 1960); V. Lidtke, *The Outlawed Party: Social Democracy in Germany, 1878–1890* (Princeton, 1966); and J. C. G. Roehl, "The Disintegration of the Kartell and the Politics of Bismarck's Fall from Power, 1887–90," *Historical Journal* 9 (1966). For an excellent essay on the effects of the Bismarck legend, see M. Stuermer, "Bismarck in Perspective," *Central European History* 4 (Dec. 1971), pp. 291–331, and the follow-up comments by Hans A. Schmitt and M. Stuermer, ibid. 6 (Dec. 1973), pp. 363–72. A good and readable account of Wilhelm II is M. Balfour, *The Kaiser and His Times* (Boston, 1964).

J. J. Sheehan, ed., *Imperial Germany* (New York, 1976), is a useful and interesting collection of essays on German domestic and foreign policy. D. S. White, *The Splintered Party: National Liberalism in Hessen and the Reich, 1867–1918* (Cambridge, Mass., 1976), and D. P. Silverman, *Reluctant Union: Alsace-Lorraine and Imperial Germany, 1871–1918* (University Park, Pa., 1972), are notable studies on much-neglected topics. G. Craig, *The Politics of the Prussian Army, 1640–1945* (Oxford, 1955), is still the standard work on the subject.

Of biographies and collections of personal papers of major figures of the Bismarck era, only the one on Holstein has been published in English. N. Rich and M. H. Fisher, eds., *The Holstein Papers*, 4 vols. (Cambridge, 1955–63), and N. Rich, *Friedrich von Holstein*, 2 vols. (Cambridge, 1965).

In German a study of Bismarck should start with his writings, *Bismarck: Die Gesammelten Werke*, 15 vols. (Berlin, 1924–35). Edited by the foremost scholars of the period (Gerhard Ritter, H. v. Petersdorff, F. Thimme, W. Andreas, W. Schuessler, and others), the work is not complete. Many of the chancellor's letters and directives on foreign policy before 1871 are in *Die auswaertige Politik Preussens, 1858–1871*, 10 vols. (Munich, 1932–45); after 1871, they are to be found in the first six volumes of *Die Grosse Politik der Europaeischen Kabinette*, 40 vols. (Berlin, 1922–27). This collection, too, is incomplete. His speeches are in H. Kohl, ed., *Bismarcks Reden*, 14 vols. (Berlin, 1892–95), and there are many published collections of his letters. A small part of the unpublished material has been microfilmed. (For a listing of these films and their locations, see *A Catalogue of Files and Microfilms of the German Foreign Ministry Archives, 1867–1920* [Oxford, 1959].) A good factual account of Bismarck's chancellorship is W. Bussman, *Das Zeitalter Bismarcks* (Frankfurt, 1968); this should be supplemented with H. U. Wehler, *Das deutsche Kaiserreich, 1871–1918* (Goettingen, 1973).

There is an extensive memoir literature by Bismarck's contemporaries (for a listing, see Born's bibliography); one of the more interesting memoirs is *Das Tagebuch der Baronin Spitzemberg*, edited by R. Vierhaus (Goettingen, 1960). Of private paper collections (*Nachlaesse*), the ones of E. L. von Gerlach, Grand Duke Frederick I of Baden, and P. Eulenburg, are the most important: H. Diwald, ed., *Von der Revolution zum Norddeutschen Bund. Aus dem Nachlass von Ernst Ludwig von Gerlach*, 2 vols. (Goettingen, 1970); W. P. Fuchs, ed., *Grossherzog Friedrich I von Baden und die Reichspolitik, 1871–1907*, 3 vols. (Stuttgart, 1968–); and J. C. G. Roehl, ed., *Philipp von Eulenburgs Politische Korrespondenz* (Boppard, 1976), the first of a three-volume work.

Of the many major biographies those of E. Eyck, *Bismarck: Leben und Werk*, 3 vols. (Zuerich, 1941–44), and A. O. Meyer, *Bismarck: Der Mensch and der Staatsmann* (Stuttgart, 1949), present two opposing views. The former presents a liberal interpretation, while the latter reflects the traditional, conservative-national approach. The two works appeared almost simultaneously in the early post–World War II period and triggered a spirited debate among German historians. Some of the more important contributions to this debate are: F. Schnabel, "Das Problem Bismarck," *Hochland* 42 (1949); H. Rothfels, "Probleme einer Bismarck Biographie," *Deutsche Beitraege* 2 (1948); G. Ritter, "Das Bismarckproblem," *Merkur* 4 (1950); H. v. Srbik, "Die Bismarck-Kontroverse: Zur Revision des deutschen Geschichtsbildes," *Wort und Wahrheit* 5 (1950); W. Bussman, "Wandel und Kontinuitaet der Bismarck Wertung," *Welt als Geschichte* 15 (1955); and M. v. Hagen, "Das Bismarckbild der Gegenwart," *Zeitschrift fuer Politik*, n.s. 6 (1959). Some of these essays are printed in L. Gall, ed., *Das Bismarck-Problem in der Geschichtsschreibung nach 1945* (Cologne, 1971).

On Bismarck's early period, E. Marcks, *Bismarcks Jugend, 1815–1848* (Stuttgart, 1915), is still the best, and K. Groos, *Bismarck im eigenen Urtel: Psychologische Studien* (Stuttgart, 1920), is a valuable contribution. Bismarck's views and activities during the 1848 Revolution are well described by G. A. Rein, "Bismarcks gegenrevolutionaere Aktion in den Maerztagen 1848," *Welt als Geschichte* 13 (1953). An indispensable source for contemporary literature on the unification is K. G. Faber, *Die nationalpolitische Publizistik Deutschlands von 1866 bis 1871: Eine kritische Bibliographie*, 2 vols. (Duesseldorf, 1963), which is a continuation of Hans Rosenberg, *Die nationalpolitische Publizistik Deutschlands vom Eintritt der Neuen Aera in Preussen bis zum Ausbruch des Deutschen Krieges* (Munich, 1935).

The centenary of the founding of the German Reich has produced a large number of articles and essays; some of these are printed in: T. Schieder and E. Deuerlein, eds., *Reichsgruendung, 1870/71: Tatsachen, Kontroversen, Interpretationen* (Stuttgart, 1970); W. Hofer, ed., *Europa und die Einheit Deutschlands: Eine Bilanz nach 100 Jahren* (Cologne, 1970); H. Boehme, ed., *Probleme der Reichsgruendungszeit, 1848–1879* (Koeln, 1968); M. Stuermer,

BIBLIOGRAPHICAL ESSAY

ed., *Das kaiserliche Deutschland: Politik und Gesellschaft, 1870–1918* (Duesseldorf, 1970); H. Bartel and E. Engelberg, eds., *Die grosspreussisch-militaerische Reichsgruendung 1871*, 2 vols. (Berlin [East], 1971).

O. Becker, *Bismarcks Ringen um Deutschlands Gestaltung* (Heidelberg, 1958), is a detailed and thorough study of political and constitutional developments from the Revolution of 1848 to the unification. H. Boehme, *Deutschlands Weg zur Grossmacht: Studien zum Verhaeltnis von Wirtschaft und Staat waehrend der Reichsgruendungszeit* (Cologne, 1966), is a similar treatment of economic policies and their impact on the unification from 1848 to 1878. The most comprehensive work on German constitutional history is E. R. Huber, *Deutsche Verfassungsgeschichte seit 1789*, 4 vols. (Stuttgart, 1957–69). (See, however, R. Dietrich's criticism of Huber's work in his "Das Reich, Preussen und die Einzelstaaten bis zur Entlassung Bismarcks," in D. Kurze, ed., *Aus Theorie und Praxis der Geschichtswissenschaft: Festschrift fuer Hans Herzfeld* [Berlin, 1972], pp. 236–56, especially p. 242, fn. 6, and pp. 246–47.) E. W. Boeckenfoerde, ed., *Moderne Deutsche Verfassungsgeschichte, 1815–1918*, (Cologne, 1972) is a collection of essays; of particular interest for the Bismarck period is T. S. Hamerow, "Die Wahlen zum Frankfurter Parlament," pp. 215–36; K. Griewank, "Ursachen und Folgen des Scheiterns der deutschen Revolution von 1848," pp. 40–62; and H. O. Meisner, "Bundesrat, Bundeskanzler, und Bundeskanzleramt (1867–71)," pp. 76–94. K. H. Hoefele, *Geist und Gesellschaft der Bismarckzeit, 1870–1890* (Goettingen, 1967), presents a good selection of interesting readings of the period.

One of the best historiographical essays on the German unification is E. Fehrenbach, "Die Reichsgruendung in der deutschen Geschichtsschreibung," in the Schieder and Deuerlein collection. Other noteworthy articles on the unification are L. Gall, "Staat und Wirtschaft in der Reichsgruendungszeit," *Historische Zeitschrift* 209 (1969), and W. Zorn, "Wirtschafts- und Sozialgeschichtliche Zusammenhaenge der deutschen Reichsgruendungszeit 1850–70," *Historische Zeitschrift* 197 (1963), which deal with the social and economic aspects. H. Bartel, "Die Reichseinigung in 1871 in Deutschland—ihre Geschichte und Folgen," *Zeitschrift fuer Geschichtswissenschaft* 16 (1968), is an East German appraisal, as is E. Engelberg, ed., *Im Widerstreit um die Reichsgruendung: Eine Quellensammlung zur Klassenauseinandersetzung in der deutschen Geschichte von 1849 bis 1871* (Berlin [East], 1970). G. Ritter, "Grossdeutsch und Kleindeutsch im 19. Jahrhundert," in W. Hubatsch, ed., *Schicksalswege deutscher Vergangenheit* (Duesseldorf, 1950), is a review of the greater and lesser German solutions leading toward unification.

The centenary of the Austro-Prussian War of 1866 also produced a number of interesting articles. H. J. Schoeps, "Der Frankfurter Fuerstentag und die oeffentliche Meinung in Preussen," *Geschichte in Wissenschaft und Unterricht* 19 (1968), and W. Real, "Oesterreich und Preussen im Vorfeld des Frankfurter Fuerstentages," *Historisches Jahrbuch* 2 (1966), deal with the meeting of the German princes at Frankfurt in August 1863. T. Schieder, W. Bussmann, H. Hantsch, "Entscheidungsjahr 1866," *Das Parlament* 24 (1966), and E. Deuerlein, W. Poels, "Entscheidungsjahr 1866," *Das Parlament* 25 (1966), discuss the significance of 1866 for German history. Also on this subject are: K. G. Faber, "Realpolitik als Ideologie: Die Bedeutung des Jahres 1866 fuer das politische Denken in Deutschland," *Historische Zeitschrift* 203 (1966); K. Bosl, "Die deutschen Mittelstaaten in der Entscheidung von 1866," *Zeitschrift fuer Bayerische Landesgeschichte* 3 (1966): and K. H. Hoefele, "Koeniggraetz und die Deutschen von 1866," *Geschichte in Wissenschaft und Unterricht* 17 (1966). H. A. Winkler, *Preussischer Liberalismus und deutscher Nationalstaat, 1861–1866* (Tuebingen, 1964), deals with the split among German liberals in the wake of the constitutional conflict and Prussia's victory over Austria, while M. Gugel, *Industrieller Aufstieg und buergerliche Herrschaft: Soziooekonomische Interessen und politische Ziele des liberalen Buergertums in Preussen zur Zeit des Verfassungskonflikts, 1857–1867*, (Cologne, 1975), examines the political aims and the social and economic interests of the liberal bourgeoisie in connection with the constitutional conflict.

On the Prussian-Italian alliance of 1866, its origins and subsequent relations, R. Lill has written three interesting pieces. "Die Vorgeschichte der preussisch-italienischen Allianz (1866)," *Quellen und Forschungen aus italienischen Archiven und Bibliotheken* 42–43 (1963); "Beobachtungen zur preussischitalienischen Allianz (1866)," ibid. 44 (1964); and "Die italienisch-deutschen Beziehungen 1869–76," ibid. 46 (1966).

The Hohenzollern candidature for the Spanish throne and the origins of the Franco-Prussian War of 1870 have attracted the interest of German historians, especially in view of newly discovered documents. J. Dittrich, "Ursachen und Ausbruch des deutsch-franzoesischen Krieges 1870/71," in Schieder and Deuerlein, eds., *Reichgruendung 1870/71* (Stuttgart, 1970), contains a good historiography of the origins of the war, while his larger, earlier study, *Bismarck, Frankreich und die spanische Thronkandidature der Hohenzollern: die "Kriegsschuldfrage" von 1870* (Munich, 1962), presents new documents from the Sigmaringen archives. J. Becker, "Zum Problem der Bismarckschen Politik in der Spanischen Thronfrage 1870," *Historische Zeitschrift* 212 (1971), is based on newly discovered material. E. Kolb, *Der Kriegsausbruch 1870: Politische Entscheidungsprozesse und Verantwortlichkeiten in der Julikrise 1870* (Goettingen, 1970), a defense of Bismarck, is critically reviewed by S. W. Halperin (*Journal of Modern History* 45 [1973]).

New interpretations and a lively exchange of opinions have arisen on the topic of the annexation of Alsace-Lorraine following the Franco-Prussian War: W. Lipgens, "Bismarck, die oeffentliche Meinung und die Annexion von Elsass und Lothringen 1870," *Historische Zeitschrift* 199 (1964); L. Gall, "Zur Frage der Annexion von Elsass und Lothringen 1870," *Historische Zeitschrift* 206 (1968); W. Lipgens, "Bismarck und die Frage der Annexion 1870: Eine Erwiderung," *Historische Zeitschrift* 206 (1968); and E. Kolb, "Bismarck und das Aufkommen der Annexionsforderung 1870," *Historische Zeitschrift* 209 (1969).

The most recent study of Bismarck's foreign policy is by A. Hillgruber, *Bismarcks Aussenpolitik* (Freiburg, 1972). A. S. Jerussalimski, *Bismarck: Diplomatie und Militaerismus* (Berlin [East], 1970) looks at the chancellor and his foreign policy from a Marxist point of view. A detailed criticism of the West German, bourgeois historiography of Bismarck's foreign policy is H. Wolter, "Neue Aspekte in der buergerlichen Historiographie der BDR zur Bismarckischen Aussenpolitik 1871 bis 1890," in *Jahrbuch fuer Geschichte* 10 (1974), pp. 507–39. A. Novotny, *Quellen und Studien zur Geschichte des Berliner Kongresses 1878*, vol. 1, *Oesterreich, die Tuerkei und das Balkanproblem im Jahre des Berliner Kongresses* (Graz and Cologne, 1957), presents a summary of documents and a useful historiographical account of the literature up to 1957. H. U. Wehler's interpretation of the chancellor's colonial policy, in *Bismarck und der Imperialismus* (Cologne, 1969), gave rise to a keen controversy. (See, in this connection, G. W. F. Hallgarten, "War Bismarck ein Imperialist? Die Aussenpolitik des Reichsgruenders im Licht der Gegenwart," *Geschichte in Wissenschaft und Unterricht* 22 [1971]; H. U. Wehler, "Noch einmal: Bismarcks Imperialismus. Eine Entgegnung auf G. W. F. Hallgarten," ibid. 23 [1972]; and G. W. F. Hallgarten, "Wehler, der Imperialismus und ich: Eine geharnischte Antwort," ibid. 23 [1972].) From the German Democratic Republic, K. Guettner, *Die Anfaenge der deutschen Kolonialpolitik in Ostafrika* (Berlin [East], 1959) presents new material from the Potsdam archives on the beginnings of German colonial policy in East Africa, and M. Nussbaum, *Vom "Kolonialenthusiasmus" zur Kolonialpolitik der Monopole* (Berlin [East], 1962), deals with colonial policies from Bismarck to Hohenlohe. K. J. Bade, *Friedrich Fabri und der Imperialismus in der Bismarckzeit: Revolution-Depression-Expansion* (Zuerich, 1975), focuses on the father of the German colonial movement who, for a time, became Bismarck's informal advisor.

More specialized studies of Bismarck's foreign policy are: F. Schnabel, "Bismarck und die klassische Diplomatie," *Aussenpolitik* 3 (1952); R. Wittram, "Bismarcks Russlandpolitik nach der Reichgruendung," *Historische Zeitschrift* 186 (1958); S. Kumpf-Korfes, *Bismarcks "Draht nach Russland": Zum Problem der sozial-oekonomischen Hintergruende der russischdeutschen Entfremdung im Zeitraum von 1878 bis 1891* (Berlin [East], 1968); H. Philippi, "Beitraege zur Geschichte der diplomatischen Beziehungen zwischen dem Deutschen Reich und dem Heiligen Stuhl 1872–1909," *Historisches Jahrbuch* 82 (1963); M. Winckler, "Der Ausbruch der 'Krieg-in-Sicht' Krise vom Fruehjahr 1875," *Zeitschrift fuer Ostforschung* 14 (1965); and M. Winckler, "Zur Entstehung und vom Sinn des Bismarckschen Buendnissystems," *Die Welt als Geschichte* 2 (1963).

BIBLIOGRAPHICAL ESSAY

On domestic policy, H. Rosenberg, *Grosse Depression und Bismarckzeit: Wirtschaftsablauf, Gesellschaft und Politik in Mitteleuropa* (Berlin, 1967), is a significant extension of the author's article mentioned earlier. R. Morsey, *Die oberste Reichsverwaltung unter Bismarck, 1867–1890* (Muenster, 1957), is a thorough study of the higher levels of administration of the Bismarck period. M. Stuermer, *Regierung und Reichstag im Bismarckstaat, 1871–1880. Caesarismus oder Parlamentarismus* (Duesseldorf, 1974), deals with the constitutional dilemma and the role of the Reichstag and is a major contribution toward a better understanding of Bismarck's domestic policies. The question of Bonapartism in Bismarck's policies is discussed by A. Mitchell, "Bonapartism as a Model for Bismarckian Politics," with comments by O. Pflanze, C. Fohlen, and M. Stuermer, in the *Journal of Modern History* 49, no. 2 (June 1977): 181–209.

A significant study on German local government and administration is H. Heffter, *Die Deutsche Selbstverwaltung im 19. Jahrhundert* (Stuttgart, 1969). W. Fischer, *Wirtschaft und Gesellschaft im Zeitalter der Industrialisierung* (Goettingen, 1972), deals with the development of business and industrial organizations and their relationship to the government.

On the *Kulturkampf*, A. Constabel, *Die Vorgeschichte des Kulturkampfes: Quellenveroeffentlichung aus dem Deutschen Zentralarchiv* (Berlin [East], 1956), presents a collection of documents from the East German state archives. H. Bornkamm, *Die Staatsidee im Kulturkampf* (Muenchen, 1950), is a short account of Bismarck's motives and the political ideas surrounding this struggle. G. Franz, *Kulturkampf: Staat und Katholische Kirche in Mitteleuropa von der Saekularisation bis zum Abschluss des Preussischen Kulturkampfes* (Muenchen, 1954), puts the struggle into its European context and stresses the domestic as well as the international aspects. R. Ruhenstroth-Bauer, *Bismarck und Falk im Kulturkampf* (Heidelberg, 1944), uses the Falk *Nachlass*, the reports of the Wuerttemberg and Baden representatives, and material from the files of the former Prussian Secret State Archives.

On Bismarck's anti-Socialist crusade and on Germany's Social Democratic party in general, most of the more recent studies have been published in the German Democratic Republic. E. Kundel, *Marx und Engels im Kampf um die revolutionaere Arbeitereinheit: Zur Geschichte des Gothaer Vereinigungskongresses von 1875* (Berlin [East], 1962), deals with the Gotha Congress. K. A. Hellfaier, *Die deutsche Sozialdemokratie waehrend des Sozilistengesetzes, 1878–1890* (Berlin [East], 1959), describes the activities of the party during its illegal period. Outside the DDR, W. Pack, *Das parlamentarische Ringen um das Sozialistengesetz Bismarcks, 1878–1890* (Duesseldorf, 1961), presents a balanced account of the parliamentary struggle over the anti-Socialist laws, and W. Poels, "Staat und Sozialdemokratie im Bismarckreich," *Jahrbuch fuer die Geschichte Mittel- und Ostdeutschlands* 13–14 (1965), is a useful survey.

Bismarck's relationship with the German press is dealt with by E. Naujoks,

"Bismarck und die Organisation der Regierungspresse," *Historische Zeitschrift* 206 (1967), and by D. Brosius, "Welfenfonds und Presse im Dienste der preussischen Politik in Hannover nach 1866," *Niedersaechsisches Jahrbuch fuer Landesgeschichte* 36 (1964). N. v. d. Nahmer, *Bismarcks Reptilienfonds* (Mainz, 1968), discusses the chancellor's secret press fund.

There is a considerable amount of literature on Bismarck's personality, his political and social views, his religion, and anything else that might explain his actions and thoughts. L. v. Muralt, *Bismarcks Verantwortlichkeit* (Goettingen, 1955), describes him as a responsible, Christian statesman. G. A. Rein, *Die Revolution in der Politik Bismarcks* (Goettingen, 1957), deals with the "revolutionary" aspects of the chancellor's policies, such as his introduction of universal manhood suffrage, a possible alliance with Lassalle's workers' movement, and the workmen's insurance and compensation legislation of the 1880s. H. Kober, *Studien zur Rechtsanschauung Bismarcks* (Tuebingen, 1961), discusses Bismarck's attitude toward law, while H. Loesener, *Grundzuege von Bismarcks Staatsauffassung* (Bonn, 1962), deals with his political and constitutional views. G. A. Rein, "Bismarcks Royalismus," *Geschichte in Wissenschaft und Unterricht* 5 (1954), examines his attitude toward the monarchy.

Some attention has been paid in recent years to Bismarck's alleged plans for a coup d'état. W. Poels, *Sozialistenfrage und Revolutionsfurcht in ihrem Zusammenhang mit den angeblichen Staatsstreichplaenen Bismarcks* (Luebeck, 1960), treats this subject in connection with the Socialist question in the late 1880s and early 1890s. J. C. G. Roehl, "Staatsstreichplaene oder Staatsstreichbereitschaft? Bismarcks Politik in der Entlassungskrise," *Historische Zeitschrift* 203 (1966), looks at it at the time of Bismarck's dismissal, while M. Stuermer, "Staatsstreichgedanken im Bismarckreich," *Historische Zeitschrift* 209 (1969), examines the implications of the idea of a coup d'état throughout Bismarck's tenure of office.

Index

A

Acton, John Emerich Edward
  Dalberg, Acton, Lord, 71
Agricultural revolution: spread of, 2
Alexander II, Czar of Russia (1855–
  81): meets Wilhelm at Breslau
  (1859), 30; and Bismarck, 30; and
  Bismarck's plan to reform North
  German Confederation, 57; and
  Prussian territorial acquisitions,
  61; meeting with Francis Joseph I
  at Schoenbrunn (1873), 106; meet-
  ing with Wilhelm I and Francis
  Joseph I at Berlin (1872), 106;
  meeting with Wilhelm I at St.
  Petersburg (1873), 106
Alexander III, Czar of Russia
  (1881–94): and Congress of Berlin,
  112
Alsace-Lorraine: annexation of, 73,
  74, 79–81 passim; effects of annexa-
  tion on French-German relations,
  80–81; mentioned, 77, 84
Altmark, 2
Alvensleben, Gustav von, Gen., 45
Alvensleben Convention: terms of,
  45, 46; withdrawal of, 46
Ancillon, Joseph, 4
Andrassy, Gyula von, Count: resigna-
  tion of, 113; mentioned, 110
Anti-Semitism: and Bismarck, 6, 9,
  102; in Germany, 102–3
Anti-Socialism: Bismarck's, 83, 124;
  legislation, 95–96, 125
Arnim, Harry von, 78
Arnim, Malvine (nee Bismarck), 5

Arnim-Boitzenburg, Count, 4
Augusta, Queen of Prussia (1861–70),
  Empress of Germany (1871–88):
  enmity toward Bismarck, 18, 19,
  40; mentioned, 32, 84, 86
Augustenburg, Duke of: Prussian
  break with, 52; mentioned, 49, 53,
  54
Austria: attempts to join Customs
  Union, 46; and reorganization of
  German Confederation, 46–47; alliance with Prussia on Schleswig-
  Holstein, 49; armistice with Denmark (1864), 49–50; settlement of
  Schleswig-Holstein, 50; Schmerling-Belcredi government, 52; secret convention with France ceding
  Venetia, 56; and Bismarck's plan to
  reform Confederation, 57;
  strengthens border defenses
  against Prussia, 57; effect of formation of North German Confederation on, 67; and German unification,
  104; alliance with Germany (1879),
  105, 106, 112; expansion into Balkans, 109; Reichstadt agreement
  with Russia (1876), 110; joins Three
  Emperors' Alliance, 114; alliance
  with Rumania, 115; alliance with
  Serbia, 115; joins Triple Alliance,
  115; railroad building in Balkans,
  116; mentioned, 1, 11, 14, 16, 18,
  20–33, 42, 45–49, 50–62, 66–69,
  71, 72, 79, 84, 104–6, 108–19
Austro-Prussian war: events of, 60;

INDEX

INDEX

INDEX